A CHOICE OF ORNAMENTS

NICOLAS BENTLEY

A Choice of Ornaments

READERS UNION
ANDRE DEUTSCH
London 1961

This Readers Union edition was produced in 1961
for sale to its members only by Readers Union Ltd
at Aldine House, 10-13 Bedford Street, London
W.C. 2 and at Letchworth Garden City, Herts.
Full details may be obtained from our London
address. The book is set in 11 pt Bembo type and
has been reprinted by Drukkerij Holland N.V.,
Amsterdam.
It was first published by André Deutsch Ltd.

LET that which I borrow be survaied, and then tell me whether I have made good choice of ornaments, to beautifie and set foorth the invention, which ever comes from mee. For, I make others to relate (not after mine owne fantasie, but as it best falleth out) what I cannot so well expresse, either through unskill of language, or want of judgement. I number not my borrowings, but I weigh them. And if I would have made their number to prevaile, I would have had twice as many. They are all, or almost all of so famous and ancient names, that me thinks they sufficiently name themselves without mee. If in reasons, comparisons and arguments, I transplant any into my soile, or confound them with mine owne, I purposely conceale the Author, thereby to bridle the rashnesse of these hastie censures, that are so head long cast upon all manner of compositions ...

MICHEL DE MONTAIGNE, *Essays*, Book II

CONTENTS

ACKNOWLEDGEMENTS

I SHOULD like to thank the following authors, publishers and owners of copyrights for kindly giving me their permission to quote the extracts that I have selected:

George Allen & Unwin Ltd, *A Modern Symposium* by G. Lowes Dickinson, and *The Path to Rome* by Hilaire Belloc; Edward Arnold & Co., *A Passage to India* and *Where Angels Fear to Tread*, both by E. M. Forster; The British Broadcasting Corporation, *An Imaginary Journey* by Laurie Lee; Jonathan Cape Ltd and the Trustees of the T. E. Lawrence estate, *Seven Pillars of Wisdom* by T. E. Lawrence; Cassell & Co. Ltd, *The Goncourt Journals* (translated by Lewis Galantière); Bruno Cassirer Ltd, *Art and Connoisseurship* by Max J. Friedlander; Chatto & Windus Ltd, *Amateur Sailor* by Robert Harling, and *Eminent Victorians* by Lytton Strachey; Constable & Co. Ltd, *Those Days* by E. C. Bentley; The Cresset Press Ltd, *A Land* by Jacquetta Hawkes, and *There Is No Return* by Philip Jordan; André Deutsch Ltd, *The Bombard Story* by Alain Bombard, *A Cure for Serpents* by Alberto Denti di Pirajno, and *Put Off Thy Shoes* by Elizabeth Hamilton; The Dropmore Press, *The English Sense of Humour* by The Hon. Sir Harold Nicolson; Gerald Duckworth & Co. Ltd, *New Cautionary Tales* by Hilaire Belloc, and *The Pleasures of Poetry* by Dame Edith Sitwell; *Encyclopaedia Brittanica*, 'Alexander the Great' by E. R. Beavan, and 'Crimean War' by F. J. Hudlestone and E. W. Sheppard; William Heinemann Ltd and the Executrix of the late Maurice Baring, *Lost Lectures* and *The Puppet Show of Memory;* and Mrs Sybil Bolitho Fearnley, *Twelve Against the Gods* by William Bolitho; and *Father and Son* by Sir Edmund Gosse, and *The Summing Up* by W. Somerset Maugham; the Controller of Her Majesty's Stationery Office, *Front Line, 1940–41;* The Hogarth Press Ltd, *Channel Packet* by Raymond Mortimer, *Orlando* by Virginia Woolf, and *What I Believe* by E. M. Forster; Hollis & Carter Ltd, *Still Talking at Random* by Douglas Woodruff; Hutchinson & Co. Ltd, and Miss Dorothy Collins, *Autobiography* by G. K. Chesterton, and *Jazz in Perspective* by Iain Lang; Ives Washburn Inc., *Al Capone* by Fred D. Pasley; Michael Joseph Ltd, *A House of Children* by Joyce Cary, and *My Father in China* by James Burke; Keith Prowse Music Publishing Co. Ltd, *Chu Chin Chow* by Frederick Norton; John Lane the Bodley Head Ltd, *Life Class* by Ludwig Bemelmans; Macmillan & Co. Ltd and Mrs George Bambridge, *A Diversity of Creatures* by Rudyard Kipling; and Mademoiselle Jeanne Bergsen, *Laughter* by Henri Bergsen, and *Far From the Madding*

10 ACKNOWLEDGEMENTS

Crowd by Thomas Hardy and *Great Morninq* by Sir Osbert Sitwell; John Murray Ltd, *Landscape into Art* by Sir Kenneth Clark, and *Selected Poems* by John Betjeman; Odhams Press Ltd, *My Early Life* by The Rt. Hon. Sir Winston S. Churchill; A. D. Peters Ltd, *The Road to Oxiana* by Robert Byron; James Pope–Hennessy Esq., *America is an Atmosphere;* the Public Trustee, *The Old Wives' Tale* by Arnold Bennett; Dame Edith Sitwell, *The English Eccentrics;* Oxford University Press and Mrs D. Newton–Wood, *Romance* by W. J. Turner.

I should also like to thank the following editors and authors: of *The Bookseller* for allowing me to quote from an article by 'O.P.', (August 6, 1956); of *Harper's Bazaar* for extracts from Raymond Mortimer's article on the paintings of Graham Sutherland (April, 1948); of *The Listener* for extracts from 'The Importance of Being Greedy' by The Hon. Sir Harold Nicolson (February 8, 1951) and 'Making Eyes' by J. Dance (April 13, 1943); of the *Evening Standard* for the passage from Sir Richard Livingstone's 'Where Do We Go From Here?' (May 13, 1947); of *The Observer* for extracts from articles by C. A. Lejeune (December 24, 1944), and Edwin Muir (March 20, 1955); of *The Sunday Times* for extracts from articles by Sir Desmond MacCarthy (January 28, 1951) and Miss Elizabeth Nicholas (September 29, 1958); and of *The Times* for quotations from an article on *The Passions* (April 10, 1943), the account of General de Gaulle's reception by the Bey of Tunis (June 28, 1943), and for a letter from 'Yorkist' (June 6, 1944).

INTRODUCTION

WHEN I was a small boy I used to mark the pages of my books with coloured chalks whenever a passage struck my imagination or seemed for some reason worth recording, and I still remember the effect of those tropical greens and acid pinks, those streaks of Parma violet, those hues of sunflower and geranium, that defaced the pages of my *Puss in Boots* and my *John Gilpin*, and of *Carrots, Just a Little Boy*, and a book called, I think, *Bluebell*, of which the only thing that I now recall is that its pale blue cover was embossed in gold with the head of a sickly looking child with a haircut like a French poodle's. These books were among my earliest favourites, and the habit of marking their pages, which my parents rashly allowed to go unchecked, developed later into the vice that made it possible for me to produce this book. The only claim I make for it is that while I was putting it together, which I did in my spare time over a long period, the writing and compiling of it gave me a great deal of enjoyment. My aim, in fact, was no more exalted than that of most miscellanists; it was simply the pleasure of backing my own fancy. But by way of introduction and comparison I have backed my fancies here and there with opinions of my own, or set an account of some personal experience alongside one that I have quoted.

It may seem odd but it is nevertheless true to say that my tastes in literature have really changed very little since I first began to read. They are still largely instinctive rather than cultivated, and enthusiastic rather than critical, and on the whole they remain unaffected by the prevailing winds of criticism or fashion. I mention this not with satisfaction, nor because some defence of it may seem necessary, but only to explain what might otherwise strike some readers as quixotic or even absurd in my choice of material.

My original intention, after I ceased marking my books with coloured chalks and took to pencil, was to keep a notebook, merely for my own interest, of some of these passages, and it was not until after I had started doing this that I began to see a possibility of attempting something more ambitious. Few things give a truer picture of a man's character and disposition, or of the cast of his intellect, than what he chooses to read for his own enjoyment. So in a sense this book may be regarded as a self-portrait, framed, if you like, with personal comments, though these are distributed so freely and in so haphazard a way that such an analogy may seem misleading. Perhaps it would be nearer the mark to compare the result with those self-revealing doodles that one makes on a sheet of blotting-paper in moments of abstraction.

At first I thought that by a judicious arrangement of the material something more like an autobiography might emerge. I admit I was taken by the example of Miss Alice B. Toklas. To get a collection of other people to write my autobiography for me seemed an excellent plan, especially as I knew that those on whom I should be able to rely would include Montaigne, Burton, Herrick, Pepys, Rousseau, Byron, De Quincey, the Goncourts, Samuel Butler, E. M. Forster, Joyce Cary and Dame Edith Sitwell, among a host of others as candid and as perceptive as the most self-critical subject could desire. I was also well aware that few of us have a strict enough regard for truth, particularly in relation to our own affairs, or are capable of seeing ourselves with the necessary detachment, to write a completely honest autobiography. So it seemed to me that by getting so distinguished a company to explore my state of mind and express their conclusions in an orderly manner I should be saving myself much of the tedium and embarrassment that I find inseparable from the process of self-analysis.

It would also save me, I hoped, from the accusation of a bias towards discretion, which is one that to my mind too often bedevils the autobiographer. It is not necessary to be able to write as well as Sir Winston Churchill in order to be as readable, but neither his eloquence nor his authority would have compensated for the emasculation of his war memoirs by too strict a regard for delicacy. Nor does the over-nice biographer pay a just tribute to the memory of his subject if the impression that emerges falsifies the picture by which posterity will judge him. It may well be that a man's ability to overcome some unsuspected weakness will sometimes seem nobler than his recorded achievements; nor, I think, should the more trivial aspects of personality and appearance be suppressed merely because they may happen to be unattractive. Consequently, in the portrait which I hope will emerge here—at least by implication—truth rather than self-deluding flattery is what I have aimed at. And if the final effect seems to suggest someone who is inconsistent, prejudiced and conservative in taste, this is likely to be a good deal nearer the mark than if I were made to seem impartial, decisive and intellectually enterprising. These are characteristics which I dare say would enable one to produce a scholarly and well-balanced book, but it would be one that would reflect very little of my own personality. However, whether the likeness that emerges will seem a credible one, or whether those who know me will think it too flattering, the blame cannot justly be called mine; it must be laid at the door of Montaigne, Pepys, de Quincey, Byron, etc.

It must be apparent by now that among other trials the reader will have to face is a tendency for me to digress. For me, as for Tristram Shandy, 'digressions, incontestably, are the sunshine;—they are the life, the soul of reading'. You will find them abounding here, because it is through one's habits of reading that one's habits of writing are usually developed, and this inclination to dart hither and thither reflects the rather inconsequential approach that I have always had towards reading.

One of the difficulties about a book of this sort is not, as is so often the writer's difficulty, how to begin it, but where to end it. Considerations of size, not to mention those of the reader's patience, gave me some idea of what its length should be, but no hint of the way to set about choosing my material from all that I had accumulated. This problem I never really succeeded in solving beyond making a rough and ready division of my quotations under broad subject headings, in the hope that this would eventually enable me to produce a discursive essay on each theme. As it turned out, discursive is rather too modest an adjective; and here I would suggest that unless you feel a readiness to enjoy the form of literary hop-scotch that resulted, now is the time to stop reading.

For those who may feel inclined to persist, some explanation of my reasons for marking this or that passage may be of interest. As a rule, my pencil was applied when what I happened to be reading put me in mind of my enjoyment, or sometimes of my endurance, of a similar sort of experience; or it may have been that it aroused the same sort of emotional response as that of the character it involved. This trick of self-identification is, of course, one that most people play upon themselves in varying degrees, and although while reading I no longer mouth, gesticulate and reel as often as I did when I was a small boy, I can still 'romance myself', as Walpole put it, describing this amiable form of self-delusion, into another and more exciting world. At other times my pencil was applied probably because a description of some scene or circumstance drew my imagination so closely to it that I had the feeling of having seen or heard it all before; a vicarious form of re-association that has a distinct pleasure of its own. Sometimes, in a gesture of Olympian patronage, I marked passages merely to indicate my agreement with what had been said.

It is largely through my being indifferently educated—for which those who tried to teach me are less to blame than my own unresponsiveness—that I was late in acquiring a good deal of what it now seems to me should form the standard intellectual equipment of a moderately cultivated man. It was not until I was thirty, for instance, that under the necessity of spending a week or two in bed I began dissecting *The Anatomy of Melancholy*, and although a good many of its allusions are no doubt lost on me through my meagre knowledge of the classics, few books have given me such a long-lasting reward. I was forty at least before I came to have more than a nodding acquaintance with Chaucer, and but for Professor Coghill's persuasive efforts our relations might still have been as distant as before; while Montaigne, Rousseau, Stendhal, de Quincey, Dostoievsky and Ruskin were among many others of whom I knew little—and still do not know nearly enough— at that impressionable age when, if only I had been of a more scholarly disposition, acquaintance might easily have ripened into friendship.

It would be dishonest to pretend that I do not regret this, but it would be snobbish to make out that I am ashamed of it; the inclinations of one's taste in literature seem to me as natural a thing as a preference for feeling well-fed rather than hungry. That I used to read a good deal more frivolously when I was younger, and therefore no doubt less profitably, is true; but if *The Diary of a Nobody*, Barry Pain, W. W. Jacobs, Michael Arlen and P. G. Wodehouse do not seem to offer a promising liaison with Kafka, Sartre or Ivy Compton-Burnett, they undoubtedly aided my return journey to writers such as Sterne, Stevenson, Tennyson and Hardy, against whom a regimen of forcible feeding while I was at school had caused me revolt.

My original intention was to omit poetry from these pages, being, like most people, less responsive to it than to prose. But I realised that to do this would have falsified my portrait, because although I am less certain of my poetic likes and dislikes—or rather of my reasons for them—there is a great deal of poetry that I enjoy, even when, as often happens, it leaves me mystified. My ignorance of poetic rules and of the subtleties of their application means that inevitably I lose much that is significant; but a greater bar to my appreciation has been a mixture of laziness and impatience, and the understanding of a quick and greedy reader, such as I am, will often founder on submerged obstacles in the form of imagery, symbolism and allusion, leaving large areas of desolation in the regions of his poetic experience. And here I should like to pay a debt long overdue. For helping me to overcome some of these difficulties I owe much to Dame Edith Sitwell. Her loving study of Pope, and her own *Anthology*, as well as her *Pleasures of Poetry*, with its beguiling introduction, have helped immeasurably to increase my powers of appreciation, if not of discrimination. The clarity and persuasiveness of her style, and her immense love and

knowledge of the subject would make it difficult even for the most
prose-bound reader to remain indifferent to its appeal.

I wish, however, that I did not find it so hard to enjoy contemporary
poetry, or at least a good deal of it. But because I sometimes do not
understand it, this does not mean that I believe the writers of such
poetry to be phoneys or fakers, as do some of their critics, who, to
judge from their comments, are no better informed about it than
I am. To my mind it would be an impertinence to doubt the sincerity
of poets such as William Carlos Williams or E. E. Cummings, or
indeed of anyone who has spent a lifetime in studying poetry. But
most of the poems of theirs that I have read, and admittedly I have
not read a great many, seem to me to bear very little relation to poetry.
I have been told that one of the objects of such poets is to emancipate
poetry from the bonds of romantic imagery and from worn-out forms
in which European traditions have for so long confined it, which is
an aim that I can understand. What I cannot understand is why these
would-be emancipators seem so often to give meaningless utterance,
or when what they have to say is intelligible, that it should hardly
seem worth saying. I am ready to allow, though, that my failure to
understand these poets lies in me rather than in them, since my enjoyment of contemporary music and painting remains comparatively
unaffected by the fact that the fingers of my mind often seem inade-
quate to grasp what is going on. In music the twelve-tone scale, though
less agreeable to my ears than the one on which Bach relied, can still
be used for effects that stimulate and absorb one's faculties of enjoyment
without yielding much of a clue to the composer's intentions. In
painting too the same sort of thing may occur. Klee, for example,
is an artist whose purpose often eludes me; yet I would as soon live
with Klee pursuing what Ben Shahn has described as 'the innuendoes
of accidental forms' as with the work of almost any other artist of
his epoch.

But I have digressed long enough. Miscellanists, however objective
they intend to be, can hardly help showing now and again some
unpremeditated bias. For myself I cannot even plead an objective
intention. Personal taste may not be a sound or systematic basis for a
miscellany, but it is the only one I have to offer, and if the lines I have
chosen from the *Essay on Man*, or the account of the Eatanswill
election, are too hackneyed for some tastes, I have included them
because I find that no amount of re-reading seems to stale Pope's
majestic irony or Dickens' satire. At the same time, I have tried to
strike a balance between what is likely to be new to a good many

readers and what I hope will not be too well-known to others to stand repetition.

One problem that exercised my mind a good deal was how to identify my quotations clearly but not obtrusively, as my aim has been to preserve the continuity of the various sections of the book with as little interruption of interest as possible. Each extract is therefore numbered and at the end of each section there is a corresponding list of the sources.

Early Years

*

There was a time when meadow, grove, and stream,
The earth, and every common sight,
    To me did seem
Apparelled in celestial light . . .
WILLIAM WORDSWORTH, *Intimations of Immortality*

ON THE sole evidence of his having written *After Blenheim*, which is one of the few poems by Southey that I can remember having read, I always suspected him of being a bit of an ass. This idea was confirmed for me when I came across a saying of his that 'the days of childhood are but days of woe.' [1] If ever there is an opportunity for happiness in life it is surely when one is a child. As far as I can tell, most of the children I know are happy most of the time, and I should have thought that generally speaking this is true of others. They have not yet learnt that the happiness of one person must almost always involve some measure of unhappiness for another; the communist, for instance. Most people would associate with the idea of happiness some degree of free will. But communists, or such of them as I have met, seem to be genuinely angered by any sign of independent thought or action in the sphere of morals, of education, and a good many other things touching pretty closely on human happiness. Or take those who believe in the tenets of the Lord's Day Observance Society. Such persons seem sincerely, if rather self-righteously, upset by things that give innocent enjoyment to multitudes of others. Take the parent who reproves the child for amusing itself by some form of desecration or destruction. Was there ever a more certain cause of alarm and despondency in the nursery? Wherever the roots of happiness are to be observed, there one cannot help perceiving also the seeds of unhappiness. But luckily it is not until we begin to grow up that we become aware of this. Most of us could probably say with some truth that our earliest years were indeed our happiest. The universal anxieties of the adult world have not yet thrown their shadows on the mind. There are not yet any of those lurking sensations, such as of being selfish or unkind, or lacking in responsibility or discretion, that so often plague one in later life.

On the whole, I had a very happy childhood, without, I hope, being more selfish or unkind or irresponsible than most children naturally are. I think it was not until I began going to school that I got hold of the fact that happiness is relative and disappointment a recurring factor to which one has got to learn to adjust one's expectations. The failure to understand this at a fairly early age or, more often, an inability to make the adjustment soon enough, seems to me a cause of much adolescent misery, as well as of a good deal of the unhappiness that occurs in later life.

There were always a few boys at school—significantly, perhaps, they were mostly of a cerebral and unathletic type—who never seemed to get to grips with life, and they suffered accordingly. I was never particularly athletic myself, but I was certainly far from being of the cerebral type, and those who belonged to it I baited with a ferocious glee. I have since learnt to be deeply ashamed of this, for although some of my victims may have deserved what they got, there were others who certainly did not, and to these I offer my apologies.

As one grows older and the horizons of sensation and experience grow wider, one is inclined to think—also perhaps because memory is short—that the sorrows of early childhood, being themselves short-lived, are therefore trivial. I do not believe this. At no time of life does one feel things more deeply, or for that matter enjoy them more intensely, than at this period, before sophistication has set in and before one has learnt what time can do to lessen suffering.

Not having been, in any sense that I am aware of, an abnormal child, I assume that I had a normal child's share of suffering and disappointment. Yet I find that I have happily and conveniently forgotten most of the causes, though I well remember some of my joys. I don't think anything has ever given me more intense pleasure than some of my playthings. I still remember with the deepest affection an Eskimo doll whose clothing could be put on and taken off. There was an American fire engine, too, which ran about by some mysterious means that I never understood, making a very satisfactory and authentic sound of wailing as it did so. And there was a whole regiment of *cuirassiers*, complete with trumpet-majors, which came from *Le Nain Bleu* in Paris. How I loved them! Then there were 'occasions', such as my first pantomime, with Clarice Mayne as the principal boy. Felicity, I thought, could reach no higher plane. And in a way I was right, because I have never enjoyed going to the theatre more than I did on that occasion.

Then, of course, there was Christmas. 'I suppose everyone has his own picture of Christmas, and I suppose it is always a picture fixed by the eyes of a child. Christmas to me is *While Shepherds Watched* and the night of Christmas Eve; the prick of holly through my pina-fore; a glimpse of a spangled tree through a forbidden door; a sense of grown-ups bustling downstairs, and myself trying feverishly to sleep with a limp cashmere stocking at the foot of my bed; and then, in the small hours, groping for that stocking in the dark; finding it, fat and crackling; and settling down at last to true sleep, to wake with the sound of church bells ringing.' [2]

Christmas at that age is also, of course, the season of balls and parties. There was one at the Portman Rooms that I remember, a fancy dress party in aid of the Waifs and Strays Society, with which an uncle of mine was connected. On the way there I was sick in the cab from excitement, and coming home I was sick again, probably from the reaction. But in between I was in heaven. That particular kind of heaven is one that can only be reached through childhood, nor do you have to be in a state of grace to achieve it. In fact, a state of grace would be a handicap because what one has to do is to abandon utterly, and as only a child can, every vestige of self-consciousness. Only then is it possible to work oneself up into the necessary state of blissful frenzy. Striking what must surely have been a vein of truthful reminiscence, Joyce Cary synthesized this process with touching and at the same time hilarious exactitude in his description of the party in *A House of Children*:

'Kathy ... began at once, with anxious and responsible care, to teach me the steps while I was as polite and deferential with her as if she had been another of the strange girls who, in puffed silk sleeves and frilled and tucked frocks, soberly danced or conversed round me, frowning over their partners' shoulders with looks of preoccupation and anxiety ...

'I danced with Kathy for a long time and thanked her effusively for teaching me the steps. Afterwards we went through a lancers together where all the girls, with shrill angry voices, cried out instructions to their partners, and thrusting them furiously away at the end of each figure, shouted: "Grand chain—do think what you're doing".

'All of us were instructors or pupils: one saw nothing but humble-looking boys carefully performing awkward motions and little girls beckoning at them or blushing for them. At the end of the dance loud angry discussions broke out about who had spoilt what figure and who had torn somebody's frock. The loud voices and frowning faces and angry gestures were those of a fight. Yet when someone proposed another set we clapped and cried out in chorus: "Please, please". All faces were full of eagerness, as if for a treat. We wanted it all again, anxieties, reproaches, instruction. I suppose we felt that this was life, that we were finding out how to do it; and that the finding out was itself engrossing. We had not come to the party for pleasure, but to be engrossed.

'Some time during these dances I fell in love with Kathy—I kept on looking at her and laughing with pleasure. She seemed to me charming, kind; the nicest girl I had ever met. I began to prance round her as I used to jump aimlessly round my father's legs, running into him. Kathy was gravely delighted. At nine she was far more mature than I, and I dare say her feelings were deeper and stronger. She kept on restraining my wild leaps, smiling in an embarrassed way and saying, "You must dance the steps". But her voice was full of apology, and when the dance was over we walked into the passage with our arms round each other's waists and agreed we would never love anyone else. Kathy kept saying: "But do you really want to marry me?" and every time I assured her she sighed deeply and murmured: "Oh, dear, isn't it lovely here, isn't it a lovely party? It's the loveliest day of my life." We even kissed each other, and I could see that this meant a great deal to Kathy: it was a pledge.

'After tea, of course, all our decorum, our sense of an important occasion, vanished. I had sat next to Kathy at tea and we had even held hands, feeding ourselves with the other: but suddenly I jumped down and darted away from her, with a tribe of boys. Drunk with sugar-cake and sweets, wearing paper caps, we flew through the rooms yelling, often revolving on our axes, pirouetting because we knew we would soon reach the end of the rooms, and be obliged to turn back...

'Some time later I ... now free from responsibility, and, as I say, partly drunk, danced a Roger de Coverley, in which several children were battered into tears. We leaped together, stamped our feet, and when the time came to pass under the hands of the top couple, ran our heads against the behinds of the couple in front, and tried to push them down.

'I was especially excited to recognise Kathy in the line of girls opposite me, two or three down. She was not drunk. She had been too busy at tea, giving me the best cakes, to eat much herself. She kept looking at me with a perplexed, mournful expression, and these looks caused me explosions of laughter, not malicious, but purely drunken. Indeed I felt guilty towards Kathy, but my guilt, like all my other reactions, passed at once into wild leaps and shouts of laughter; into a desire for violence. Our dance grew into a war dance. Some of the girls, except the older ones like Kathy, were rougher than the boys. My partner, a fat creature with a red doll-like face, shrieked like an engine whistle, and then uttering an insane laugh, with protruded stomach and arms held back, rushed against me and bumped into me so violently that I nearly fell. But I got the idea and I also began to bump my stomach against my neighbour's. All of us danced the whole time with our own steps. Even when I stood in the line, watching the end boy and the end girl preparing their *pas de deux* between the lines, I jumped up and down, yelled, and hopped in complete circles, turning my back on the rest. All of us were trying to make as much noise and turmoil as possible, because the noise, as we had discovered, and the wildness of our own kicks and prances, were themselves exciting.'[3]

Something of the same phrenetic spirit of this occasion is reflected by Dickens in a letter to his friend Mrs Richard Watson:

'A week or so ago I took Charley and three of his schoolfellows down the river gipsying. I secured the services of Charley's godfather (an old friend of mine, and a noble fellow with boys), and went down to Slough, accompanied by two immense hampers from Fortnum and Mason, on (I believe) the wettest morning ever seen out of the tropics.

'It cleared before we got to Slough; but the boys, who had got up at four (we being due at eleven), had horrible misgivings that we might not come, in consequence of which we saw them looking into the carriages before us, all face; their countenances lengthened to that surprising extent. When they saw us the faces shut up as if they were upon strong springs, and their waistcoats developed themselves in the usual places. When the first hamper came out of the luggage-van, I was conscious of their dancing behind the guard; when the second came out with bottles in it, they all stood wildly on one leg. We then got a couple of flys to drive to the boat-house. I put them in the first, but they couldn't sit still a moment, and were perpetually flying up and down like the toy figures in the sham snuff-boxes. In this order we went on to "Tom Brown's the tailors", where they all dressed in aquatic costume, and then to the boat-house, where they all cried in shrill chorus for "Mahogany"—a gentleman so called by reason of his sunburnt complexion, a waterman by profession. (He was likewise called during the day "Hog" and "Hogany", and seemed to be unconscious of any proper name whatsoever.) We embarked, the sun shining now, in a galley with a striped awning, which I had ordered for the purpose, and all rowing hard, went down the river. We dined in a field; what I suffered for fear those boys should get drunk, the struggles I underwent in a contest of feeling between hospitality and prudence, must ever remain untold. I feel, even now, old with anxiety of that tremendous hour. They were very good, however. The speech of one became thick, and his eyes too like lobsters' to be comfortable, but only temporarily. He recovered and I suppose outlived the salad he took. I have heard nothing to the contrary, and I imagine I should have been implicated on the inquest if there had been one. We had tea and rashers of bacon at a public-house, and came home, the last five or six miles, in a prodigious thunder-storm. This was the great success of the day, which they certainly enjoyed more than anything else. The dinner had been great, and Mahogany has informed them, after a bottle of light champagne, that he never would come up the river "with ginger

company" any more. But the getting so completely wet through was
the culminating part of the entertainment. You never in your life
saw such objects as they were; and their perfect unconsciousness that
it was at all advisable to go home and change, or that there was anything
to prevent their standing at the station two mortal hours to see me
off, was wonderful. As to getting them to their dames with any sort
of sense that they were damp, I abandoned the idea. I thought it a
success when they went down the street as civilly as if they were just
up and newly dressed, though they really looked as if you could have
rubbed them to rags with a touch, like a saturated curl paper.' [4]

In another letter, also to Mrs Watson, Dickens describes an outing
to the Great Exhibition with another party of children:

'The school was composed of a hundred "infants", who got among
the horses' legs in crossing to the main entrance from the Kensington
Gate, and came reeling out from between the wheels of coaches un-
disturbed in mind. They were clinging to horses, I am told, all over the
park. When they were collected and added up by the frantic monitors,
they were all right. They were then regaled with cake, etc., and went
tottering and staring all over the place; the greater part wetting their
forefingers and drawing a wavy pattern on every accessible object.
One infant strayed. He was not missed. Ninety and nine were taken
home, supposed to be the whole collection, but this particular infant
went to Hammersmith. He was found by the police at night, going
round and round the turnpike, which he still supposed to be a part of
the Exhibition. He had the same opinion of the police, also of Hammersmith workhouse, where he passed the night. When his mother came
for him in the morning, he asked when it would be over? It was a
great Exhibition, he said, but he thought it long.' [5]

This state of being in a waking dream, of being fully aware that life
is going on around one, but of feeling at the same time that what is
taking place in one's imagination has the greater reality, was by no
means uncommon to me as a child and is probably the experience of
most children. It is one that strikes them most forcibly at the time
when they begin to discover the mysterious power that words are
capable of exerting over the imagination, a discovery that comes as a
startling but pleasurable shock.

> *When I was but thirteen or so*
> *I went into a golden land;*
> *Chimborazo, Cotopaxi*
> *Took me by the hand.*

My father died, my brother too,
*   They passed like fleeting dreams.*
I stood where Popocatapetl
*   In the sunlight gleams.*

I dimly heard the master's voice
*   And boys far off at play,*
Chimborazo, Cotopaxi
*   Had stolen me away.*

I walked in a great golden dream
*   To and fro from school—*
Shining Popocatapetl
*   The dusty streets did rule.*

I walked home with a gold dark boy,
*   And never a word I'd say,*
Chimborazo, Cotopaxi
*   Had taken my speech away:*

I gazed entranced upon his face
*   Fairer than any flower—*
O shining Popocatapetl,
*   It was thy magic hour:*

The house, people, traffic seemed
*   Thin fading dreams by day,*
Chimborazo, Cotopaxi
*   They had stolen my soul away.*[6]

Those are the words of a town boy like myself, and no doubt he often wished, as I did, that he could live in the country, but having been born and bred in London, I don't suppose I could have been transplanted with any great hopes of my taking root successfully. To migrate from the country to the town is much easier. For one thing, the practical problem of how to earn one's bread and butter is usually easier to solve; for another, the man who is of an enquiring turn of mind or of a gregarious disposition must sometimes find the country-man's unhurried existence irksome. The unreserved acceptance of values that are new and strange, and of a stranger physical peace, is seldom to be found in one who is rooted by habit and instincts to an urban way of life. One of the few people I have ever known of whom it could truthfully be said that he gave the impression of feeling equally at home in London and in the country was Robert Byron, that brilliant and lamented figure whose disappearance during the war cheated the world of a writer bound for that shelf on the slopes of Parnassus where Doughty sits with Lawrence of Arabia and others of a small and select company. It is difficult to think of Robert, so urban in appearance, so fastidious in manner, as being anything but the most sophisticated, the most cosmopolitan of beings. Yet it was his intention, if he had had a son, to see that he 'shall salute the lords and ladies who unfurl green hoods to the March rains, and shall know them afterwards by their scarlet fruit. He shall know the celandine, and the frigid, sightless flowers of the woods, spurge and spurge laurel, dogs' mercury, wood-sorrel and queer four-leaved herb-paris fit to trim a bonnet with its purple dot. He shall see the marshes gold with flags and kingcups and find shepherd's purse on a slag-heap. He shall know the tree-flowers, scented lime-tassels, blood-pink larch-tufts, white strands of the Spanish chestnut and tattered oak-plumes. He shall know orchids, mauve-winged bees and claret-coloured flies climbing up from mottled leaves. He shall see June red and white with ragged robin and cow parsley and the two campions. He shall tell a dandelion from sow thistle or goat's beard. He shall know the field flowers, lady's bedstraw and lady's slipper, purple mallow, blue chicory and the cranesbills—dusky, bloody and blue as heaven. In the cool summer wind he shall listen to the rattle of harebells against the whistle of a distant train, shall watch clover brush and scabious nod, pinch the ample veitches, and savour the virgin turf. He shall know grasses, timothy and wag-wanton, and dust his finger-tips in Yorkshire fog. By the river he shall know pink willow-herb and purple spikes of loosestrife, and the sweetshop smell of water-mint where the rat dives silently from its hole. He shall know the velvet leaves and yellow spike of the old dowager, mullein, recognize the whole company of thistles, and greet the relatives of the nettle, wound-wort and horehound, yellow rattle, betony, bugle and archangel. In autumn, he shall know the hedge lanterns, hips and haws and bryony. At Christmas he shall climb an old apple-tree for mistletoe, and know whom to kiss and how.

'He shall know the butterflies that suck the brambles, common whites and marbled white, orange-tip, brimstone, and the carnivorous clouded yellows. He shall watch fritillaries, pearl-bordered and silver-washed, flit like fireballs across the sunlit rides. He shall see that family of capitalists, peacock, painted lady, red admiral and the tortoiseshells, uncurl their trunks to suck blood from bruised plums, while the purple emperor and white admiral glut themselves on the bowels of a rabbit. He shall know the jagged comma, printed with a white c, the manx-tailed iridescent hair-streaks, and the skippers demure as charwomen on Monday morning. He shall run to the glint of silver on a chalk-hill blue—glint of a breeze on water beneath an open sky— and shall follow the brown explorers, meadow, brown argus, speckled wood and ringlet. He shall see death and revolution in the burnet moth, black and red, crawling from a house of yellow talc tied half-way up a tall grass. He shall know more rational moths, who like the night, the gaudy tigers, cream-spot and scarlet, and the red and yellow under-wings. He shall hear the humming-bird hawk moth arrive like an air-raid on the garden at dusk, and know the other hawks, pink sleek-bodied elephant, poplar, lime, and death's head. He shall count the pinions of the plume moths, and find the large emerald waiting in the rain-dewed grass.

'All these I learnt when I was a child and each recalls a place or occasion that might otherwise be lost. They were my own discoveries. They taught me to look at the world with my own eyes and with attention. They gave me a first content with the universe. Town-dwellers lack this intimate content, but my son shall have it.' [7]

The things that taught Robert Byron to look at the world with his own eyes instead of through spectacles coloured with the impressions of other observers were the same simple things that taught Thomas Bewick to use his eyes. Bewick's *Memoir* of his life has much the same charm as his illustrations; and what more could a reader ask? His moral and political views, like those of many people who lead a simple and retired life, are dogmatic rather than well-informed. But when he looks back on his boyhood in its wild Northumbrian setting it is with that fresh and felicitous vision that very few of us are born with and none of us can acquire if we have not got it.

'From the little window at my bed-head, I noticed all the varying seasons of the year; and, when the spring put in, I felt charmed with the music of birds, which strained their little throats to proclaim it. The chief business imposed upon me as a task, at this season, was my being set to work to "scale" the pastures and meadows; that is, to spread the mole-hills over the surface of the ground. This, with gardening and such like jobs, was very hungry work, and often made me think dinner was long in coming; and, when at last it was sent to me, I sat down on the "lown" side of a hedge and ate it with a relish that needed no sauce.

'As soon as the bushes and trees began to put forth their buds, and make the face of nature look gay—this was the signal for the angler to prepare his fishing tackle. In doing this I was not behind hand. Fishing rods, set gads, and night lines were all soon made fit for use, and with them, late and early, I had a busy time of it, during the summer months, until the frosts of autumn forbade me to proceed. The uneasiness which my late evening wadings by the waterside gave to my father and mother, I have often since reflected upon with regret. They could not go to bed with the hopes of getting to sleep, while haunted with the apprehension of my being drowned; and well do I remember to this day my father's well-known whistle, which called me home. He went to a little distance from the house, where nothing obstructed the sound, and whistled so loud, through his finger and thumb, that in the still hours of evening it might be heard echoing up the vale of the Tyne, to a very great distance. This whistle I learned to imitate, and answered it as well as I could, and then posted home.' [8]

One would not imagine from reading his *Memoir* that Bewick took much interest in people as individuals. With the marvellous clarity of his gaze concentrated on external phenomena, it was the outward appearance, not the inward significance, of what he saw that absorbed his interests. That is why his illustrations, unlike those of Goya, or of Daumier, leave one spellbound in admiration of their skill but also leave one's feelings intact. All through his life Bewick seemed to retain this child-like awareness of his surroundings and of the people he met, and because of it was able to reflect what he saw with such enchanting if formal fidelity, for most children are wonderfully observant. But the accumulation of interests and responsibilities and impressions that is part of the business of growing up tends to disperse one's faculties, and none more rapidly than the power of visual observation. 'I do not suppose one ever in after life knows people so intimately as those with whom one's childhood and early youth have been passed. One's family, the servants with whom so much of a child's life is spent, one's masters at school, other boys and girls—the boy knows a great deal about them. He sees them with directness. Adults discover themselves, consciously and unconsciously, to the very young as they never do to other adults. And the child, the boy, is aware of his environment, the house he lives in, the countryside or the streets of the town, in a detail that he can never realize again when a multitude of past impressions has blurred his sensibilities.' [9]

This process begins almost as soon as the first workings of the imagination, which endow one's surroundings with qualities as

fabulous as they are exciting. For me no Texas canyon could ever be
more real than a certain dusty stretch of railway embankment behind
the house where I lived as a child, which was known to me and my
friends as the Gulch, without any of us, I think, having much idea of
what a gulch really was. I had a wooden sword, too, that was covered
with silver paper and was made for me by the Japanese cook of a friend
of ours. I was strongly influenced at this time by a brilliantly coloured
history of the Forty-Seven Ronins, whose oaths were sworn upon the
hilt of a similar weapon, and when the Gulch was not in use as a hide-
out for cattle-rustlers, it became the camp of a blood-thirsty set of
samurai.

   Being, as any self-respecting small boy must be, a passionate collec-
tor, I accumulated during these brief years a considerable assortment
of small objects, such as flints and nails and bottle-tops, that I found
in the Gulch and elsewhere, which I hoarded in tin boxes in the
expectation of their coming in useful for some purpose or other later
on. To what uses, if any, they were finally put I now forget, but I
am sure they served me as well in my imagination as if they had been
articles of practical use or immense value, and there was hell to pay
when one day a friend of mine filched some of these treasures. Such is
the power of imagination.

> *My little Son, who look'd from thoughtful eyes,*
> *And moved and spoke in quiet grown-up wise,*
> *Having my law the seventh time disobey'd,*
> *I struck him, and dismiss'd,*
> *With hard words and unkiss'd,*
> *His Mother, who was patient, being dead.*
> *Then, fearing lest his grief should hinder sleep,*
> *I visited his bed,*
> *But found him slumbering deep,*
> *With darken'd eyelids, and their lashes yet*
> *From his late sobbing wet.*
> *And I, with moan,*
> *Kissing away his tears, left others of my own;*
> *For, on a table drawn beside his head,*
> *He had put, within his reach*
> *A box of counters and a red-vein'd stone,*
> *A piece of glass abraded by the beach*
> *And six or seven shells,*
> *A bottle with bluebells*

And two French coins, ranged with careful art,
To comfort his sad heart . . .[10]

As a rule, only persons with under-developed egos, unless they happen to be teachers or psychiatrists of unusual perception, seem to have more than an inkling of the states of mind which differentiate the child from the adult. The instincts of childhood persist through life, re-coloured and re-fashioned by adult experience, but because we tend—though perhaps less eagerly as we move towards old age—to live in the present rather than in the past or the future, the effort of recapturing the essence of one's youth, with its perpetual quickening of the senses and the imagination, is one that few people are capable of making. We forget that the 'eight year old world has no language problems, no passports or barriers, no restraint and no money. It is as flat as a ribbon, about a million miles long, and scarcely wider than the garden path. It begins in the corner of the bedroom, among stuffed elephants and German helmets, and throws into space a gaudy coloured line—a line throbbing with circus freaks and horrors.

'In the perspectives of this world there are no distances or vistas, only details of animals and men, close at hand and awfully regarded. Conjured up by the tales of uncles, by black nights in bed, by facts half heard, half understood, its countries and continents, teeming with crazed inhabitants, lie as compact as railway stations along the path of my journey. And through this world I travel alone, armed with eyes for stretching, tongue for drying up, sticks for prodding, and legs for flying fast when things get out of hand.

. . . the world itself lies open to exploration by all kinds of conveyances—by feet, by memory, by hope and speculation.

'First of course comes England, the home country, the limit of what is familiar. The entire realm lies immediately outside the house and stretches no further than the village edge. It consists of a few wild flowers, a mass of jungly grass, an anthill, an oak tree, a bees' nest, and a flake-stone quarry clustered with Roman snails.

'This detailed landscape is all I know of England. It is home, the country we sing at school; and every event of history can be sited somewhere among its fields. King Charles once hid in that oak tree, King Rufus was murdered in that dusty wood, all battles were fought on that brambled bank, and every Queen was born here. I accept all these facts without question, for England beyond the boundaries of the familiar parish is unimaginable.

'It is past these frontiers, past the stream and the quarry and the end of the lane, that the strange lands begin, the world of foreigners and abroad.

'It begins in a cloud of darkness, in a grove of evergreens a mile away, deep down in a neighbouring valley. For that is the home of the Druids, tall green-faced men in silver shirts who spend their days motionless among the pine cones plucking at tinny harps and sneezing. I avoid that grove as I would the dark of hell, for it is the first pit in the path of the world traveller. Once fall into the hands of these lank-limbed men and you are lost for ever. For they will choke you with larch dust, poison your eyes with berries, kill you to a slow music, and thread your head on a harp string like a bead. It is a terrible place, as my grandmother has made quite clear.

'Yet go beyond these evergreens and you are still not out of the wood. For here lies a country of still more mortal danger, where live the Welsh, the terrors of these valleys. They are short-legged men, cunning as Blackfoot Indians, and they run like foxes through the twilight grasses, their mouths full of chicken feathers and their hands with strangled rabbits. When they are not raiding the fields they run up and down hills singing. I am not a Welshman, and when I hear this singing I have been taught to fly. Otherwise I hide in bushes and watch them closely as they pass, feeling my scalp tingle at their strangeness and thanking my stars I am neither fowl nor rabbit.

'Outside the village walls these Welsh and Druids press upon one closely and are the first denizens of the foreign world. But beyond their territory and over the hill there lies a grey stone town where an aunt lives among the savages. The women of this town make strong wines by boiling such things as oak leaves, harebells, dandelions and mice. The men wear sacks and gaiters, talk with stones in their mouths, and strike sparks from the road as they walk. They shout a lot, too, and smell of horses, and spend their time either fighting each other with cabbage stalks or sleeping drunkenly in sunny graveyards . . .

'By the time one has skirted the Welsh and penetrated to the village of my aunt one has reached, as it were, the regions of Ultima Thule, the limits of the known lands. Beyond that the world is charted only by legends, an abyss of magic and mystery.

'First there is a hundred miles of howling void, a desert of nothing-ness about which nothing is known. Then, out of this steamy un-tracked wilderness, the city of London raises its scarlet towers, floating in space like an enchanted island. This London, of course, with its hollow, drum-like name, is neither England nor abroad but something on its own, a walled fantasy of remembered tales. Within its limits

stirs the greatest concentration of life ever to have been witnessed by
human eyes. A roar is heard, as of a great pot boiling, chimneys pour
sulphur into the heavy sky, banners and gory heads droop from the
walls, and the streets are full of crusaders and crooks, poets and pick-
pockets, and slit-eyed Chinamen smoking opium on the pavements.
It is neither night or day here, but a rouged perpetual twilight, during
which several notable calamities are all happening at once. There are
at least a dozen houses on fire, all burning merrily. A plague cart of
corpses creaks its way to the river. A policeman drops into a sewer
after a spy, while a heretic roasts slowly on a spit nearby. Buses, horse
broughams and Roman chariots jostle each other on the crossings;
pale queens in black ride weeping to the Tower, and large on a rooftop,
livid against the sky, a headman fondles his shining axe. London,
in fact, is neither place nor city, nor the abode of mortal men: it is a
depository of fact and drama, a rag-book history lying in the flames,
its black charred pages turning slowly.

'But leaving London and striking far afield, we are next confronted
by the hot damp wastes of Africa. Africa, to my eight years' eyes, is
no more than a tangled trail through a forbidden wood, but limitless
in length, a sick green country of apparitions, a hunter's hell and
paradise. One hacks one's way through tunnels of wild gooseberries,
through barbed wire tangles of bleeding briars, through fevered banks
of nightshade. The pathway is stamped with fearsome tracks and
throbs with drums and headache. Coils of black snakes unlace one's
boots and the wet tongues of crocodiles lick one's blistered feet. All
the animals of Noah beset this Afric path: their eyes in the undergrowth
ripen like poisoned berries, their teeth shine like thorns, their voices
scream and chuckle. Huge elephants flap their rhubarb leaves of ears,
rhinos raise oak-tree snouts out of the swamp, the sky is black with
leaping apes and leopards, and a jaguar, growling in his hole, sucks the
warm juices from a hunter's head.

'This Africa is a test for heroes, hostile, deadly, reeking of fangs and
fevers. One never travels here except with a sense of mission, to effect
a rescue, to explore new territory, to find a new mountain or an ancient
treasure. Again there are no visible distances here, only the narrow
trail and the taunting jungle. And night and day one travels it alone,
feeling neither hunger nor exhaustion, conscious only of the threat in
every leaf, the pitiless continent hungering for one's bones.

'But worse than the bare-toothed beasts in the undergrowth, worse
even than the Druids back home, are the multitudinous bushmen that
infect one's path. They come at you from all sides and in all sizes

—knee-high pygmies blowing darts, Congo-cannibals with poisoned spears, bouncing Bantus with butchers' knives, and giant Zulus dressed all in blood and feathers. They hunt you tirelessly, abandoning everything to the joy of the chase. They taunt you with drums and lead you into swamps hissing with adders. They hang from the trees and whisper in your ear, promising you untold torments. And finally they surround you, their eyes in every bush—and you know at last you are trapped.

'But the beauty of this great Africa . . . is that as soon as things get too hot for you there is always a pathway down which you may turn to arrive back home in a couple of minutes.

'Let us leave Africa now to its solitary hunters, to its lizards, rocks, and monkeys' tails encircling the moon. The cannibals lick their lips and steal away, the death drums fade, the lions yawn and sleep, made fat on our lost friends. But we are alive, and the world waits, and Africa will keep.

'For next to Africa we have the Sea, that great surge of adventure, that deep blue space among the islands, through which we sail on an upright elmtree, peering high from its topmost boughs for pirate sails and serpents. The seas of the world are legends through which we ride immortal. Here we assume the mastery of our fates, climb rigging, give orders, sail nowhere, and clash continually with passing ships in brave and bloodless warfare. In these deep waters, storm-whipped and mountain high, ships sink but to rise again and no one ever drowns. Enemies may be bound, blind-folded, cast overboard and fed to the fish, but they always reach the shore alive, or return to flight again . . . Whales and sharks seize vessels in their teeth, crush them like biscuits and tear them like paper bags. Rocks writhe like living beasts to impale one's timbers. Volcanoes open in the waves to engulf one with steam and fire. Yet somehow one always escapes scot free. For this sea is a friendly monster, designed only to excite, and after each calamity the waves are dotted with the rafts of mariners happily drifting home.

'Beyond and among the seas lie the countries discovered by my uncles. One is India, another the Arctic, and they both lie cheek by jowl. India approaches in the shape of a jewelled elephant, with a tiger on its back. On the back of the tiger rides my Uncle Charles, fighting the beast with his bare hands. I am glad to see him and in no way surprised at his occupation, for his great brown hands were made for fighting tigers. He is as good as a circus, is Uncle Charles, and his tough, leather-skinned body is tattooed all over with exotic fancies.

Cobras are coiled around his arms, there are palm trees and temples upon his chest, birds and flowers climb up his back, and a half-clad dancing girl writhes on the mobile muscles of his belly. He is a king of India, tamer of elephants and rider of wild black horses. His friends are the dark magicians who live in the sandy caves. They produce bells out of the air, swallow smoke and flames, beat drums, sing, and run swords through their bloodless hearts. This India is more fun to be than anywhere else. It smells of hot tea and pepper, and everything one sees is a conjuring trick. Snakes dance to music, cows wear beads and speak, hawks fly to your hand with rubies in their mouths, and the wildest tigers, at a word from my uncle, immediately become hearthrugs. It is a good place to be.

'Nearby, in the Arctic, I meet another uncle, who is squat, hairy and old. It is a white place here and sparkling cold, for this is the storage house of all our winters and all the frosts and snows of the world fly here when the thaws set in. My arctic uncle has silver whiskers and is dressed like a bear. He cuts holes in the ice and pulls out shining fish. When he speaks smoke pours out of his nostrils, and standing in the snow he looks like an ancient photograph, smudged black with lines and creases.

'I like it in the Arctic for it is white and curved like the top of a balloon. Through the ice one can see the broad brown faces of eskimos, smiling and eating candles. Polar bears, like snowmen, swim around under water. There are dogs and wolves and houses of ice like bells, but the best of this place is the abundant cold and the fact that one is higher here than anywhere else on earth.

'As for the rest of the world, it is spread out thin, more distant, and rarely observed, lacking in uncles. There is Australia, of course, where men and rabbits walk like flies on the ceiling fields. There are the underground regions, full of molten fire and skeletons. There are islands of golden sand, covered with bananas and liquorice, mountains gashed by stars, deserts of storm and whirlwind, lakes full of dragons, and countries propped up on beanstalks, full of billowing princesses and giants with hands like trees.

'The furthest countries are the best and most fearsome. In far off Spain, for instance, they will nail you to the wall, screw diamonds in your eyes and give you hot gold to drink. In America they slice off the top of your head, or slash your veins and call you brother. In the jungles of Peru they make you King, fall down and worship you and feed you on roasted liquorice.

'But beyond all these we come to the edge of the world, and the grass-grown cliff drops sheer into the dark. Comets and stars roll musically by, and every thought has wings. I am armed now with a spaceman's eyes, with the nerve of a god and the hopefulness of angels. I have renounced all human associations. I am the Solitary, shining with light and power. The world is behind me. The garden path leads outward to the moon.' [11]

It requires the poet's glowing and prismatic vision, as well as the poet's tongue, to recreate such a picture of the rich excitements of being a small boy, and one can hardly help feeling a pang of sympathy for little boys whose upbringing denies them the sort of experiences that feed such an imagination.

How different must have been the childhood dreams of Edmund Gosse, whose *Father and Son* is to my mind one of the best auto-biographies ever written. It tells of a childhood spent in the austere shadow of the Plymouth Brethren, to which sect both his parents were staunch and positive adherents. That Gosse survived the rigours of such an upbringing, and could even write about it in later life not only with detachment but with the gentlest of irony, is a tribute to the generosity and resilience of his emotions. His mother died when he was seven, leaving him to the mercy, as no doubt it seemed to her, of his father, a remote and complicated zoologist, tortured by the problems with which an inflexible adherence to religious principles confronted him in a materialistic world. Perhaps it was in an attempt to subdue the pangs of conscience that arose from a sense of his own inadequacy that he persuaded himself of his son's moral and intellectual fitness to become a full-fledged 'Brother' at the age of ten. After an intensive period of training in dogmatic theology, the little lamb was considered ready for the slaughter and was carted off by his father, accompanied by his governess, Miss Marks, and a friend of hers, Miss Burmington, known as Mary Grace, to the 'Room' where a neighbouring sect of the Brethren met to worship God with stern and uncompromising fanaticism.

'My public baptism was the central event of my whole childhood. Everything, since the earliest dawn of consciousness, seemed to have been leading up to it. Everything, afterwards, seemed to be leading down and away from it. The practice of immersing communicants on the sea-beach at Oddicombe had now been completely abandoned, but we possessed as yet no tank for a baptismal purpose in our own Room. The Room in the adjoining town, however, was really quite a large chapel, and it was amply provided with the needful conveniences. It was our practice, therefore, at this time, to claim the hospitality of our neighbours. Baptisms were made an occasion for friendly relations between the two congregations, and led to pleasant social intercourse. I believe that the ministers and elders of the two meetings arranged to combine their forces at these times, and to baptise communicants from both congregations.

'The minister of the town meeting was Mr S., a very handsome old gentleman, of venerable and powerful appearance. He had snowy hair and a long white beard, but from under shaggy eyebrows there blazed out great black eyes which warned the beholder that the snow was an ornament and not a sign of decrepitude. The eve of my baptism at length drew near; it was fixed for October 12, almost exactly three weeks after my tenth birthday. I was dressed in old clothes, and a suit of smarter things was packed up in a carpet-bag. After night-fall, this carpet-bag, accompanied by my Father, myself, Miss Marks and Mary Grace, was put in a four-wheeled cab, and driven, a long way in the dark, to the chapel of our friends. There we were received, in a blaze of lights, with a pressure of hands, with a murmur of voices, with ejaculations and even with tears, and were conducted, amid unspeakable emotion, to place of honour in the front row of the congregation.

'The scene was one which would have been impressive, not merely to such hermits as we were, but even to worldly persons accustomed to life and to its curious and variegated experiences. To me it was dazzling beyond words, inexpressibly exciting, an initiation to every kind of publicity and glory. There were many candidates, but the rest of them,—mere grown-up men and women,—gave thanks aloud that it was their privilege to follow where I led. I was the acknowledged hero of the hour. Those were days when newspaper enterprise was scarcely in its infancy, and the event owed nothing to journalistic effort. In spite of that, the news of this remarkable ceremony, the immersion of a little boy of ten years old "as an adult", had spread far and wide through the county in the course of three weeks. The chapel of our hosts was, as I have said, very large; it was commonly too large for their needs, but on this night it was crowded to the ceiling, and the crowd had come—as every soft murmurer assured me—to see *me*.

'There were people there who had travelled from Exeter, from Dartmouth, from Totnes, to witness so extraordinary a ceremony. There was one old woman of eighty-five who had come, my neighbours whispered to me, all the way from Moreton-Hampstead, on purpose to see me baptized. I looked at her crumpled countenance with amazement, for there was no curiosity, no interest visible in it. She sat there perfectly listless, looking at nothing, but chewing between her toothless gums what appeared to be a jujube.

'In the centre of the chapel-floor a number of planks had been taken up, and revealed a pool which might have been supposed to be a small swimming-bath. We gazed down into this dark square of mysterious waters, from the tepid surface of which faint swirls of vapour rose. The whole congregation was arranged, tier above tier, about the four. straight sides of this pool; every person was able to see what happened in it without any unseemly struggling or standing on forms. Mr S. now rose, an impressive hieratic figure, commanding attention and imploring perfect silence. He held a small book in his hand, and he was preparing to give out the number of a hymn, when an astounding incident took place.

'There was a great splash, and a tall young woman was perceived to be in the baptismal pool, her arms waving above her head, and her figure held upright in the water by the inflation of the air underneath her crinoline which was blown out like a bladder, as in some extravagant old fashion-plate. Whether her feet touched the bottom of the font I cannot say, but I suppose they did so. An indescribable turmoil of shrieks and cries followed on this extraordinary apparition. A great many people excitedly called upon other people to be calm, and an instance was given of the remark of James Smith that

> *He who, in quest of quiet, 'Silence !' hoots*
> *Is apt to make the hubbub he imputes.*

'The young woman, in a more or less fainting condition, was presently removed from the water, and taken into the sort of tent which was prepared for candidates. It was found that she herself had wished to be a candidate and had earnestly desired to be baptized, but that this had been forbidden by her parents. On the supposition that she fell in by accident, a pious coincidence was detected in this affair; the Lord had pre-ordained that she should be baptized in spite of all opposition. But my Father, in his shrewd way, doubted. He pointed out to us, next morning, that, in the first place, she had not, in any sense, been baptized, as her head had not been immersed; and that, in the second place, she must have deliberately jumped in, since, had she stumbled and fallen forward, her hands and face would have struck the water, whereas they remained quite dry. She belonged, however, to the neighbour congregation, and we had no responsibility to pursue the enquiry any further.

'Decorum being again secured, Mr S., with unimpaired dignity, proposed to the congregation a hymn, which was long enough to occupy them during the preparations for the actual baptism. He then retired to the vestry, and I (for I was to be the first to testify) was led by Miss Marks and Mary Grace into the species of tent of which I have just spoken. Its pale sides seemed to shake with the jubilant singing of the saints outside, while part of my clothing was removed and I was prepared for immersion. A sudden cessation of the hymn warned us that the Minister was now ready, and we emerged into the glare of lights and faces to find Mr S. already standing in the water up to his knees. Feeling . . . almost infinitesimally tiny as I descended into his Titanic arms, I was handed down the steps to him. He was dressed in a kind of long surplice, underneath which—as I could not, even in that moment, help observing—the air gathered in long bubbles which he strove to flatten out. The end of his noble beard he had tucked away; his shirt-sleeves were turned up at the wrist.

'The entire congregation was now silent, so silent that the uncertain splashing of my feet as I descended seemed to deafen me. Mr S., a little embarrassed by my short stature, succeeded at length in securing me with one palm on my chest and the other between my shoulders. He said, slowly, in a loud, sonorous voice that seemed to enter my brain and empty it, "I baptize thee, my Brother, in the name of the Father and of the Son and of the Holy Ghost!" Having intoned this formula, he then gently flung me backwards until I was wholly under the water, and then—as he brought me up again, and tenderly steadied my feet on the steps of the font, and delivered me, dripping and spluttering, into the anxious hands of the women, who hurried me to the tent—the whole assembly broke forth in a thunder of song, a paean of praise to God for this manifestation of his marvellous goodness and mercy.' [12]

Gosse's father was a poor man by the standards of his own respectability, though money meant very little to him, in spite of his being inordinately selfish, or to be more precise, inconsiderate. But it was not poverty that forced such stringent physical and intellectual limitations on Gosse's childhood; it was bigotry. Mark Twain, who came of a family considerably worse off than Gosse's, led a rough life, it is true, but a free and happy one in the widest sense of both terms. How otherwise could he have written *Huckleberry Finn*, which I think I should be better pleased to have written than almost any book I have ever read?—pleased both in the sense of having enjoyed the writing of it and because of the pleasures it has given to generations of readers, as well as to readers of all generations. I suppose I was about ten or eleven when I first read it, and it is still capable of giving me as much pleasure now as it did then, if not more, for although the first, fine, careless rapture has worn off, I missed a good deal of its irony and of its pathos then, nor did I appreciate how accurate it was in its observation of men and nature. It shows, as few other books show except by the measure of their failure, what a rare ability it is in a grown-up to remember *truthfully* how one thought and felt as a child. Dickens had it, of course, in a remarkable degree; and to a lesser extent, and rather unexpectedly perhaps, so had Kipling. On the other hand, Hans Andersen, in whom it might have been expected, seems to have possessed it hardly at all. Why is this, I wonder? Perhaps some child psychologist lighting upon these lines will feel prompted to write and tell me. I hope not. But let us go along now with Huck and Tom and the rest of the Gang:

'When Tom and me got to the edge of the hill-top, we looked away down into the village and could see three or four lights twinkling, where was sick folks, maybe; and the stars over us was sparkling ever so fine; and down by the village was the river, a whole mile broad, and awful still and grand. We went down the hill and found Jo Harper, and Ben Rogers, and two or three more of the boys, hid in the old tan-yard. So we unhitched a skiff and pulled down the river two mile and a half, to the big scar on the hillside, and went ashore.

'We went to a clump of bushes, and Tom made everybody swear to keep the secret, and then showed them a hole in the hill, right in the thickest part of the bushes. Then we lit the candles and crawled in on our hands and knees. We went about two hundred yards, and then the cave opened up. Tom poked about amongst the passages and pretty soon ducked under a wall where you wouldn't a noticed that there was a hole. We went along a narrow place and got into a kind of room, all damp and sweaty and cold, and there we stopped. Tom says:

'"Now we'll start this band of robbers and call it Tom Sawyer's Gang. Everybody that wants to join has got to take an oath, and write his name in blood."

'Everybody was willing. So Tom got out a sheet of paper that he had wrote the oath on, and read it. It swore every boy to stick to the band, and never tell any of the secrets; and if anybody done anything to any boy in the band, whichever boy was ordered to kill that person and his family must do it, and he mustn't eat and he mustn't sleep till he had killed them and hacked a cross in their breasts, which was the sign of the band. And nobody that didn't belong to the band could use that mark, and if he did he must be sued; and if he done it again he must be killed. And if anybody that belonged to the band told the secrets, he must have his throat cut, and then have his carcass burnt up and the ashes scattered all around, and his name blotted off of the list with blood and never mentioned again by the gang, but have a curse put on it and be forgot, for ever.

'Everybody said it was a real beautiful oath, and asked Tom if he got it out of his own head. He said, some of it, but the rest was out of pirate books, and robber books, and every gang that was high-toned had it.

'Some thought it would be good to kill the *families* of boys that told the secrets. Tom said it was a good idea, so he took a pencil and wrote it in. Then Ben Rogers says:

'"Here's Huck Finn, he hain't got no family—what you going to do 'bout him?"

'"Well, hain't he got a father?" says Tom Sawyer.

'"Yes, he's got a father, but you can't never find him, these days. He used to lay drunk with the hogs in the tan-yard, but he hain't been seen in these parts for a year or more."

'They talked it over, and they was going to rule me out, because they said every boy must have a family or somebody to kill, or else it wouldn't be fair and square for the others. Well, nobody could think of anything to do—everybody was stumped, and set still. I was most ready to cry; but all at once I thought of a way, and so I offered them Miss Watson—they could kill her [Miss Watson being 'a tolerable slim old maid with goggles' and sister of Huck's foster-mother, the widow Douglas]. Everybody said:

'"Oh, she'll do, she'll do. That's all right. Huck can come in."

'They all stuck a pin in their fingers to get blood to sign with, and I made my mark on the paper.

'"Now," says Ben Rogers, "what's the line of business of this Gang?"

'"Nothing, only robbery and murder," Tom said.

'"But who are we going to rob? Houses—or cattle—or—"

'"Stuff! Stealing cattle and such things ain't robbery, it's burglary," says Tom Sawyer. "We ain't burglars. That ain't no sort of style. We are highwaymen. We stop stages and carriages on the road, with masks on, and kill the people and take their watches and money."

'"Must we always kill the people?"

'"Oh, certainly. It's best. Some authorities think different, but mostly it's considered best to kill them. Except some that you bring to the cave here and keep them till they're ransomed."

'"Ransomed? What's that?"'

'"I don't know. But that's what they do. I've seen it in books; and so of course that's what we've got to do."'

'"But how can we do it if we don't know what it is?"'

'"Why blame it all, we've *got* to do it. Don't I tell you it's in the books? Do you want to go to doing different from what's in the books, and get things all muddled up?"'

'"Oh, that's all very fine to *say*, Tom Sawyer, but how in the nation are these fellows going to be ransomed if we don't know how to do it to them? That's the thing *I* want to get at. Now what do you *reckon* it is?"'

'"Well, I don't know. But per'aps if we keep them till they're ransomed it means that we keep them till they're dead."'

'"Now, that's something *like*. That'll answer. Why couldn't you said that before? We'll keep them till they're ransomed to death—and a bothersome lot they'll be, too, eating up everything and always trying to get loose."'

'"How you talk, Ben Rogers. How can they get loose when there's a guard over them, ready to shoot them down if they move a peg?"'

'"A guard? Well, that *is* good. So somebody's got to set up all night and never get any sleep, just so as to watch them. I think that's foolishness. Why can't a body take a club and ransom them as soon as they get here?"'

'"Because it ain't in the books so—that's why. Now Ben Rogers, do you want to do things regular, or don't you?—that's the idea. Don't you reckon that the people that made the books knows what's the correct thing to do? Do you reckon *you* can learn 'em anything? Not by a good deal. No, sir, we'll just go on and ransom them in the regular way."'

'"All right. I don't mind; but I say it's a fool way, anyhow. Say —do we kill the women, too?"'

'"Well, Ben Rogers, if I was as ignorant as you I wouldn't let on. Kill the women? No—nobody ever saw anything in the books like that. You fetch them to the cave, and you're always as polite as pie to them; and by-and-by they fall in love with you and never want to go home any more."'

'"Well, if that's the way, I'm agreed, but I don't take no stock in it. Mighty soon we'll have the cave so cluttered up with women, and fellows waiting to be ransomed, that there won't be no place for the robbers. But go ahead, I ain't got nothing to say."

'Little Tommy Barnes was asleep, now, and when they waked him he was scared, and cried, and said he wanted to go home to his ma, and didn't want to be a robber any more.

'So they all made fun of him, and called him cry-baby, and that made him mad, and he said he would go straight and tell all the secrets. But Tom give him five cents to keep quiet, and said we would all go home and meet next week and rob somebody and kill some people.

'Ben Rogers said he couldn't get out much, only Sundays, and so he wanted to begin next Sunday; but all the boys said it would be wicked to do it on Sunday, and that settled the thing. They agreed to get together and fix a day as soon as they could, and then we elected Tom Sawyer first captain and Jo Harper second captain of the Gang, and so started home." [13]

Mark Twain was about fifty, I believe, when he wrote *Huckleberry Finn*, but he was not too old to get back into the skin of his boyhood. It is when a writer is getting on in years that one finds it difficult to imagine his having ever experienced the same sort of joys and sorrows, the same fears, passions, mysteries and revelations that come to one as a child. It is doubly difficult when he is someone so monumental, complex, erudite and irretrievably adult as Ruskin, and yet in recording the observations and sensations of his childhood Ruskin evokes all the small boy's pleasure and excitement at travelling by coach:

'Now the old English chariot is the most luxurious of travelling carriages, for two persons, or even for two persons and so much of third personage as I possessed at three years old. The one in question was hung high, so that we could see well over stone dykes and average hedges out of it; such elevation being attained by the old-fashioned folding steps, with a lovely padded cushion fitting into the recess of the door,—steps which it was one of my chief travelling delights to see the hostlers fold up and down; though my delight was painfully alloyed by envious ambition to be allowed to do it myself:—but I never was,—lest I should pinch my fingers.

'The "dickey" . . . was made wide enough for two, that my father might go outside also when the scenery and day were fine. The entire equipage was not a light one of its kind; but, the luggage being carefully limited, went gaily behind good horses on the then perfectly smooth mail roads; and posting, in those days, being universal, so that at the leading inns in every country town, the cry "Horses out!" down the yard, as one drove up, was answered, often instantly, always within five minutes, by the merry trot through the archway of the booted and bright-jacketed rider, with his caparisoned pair,—there was no driver's seat in front: and the four large, admirably fitting and sliding windows, admitting no drop of rain when they were up, and never sticking as they were let down, formed one large moving oriel, out of which one saw the country round, to the full half of the horizon. My own prospect was more extended still, for my seat was the little box containing my clothes, strongly made, with a cushion on one end of it; set upright in front (and well forward), between my father and mother. I was thus not the least in their way, and my horizon of sight the widest possible. When no object of particular interest presented itself, I trotted, keeping time with the postboy on my trunk cushion for a saddle, and whipped my father's legs for horses; at first theoretically only, with dexterous motion of wrist; but ultimately in a quite practical and efficient manner, my father having presented me with a silver-mounted postillion's whip . . .

'The mode of journeying was as fixed as that of our home life. We went from forty to fifty miles a day, starting always early enough in the morning to arrive comfortably to four o'clock dinner. Generally, therefore, getting off at six o'clock, a stage or two were done before breakfast, with the dew on the grass, and the first scent from the hawthorns; if in the course of the midday drive there were any gentleman's house to be seen,—or, better still, a lord's,—or, best of all, a duke's,—my father baited the horses, and took my mother and me reverently through the state rooms; always speaking a little under our breath to the housekeeper, major domo, or other authority in charge; and gleaning worshipfully what fragmentary illustrations of the history and domestic ways of the family might fall from their lips.' [14]

Ruskin's childhood seems to have been as happy as his maturity was miserable, and if later on his vision of life became clouded by the turmoil of his emotions, his dreams as a child were lapped in a sense of security which the conditions of our own day and age make it hard for us to communicate to our children, and therefore the more imperative that we try to do so.

> *Golden slumbers kiss your eyes;*
> *Smiles awake you when you rise.*
> *Sleep, pretty wantons, do not cry,*
> *And I will sing a lullaby:*
> Rock them, rock them, lullaby.

Care is heavy, therefore sleep you;
You are care, and care must keep you.
Sleep, pretty wantons, do not cry,
And I will sing a lullaby:
Rock them, rock them, lullaby.[15]

SOURCES

1 Robert Southey, *The Retrospect*.
2 C. A. Lejeune, *The Observer*, December 24, 1944.
3 Joyce Cary, *A House of Children*.
4 Charles Dickens, letter to Mrs Richard Watson.
5 Ditto.
6 W. J. Turner, *Romance*.
7 Robert Byron, 'All These I Learnt', from *Little Innocents*.
8 Thomas Bewick, *A Memoir*.
9 W. Somerset Maugham, *The Summing Up*.
10 Coventry Patmore, *The Unknown Eros*.
11 Laurie Lee, *An Imaginary Journey*.
12 Sir Edmund Gosse, *Father and Son*.
13 Mark Twain, *Huckleberry Finn*.
14 John Ruskin, *Praeterita*.
15 Thomas Dekker, *Lullaby*.

Reading and Writing

*

My early and invincible love of reading ... I would not
exchange for the treasures of India.

EDWARD GIBBON, *Memoirs of my Life and Writings*

'EVEN before I could read comfortably by myself, my interest in books was stimulated by listening to my elders as they read aloud. The magic of words and cadence, the purely sensuous pleasure of melodious sound, stirred me from the time when I was quite a child,' [1] and still, 'when by the aid of some historic vision and local circumstance I can romance myself into pleasure, I know nothing transports me so much.' [2]

I don't remember how old I was when I first learnt to read, but I know that in this respect, though certainly not in any other field of learning, I was rather precocious. I read anything and everything I could lay hands on, and far from being scared or bored by the stacks of books that were in the house, and in my grandfather's study where I spent a good deal of my time, the more I read, the stronger my appetite became. I can only remember one instance of anything like a ban being placed on what I chose to read. On that occasion—I must have been about ten at the time—I had found a copy of a magazine called *The London Mail* lying in a ditch near the cottage that we had taken for the holidays. It was, as I learnt later on, a feeble imitation of what *La Vie Parisienne* was like in those days, though the drawings were not as good. Without actually forbidding me to read it, my father implied that he would rather I did not, and I obeyed him. No doubt he was right, though the naivety of childhood is usually its own protection against smut.

As one grows older there is no such protection against unexpected assaults on one's susceptibilities. Now and again, perhaps because of the generation I belong to, mine are given a jolt—which I cannot help feeling is often intentional—when I find an author indulging in the use of obscene language. The problem of how to convey an impression of such language without giving the offence that its appearance is liable to cause is probably one of the oldest in the history of literature, but that it can be effectively solved is shown by Shakespeare and no doubt by earlier as well as later writers, among them Goldsmith, Crabbe, Dickens, Kipling and Damon Runyon. To me it seems the sign of a second-rate imagination to assume that the impact of an obscene word can only be conveyed by showing it in cold print. One of the few books for which to my mind there seems some justification for its obscenity is *Ulysses*. Joyce's exploration of the subconscious mind may not be as detailed or as acute as Proust's, but it does have a serious psychological purpose. I am not suggesting that this is a convincing argument for obscenity in other novels of this type, only that in *Ulysses* there seems more to be said for it than in, for instance, those apparently endless epics of life in the armed forces in which certain less gifted authors, especially in America, seem bent on showing how indifferent are the talents they possess.

An influence that seems likely to have had a more baleful effect than obscenity is the pessimism that was prevalent among certain influential writers of my youth. For those susceptible to it, causes for pessimism are never difficult to find, though I am sure these writers were not alone in their misgivings, or that their personal sufferings were not genuine. But the idea that my inmost thoughts about myself could have the same or indeed anything like as much fascination for other people as they have for me is unthinkable, and when I come across it in other writers it inevitably smacks to me of exhibitionism. The analytical pessimists of the 'twenties and 'thirties who took their souls out, washed them publicly and then hung them on the line, did so presumably in the assumption that it would be of general interest for them to explain why they felt so fed up with life. This, of course, is an idiotic generalization, like most generalizations, and may even seem to impugn the sincerity of writers such as those I am thinking of, Gide, Lawrence, Huxley, etc. (though Huxley was partially redeemed in my eyes by his sardonic sense of the ridiculous); all of them brilliant, powerful, perceptive and intellectually enterprising, but too preoccupied for my taste with the origins of their own discontents and consequently inclined to elevate introspection above a general regard for the problems of humanity, which is a more enduring mark of greatness in an author. That is why a writer such as François Mauriac appeals to me, while certain others no less gifted leave me cold. Flaubert was intensely self-absorbed, so was Turgenev, and so was Dickens, and as it is the natural tendency of creative beings to look inwards for their inspiration, where feelings are at their most intense, they all drew heavily on their emotions while they were at work. But it is the ability of such writers to transmute the individual intensity of their feelings into sensations such as we have all experienced that gives their work its universal character and its universal appeal.

The kind of problems with which Mauriac deals are problems of morality and conscience, not petty personal conflicts, and it is a sign of his genius that such conflicts in his characters are lifted from the domestic rut and exemplified as problems of perpetual significance. They are not problems that could ever be as easily solved as those that beset the characters in Simenon's novels, for instance, for whom the decisive answer is usually given by a bullet. To solve the sort of problems that face Mauriac's characters, if indeed they are soluble at all, requires patience, self-examination, charity and understanding. As he himself has said, 'Time, which always spells defeat for love, treats hate more slowly'.[3] Death, if that happens to be the chosen solution, will not come from a gun but is more likely to be the living death of the cloister, or suffocation in the Stygian twilight of existence with a paralytic but enduring spouse, or with a conscience that is dead but won't lie down; solutions more common in the lives of most of us, and perhaps no less terrible than the solution of violence.

Although their preoccupation with gloom tends to show itself in a more universal and less personal form of grouch, the angry young men of the fifties exhibit much the same streak of pessimism as was shown by some of their elders. If anything, reasons for universal discontent and anxiety are stronger now than they were then, although, oddly enough, it is not for this reason, or so I believe, that most of the angry young men feel as they do. It is easy perhaps for those who do not share their irritation and contempt, or at least do not care to show it, though possibly feeling no less anxious or discontented themselves, to be flippant about angry young men, but I do not intend to be flippant in saying that I believe an important cause of their behaviour is that in childhood they probably had their bottoms smacked either too little or too much. Their attitude towards life is that of someone who has been either spoilt or neglected. A boy who has been sensibly brought up without either excessive love or discipline and in reasonably happy surroundings does not develop into an angry young man, unless he is suffering from some psychological disturbance.

An acrid wit, usually exercised at the expense of other people, is a characteristic that also derives from being either spoilt or neglected. How seldom does one come across an angry young man whose sense of humour extends far enough to embrace his own introspective self? Why is this? Why is it that introspection and geniality seem so seldom to go together? Why, when a modern writer looks into his heart or examines his conscience, does he invariably tend to seek out the dark places and ignore the light? Is it because of temperament or circumstance? Because of heredity or climate—or what? One is tempted to think of the obvious reason and put it down to our living in the Age of Anxiety. But is that the real reason why 'a morbid, withering, deadly, antisocial sirocco, loaded with moral and political despair, breathes through all the groves and valleys of modern Parnassus'?[4] I think not, for thus was Peacock lamenting the state of intellectual

affairs in 1817, though his words might just as well have been uttered
a hundred and thirty years later. The wonder of it is that, even so,
I am never able to find time to read everything that inclination and
experience point to as likely to be worth while. There are whole tracts
of classical literature, for instance, of which when my father was a boy
at least a smattering of knowledge was necessary if one wished to be
thought properly educated, but of which I know next to nothing.
I suppose the truth is that I never was properly educated, successive
masters having abandoned in despair their attempts to interest me in
any systematic form of learning. Not that I set much store by being
able to count myself to a large extent self-educated, as some do who
have got most of their learning away from school. I should have been
immensely pleased, and proud too I daresay, to have had the kind of
mind that would have won me a scholarship to Eton or Winchester.
But as it is, the gaps in my learning, and especially in my reading,
appal me.

Yet, 'to read freely, extensively, has always been my ambition, and
my utter inability to study has always been to me a subject of grave
inquietude—study as contrasted with a general and haphazard gathering
of ideas taken in flight. But in me the impulse is so original to frequent
the haunts of men that it is irresistible . . . I watch the movement of
life . . . Contact with the world is in me the generating force: without
this contact what invention I have is thin and sterile . . .' [5] But this
does not prevent my feeling genuinely uneasy when I think of the
extent of my ignorance about the works of Plato, Aristotle, Homer,
Virgil, Dante and heaven knows who else. The realization of this often
fills me with gloom and to try to take my mind off it I turn to *The
Diary of a Nobody* or to Thurber or Raymond Chandler, to books
which themselves have something of the movement of life in them
and which reflect the author's contact with the visible and familiar
world. I am not even as well read in the Bible as I should like to
be. However, if I am a less good Christian for that, perhaps I have
benefited from my ignorance in other ways. 'To my mind King
James's Bible has been a very harmful influence on English prose.
I am not so stupid as to deny its great beauty. It is majestical. But the
Bible is an oriental book. Its alien imagery has nothing to do with us.
Those hyperboles, those luscious metaphors, are foreign to our genius.
I cannot but think that not the least of the misfortunes that the Secession
from Rome brought upon the spiritual life of our country is that this
work for so long a period became the daily, and with many the only,
reading of our people. Those rhythms, that powerful vocabulary, that

grandiloquence, became part and parcel of the national sensibility. The plain, honest English speech was overwhelmed with ornament. Blunt Englishmen twisted their tongues to speak like Hebrew prophets. There was evidently something in the English temper to which this was congenial, perhaps a naïve delight in fine words for their own sake, an innate eccentricity and love of embroidery, I do not know; but the fact remains that ever since, English prose has had to struggle against the tendency to luxuriance. When from time to time the spirit of the language has reasserted itself, as it did with Dryden and the writers of Queen Anne, it was only to be submerged once more by the pompousities of Gibbon and Dr Johnson. When English prose recovered simplicity with Hazlitt, the Shelley of the letters, and Charles Lamb at his best, it lost it again with de Quincey, Carlyle, Meredith and Walter Pater. It is obvious that the grand style is more striking than the plain. Indeed, many people think that a style that does not attract notice is not style. They will admire Walter Pater's, but will read an essay by Matthew Arnold without giving a moment's attention to the elegance, distinction and sobriety with which he set down what he had to say.' [6]

Not everyone will share this respect for Matthew Arnold, though perhaps one should make a distinction between his prose and his poetry. To me, and to my loss, no doubt, both are equally unreadable, though I admit the sobriety and even the elegance of the prose. But it is comforting to know that my opinion of the poetry at least is shared by a critic for whom I have so deep a respect as Dame Edith Sitwell:

'If we consider the poetry written in this present age,' she says, 'and the standards of value given to us by those who would be our guides, we shall find that there is a general misapprehension of the aims and of the necessities of poetry; and this misapprehension has arisen in part from the fact that many respectable persons, but very few poets, are encouraged to write it . . .

'A large section of the public has not yet recovered from the cold, damp mossiness that has blighted the public taste these last forty, fifty, or even sixty years . .   This general blighting and withering of the poetic taste is the result of the public mind having been overshadowed by such Aberdeen-granite tombs and monuments as Matthew Arnold, —is the result, also, of the substitution of scholar for poet, of school inspector for artist . .

'It is a terribly informing task to read any anthology published during the last fifty years; to read, let us say, *The Oxford Book of English Verse*. How strange is the contrast between the beginning of such an anthology, with the great poems of the past, included, no doubt, because it is not possible for anyone, however insensitive to the structure and texture of poetry, to exclude them, and the poems which follow. The former are now generally accepted; they have passed into the consciousness of our race, though nobody, with the exception of those few people who care for poetry, would dream of thinking about them. Having read those great poems, let us read some of the poems which were written shortly after the time of Swinburne, and which may have been admitted to the book in a spirit of fatigue or despair. What do we find? Matthew Arnold's chilblained, mittened musing and T. E. Brown's appalling poem, "A garden is a lovesome thing, God wot . . ."' [7]

I wish that more literary critics were as straightforward and as uncompromising as Dame Edith. Sometimes I find myself having to dig about in a mass of clever verbiage in order to find out what some critic thinks about an author or his work. And there is another sort of critic I could happily do without—the sort who takes elaborate pains to demolish a book that is of little or no importance. When a well known author writes a bad book, or when an obscure one produces something that is worth serious consideration, although one may flatly disagree with what he has to say, it seems to me justifiable to criticise what has been written without pulling one's punches. But if you get hold of a book by someone who is quite unknown, and after reading a page or so it becomes clear that he always will be, it seems caddish to demolish the poor creature's work by an ironic analysis of its defects. Yet often one sees some piddling little novel, written no doubt with tears and the best of intentions, being dissected with a loving care that shows merely how large is the critic's conceit and how small his charity. Considering how few are the literary critic's rewards, most of them I think set out to be as helpful as they can, and except for the few who like showing off now and again at the expense of some poor devil who is obviously not a worthy target, literary criticism, at least as it is practised in England, is an admirable time-and-labour-saving process. 'It is, at any rate, the quickest means to some knowledge of many books about which we should otherwise know nothing, and of famous writers about whom we should form crude notions if we relied entirely on our own scrappy acquaintance with their works. Of course, second hand knowledge can never be as personally satisfying as direct knowledge, but it is preferable to ignorance, or presumption, the alternative.' [8]

To be a regular critic of any of the arts, especially one who writes on a newspaper, and at the same time to preserve one's critical balance as well as one's integrity, cannot be easy. Both are liable to be overthrown sooner or later by the cataract of mediocrity. Also 'there is an impersonality in a newspaper, that insensibly affects the writer,' [9] even the critic, however honestly and with whatever determination he tries to escape its influence. 'People who write much for the press seem to lose the faculty of seeing things for themselves; they see them from a generalized standpoint often vividly, sometimes with hectic brightness, yet never with that idiosyncrasy which may give only a partial picture of the facts, but is suffused by the personality of the observer. The press, in fact, kills the individuality of those who write for it.' [10]

Why this should happen—and I think that more often than not it is true—is partly to be explained by the fact that the writing of 'good prose is an affair of good manners,' [11] and journalists are not on the whole the most polite of men. They cannot afford to be. Man is by nature an inquisitive animal and the desire to know what is happening to his neighbour is a universal trait. It did not take either Hearst or Northcliffe long to see that there was a mint of money to be made out of exploiting this weakness, and so it became the journalist's two-way function to appease and at the same time stimulate the public's curiosity; to which end, as *Time* magazine has taken infinite pains to show, good prose is sometimes more of a hindrance than a help. Or take the example of Gertrude Stein. Not that I believe the eccentricities of her writing were evolved with the idea solely of attracting attention, although when attention came she seemed to enjoy it. But I think she was too conscientious and too sincere a writer to want publicity for its own sake. She was an interesting and original writer not because of her syntactical whims, but in spite of them. Highly cultivated and with acute powers of observation, she also had a mind often startling in its lucidity, and an enormous appetite for people and experience. Above all, she had what seems to me a beautifully balanced sense of humour. With these qualities, added to a whole-hearted study and pursuit of literature, for which she apparently felt she had an almost Heaven-sent vocation, it would be surprising if she were not worth some consideration as a writer. Yet she has usually been derided or ignored, except by the more perspicacious critics. That she wrote a good deal of gibberish is incontestable, but along with it, or rather, before her ego expanded and her style degenerated, she also wrote two or three books that have almost certainly had their influence on literary form in America, and consequently on contemporary writing in

Europe. But in England her achievements in this direction have been partially obscured by her egocentricity. The English are circumspect in the matter of genius, particularly when it is self-proclaimed, and Gertrude Stein, though she was not a genius, lived in the happy though harmless illusion that that was exactly what she was. The mistake she made was in losing no opportunity of asserting this belief, which was a pity because her writing was often good enough not to need her own advocacy of it or the stupid embellishments with which she sometimes spoilt passages of good clean prose. And good clean prose is not so easy to produce as may be thought by anyone who has not tried to write it.

'Good prose,' says Somerset Maugham, 'is, unlike verse, a civil art. Poetry is baroque. Baroque is tragic, massive and mystical. It is elemental. It demands depth and insight. I cannot but feel that the prose writers of the baroque period, the authors of King James's Bible, Sir Thomas Browne, Glanville, were poets who had lost their way. Prose is a rococo art. It needs taste rather than grandeur. Form for the poet is the bit and the bridle without which (unless you are an acrobat) you cannot ride your horse; but for the writer of prose it is the chassis without which your car does not exist. It is not an accident that the best prose was written when rococo, with its elegance and moderation, at its birth attained its greatest excellence. For rococo was evolved when baroque had become declamatory and the world, tired of the stupendous, asked for restraint. It was the natural expression of persons who valued a civilized life.' [12]

The implication of this seems to be that the best writing of any age reflects the standard of its civilization. But I question whether this is really so. American literature, it seems to me, is slowly but surely stealing a march on our own; I am speaking of contemporary writing, of course. It not only shows enormous vitality but is often subtle in both perception and imagination; in outlook and idiom it has a distinct native freshness; and it has got something to say. These are qualities which at the present time seem to be rather in the doldrums on this side of the Atlantic. And yet I believe that we are still more civilized, in the sense in which Maugham uses that expression, than the Americans, whom, by and large, I love and admire nevertheless. Yet in spite of their barbarity—and I really do not feel this is too strong a word for a nation which, within the span of a single generation, allowed power to accrue to such men as Huey Long, Al Capone, Father Coughlan and Senator McCarthy—in spite of this, the buds of true literary genius are undoubtedly beginning to unfold in American literature. And in case this should seem patronizing—though nothing could be further from my intention—I would point out that Chaucer died nearly four hundred years before Washington Irving was born, and that 'the true hallmark of a great creative artist . . . is that his work is not only of contemporary, but also of universal significance, and that with the passing of time the contemporary problems, which seemed to him so important, tend to recede into the background, while the universal significance of his work comes more and more to the fore.' [13]

That is true enough. But when a writer begins to talk about universal significance I feel the time has come to examine his terms of reference. What precisely does universal significance mean? It can mean that the writer is a man of profound and enduring wisdom; or it can mean that he is a no less profound bore. Martin Tupper was strong on universal significance, so was Ella Wheeler Wilcox, and theirs was a fate with which I imagine not many people would quarrel nowadays, though it is fair to remember that each of them in their day gave widespread if rather unsophisticated pleasure. And if 'literary charm, arising out of a desire to please, excludes those flights of intellectual power which are so much more rewarding than pleasure,' [14] I do not suppose either of them had an inkling of what they were missing. Yet 'literary charm', so long as it does not arise simply from a desire to please, and so appear self-conscious, is an admirable, I would even say an enviable, thing. For I believe that 'writing is not literature unless it gives the reader a pleasure which arises not only from the things said, but from the way in which they are said'.[15] That is for me one of the troubles about reading books that have been translated. I do not underestimate the difficulties of the translator. It must be very hard indeed to convey a writer's meaning without losing something of the subtlety or precision that derive from the characteristics of his style. Only if one knows the author's language thoroughly can one judge a translation objectively. Otherwise it must seem either good or bad according to the degree of pleasure, or the reverse, that it gives, and it is very seldom that I have the feeling that what I am getting is probably something very like to the original. There is usually a stilted air about the thing, as though one were listening to an intelligent foreigner speaking in one's own tongue; though the grammar appears impeccable, there is a faint but distracting hint of a foreign accent. I know this is an illogical and perhaps pedantic prejudice, but there is another objection, and I think a more valid one, to reading a translated book.

'It has become a convention that masterpieces of other ages and civilizations should be translated into the ordinary vocabulary of the present time. There is one main argument in support of this: that the general reader will at least understand what the translator says, whether he catches the accent of the original or not. The argument against is that no good writer in any age has confined himself to the popular vocabulary, even when he has dealt with contemporary affairs. He chooses his own speech, employing it traditionally if he is a traditionalist, or in some new way if he is an innovator. His individuality determines his choice.

'If then we turn Homer or Dante or Montaigne into contemporaries we shall certainly lose something which is essential in them. And if we do that, there is no reason why we should not modernise our own writers as well, Sir Thomas Browne, for example, or Gibbon; nor any reason why we should not repaint Giotto or Cézanne, to make them quite current, or reconstitute St Mark's and St Paul's, or write up-to-date scores for Mozart and Beethoven. The new fashion in translation is probably an aberration of the historical sense. The great masterpieces exist in their own periods and for all time. To turn them into contemporary works is really to falsify them, and put them beyond real comprehension by making them appear to be perfectly comprehensible to everyone.' [16]

It must be a similar sort of aberration that results in the squeezing of books as though they were lemons from which the essence can be extracted and what is left over thrown away. Only a rather stupid or lazy-minded person, probably one who is both, would suppose that a novel like *War and Peace* can be compressed for the easy enjoyment of others as lazy as himself and still retain the impress and the scope of Tolstoy's imagination. 'Anything which encourages people to believe that great works of literature can be predigested, softened up, made easy, or incapsulated, seems to me to do no service to anybody. There is no substitute for Shakespeare, or Milton, or Dante, and reading them with the attention they demand and deserve can never be anything but hard work.' [17] I cannot deny that mental laziness has had a good deal to do with my by-passing many of the ancient classics, though I think this is not wholly through lack of concentration. There is also something in me that mysteriously reacts against the mythological concept, which is no doubt why I have never been able wholly to enjoy Wagner. Whatever it is, this defect must be fairly deep-seated because it first proclaimed itself when at an early age I began to show a marked disinterest in fairy stories. Indeed, it seems that I must have been more progressive in my reading habits then than I am now. How discouraging it is to be still young enough to notice how early in life one's ideas begin to ossify, and yet too old to prevent their doing so. My attitude towards books is like Montaigne's, 'I make no other use of them than those who know them not. I enjoy them, as a miser doth his gold; to know that I may enjoy them when I list, my mind is settled and satisfied with the right of possession. I never travel without bookes, nor in peace nor in warre: yet I doe passe many dayes and moneths without using them. It shall be anon, say I, or to-morrow, or when I please; in the meane while time runnes away, and passeth without hurting me. For it is wonderfull what repose I take, and how I continue in this consideration, that they are at my elbow to delight me when the time shall serve; and in acknowledging what assistance they give unto my life. This is the best munition I have found in this human peregrination, and I extremely bewaile those men of understanding that want the same. I accept with better will other kindes of ammusements, how slight soever, forsomuch as this cannot faile me. At home I betake me somewhat oftner to my library, whence all at once I command and survey all my household.' [18]

Montaigne kept his library in a tower, and there is a lot to be said for keeping all of one's books together. Yet a room that has none gives me the feeling of its being not properly furnished. I like to be able to pick up and dip into a book wherever I may happen to be. For instance, 'I have always had a fancy for reading while eating, if I am alone; it supplies the want of society. I devour alternately a page and a morsel. It seems as if my book were dining with me.' [19] I do not much mind what sort of book it is, though 'historians are my right hand; for they are pleasant and easie: and there withall, the man with whom I desire generally to be acquainted, may more lively and perfectly be discovered in them, than in any other composition: the variety and truth of his inward conditions, in grosse and by retale: the diversitie of the meanes of his collection and composing, and of the accidents that threaten him. Now, those that write of men's lives, forasmuch as they ammuse and busie themselves more about counsels than events, more about that which commeth from within, than that which appeareth outward; they are fittest for me . . .' [20]

Having less time to read than I should like to have, I tend to be rather restricted, perhaps even too conservative, in my choice of books, particularly where fiction is concerned. A class of novel, for instance, that I willingly forego nowadays, although when I was younger I doted on it, is the detective story, especially of the English variety.

As a form of so-called escapist literature there is not much to recommend such stories as a rule, if you discount the deductive element. With few exceptions, the characters and circumstances are usually so lacking in either reality or imagination that they would be intolerable to read about without this special stimulus. The excruciating falsity of the dialogue usually kills stone dead any character who may have seemed to have some element of plausibility or life about him before he opened his mouth. This, with all the painful contrivances, the pedantry, and above all the shattering facetiousness of the average whodunit deprives me of any possibility of its enjoyment. And if there is one sort that I find more boring than the rest it is the kind written by English gentlewomen whose lives have never been blemished by contact with any form of crime or violence. No word of theirs that I have ever read could possibly be considered as being in bad taste, let alone suggestive of depravity or of a knowledge of sin, though to my mind nothing could be more depraved or in worse taste than murder. Except for Wilkie Collins, Emile Gaboriau and a handful of their followers, very few authors who have tried their hands at detective stories seem to have any real knowledge of how detectives work. They show little interest in the characters they create, or in fact in human beings generally. Their interest is in gimmicks, in the ingenuities of the plot, in showing off a knowledge of wine or Etruscan art or something equally esoteric. The author of the thriller, with which the detective story is often and easily confused, is at least interested in thrills, and though he may be less gifted in the academic line, he does at least write out of his imagination, sometimes even out of his experience; and as a reservoir for the creation of character and for motives of human behaviour, the imagination, however highly coloured, is likely to be more reliable than a nose that can distinguish infallibly between a Chambertin '47 and a Richbourg '49.

Few thriller-writers seem to me as interesting or as readable as Raymond Chandler, though I suspect that his preoccupation with violence sometimes defeats its end (which is the simple and virtuous one of showing that crime doesn't pay) and obscures his merits as a writer from readers who might appreciate them better if they were not repelled by the beating up and bumping off that seem inseparable from his stories. And yet one knows, if you follow, as I do with unabashed interest, the American gangster saga, that Chandler's brutalities are small and unimaginative compared to the real thing. The advantage that he has over most of his imitators, and a large and dismal crew they are, is not so much that he is more original or more ingenious—I

find his books, few though they are, almost too much alike and sometimes too complicated to follow easily—but that in his observation and
understanding of human nature, in his bare-boned gift of narrative, and
in his handling of the spoken word, he makes most other practitioners
in this field look like amateurs. He does not see murder as a subject
merely for ingenious deduction or erudite joking, but for what it is,
a disgusting abberration, and he writes about it accordingly, with
results that offer no compromise to the reader's susceptibilities about
vice or violence.

When I am in the mood for reading—and if it were not that necessity
finds other things for me to do, I think I could take happily to a
life of idle scholarship—it does not much matter what sort of book is in
front of me, so long as it is something for my imagination to bite on.
For, as Carlyle says, 'of the things which man can do or make ...
by far the most momentous, wonderful and worthy are the things
we call Books! Those poor bits of rag-paper with black ink on
them!—from the Daily Newspaper to the sacred Hebrew Book, what
have they not done, what are they not doing!—For indeed, whatever
be the outward form of the thing (bits of paper, as we might say, and
black ink), is it not verily ... the highest act of man's faculty that
produces a Book? It is the *Thought* of man: the true thaumaturgic
virtue; by which man works all things whatsoever. All that he does,
and brings to pass, is the vesture of a Thought. This London City,
with all its houses, palaces, steam engines, cathedrals, and huge immeasurable traffic and tumult, what is it but a Thought, but millions
of Thoughts made into One;—a huge immeasurable Spirit of a
Thought, embodied in brick, in iron, smoke, dust, Palaces, Parliaments,
Hackney Coaches, Katherine Docks, and the rest of it! Not a brick was
made but some man had to *think* of the making of that brick.—The
thing we called "bits of paper with traces of black ink", is the *purest*
embodiment a Thought of man can have ... it is in all ways, the
activest and noblest.' [21]

I am not sure that I go the whole way with Carlyle on that. Of
course, he is speaking of the highest and noblest in literature. But
unfortunately a good deal of the highest and noblest is lost on me.
'One need not necessarily understand,' as Maurice Baring remarked,
'in order to enjoy. As a child I remember enjoying Shelley's poem
about Arethusa without having the slightest idea what it meant,
without even knowing that it was about a water nymph being pursued
by a river god; and now that I am disappointed, bald and fifty-seven,
and, notwithstanding that, no nearer Heaven, I can enjoy some of the

poems of T. S. Eliot without being quite certain I have caught his train of thought, or that I can trace each erudite allusion without (and still less with) the help of his notes. But . . . I can read almost any verse with pleasure, bad verse as well as good verse; and I am not surprised when I find others who share this taste.' [22]

It is rare to find a man of erudition and scholarly tastes with an appetite as indiscriminately eager as Maurice Baring's, and personally I find it most refreshing, though I can well imagine that to the true-blue pedantic literary don Baring's brand of scholarship would probably seem pretty haphazard; which is the sort of attitude that puts this type of don at a disadvantage with lesser men. The trouble with dons as a rule is that they spend too much time imbibing other people's opinions. Yet if one is fond of books it is easy enough to understand, even to envy, the don's deliberate seclusion, his capacity for reading, his genuine love of books and his life-long preoccupation with them. 'The habit of reading is the only enjoyment in which there is no alloy; it lasts when all other pleasures fade.' [23] So said Trollope, and it is one of the few points on which I find myself in agreement with him. But then I made a bad start; I began by reading his *Autobiography*. This shows him not only as self-righteous, which is bad enough, but as self-satisfied, which is worse, and in an artist unforgivable. It shows him comfortably content with the English bourgeoisie and happy to be a member of it. No doubt it is better to be happy than unhappy in the station of life to which providence directs you, but for a professional writer who aspires to be something better than a hack, the climate of thought and opinion among the middle class mass is hardly conducive to the production of a major or even a minor masterpiece. The middle class mass has certain virtues that are to be envied and some that are to be much admired. It is a very fine thing in its way, this mass; but its way is not the way to Parnassus and it can sometimes be cruel and obtuse and indifferent towards those who want to try to get there. Not that Trollope, to do him justice, made any pretence about trying to scale the heights. He wrote to make money, as most authors do. I have no objection to this, but what I do object to is Trollope's approach to the job, which was that of a factory hand with one eye on the clock. The wonder of it is that in such circumstances he was able to produce anything that has remained worth reading. After I had read the *Autobiography*, I tried *The Warden*, then *Phineas Finn* and then *Barchester Towers;* but it was no good: the author's ugly image, symbolising the heavy-handed materialism of his beliefs, kept obtruding itself, and in the end I gave up.

It may seem foolish to be so subjective, but reading, as I mostly do, for my own pleasure, I set out in a different frame of mind from that of the reader who embarks on a work that requires a critical and dispassionate approach for its proper understanding. I am firmly of the belief that 'a man ought to read just as inclination leads him; for what he reads as a task will do him little good.' [24]

SOURCES

1   The Hon. G. W. E. Russell, *Fifteen Chapters of Autobiography.*
2   Horace Walpole, letter to Lady Ossory, August 11, 1778.
3   François Mauriac, *A Woman of the Pharisees.*
4   Thomas Love Peacock, *Nightmare Abbey.*
5   George Moore, *Confessions of a Young Man.*
6   W. Somserset Maugham, *The Summing Up.*
7   Dame Edith Sitwell, *The Pleasures of Poetry.*
8   Sir Desmond MacCarthy, *The Sunday Times,* January 28, 1951.
9   See 6.
10   Ibid.
11   Ibid.
12   Ibid.
13   David Magarshack, introduction to *Crime and Punishment,* Penguin edition.
14   Palinurus, *The Unquiet Grave.*
15   Stopford Brooke, *A Primer of English Literature.*
16   Edwin Muir, *The Observer,* March 20, 1955.
17   'O.P.', *The Bookseller,* August 6, 1956.
18   Michel de Montaigne, *Essays,* Book II.
19   *The Confessions of Jean-Jacques Rousseau.*
20   See 18.
21   Thomas Carlyle, *On Heroes.*
22   Maurice Baring, *Lost Lectures.*
23   Anthony Trollope, *An Autobiography.*
24   Samuel Johnson, Boswell's *Life.*

Essay on man

*

Man is the only animal that laughs and weeps; for he is the
only animal that is struck by the difference between what
things are, and what they ought to be.

WILLIAM HAZLITT, *Lectures on the English Comic Writers*

I ONCE read a book by Freud. I was a student at the time and was tremendously impressed by it. Now I cannot even remember its name, let alone what it was that so impressed me. Looking back, I wonder why I read it at all, not being then, as one so often is at such an age, introspectively inclined. I was, and in some respects still am, too frivolous ever to make the grade as a man of intellectual purpose. Except when I am at work, either writing or drawing, or absorbed in looking at a work of art or nature (my preference for them being in that order) or when I am feeling depressed or out of sorts, or have a fancy to be solitary, except on occasions such as these, the temptation to upset someone's gravity, to disorganize the proceedings with some remark not strictly appropriate, or to prolong an argument merely for the enjoyment of arguing, are temptations that I usually find it hard to resist. Or else my mind begins to wander. At meetings, to which from time to time I am summoned and dutifully attend, I sit in a state of rapt inattentiveness, thinking of other things; the skyline outside the window maybe, and compare it with the skyline of Paris on just such an afternoon, or of Elsinore as I once saw it gleaming in the dusk across the Baltic, or of New York in the autumn dawn; and my thoughts, which ought to be firmly fixed on the agenda, turn to that evening with Philippa at the Blue Room on—was it on 46th or 52nd Street?—and the girl who sang with a voice that reminded us so warmly, so enchantingly, of Yvonne Printemps. Time's winged chariot has thumped its way down a score of years at least since *Violettes Imperiales*, which ought to have been but was not (I think) by Offenbach, though it had the same romantic effervescence as *Gaieté Parisienne*, as *Beau Danube*, with its moment of magical poignancy as the grey hussar hesitates, listens, as though to the music of another sphere, and then leans into the waltz. In all romantic ballet there is nothing more transporting than Massine was at that moment. Oh, shades of the Garden, with its gilt Victorian setting and red-striped wallpaper, and supper afterwards at Rules. Why this fondness of mine, I wonder, for fish and game in preference to good red meat? Is it something atavistic? And for beans, and broccoli, and brandy? How right Johnson was giving it pride of place among the hierarchy of liquors. Right, too, in defining happiness as riding with a pretty woman in a post-chaise—or was it driving? Either way, Stubbs is the man it calls to mind, and you can keep the rest of the British School, or almost all of it. But what of the one at Athens? How shall I ever get to Greece? Cyprus too I must see one day, and Turkey. What a lot I seem to have been missing! And Venice again, with its never-ending beauties, sights, sounds, and surprises, not forgetting Peggy Guggenheim and the collection, and dining late at Quadri's in the warm September night beside the open window, with the band rattling through *Semiramide* in the piazza, then on to Harry's Bar and will all those in favour of the motion kindly signify in the usual manner?

So back with a jerk to realities that are often so much less real to me than the miracle of Vermeer's vision, of Renoir's pigment, or the ethereal fantasies of Turner, or than the pictures that the mind's eye retains from its earliest years, from *The Tailor of Gloucester*, *Tom Sawyer*, Sherlock Holmes and the world of Jules Verne. Maybe it is because so large a share of my leisure thoughts, and often those while I am not at leisure, are absorbed by matters of this sort that I have not much time—and let's face it, not much inclination—for self-analysis, except when it has the specific object of resolving some problem of my emotions or behaviour. I know this *ad hoc* approach is all wrong and probably leads me to draw a number of erroneous conclusions, but I cannot work up enough interest in my own psychological state to make it worth the effort of long investigations. So 'what shall I compare it to, this fantastic thing I call my Mind? To a waste-paper basket, to a sieve choked with sediment, or to a barrel full of floating froth and refuse?

'No, what it is really most like is a spider's web, insecurely hung on leaves and twigs, quivering in every wind, and sprinkled with dew-drops and dead flies. And at its centre, pondering ... sits motionless the spider-like and uncanny Soul.' [1] Perhaps it is that I am too fatalistic, too ready to accept without question what the Gods have dished out to me, to make the effort towards a better understanding of how my mind works. Perhaps if I were more aware of myself, of what it is in my make-up that impels me now towards one sort of folly, now towards another, I might be able to take steps to rectify the position. But the truth is that I haven't a clue. Here I am, if it doesn't sound too grandiloquent, a creature

> *Placed on this isthmus of a middle state,*
> *A being darkly wise and rudely great:*
> *With too much knowledge for the Sceptic side,*
> *With too much weakness for the Stoic's pride,*
> *Alike in ignorance, his reason such,*

Whether he thinks too little or too much;
Chaos of thought and passion, all confused;
Still by himself abused or disabused;
Created half to rise, and half to fall;
Great Lord of all things, yet a prey to all;
Sole judge of truth, in endless error hurled;
The glory, jest, and riddle of the world.[2]

The sort of person I imagine myself to be—only a mystic or a lunatic could feel with certainty that he knows the whole truth about himself—is one of those rather restless beings for whom action is in itself some sort of reward, or perhaps more truthfully, some sort of palliative. I think also that there is 'an essential difference of character in mankind, between those who wish *to do*, and those who wish *to have* certain things,' [3] and that it is to the first of these categories that I belong. I enjoy the possession of certain objects that give me pleasure by their appearance, and, though less often, by their associations, and although I regret it when something gets damaged or broken, I cannot honestly say that their destruction means much to me and I quickly forget my attachment. Hazlitt remarked that he sometimes observed 'persons expressing a great desire to possess fine horses, hounds, dress, equipage, etc. and an envy of those who have them. I myself have no such feeling, nor the least ambition to shine, except by doing something better than others. I have the love of power but not of property. I should like to be able to outstrip a greyhound in speed; but I should be ashamed to take any merit to myself from possessing the fleetest greyhound in the world. I cannot transfer my personal identity from myself to what I merely call *mine*. The generality of mankind are contented to be estimated by what they possess, instead of what they are.' [4]

Of course, I am not really as disinterested as this would make me out to be. I am too much of a sybarite for one thing, too fond of sensory pleasures. Yet attached as I am to my *lares* and *penates*, it is the pleasure they give *me* that counts, not the delight or the admiration, or the envy, they arouse in others. I sometimes think that this tendency makes me too indifferent to criticism and less receptive to fresh ideas than is good for me. And when I realize this I am seized with a sense of atrophy, of inadequacy. ' "I must really improve my mind", I tell myself, and once more begin to patch and repair that crazy structure. So I toil and toil on at the vain task of edification, though the wind tears off the tiles, the floors give way, the ceilings fall, strange birds build untidy nests in the rafters, and owls hoot and laugh in the tumbling chimneys.' [5] Not that I aim at perfection, because 'perfection has one grave defect: it is apt to be dull.'[6] It may give you a good opinion of yourself, but is likely to leave you without much sense of humour about your own affairs. And if you cannot afford to be laughed at, you are on very uncertain ground when it comes to making jokes at the expense of other people; which are the only jokes worth making, because only human beings are afflicted with a sense of their own dignity. Humour is an affair of the intelligence, not of the heart. You cannot allow your sympathies to become engaged by the predicaments of a comedian, as they would be in real life, because you cannot laugh at someone for whom you are feeling sorry. It is not merely a question of pretence. One is not less moved by the tragic situations of Oedipus or Hamlet because one knows that they are not real, but here one is willingly and deliberately suspending intelligence in favour of emotion. 'In a society composed of pure intelligences there would probably be no more tears, though perhaps there would still be laughter; whereas highly emotional souls, in tune and unison with life, in whom every event would be sentimentally prolonged and re-echoed, would neither know nor understand laughter. Try, for a moment, to become interested in everything that is being said and done; act, in imagination, with those who act, and feel with those who feel; in a word, give your sympathy its widest expansion: as though at the touch of a fairy wand you will see the flimsiest of objects assume importance, and a gloomy hue spread over everything. Now step aside, look upon life as a disinterested spectator: many a drama will turn into a comedy. It is enough for us to stop our ears to the sound of music, in a room where dancing is going on, for the dancers at once to appear ridiculous. How many human actions would stand a similar test? Should we not see many of them suddenly pass from grave to gay, on isolating them from the accompanying music of sentiment? To produce the whole of its effect, then, the comic demands something like a momentary anaesthesia of the heart. Its appeal is to intelligence, pure and simple.' [7]

I said just now that I was not much interested in self-analysis for its own sake. As a means of self-discovery I know that it has its uses, and because humour has always been part of my trade I have tried from time to time, though not very systematically, to explore the workings of my own sense of humour. It has usually proved a dis-couraging though perhaps not wholly unprofitable experience. That the Englishman's sense of humour is not quite like that of anyone else is a proposition not to be easily denied. It seems to me in some respects a rather poor mechanism compared to the Frenchman's, or to the American's more oblique and astringent sense. I am abashed, therefore, to realize how much of the Englishman's sense of humour I share. For example, 'the disquiet with which ... the English react to the unfamiliar. It is interesting, for instance, to observe how large a part is played in English laughter by the factor of recognition. A music-hall audience ... will respond immediately to the recognizable, and will laugh aloud at stock jokes, repetition, mimicry, personifications, references to food or drink, and any allusion to the topical.

'This desire to economise in mental and psychic effort also explains the tendency of the English to regard as comic, insincere or pretentious anything which they do not happen personally to understand. Apart from the self-protective element in such laughter there is also the instinct to dismiss as unimportant any subject which requires for its understanding concentrated mental effort. This inclination to ridicule the difficult can be observed in the normal reaction of the Englishman to innovations in art, literature and even politics. It can also be noticed in his hatred of conceptual logic, a hatred which finds an outlet in the strangest of all the many manifestations of the English sense of humour, namely the national love of nonsense,' [8] a thing incomprehensible, for instance, to the French, in whom there is a deep-seated sense of logic.

The popular conception of the difference between ourselves and the French in what each of us finds amusing is that while they appreciate wit, we enjoy humour. Well, what is the difference between wit and humour? The essential difference, I should say, 'is that, whereas wit is always intentional, humour is always unintentional. Wit possesses an object; it is critical, aggressive and often cruel; it depends for its success upon condensation, revelation, suddenness and surprise, and it necessitates a quick and deliberate motion of the mind; it is not a private indulgence but invariably needs an audience; it is thus a social phenomenon. Humour on the other hand has no object; it does not seek to wound others, it seeks only to protect the self; it is not a sword but a shield. So far from entailing an expenditure of intellectual or psychic effort, it seeks to economise that effort; it does not depend on suddenness or surprise, but is contemplative, conciliatory, ruminating; and it is largely a private indulgence and does not require an audience for its enjoyment.

'The sense of humour is for these reasons more akin to aesthetics than it is to the appreciation of wit or satire. The sense of humour, like aesthetics, is not limited by service to any particular purpose; it has a non-determining character. Like aesthetics also it is largely intuitive, and possesses a logic of the fancy which is wholly different from, and even opposed to, conceptual logic. Thus whereas wit is the product of imagination and seeks by mental energy and speed to discover similarities in dis-similar things, humour is the play of fancy and is content with the comparatively effortless recognition of dissimilarity in similar things.

'It is this presence or absence of an object and an intention which also distinguishes humour from satire and irony. Humour essentially is a receiving station, not a transmitter; it observes human frailty indulgently and without bothering to correct it; irony and satire have a nobler and more didactic purpose. Whereas irony, being critical and pessimistic, demonstrates the difference between the real and the ideal, humour, being uncritical and optimistic, either ignores the difference, or pretends that it is not, after all, so very important.' ⁹

Though the inclination of my sense of humour is decidedly in the direction of irony, I refuse to regard myself, no matter in what light others may think they see me, as a pessimist. I am an aspiring creature and well aware of it, but not ambitious enough for that. 'Despair is the price one pays for setting oneself an impossible aim. It is, one is told, the unforgiveable sin, but it is a sin the corrupt or evil man never practises. He always has hope,' ¹⁰

> . . . the thing with feathers
> That perches in the soul,
> And sings the time without the words
> And never stops at all . . .¹¹

'He never reaches the freezing point of knowing absolute failure. Only the man of goodwill carries always in his heart this capacity for damnation.' ¹²

In my own heart I carry an awareness of certain grave defects in my character which I am frequently ashamed of, my weakness in trying to overcome them being one, but it has never occurred to me that by conventional standards I may seem a corrupt or evil man. Yet life, with its infinity of disappointments and frustrations, still seems to renew its offers of hope, though 'it is seldom that we find either men or places such as we expect them. He that has pictured a prospect upon his fancy, will receive little pleasure from his eyes; he that has anticipated the conversation of a wit, will wonder to what prejudice he owes his reputation. Yet it is necessary to hope, though hope should always be deluded; for hope itself is happiness, and its frustrations, however infrequent, are yet less dreadful than its extinction.' [13]

If that is the voice, as some might think, of unreasoning optimism, it is a voice curiously characteristic of the Englishman's attitude towards life. Consider the case of Micawber. To what other race could he have belonged? Is he conceivable as a German or a Spaniard, a Russian or a Chinese, an Arab or a Swede? I hardly think so, and still less can one picture him as a citizen of some South American republic. If the buttresses of hope, the reasons for universal sanguinity on which in my boyhood it seemed not unreasonable to rely, have since vanished away, and if in consequence the world has become a more dangerous and uncomfortable place, I still prefer to face up to it with the inconsequential optimism of the Englishman, however ill-founded, than with the stern materialistic vision of the communist, or the defiant self-righteousness that hides the moral uncertainty and good intentions of so many Americans.

My father, as a schoolboy, was once asked by one of his masters what he would like to be if he were not an Englishman. His answer was, '"I should like to be an Englishman". This,' he says, 'was treated by the inquirer and by the other boys as paltering with the question; in other words, as trying to be funny; but after all, I meant it, and I still think that it was the form in which the question was put that was to blame. If I had been asked, "If you could not be an Englishman, what would you like to be?" I should have had more difficulty in framing a reply . . .

'All the same, I have never had the faintest feeling that I should like to be anything but English; not even in those days when I hardly knew what being English meant. I preferred being English as a Frenchman prefers being French, or a Chinaman prefers being Chinese. My excuse for this irrational frame of mind was, and is, what someone has called the only good excuse in the world: I could not help it. That is what patriotism has always meant to me; that it is no more credit to a man that he loves his country than that he eats, or drinks or loves his sweetheart. It ought to be taken for granted . . .

'To be a patriot is not in itself a passport to happiness. It is not agreeable to feel that one's country is misunderstood, as—from the very nature of the case, perhaps—all great countries are. It is less agreeable to feel that it is heartily disliked . . . Least agreeable is it to the patriot when his country's honour and independence and place in the world —its life, as we are prone to call it at such moments—are threatened in war that is war, and not merely some contention that threatens little more than the taxpayer's pocket.

'These are trials; and the last-named is a searching one. But at least we can endure it together, and believe in what we are fighting about. The real troubles of the patriot, as a patriot, begin only when his country takes what he feels in his heart to be the wrong turning, and adopts a policy that no reasoning, with others or himself, can make him regard as honourable.' [14]

I remember that when I was a boy more than one of my parents' friendships foundered on a divergence of opinions on the Irish question, upon which my father held decided views. One dispute in particular —it was not of his making, he was the most peaceable man I have ever known—was a cause of sincere regret throughout the rest of his life, but he believed in the validity of his opinion and would not let it be shaken, no matter what it cost him. Moral judgements are invariably the hardest to make, for in the last analysis they must depend on one's own conception of what is right and what is wrong in given circumstances. What counts therefore is not what someone in authority 'tells me I *may* do, but what humanity, reason and justice tell me I ought to do'.[15] I do not mean that where moral judgements are not involved it is necessarily easier to decide between what seems right and what you believe to be wrong, but it is easier to strike a balance. In matters of taste, for instance: if I am told, by someone whose views I respect, that a painting by some primitive master, which seems to me both hideous and inept, is a great work of art, I am prepared to admit the possibility, while sticking to my own opinion of its merits as a picture. For making some such remark I was once told that I was a Philistine. I reacted strongly, not only because I believed it to be untrue, but because the word signifies indifference as much as ignorance, and indifference is the enemy of all the arts, which, in proportion to their mystery and elusiveness, require patience and curiosity for their understanding. Nevertheless there are regions of thought and sound and form in art that remain above my comprehension. *Musique concrète*, for instance, seems to me to have as little to do with music as some of William Carlos Williams's poems seem to have to do with poetry. But I am not prepared to condemn them on that account, and that is the difference between the Philistine and the highbrow. Personally, 'I am proud to consider myself . . . a highbrow. Puzzled by this term of abuse, a visiting French author is said to have asked for explanations; and then to have exclaimed, "I understand. A highbrow is a person who prefers good books to bad ones". I would suggest further that the highbrow is a person to whom the past and the present are similarly significant and vivid. Many people can like only the newest tunes and the most recent books; others can respect nothing that is not familiar and consecrated by time. The highbrow, I hope, seeks to base his judgement on non-temporal values, and is indifferent to mere novelty or antiquity. Those who claim to enjoy Picasso but not Poussin, seem to me as untrustworthy in their taste as those who claim to enjoy Poussin but not Picasso. The highbrow depends upon the standard of excellence set by the masterpieces of the past, but does not expect their methods to be imitated by the masterpieces of the present.' [16]

That, broadly speaking, is the meaning that I attach to the word highbrow, but it is a word that one should use with care because, of course, there are bad as well as good highbrows. By the good highbrow I mean 'the man who is well educated and glad of the fact without thrusting it down other people's throats, who, without being ashamed of his knowledge, his intellectual or artistic superiority, or his gifts and aptitudes, does not use them as a rod to beat others with, and does not think that because he is the fortunate possessor of certain rare gifts or talents, he is therefore a better or a more useful man: such is the good highbrow . . .

'Now we come to the bad highbrow, which no highbrow will admit that he can be: but, as a Master of Trinity once said, we are none of us infallible, not even the youngest of us. And the moment we fall into the temptation of despising the interests and the recreations of others, however futile they may seem to us, we become bad high-brows . . .

'The worst faults of the bad highbrow are not (putting aside his knowledge, learning, scholarship or culture, which are not faults at all, but the gifts of Heaven, if they are genuine, and the curse of the devil if they are false) his pride, arrogance and narrow-mindedness; but his envy of others who are either highbrows like himself and possibly better ones, or, worse still, his envy of others who are not highbrows at all, but people who are amusing themselves in their own way. If you want to know what envy is, said Lord Beaconsfield, you should live among artists; but were he alive now he would have said you must live among highbrows. But the bad highbrow is not a new thing: he is as old as the hills. Aristophanes knew him and satirised him; Molière knew him, male and female, and shot some of his most pointed arrows at the species, fixing them to remain for ever before our delighted gaze.' [17]

I hope that I am not a bad highbrow, yet sometimes, when I meet someone whose powers of understanding and appreciation are shown to be markedly superior to mine, I am conscious of the fact that I am envious of his possessing so high a degree of intellectual poise and equipment. But you cannot have it both ways; I realize that I am not suited either by disposition or intellect to the life of a scholar, and I have tried to do the best I can with the clay from which I was made. After all, what does it signify?

> *Like to the falling of a star,*
> *Or as the flights of eagles are,*
> *Or like the fresh spring's gaudy hue,*
> *Or silver drops of morning dew, . . .*
> *Even such is Man, whose borrowed light*
> *Is straight call'd in and paid to night.*
> *The wind blows out, the bubble dies,*
> *The spring entombed in autumn lies;*
> *The dew dries up, the star is shot,*
> *The flight is past,—and Man forgot.*[18]

SOURCES

1   Logan Pearsall Smith, *Trivia.*
2   Alexander Pope, *Essay on Man.*
3   William Hazlitt, *Characteristics.*
4   Ibid.
5   See 1.
6   W. Somerset Maugham, *The Summing Up.*
7   Henri Bergsen, *Laughter.*
8   Sir Harold Nicolson, *The English Sense of Humour.*
9   Ibid.
10 Graham Greene, *The Heart of the Matter.*
11 Emily Dickinson, *Hope is the Thing with Feathers.*
12 See 10.
13 Samuel Johnson, *The Idler.*
14 E. C. Bentley, *Those Days.*
15 Edmund Burke, *Short Sayings.*
16 Raymond Mortimer, *Channel Packet.*
17 Maurice Baring, *Lost Lectures.*
18 Henry King, *On the Life of Man.*

The Last Argument

*

They now to fight are gone,
Armour on armour shone,
Drum unto drum did groan,
  To hear was wonder;
That with the cries they make
The very earth did shake
Trumpet to trumpet spake,
  Thunder to thunder.
MICHAEL DRAYTON, *The Battle of Agincourt*

IT is sometimes hard for an unbeliever like myself to be optimistic about the possibilities of everlasting peace—and I am not being cynical: it is hard, but not impossible. I mean that my scepticism of the religious view leaves me without much interest in what may happen hereafter. It is the physical fate of mankind—in fact, to be honest about it, of myself—that preoccupies my thoughts about the future, not the hypothetical existence of a celestial utopia. Faced with the indifference of the communist world to the feelings and aspirations of the rest of humanity, faced with its open and avowed antagonism to all concepts of right and wrong, of good and bad, except its own, it is not easy to see how a more peaceful form of co-existence can ever be achieved than the state of uneasy truce under which we now exist. Nor do the overpowering bromides of Western statesmen help to clear one's vision. Not that one can blame the poor devils, I suppose, except for their unerring pomposity. Why is it that so often when a man gets on his hindlegs to make a speech, no matter how sensible his views or honest his intentions, he makes himself sound like an idiot by adopting an orotund manner of speech quite unlike his ordinary way of talking? Western statesmen are the impotent victims of their own proud independence, with its resultant and inevitable conflict of ideas and reliance on compromise and expediency, neither of which seem to offer satisfactory safeguards against annihilation.

Ten years of my life have been years of war, and it looks as though I shall spend the rest of it in apprehension, probably never very far below the surface, of an experience far worse than any that war has yet disclosed. Logically, this ought to have been enough to sicken me of the subject, but with a perversity that many people seem to share, I still find enjoyment in reading of battles and of the spirit of men under arms; not that anything can ennoble so beastly a thing as war, though imaginative words and the perspective of time may lend it a spurious glamour. Thermopylae may sound magnificent in the telling, so may Roncesvalles, and Agincourt, and Lepanto, but I doubt that any man who fought in battles such as these was better off than if he had landed on the beach at Anzio or dropped from the skies at Arnhem. The horrors of warfare do not change as much with the passage of time as propagandists like to make out, except that its horrors encircle the innocent in ever greater numbers. Indeed, pain and mutilation were more to be feared in the fifteenth century than they are in the twentieth.

74

But it all comes down to the same thing: nothing but the soldier's plain courage can ever redeem what is and must always be a sordid trade. Whatever ancient glamour war may once have had for Englishmen departed finally when conscription came. Of those who belonged to the generation before my own, many had already had the scales struck from their eyes. One of them was J. B. Morton, who, during that fateful weekend in August 1914, was at a house party in Sussex, and all that sunny Saturday was playing cricket:

'That match is a vivid memory, in a setting of quiet fields and ancient trees. There was a great meal afterwards, and beer and songs. And that was the end of the old world. It was the end of a careless light-heartedness, and of a kind of innocence. One came to manhood through a terrible gate, and suddenly, without the preparation that had been expected. Boyhood, in those days, did not pass quietly into manhood, but was rent away in a gun-flash, and departed for ever in a single night of violence.' [1]

The eye-witness, however inarticulate, must always have an advantage over the academic historian: the advantage of experience. No one, to my mind, compares with Gibbon as a war historian, and yet, in spite of his rich and animating detail, in spite of his lucidity and the simple patterns to which he can reduce a complicated strategy, it is difficult to imagine that the events he describes were not created out of his stupendous imagination. The grandeur and sobriety of his style, almost as much as the passage of time, may have something to do with this, but the fact remains that one can read Gibbon unmoved by anything except admiration for his genius. Take, for instance, his description of the march of Julian's legions through Mesopotamia in their attack on the Persian empire. In spite of the impression of a more or less orderly progress with which he invests this immense undertaking, involving the transport of huge armies across the Euphrates and the Tigris, it can hardly have been a picnic for the P.B.I. of the Roman army, girt with armour and forced to march many miles a day in great heat and through inhospitable country.

Julian set out from Antioch in March, A.D. 363. His army, 'the most numerous that any of the Caesars had ever led against Persia, consisted of sixty-five thousand effective and well-disciplined soldiers. The veteran bands of cavalry and infantry, of Romans and Barbarians, had been selected from the different provinces; and a just pre-eminence of loyalty and valour was claimed by the hardy Gauls, who guarded the throne and person of their beloved prince. A formidable body of Scythian auxiliaries had been transported from another climate, and almost from another world, to invade a distant country, of whose name and situation they were ignorant. The love of rapine and war allured to the Imperial standard several tribes of Saracens, or roving Arabs, whose service Julian had commanded, while he sternly refused the payment of the accustomed subsidies. The broad channel of the Euphrates was crowded by a fleet of eleven hundred ships, destined to attend the motions and to satisfy the wants, of the Roman army. The military strength of the fleet was composed of fifty armed galleys; and these were accompanied by an equal number of flat-bottomed boats, which might occasionally be connected into the form of temporary bridges. The rest of the ships, partly constructed of timber, and partly covered with raw hides, were laden with an almost inexhaustible supply of arms and engines, of utensils and provisions. The vigilant provision of Julian had embarked a very large magazine of vinegar and biscuit for the use of the soldiers, but he prohibited the indulgence of wine and rigorously stopped a long string of superflous camels that attempted to follow the rear of the army . . .

'From the moment that the Romans entered the enemy's country, the country of an active and artful enemy, the order of march was disposed in three columns. The strength of the infantry, and consequently of the whole army, was placed in the centre, under the peculiar command of the master-general Victor. On the right, the brave Nevitta led a column of several legions along the banks of the Euphrates, and almost always in sight of the fleet. The left flank of the army was protected by the column of cavalry . . . and the ranks, from a motive either of use or ostentation, were formed in such open order that the whole line of march extended almost ten miles.

'The ordinary post of Julian was at the head of the centre column; but as he preferred the duties of a general to the state of a monarch, he rapidly moved, with a small escort of light cavalry, to the front, the rear, the flanks, wherever his presence could animate or protect the march of the Roman army. The country which they traversed, from the banks of the Chaboras to the cultivated lands of Assyria . . . was a plane throughout, as even as the sea, and full of wormwood; and if any kinds of shrub or weeds grew there, they had all an aromatic smell; but no trees could be seen. Bustards and ostriches, antelopes and wild asses appeared to be the only inhabitants of the desert, and the fatigues of the march were alleviated by the amusements of the chase. . .'

After reducing by siege the cities of Perisabor and Maogamalcha, which lay on their route, the army finally reached the banks of the

Tigris, having marched some seven hundred miles from their starting point.

'As it became necessary to transport the Roman army over the Tigris another labour presented itself, of less toil, but of more danger than the preceding expedition. The stream was broad and rapid; the ascent steep and difficult; and the entrenchments which had been formed on the ridge of the opposite bank, were lined with a numerous army of heavy cuirassiers, dexterous archers, and huge elephants who. . . could trample with the same ease a field of corn or a legion of Romans. In the presence of such an enemy the construction of a bridge was impracticable; and the intrepid prince, who instantly seized the only possible expedient, concealed his design till the moment of execution from the knowledge of the Barbarians, of his own troops and even of his generals themselves. Under the specious pretence of examining the state of the magazines, fourscore vessels were gradually unladen, and a select detachment, apparently destined for some secret expedition, was ordered to stand to their arms on the first signal . . .

'As soon as the hour of supper was passed, the emperor summoned the generals to his tent and acquainted them that he had fixed that night for the passage of the Tigris. They stood in silent and respectful astonishment; but when the venerable Sallust assumed the privilege of his age and experience, the rest of the chiefs supported with freedom the weight of his prudent remonstrances. Julian contented himself with observing that conquest and safety depended on the attempt; that, instead of diminishing, the number of their enemies would be increased by successive reinforcements, and that a longer delay would neither contract the breadth of the stream, nor level the height of the bank.

'The signal was instantly given and obeyed: the most impatient of the legionaries leaped into five vessels that lay nearest to the bank, and as they plied their oars with intrepid diligence, they were lost after a few moments in the darkness of the night. A flame arose on the opposite side, and Julian, who too clearly understood that his foremost vessels in attempting to land had been fired by the enemy, dexterously converted their extreme danger into a presage of victory. "Our fellow-soldiers," he eagerly exclaimed, "are already masters of the bank; see—they make the appointed signal: let us hasten to emulate and assist their courage". The united and rapid motion of a great fleet broke the violence of the current, and they reached the eastern shores of the Tigris with sufficient speed to extinguish the flames and rescue their adventurous companions. The difficulties of a steep and lofty ascent were increased by the weight of armour and the darkness of the night. A shower of stones, darts and fire was instantly discharged on the heads of the assailants, who, after an arduous struggle, climbed the bank and stood victorious upon the rampart. As soon as they possessed a more equal field, Julian, who with his light infantry had led the attack, darted through the ranks a skilful and experienced eye; his bravest soldiers, according to the precepts of Homer, were distributed in the front and rear; and all the trumpets of the Imperial army sounded to battle. The Romans, after sending up a military shout, advanced in measured steps to the animating notes of martial music; launched their formidable javelins; and rushed forwards with drawn swords, to deprive the Barbarians, by a closer onset, of the advantages of their missile weapons. The whole engagement lasted above twelve hours; till the gradual retreat of the Persians was changed into a disorderly flight.' [2]

It is easy to write of victory with pride, more difficult to write of defeat without bitterness. It may be argued, I suppose, that Dunkirk was a victory, if the exploitation of circumstance rather than the deliberate achievement of calculated ends can be called a victory. That it was a victory of the spirit, perhaps the greatest in our history, considering the odds, can never be denied. What the evacuation was like and how it felt to be there has nowhere been better described than in an account given by Robert Harling, who was there in one of a string of lifeboats towed by a river tug:

'With eleven other boats in charge of Thames tug *Moon* IV we moved off down river, a strange cortège, nestling in the wake of the fussing tug with its two small white stern lights. Midnight donged on one of the riverside churches. The river and the night were wholly merged . . .

'We divided ourselves into watches . . . I had had a short nap on the quayside and offered to take first watch and Rhodes agreed . . . It was already chilly after the hot day and later it would be chillier, I thought, and chose to be cold steering rather than cold trying to sleep . . .

'Dawn was cold and grey, discounting any thrill the dark night had given to our purpose. We lay off the coast. The Kentish cliffs were dulled in colour and in outline. All the tugs were lying offshore, a fleet of nondescripts with their attendant fleet of old lifeboats. Against the bleak dawn the silhouettes were like insects upon the sea, too small, without the dignity of boats. We all sat up, rubbing and slapping our limbs to quicken deadened blood . . . Pink streaks lay along the sea's rim and rose uneasily into the world. "Sailor's warning," murmured Rhodes . . . A keen but not uncomfortable breeze blew from the east.

"Christ, I hope they're doing something about grub," said Rhodes. Then suddenly, with the swift passage of rumour, we heard breakfast was on its way. Stores were passed from each tug to its dependent boats . . . new bread, cheese, butter, jam, tinned fruit and hard-boiled eggs . . .

'Some time after eight o'clock we got under way. . . . The wind was still keen, but the forebodings of the red sky of the early morning seemed to have been an insubstantial omen, for there was already a touch of warmth in the morning air . . .

'All through the afternoon we passed our own ships returning with men. British and French destroyers, sloops, trawlers, drifters and motor boats were on their way back. They were packed tight with masses of khaki figures lining the decks, crowded to the ropes or bulwarks . . .

'In the middle of one of the discussions which started from time to time, our starboard companion-boat swung round, crashed into us at what seemed terrific speed, forcing us far over, so that we lay dangerously upon our beam. The other boat buried her port side completely under water. Three ratings were hurled into the sea. The fourth yelled and hung on to a thwart. I saw two go clean under our boat; the other was caught as he was swept past a boat astern. I looked to port; two white faces were carried astern very swiftly.

'One still wore a tin helmet, and the other yelled fearfully. I think he yelled "I can't swim!" but he went down once and was gone. Voices cried frantically to the tug. She swung round quickly to port; as skilful and as swift a turn as a London taxi-driver's. Engines were slowed for the search. One was picked up. The other had gone. The tug cruised around for about ten minutes, but it was a vain search and we turned once again to our course. The third man was shivering in the boat which had picked him up; the fourth, who had kept to the boat, looked an unnerved creature and was now baling furiously . . .

'The sight of the drowning man hurtling past the boat had rather upset me, and, indeed, it seemed to have cast a gloom over the whole fleet. The man had drowned so quickly and so easily . . .

'An hour later we were nearing the French coast. Subtly the feeling in the boat changed. There was a nervous tenseness amongst us; we no longer talked, but stared ahead . . . We were moving up the coast with a stranger miscellany of craft than was ever seen in the most hybrid amateur regatta: destroyers, sloops, trawlers, motor boats, fishing boats, tugs, Dutch schuits. Under the splendid sun they seemed like craft of peace journeying upon a gay occasion, but suddenly we knew we were there, for Rhodes said, "There they are, the bastards!" . . .

There were over fifty German planes ... flying very high. I got a heavy sick feeling right down in the stomach. The bombs dropped out of the cloudless sky. We watched them fall as the planes directed their principal attack upon two destroyers. The destroyers seemed to sit back on their buttocks and spit flames; the harsh cracks of their ack-ack guns were heartening. Then we got the kick from the bombs as their ricochet came up through the sea. Our little boat rocked and lifted high out of the water. One, two, three, four ... we waited, counting them and held tight to the gunwale. I noticed Wimble's face. It was white; I guessed my own was too. I toed off my boots as I steered; if we were going overboard, I preferred to travel light ... Far above us the German formations broke. Some came down in steep dives ... One came low, machine-gunning a tug and its towed lifeboats. Then came another. We knew it was coming our way. It was crazy to sit there, goggle-eyed and helpless, just waiting for it, but there seemed singularly little else to do. The seconds were hours. "Wait for it and duck!" shouted Rhodes above the roar of the engines. "Now! and bale like bloody hell if he hits the boat." We ducked. The rat-a-tat of the bullets sprayed round the stern boats of our little fleet; the two Lewis guns in the tug answered gamely as the plane zoomed up ... It had been a short burst and a lively one ...

'We had no more machine-gunning that afternoon. We were bombed from great heights but we were lucky; the tiny tugs moved sedately on towards the black cloud darkening the eastern sky; then we realised that this was no cloud but the pall of ruin above Dunkirk. We saw the cloud from more than ten miles offshore; it lay upon the land like a vast shadow. As we drew nearer we saw the dull red glow at its base. Out of the shadow came flashes of gunfire. From the sea our own warships answered, firing methodically into the pall ...

'Through the last two hours of the sunlight we moved up along the coast, picking our way through the deep but narrow channel ... In the twilight we watched the sappers moving like silhouetted robots among the flames ... We could see them quite clearly: tiny, deliberate creatures darting in and out of the fires. Tall cranes stood along the quays like a row of skeletal memorials to days of peace the town had so lately known; even as we watched, one of them toppled and fell ...

'Dusk deepened into night. We went on slowly, perhaps for a couple of miles. It was nearly ten o'clock when the tug finally let go her anchor ... We judged we were about half a mile offshore. Mist came with the night.

'We sat in the darkness, talking quietly ...

'"How do you like Dunkirk, Bute?" asked Rhodes.

'"I'm afraid I think it's beautiful in a rather terrifying way," said Bute.

'It was terrifying all right, said Rhodes. We looked back. To the south-west, quite near, the town burned steadily. Gunfire enclosed us. As far as we could judge, the Germans had ringed the area and were pouring metal into the town and on to the beaches. Gunfire from our own ships was pegging them back . . .

'Instructions were passed from the tug along the line of boats. Each pulling boat was to be lashed to a power boat; lashed craft were to proceed under power towards the beach . . . About two hundred yeards offshore the boats were to be unlashed, the powered boat was to let go her anchor whilst the pulling boat went in to the beach and there embarked as many men as possible. With this load she was to return to her companion-boat, transfer the men and go back again. After the second load had been taken on board, the pulling boat was again to return. Both boats were then to be lashed up again—"like nautical Siamese twins," somebody said—return to the tug, transfer the men, and once again go back to the beach to repeat the operation. This was to go on until dawn or until the tug had reached its full capacity,

'Three more ratings were sent along from the tug to take over the powered boat which had capsized during the afternoon. They seemed older and quieter than the youngsters who had previously been in the boat and were followed by an officer. In the delayed flash of a star shell I saw that he was a middle-aged lieutenant-commander, R.N.R. He took charge of things quickly and quietly. Towing lines were drawn taut; the lifeboats closed around the stern of the tug. Final instructions were called down to us. The two stern lifeboats were cast off . . . Then it was our turn. The ratings got the engine going quickly. We lashed up and cast off, Rhodes at the helm. The engine, at half-speed, seemed to be making a terrific din and for a minute or so overwhelmed the noise of the barrage . . . In those few hundred yards to the beach my habit of introspection kept my thoughts away from the prospect ahead. I knew that I did not like this sort of thing, yet knew that nothing would have kept me away. I loathed almost to the point of sickness the final agonising moments of preparation and delay, but at that moment when things began to happen, fear dropped, and I moved immediately into a trance of action . . .

'"Stop engines!" said the lieutenant-commander. "Let go anchor!"

'He stood up in the stern of the other boat and steppd across into our boat. "I'll come ashore with you," he said. He threw his tin hat in the bottom of the boat and began to flash a torch around in a casual way as if looking for a coin. "Wright! Watson! Jump in here. We'll want all hands for pulling! Don't let your anchor drag. I'll try and keep a line on where we leave you, but I don't think I'm going to be very successful. I'll flash three shorts. Give a yell when you see or hear us coming. Now cast off."

'We rowed towards the beach. I took the starboard bow oar. I had a rating on the thwart with me at the port oar. In the light of the officer's torch flash I saw that the rating was about thirty-five, with strong, heavy features. We pulled in towards the beach. "Give me an oar," said the lieutenant-commander. "I'll see what water we've got. Back oars when I give the word." We went on. He sounded with the oar. "Back!" The barrage started again. Shrapnel whistled down and hit the water. The rating beside me swung his hand across to his left shoulder and cursed sharply.

'"Catch anything, Watson?" asked the officer.

'"Yes sir, me shoulder. Nothing much, sir."

'"What? Shrapnel?"

'"Yes sir."

'"By God! Give me that tin hat!" He bent down and grabbed his hat and put it on quickly. Then he sat down. "Swing her round and run her in stern first, and mind you don't beach her..." Inland, star shells were going up all the time, hanging lazily upon the night. I watched the skipper take off his shoes and socks, and drape his shoes around his neck. "Now keep her afloat for God's sake. I'll take a walk and see if I can find any pongos..."

'He climbed over the side of the boat and waded ashore. Ten yards and he was lost in the blackness...

'We sat in the boat resting on our oars, now and then giving our blades a shove to keep the boat afloat. "I don't like this bleedin' shrapnel and I don't like the way the old man flashes' is torch around," said the rating next to me, rubbing his shoulder.

'"Was it much of a crack?" I asked.

'"Nothin' much, but it mighterbin."

'"Cheer up. Have a drink?" I handed him my flask of rum, for the night had become bitterly cold.

'"By God, mate, you muster bin born in 'eaven," he said, gulping, and passed the bottle back. "You'll be using that in a minute. What are yer? Civvie Street?"

'I said that I was. It seemed easier than an explanation concerning my immediate antecedents.

'"Why d'yer come on this bloody lark?"'
'"I had a chance, and thought I'd like to . . ."'

★ ★ ★

'"Look out! Someone coming," said Rhodes. "Keep her moving."
My eyes, too, could make out the wide black shadow, moving, darker
even than the night, down the beach.
'"Who goes there?" yelled Rhodes. There was no reply.
'"Who goes there?" more shrilly. Again there was no answer.
I gripped my oar. I remember that moment as tense, wondering
whether they were our own men or jerries.
'"Shove off!" said Rhodes decisively.
'"Ahoy, there!" said a voice through the darkness, and in a moment
the wide shadow had become men standing at the water's edge, with
the R.N.R. officer at their head.
'"I've got twenty-two men here," he said. "Take 'em off and come
straight back. Think you can find this spot again? Try and make a
rough bearing, helmsman."
'"Aye, aye, sir," said Rhodes. "I can get a line on that fire to starboard, I think, sir."
'"Good, do your best. Now help these men in."
'They waded out through the surf and stood looking at us like a pack
of pathetic, half-drowned schoolboys. They were almost too tired to
move. They unslung their rifles and haversacks, letting them slip down
and fall dully in the shallow water. In the light of the fireworks they
looked very young and worn, beaten to the edge of sanity. Some
tried to climb in, but were tired, slipped and could not make it. They
began to pull the boat down to port. We were desperate: their
combined weight might shove us down hard on the sand. I had sea-
boots on and yelled to Rhodes, suggesting I should go overboard and
help the men in.
'"O.K., old cock," said Rhodes; and then to the tommies: "Some
of you chaps get around the other side."
'I climbed overboard. The sea-boots were useless, for we were in
about two feet and water came pouring into the boots, soaking trousers
and socks. I began to help men up and over into the boat, hoisting them
up by their legs and shoving them in by their haunches . . .
'"I'm coming in now," I called to Rhodes . . . I gave the heavy
boat a last push and pulled myself in.
'"Don't be long," called the R.N.R. man, and wandered off up the
beach . . .

'We were a long time finding the powered boat. We had no torch and had to make a rough guess at our position. We were carried well down the coast ... We ran up against what seemed to be a giant Dutch vessel, hailed it and tried to get a position from them, but with no luck. We moved off again, completely lost. The mist was in patches and closed us in, although we could still see the fires above the town. Shrapnel still fell. We made a shot in the dark, rowing straight ahead. Our yelling would have wakened the dead. "Come on, you lazy bastards," somebody called across the waters. "Think this is a bloody picnic?" We knew we were there.

'Transferring the men to the powered boat was simple. We lashed up and they more or less fell across the gunwales. The whole job took less than five minutes. A few rifles were passed after the men. Then we shoved off again ...

'It was simpler going back to the shore. Rhodes knew roughly which point to steer for and could shape a rough course. We passed one of the other pulling boats. "How's things?" called Rhodes. "Not so bad," came the answer. "Got thirty of 'em 'ere." "Yus, and we're bloody well stayin' 'ere," said another voice.

'We pulled on and once again backed in. By now there was a crowd waiting ... Our R.N.R. officer was not there. Instead we were almost attacked by many Frenchmen. They were vociferous and seemed to have lost their nerve. They still carried all their equipment, seemed bigger and fitter than the tommies, and were strong enough to be able to pull themselves into the boat. They swarmed in, colliding with the oarsmen, stumbling forrard. Their chatter was unstoppable.

'"Taisez-vous, you loud-mouthed bloody frogs!" shouted Rhodes. I echoed him and the combined effect of our schoolboy French quietened them for a few moments but they could not remain that way for long ...

'Then the thing we most dreaded happened; the weight of the heavily laden Frenchmen drove us down into the sand, and we were stuck. For a moment my rage was unreasoning and ungovernable; I was wild with fury and began to push them aft and out of the boat, but once in they seemed determined to stay in. They were soldiers and landsmen and could not realise their situation. I hated them for their ignorance and their gesticulations. Now, looking calmly back on the night, it is easy to see that my passion was a compound of fear and hatred. I was scared stiff that we should be left ignominiously high and dry upon the beach, a further burden upon the boats; and there was no doubt about the short shrift we should get if captured in civilian clothes.

'Rhodes must have felt much the same way, for he grabbed a rifle and with the butt jabbed viciously at a couple of poilus. He lunged at a man clambering over the gunwale, yelling, "Debarquez! You bloody fools! Get out! Get out! Nous sommes ensablés!" . . .

'Disembarking was bitter for the Frenchmen, but it was the only way. We stood up and with our oars tried to shove deep down and away, but the boat would not shift. "We'd all better get out," said Rhodes, resigned. "I'll stay here and try to keep her off if we get her moving . . ."

'Most of the Frenchmen stood aside, dulled and senseless. Then their N.C.O. gave them pretty fierce instructions and they all came and shoved. I almost wept as I used to weep when boxing, pushing and shoving at that immovable lifeboat . . . Then suddenly and miraculously, we slipped upon the sand, the boat moved and floated. "O.K., O.K.!" called Rhodes. "I'll stay here," I said, desperate in determination to keep the boat afloat, even if my lungs burst with pushing. The Frenchmen waded out and climbed back, poor devils. In relief it was impossible to hate the men, but only the folly of language that in crisis can still keep men unfamiliar with their friends.

'We took them back and returned for more, and again we found more Frenchmen. This load had an officer with them, an official interpreter. Everything was easy. We took them off and again pulled out. We lashed up, but before we could get the engine going we had drifted down on a Dutch schuit. We hailed them and said we were going to put fifty-three Frenchmen aboard. There was some sort of protest. They said they weren't ready, but their protest died as those poilus decided to go aboard. We passed up some of our food and called good nights. The poilus blessed us with many words . . . The entente cordiale was re-established . . . In the dark night there was for a moment goodwill amongst men.

'This time we found about two hundred men lined up along the beach. The R.N.R. officer had found them huddled in the ruins of some foreshore house. They were bright with the hope that they might escape that night. We got over thirty of them in. We could take no more. The two who were next to embark stood back a pace sadly and silently, viewing their luckier mates . . .

'We worked until half-past three in the morning. I think we took off about three hundred men. We were never able to number them accurately, for we ferried many of them to other ships . . . Finally we were told to call it a day, for even the indefatigable R.N.R. officer could find no more men in his appointed sector of the beach. We were to go back in the tug itself . . . Dawn was about four, and with the dawn would come the Hun . . . There was that slumbrous feeling in the air that comes upon seaside towns in early morning before a scorcher of a day. We got under way . . .

'An hour later the bombers were at us again. We had been passed by two large French destroyers going fast towards Dunkirk. The bombers, three of them, had a go at the destroyers, but the ack-ack fire, accurate and intense, kept them high. Suddenly our towed lifeboats piled up; we had to stop engines. A rating went over the stern to cut three of them adrift. We were a grand target. One of the planes came down out of the pale sky in an almost vertical dive; in the quiet morning a whine revolting to hear. Our Lewis guns spattered. I was standing just under the wheel-house and watched the spent cases chattering down, dancing idiotically upon the deck. The R.N.R. lieutenant was at the starboard gun, I noticed. The bombs were well astern. The bomber had straightened out and zoomed off. Then a flight of Hurricanes appeared. In ten seconds the sky was clear of jerries. Some of the tommies had come to life during the scrap, but not one had risen from the deck: they were all too limp with sleep . . .

'The last hour of the journey was the antithesis of Dunkirk. Destroyers, sloops, trawlers, paddle-steamers, motor boats, launches were converging upon their homeland. There was almost gaiety astir in the ships. It was difficult to realise that we were watching one of the most overwhelming defeats in the history of warfare.' [3]

Four years after Dunkirk, on July 6, 1944, while the fighting round Caen and south of Cherbourg was at its bloodiest and most desperate, the following letter appeared in the correspondence column of *The Times*. That anyone should be capable of preserving such detachment, or that at that moment imagination could remain so deeply rooted in our historic past, reassured me—at a time when I badly needed such reassurance—not only of the invincible qualities of the English character, but of what seems to me our pecular genius for unconscious humour:

'Sir,

'It is to be hoped that thə College of Arms will shortly publish the blazon of the Princess's [Elizabeth's] arms to supplement and elucidate the incomplete description appearing in today's newspapers. What, for instance, is the tincture of the labels? All recent precedents

have been in favour of silver, but gold would be consistent with the
charges.

'In some papers, not *The Times*, it is stated that "the quarterings
of the royal arms are charged with the same distinctive labels."
Are we seriously to suppose that the outgoing Garter has inflicted
five marks of cadency on a single coat? If not, what does this odd
phrase mean?

'I am, Sir, your obedient servant,

YORKIST' 4

To lack a sense of reality must sometimes be a comforting thing.
In childhood, lacking experience, it is inevitable, and consequently one
dwells more vividly in the imagination than in reality. I was too young
to know what it was all about when I first read Campbell's *Hohenlinden*.
I only knew that for some reason or other it thrilled me in a way that
no other poem had done up till then. I read it again and again, as, in
those days, I read most things that I enjoyed, and although it may not
be a very good poem, its familiarity has not dimmed my appreciation
of it.

> On Linden, when the sun was low,
> All bloodless lay the untrodden snow;
> And dark as winter was the flow
>   Of Iser, rolling rapidly.

> But Linden saw another sight,
> When the drum beat at dead of night
> Commanding fires of death to light
>   The darkness of her scenery.

> By torch and trumpet fast array'd
> Each horseman drew his battle-blade,
> And furious every charger neigh'd
>   To join the dreadful revelry.

> Then shook the hills with thunder riven;
> Then rush'd the steed to battle driven;
> And louder than the bolts of Heaven
>   Far flash'd the red artillery.

But redder yet that light shall glow
On Linden's hills of stained snow;
And bloodier yet the torrent flow
*   Of Iser, rolling rapidly.*

'Tis morn; but scarce yon level sun
Can pierce the war-clouds, rolling dun,
Where furious Frank and fiery Hun
*   Shout in their sulphurous canopy.*

The combat deepens. On, ye Brave
Who rush to glory, or the grave!
Wave, Munich! All thy banners wave,
*   And charge with all thy chivalry!*

Few, few shall part, where many meet!
The snow shall be their winding sheet,
And every turf beneath their feet
*   Shall be soldier's sepulchre.* [5]

The mind's eye conjures its own vision of what one reads. Individual experience and the association of ideas cause one to fashion scenes and characters according to what is real or familiar. For me *Hohenlinden* evokes, quite wrongly perhaps, some sort of parallel with the scene as I imagine it to have been at Gettysburg, a name that seems to have surprisingly little relevance for many English readers in spite of its importance to the outcome of the American Civil War. But then the war itself does not seem to arouse much interest among us either, perhaps because the principles at stake seem so remote from any form of constitutional crises in our own recent history. But one Englishman who at the time took a less disinterested view was Colonel Lyon Fremantle, of the Coldstream Guards, who saw much of the battle of Gettysburg from a tree. The improbability of his being there at all is accounted for by his having chosen to spend his leave in observing the Civil War at first hand, and armed with letters of introduction to the leaders on both sides, he followed first of all the fortunes of the Confederate Army from Texas to the Potomac, then crossed the lines to see how the Yankees were faring.

A few days before the battle, together with a Captain Sorrell, of the Austrian Army, he presented himself at General Longstreet's headquarters. The day before the fighting began he had climbed a tree in order to survey the scene, and on the day itself, 'at 2 p.m. General

Longstreet advised me, if I wished to have a good view of the battle, to return to my tree . . . but until 4.45 p.m. all was profoundly still, and I began to doubt whether a fight was coming off today at all. At that time, however, Longstreet suddenly commenced a heavy cannonade on the right. Ewell immediately took it up on the left. The enemy replied with at least equal fury, and in a few minutes the firing along the whole line was heavy as it is possible to conceive. A dense smoke arose for six miles. There was little wind to drive it away, and the air seemed full of shells—each of which appeared to have a different style of going, and to make a different noise from the others . . .

'As soon as the firing began, General Lee joined General Hill just below our tree, and remained there nearly all the time, looking through his fieldglasses—sometimes talking to Hill and sometimes to Colonel Long of his staff. But generally he sat quite alone on the stump of a tree. What I remarked especially was, that during the whole time the firing continued, he only sent one message, and only received one report. It is evidently his system to arrange the plan thoroughly with the three corps commanders, and then leave to them the duty of modifying and carrying it out to the best of their abilities.

'When the cannonade was at its height, a Confederate band of music . . . began to play polkas and waltzes, which sounded very curious, accompanied by the hissing and bursting of the shells. . .

'A little before dark the firing dropped off in every direction, and soon ceased altogether. We then received intelligence that Longstreet had carried everything before him for some time, capturing several batteries, and driving the enemy from his positions; but when Hill's Florida brigade and some other troops gave way, he was forced to abandon a small portion of the ground he had won . . .' [6]

The next morning at six o'clock Colonel Fremantle rode to the field with Colonel Manning. 'The dead were being buried, but great numbers were still lying about; also many mortally wounded, for whom nothing could be done. Amongst the latter were a number of Yankees dressed in bad imitations of Zouave costume. They opened their glazed eyes, as I rode past, in a painfully imploring manner . . .

'At noon all Longstreet's dispositions were made. His troops for attack were deployed into line, and lying down in the woods; his batteries were ready to open. The general then dismounted and went to sleep for a short time. The Austrian officer and I now rode off to get, if possible, into some commanding position . . .

'Soon after passing the toll gate at Gettysburg, we found that we had got into a heavy cross-fire; shells both Federal and Confederate passing over our heads with great frequency . . . A small boy of twelve years was riding with us at the time. This urchin took a diabolical interest in the bursting of the shells, and screamed with delight when he saw them take effect. I never saw this boy again, or found out who he was . . .

'Finding that, to see the actual fighting, it was absolutely necessary to go into the thick of the thing, I determined to make my way to General Longstreet. It was then about 2.30. After passing General Lee and his staff, I rode on through the woods in the direction in which I had left Longstreet.

'I soon began to meet many wounded men returning from the front. Many of them asked in piteous tones the way to a doctor or an ambulance. The further I got, the greater became the number of the wounded. At last I came to a perfect stream of them flocking through the woods in numbers as great as the crowds in Oxford Street in the middle of the day. Some were walking alone on crutches composed of two rifles, others were supported by men less badly wounded than themselves, and others were carried on stretchers by the ambulance corps; but in no case did I see a sound man helping the wounded to the rear, unless he carried the red badge of the ambulance corps. They were still under heavy fire; the shells were continually bringing down great limbs of trees, and carrying further distruction amongst this melancholy procession.

'I saw all this in much less time than it takes to write it, and although astonished to meet such vast numbers of wounded, I had not seen *enough* to give me any idea of the real extent of the mischief . . .

'Soon afterwards I joined General Lee, who had in the meanwhile come to that part of the field on becoming aware of the disaster . . . General Lee was perfectly sublime. He was engaged in rallying and encouraging the broken troops, and was riding about a little in front of the wood, quite alone—the whole of his staff being engaged in a similar manner further to the rear. His face, which is always placid and cheerful, did not show signs of the slightest disappointment, care, or annoyance; and he was addressing to every soldier he met a few words of encouragement, such as, "All this will come right in the end; we'll talk it over afterwards; but, in the meantime, all good men must rally. We want all good and true men just now," etc.

'He spoke to all the wounded men that passed him, and the slightly wounded he exorted "to bind up [their] hurts and take up a musket" in this emergency. Very few failed to answer his appeal, and I saw many badly wounded men take off their hats and cheer him. He said to me, "This has been a sad day for us, Colonel—a very sad day; but we can't expect always to gain victories" . . .

'I saw General Willcox (an officer who wears a short round jacket and a battered straw hat) come up to him, and explain, almost crying, the battered state of his brigade. General Lee immediately shook hands with him and said cheerfully, "Never mind, General, *all this has been* MY *fault*—it is *I* who have lost this fight, and you must help me out of it in the best way you can."

'In this manner I saw General Lee encourage and reanimate his somewhat dispirited troops, and magnanimously take upon his own shoulders the whole weight of the repulse. It was impossible to look at him or listen to him without feeling the strongest admiration.' [7]

The fate of empires, through the fate of their armies, has sometimes been decided, or so I suspect, by the personalities of those in command of their soldiers. Not that Lee's bravery or generosity or imperturbability availed him much, except to gain the affection of his troops, and that in battle may count for a good deal. What this compelling quality may be it is hard to say. Some generals have it, others, because they lack that sense of fraternity that endears an officer to his men, have not. Some lack imagination, of which this intangible quality must be a part. Magnanimity in war is a noble thing, but to embrace your enemy publicly and with smiles, as Montgomery after Alamein embraced the captive von Thoma, who had lately been slaughtering the men of the 8th Army, is an act hardly calculated to encourage the spirit of your troops or your own popularity, and it is a high tribute to Montgomery's hold on the affection of his soldiers that it survived this kind of self-advertisement.

Although not a great deal is known about Alexander the Great, enough is on record to show that he undoubtedly was blessed with this elusive quality. 'Certain features—the high physical courage, the impulsive energy, the fervid imagination—stand out clear . . . That he was a great master of war is admitted' [8] too. Some idea of the man he was is shown in his conduct at the battle of Arbela, his second encounter with Darius, the Persian king, whom he had defeated not long before at Issus in Egypt. Alexander's forces, as well as his entourage, surfeited with success, were beginning to show signs of decline.

'Here . . . the morning of Alexander's adventure ends . . . His soldiers are no longer demigods, but merely rich men; his companions have become potentates who mark the change by the unheard-of vulgarity of their luxury. Such a one in the province that had fallen to him has camel loads of earth brought to him from Egypt, to rub himself when he went to the baths. Another has silver nails in his shoes. Philotas had hunting nets made a hundred furlongs broad. All of them had their grooms of the bath, their chamberlains, and some "made use of richer essences than oil" for friction after bathing. Alexander himself lived as hard as he had ever done, and sent all the treasures he captured to his mother and to his friends at home. But the weight of his success could not be lifted by mere personal asceticism. As he had done to Bucephalus, duty and responsibility saddled and mounted him, no gallop could henceforth throw them off. The adventure slipped with every gain deeper into the condition of a conquest.

'It is the morbid interest of this degeneration, the slow smothering of the light and heat of him in the sheer bulk of his gains, the slow strangulation of success, that now fills the story.

'It is not only his hope of renewing the adventure, but his clear interest, that impelled him to move his army in search of Darius. The unhappy Emperor, handsomest, tallest and most ineffectual of men, had collected a second army, the size and better than the quality of that butchered at Issus, and moved half-heartedly westwards again. The Macedonian machine was built on a plan that the corruption of its materials could not derange; once more Alexander set it in motion, and found it as supple, as swift, after a year's rust as ever. But, as if to reveal to the world the intimate, invisible change, Alexander did a simple-minded and strange thing. When he had came to scouts' distance of Darius, who was encamped in inertia at Gaugamela, a village near the site of ancient Nineveh, he with his soothsayer and spiritual confidant, Aristander, "performed some private ceremonies and offered sacrifice to Fear". Not, it is sure, to any physical or tangible Fear, but to Fear-Anxiety, Fear-Worry, the fear not of losing but of the responsibility; new and terrible companion of all his night watches henceforth.

'It is related that the noise of the Persian camp in the distance was like the bellowing of an immense sea, and that the whole horizon that night seemed to be lighted with its innumerable camp fires. Parmenio particularly was depressed by the prospect of the next day, and with most of the staff generals came to Alexander and begged him to make a night attack as his only hope, as the darkness would hide from the phalanx the hugeness of their task. Alexander, fresh from his sacrifice, made the celebrated and stupid reply, which shows how much of the old spirit the nearness of battle had restored him, "I will not steal a victory".

'Then he went to bed and slept more soundly than he had done since the Issus. Parmenio could not imitate him. At earliest dawn the old bear entered Alexander's tent and called him two or three times. "When he waked, Parmenio asked him how he could sleep like a man who had already conquered, when he had the greatest battle the world ever heard of to fight?"

'The day started badly. Dense and never-ending clouds of Bactrian cavalry, the ancestors maybe of those light-riding, demoniac Mongol horsemen which a thousand years later gave Genghis Khan the mastery of a larger but not greater world than Alexander's, beat away the wing where Parmenio commanded the cavalry. Parmenio sent a desperate message to Alexander to look to his retreat. Alexander, having yelled a contemptuous reply to the messenger, that all could hear, put on his helmet, and mounted. But for the first time in his life, this was no signal to charge. He hesitated and rode slowly to the front of the silent reserves, and addressed them. He had not gone far in his exhortation before they began to shout, and stopping to listen, he found that, "so far from needing any encouragement, they were striving to add to his confidence and to urge to attack at once". At this the son of Jupiter snatched a short javelin from the hands of a soldier and brandished it in the air, calling on Jupiter to see the deeds of his son. Then waited again.

'Meanwhile on the whole centre, the supreme trust of Darius, the army of chariots had charged. The great mass, the terror of the old world, came on with the impetus of a dam-burst, watched down the slope by the hard, pale phalanx of pikemen. Behind the frenzied horses stood, like men of stone or bronze, the Medes of the monuments, muffled to the eyes, straining for the impact. They struck the light Macedonian javelinists and bowmen. These murdered their horses with accurate fire, and then when the front was in confusion charged the chariots, in the marvellous discipline which, while it allowed the freest play to each man, co-ordinated their efforts like a football scrum. In a few minutes the charge re-formed itself and came through the struggling mass. But not a tenth, not a fiftieth of those who had begun; the phalanx opened to meet them and let them pass through, to be hamstrung in the rear. At this moment, Alexander and his men perceived flying high an eagle, the bird of Jupiter, and he immediately gave the signal for the main action. The impetuosity of the phalanx carried it at once far into the heart of the Asiatics, and Alexander was thrown up against the bodyguard of Darius. Here there was the most desperate bravery; even when they were dying the Persians held on the hoofs of their enemies' horses and tried to obstruct them with their bodies, which mounted in heaps. In the course of a very short time, during which Alexander and Darius may (as all traditions have it) have come to grips, a panic seized the Persians; they were heard shouting that their king was dead, that their gods were come out on them, and all ended in a great rout.' [9]

The events of ancient and even of comparatively recent history are too far off for us to grasp their physical realities, however hard we try. One can summon up a mental image, sometimes a very vivid one, of the scene, but that is all. The actual sense of danger, the *pain*, the *exhaustion*, the *sweat*, the *stench* of battle, still less the sense of fear and of spiritual anguish, are incommunicable. Even within a generation such recollections are apt to wither, and so begin to diminish. Those, for instance, who belonged to the generation that stood to lose most in the First World War, through their violent and precipitate transition from innocence to the full-fledged responsibility of being an adult, came by degrees to exchange resignation for the bitterness that they must have felt at being cheated of their youthful expectations. To Kipling, who understood the mind of youth as few writers, having taken on years, have understood it, that bitterness was experienced with intensity. His chauvinistic hatred must have been shared by multitudes of older people, but I feel it was probably of the generation which grew up in half the normal span that he was thinking when, in 1916, he wrote 'The Beginnings'.

At his best Kipling seems to me a majestic poet rather than a noble one. At his worst, like Elgar, who offers an obvious comparison, I should think he was unbeatable. "The Beginnings", in which he expresses a fundamental truth about the English (I should like to think it applies to me personally, though I doubt it) is not, I imagine, among the best of his poems. Perhaps I have been seduced into thinking it better than it is because of the circumstances in which I first came across it. It was in 1941, soon after the blitz, that I heard it recited by Laurence Olivier, and its impact then was stern and terrible. I felt that every word of it was true, and I hope that I was right:

> It was not part of their blood,
> It came to them very late
> With long arrears to make good,
> When the English began to hate.

They were not easily moved,
They were icy-willing to wait
Till every count should be proved,
Ere the English began to hate.

Their voices were even and slow
Their eyes were level and straight,
There was neither sign nor show,
When the English began to hate.

It was not preached to the crowd,
It was not taught by the State
No man spoke it aloud,
When the English began to hate.

It was not suddenly bred,
It will not swiftly abate,
Through the chill years ahead,
When time shall count from the date
That the English began to hate.[10]

I am not one of those who 'like a good hater'. Nothing worth doing
or having seems to me to have been achieved through hatred. Yet I
have hated as ardently as the best (or should it not be the worst?) when
it was natural to feel hatred. Killing in cold blood, except in self-
defence, calls for a hatred which is presumably of quite a different kind
to the slow, cumulative venom of which Kipling speaks. Even so, the
English do not make reliable haters. They are far too lazy for one thing,
and for another too self-absorbed, too circumscribed by the tight little,
trite little pattern of their lives. It was lucky for them that when they
most needed a strong, uncompromising hater Winston Churchill was
at hand, lucky that his hatred, of which justice and sound reason
formed the basis, did not lead him, as it led Hitler, to underrate his
opponent. Most people no doubt think of Sir Winston Churchill as a
statesman and politician, or less charitably perhaps as a politician and
statesman, forgetting that in his early days he was also a soldier and
knew what it meant to kill deliberately and at close quarters. That
experience is best described in his own story of the cavalry charge at
Omdurman, during the Sudan war, in which he took part as a subal-
tern attached to the 21st Lancers:

'Long before dawn,' he says, 'we were astir, and by five o'clock the

21st Lancers were drawn up mounted outside the zeriba . . . I was now called out from my troop to advance with a patrol and reconnoitre the ridge between the rocky peak of Jebel Surgham and the river. Other patrols from our squadron and from the Egyptian cavalry were also sent hurrying forward in the darkness. We trotted fast over the plain and soon began to breast the unknown slopes of the ridge. There is nothing like the dawn. The quarter of an hour before the curtain is lifted upon an unknowable situation is an intense experience of war. Was the ridge held by the enemy or not? Were we riding through the gloom into thousands of ferocious savages? Every step might be deadly; yet there was no time for over-much precaution. The regiment was coming on behind us, and dawn was breaking. It was already half light as we climbed the slope. What should we find at the summit? . . .

'I make one man follow a hundred yards behind, so that whatever happens, he may tell the tale. There is no sound but our own clatter. We have reached the crest line. We rein in our horses. Every minute the horizon extends . . . Veil after veil is lifted from the landscape. What is this shimmering in the distant plain? . . . these dark markings beneath the shimmer? *They are there!* These enormous black smears are thousands of men; the shimmering is the glinting of their weapons. . . In front of us is a vast array four of five miles long. It fills the horizon until it is blocked out on our right by the serrated silhouette of Surgham Peak . . . Suddenly new impressions strike the eye and mind. These masses are not stationary. They are advancing, and they are advancing fast. A tide is coming in. But what is this sound which we hear? They are cheering for God, his Prophet and his holy Khalifa. . .

'Now it is broad morning and the slanting sun adds brilliant colour to the scene. The masses have defined themselves into swarms of men, and above them dance a multitude of gorgeous flags. We see for ourselves what the Crusaders saw . . .

'We continued to pace forward over the hard sand, peering into the mirage-twisted plain in a high state of suppressed excitement. Presently I noticed three hundred yards away on our flank and parallel to the line on which we were advancing, a long row of blue-black objects, two or three yards apart. I thought there were about a hundred and fifty. Then I became sure that these were men—enemy men—squatting on the ground. Almost at the same moment the trumpet sounded "Trot", and the whole long column of cavalry began to jingle and clatter across the front of these crouching figures . . . Forthwith from every blue-black blob came a white puff of smoke, and a loud volley of musketry broke the odd stillness. Such a target at such a distance could

scarcely be missed, and all along the column here and there horses
bounded and a few men fell . . .

'On my right and left my neighbouring troop leaders made a good
line. Immediately behind was a long dancing row of lances couched
for the charge. We were going at a fast but steady gallop. There was too
much trampling and rifle fire to hear any bullets. After this glance to
the right and left and at my troop, I looked again towards the enemy.
The scene appeared to be suddenly transformed. The blue-black men
were still firing, but behind them there now came into view a depres-
sion like a shallow sunken road. This was crowded and crammed with
men rising up from the ground where they had hidden. Bright flags
appeared as if by magic, and I saw arriving from nowhere Emirs on
horseback among and around the mass of the enemy. The Dervishes
appeared to be ten or twelve deep at the thickest, a great grey mass
gleaming with steel, filling the dry water-course . . .

'The collision was now very near. I saw immediately before me, not
ten yards away, the two blue men who lay in my path. They were
perhaps a couple of yards apart. I rode at the interval between them.
They both fired. I passed through the smoke conscious that I was
unhurt. The trooper immediately behind me was killed at this place
and at this moment, whether by these shots or not I do not know.
I checked my pony as the ground began to fall away beneath his feet.
The clever animal dropped like a cat four or five feet down onto the
sandy bed of the watercourse, and in this sandy bed I found myself
surrounded by what seemed to be dozens of men. They were not
thickly packed enough at this point for me to experience any actual
collision with them . . . we seemed to push our way through as one has
sometimes seen mounted policemen break up a crowd. In less time than
it takes to relate, my pony had scrambled up the other side of the ditch.
I looked round.

'Once again I was on the hard, crisp desert, my horse at a trot. I had
the impression of scattered Dervishes running to and fro in all directions. Straight before me a man threw himself before me on the
ground . . . I saw the gleam of his curved sword as he drew it back for
a ham-stringing cut. I had room and time enough to turn my pony
out of his reach, and leaning over on the off side I fired two shots into
him at about three yards. As I straightened myself in the saddle, I saw
before me another figure with uplifted sword. I raised my pistol and
fired. So close were we that the pistol itself actually struck him. Man
and sword disappeared below and behind me. On my left, ten yards
away, was an Arab horseman in a bright-coloured tunic and steel

helmet, with chain-mail hangings. I fired at him. He turned aside. I pulled my horse into a walk and looked round again . . .

'There was a mass of Dervishes about forty or fifty yards away on my left. They were huddling and clumping themselves together, rallying for mutual protection. They seemed wild with excitement, dancing about on their feet, shaking their spears up and down. The whole scene seemed to flicker. I have an impression, but it is too fleeting to define, of brown-clad Lancers mixed up here and there with this surging mob. The scattered individuals in my immediate neighbour-hood made no attempt to molest me. Where was my troop? Where were the other troops of the squadron? Within a hundred yards of me I could not see a single officer or man. I looked back at the Dervish mass. I saw two or three riflemen crouching and aiming their rifles at me from the fringe of it. Then for the first time that morning I experienced a sudden sensation of fear. I felt myself absolutely alone. I thought these riflemen would hit me and the rest devour me like wolves. What a fool I was to loiter like this in the midst of the enemy! I crouched over the saddle, spurred my horse into a gallop and drew clear of the *mêlée*. Two or three hundred yards away I found my troop all ready faced about and partly formed up.

'The other three troops of the squadron were re-forming close by. Suddenly in the midst of the troop up sprung a Dervish. How he got there I do not know. He must have leaped out of some scrub or hole. All the troopers turned upon him thrusting with their lances: but he darted to and fro causing for the moment a frantic commotion. Wounded several times, he staggered towards me raising his spear. I shot him at less than a yard. He fell on the sand, and lay there dead. How easy to kill a man!' [11]

The charge at Omdurman, which I believe was one of the last ever made by a British cavalry regiment, now seems hardly more than an incident in a tribal skirmish. It was still possible, if you were not assailed by conscience or doubts about its morality, to see war as a sort of high adventure. But it was not long before that illusion, along with a lot of other romantic notions about war, was blown sky-high in the bombardments of Ypres, Arras and Armentières. The war that was to end all wars (who was the bland optimist who coined that self-deluding phrase?) ended, as wars always must, a good many things that it was not meant to destroy. The concept, for instance, of chivalry:

> I see the end of this crusade, the end of all
> Nobility in war, we'll never fight

As gentlemen again . . .
And that's the saddest task a man can choose;
To fight to win while knowing he must lose.[12]

It took the innate bestiality of the German temperament to rub our noses in the realization that nobility in war was at an end, and even then the lesson was not well learnt. The shattering complacency and ineptitude first of Baldwin and then of Chamberlain, and the imbecile loyalty of successive cabinets (was there a man dismayed?—apparently not)—showed how unwilling they were to accept the conclusion that war, if it ever came again, would not still be a business in which one could rely on the honour and decency of one's enemies.

Of Baldwin perhaps the less said the better, since it would be hypocritical to feign respect for the memory of a man whose earlier death might have spared us disasters to which I believe his negligence made a powerful contribution. Of Chamberlain one can only say thank God that his futility exposed itself in the nick of time. For 'war is a conflict at once of material and of wills, and its conduct requires a unique combination of technical expertise and moral force. The greater the technical problems, the more ferocious is the will needed to tear its way through them; therefore as war has grown more complex, constant conflicts have arisen between national leaders for whom war was an elemental conflict in which defeat was unthinkable and the military specialists for whom it was a technical problem soluble only by time and professional expertise.' [13]

Most people would probably find the general's impatience with the politician easier to sympathize with than the politician's apprehensions about the general, because it is easier to visualize tactical objectives than to appreciate the more complex considerations involved in over-all strategy. But generals are no freer from human failings, from procrastination, prejudice and professional jealousy, than politicians. They are no less prone to accidents of temperament than to those of circumstance. No one can say what difference it would have made if Wellington had been in command in the Crimea instead of Raglan, though Raglan's fate at the hands of Napoleon would perhaps have been easier to forecast. It is more likely that Wellington would have avoided some of the mistakes that were made, but he was an iron-bound traditionalist and what his views would have been on the use in war of the new-fangled telegraph, which had just then made its appearance, is by no means certain.

For sheer and often unnecessary brutality the Crimean War must be among the worst that the English have ever got themselves involved in. Yet it was conducted in a manner that sometimes makes it seem in retrospect grimly hilarious.

'This distinctly formidable enterprise was certainly undertaken ... *à cœur léger*. Little was known of the country; as Prince Albert most sensibly put it, "the first difficulty is the absence of all information as to the Crimea itself". Even the more volatile French court realized this; the great Napoleon was consulted by means of a planchette; two sketches of Sevastopol and Balaklava by Raffet were carefully studied as the possible basis of a plan of campaign; and the great strategical authority, Jomini, was sought out in the Café Anglais, where, despite the cheerfulness of his surroundings, he could only prophesy disaster. The British cabinet, however, observing from a cursory glance of the map that the Crimea was a peninsula, conceived that there could be nothing easier than for the British fleet to cut it off from the mainland by commanding the isthmus with its guns—nor could there have been but for the fact subsequently discovered, that the depth of the sea on either side of this isthmus was little more than two or three feet ...

'The British commander, Lord Raglan, the Fitzroy Somerset of the Peninsula War, had seen no service since 1815, [thirty-nine years earlier] and had spent most of his time at the Horse Guards; a courtly and polished gentleman, his chief merit was that, despite his incurable habit throughout the campaign of referring to his enemy as "the French", he was admirably adapted to lessen the friction inevitable in coalition wars ... The most remarkable thing about the British divisional generals was their age; all with the exception of the Duke of Cambridge were approaching seventy, and were of the stock and pipeclay school.

'On September 7th the combined forces embarked at Varna, 57,000 in all, the largest expedition that had ever set out for war overseas. The "Caradoc", having on board Raglan, Burgoyne and Brown, preceded the flotilla to look for a likely landing place and steamed so close to the Crimean coast that Russian officers could be seen looking at her through their telescopes, and "on perceiving this the English officers took off their hats and bowed". The Russian governor of Eupatoria, close to which the Allies decided to land, was equally punctilious; on receiving the formal summons to surrender, he first fumigated the document, then read it, and, realizing that he must yield to superior numbers, insisted that the British and French troops on landing must consider themselves in strict quarantine, the dis-embarkation took place unopposed, and without a hitch ...

'The English army at this time knew neither training nor manoeuvres outside the barrack square; the "picnics" in Surrey, as field days were then called, had taught it little or nothing. Its generals were, as Lord Wolseley said of those of Wellington's day, "mostly duffers", but the men were of that tough stolid stock whose "phlegm" throughout the Peninsula and at Waterloo had never admitted defeat . . . The Russian army was ever behind the times. The regiment belonged to the colonel, not the colonel to the regiment; peculation and corruption were rife in all its branches; and its tactics were still based on Suvorov's motto, "The bullet's a fool, the bayonet's a fine boy". The Russian soldier was . . . so indifferent a marksman . . . that at the Alma the men in the rear rank fired over the heads of those in the front. His obstinate courage was, however, proverbial, and his priests with the ikons accompanied him onto the battlefield to encourage him to fight to the death.

'The advance towards Sevastopol, about thirty miles away, began on September 19th, the French on the right next to the sea, the British inland; the French complained—not for the first or the last time in history—of British slowness. Next day the battle of the Alma was fought. As no combined plan of attack on the Russian position behind the Alma river had been arranged beforehand, co-operation between the Allies was conspicuous by its absence, and they fought two actions side by side. Generalship was equally absent on the side of the Russians where "no one received any orders and every man did what he thought best". The steady advance of the British up the slope across the river made an unforgettable impression on the French general, Canrobert; they went forward, he said, "as though they were in Hyde Park!" Some years later, at a Court ball given in Paris in honour of Queen Victoria and the Prince Consort, as he watched the careful precision with which Her Majesty went through the complicated manoeuvres of a quadrille, never faltering, never missing a step, memories of the Alma came back to him, and he cried, "The British fight as Victoria dances".

'The battle was an Allied victory, but as the French cavalry had not yet been landed and Raglan was resolved "to keep his in a band box", there was no pursuit . . . On the 23rd, the advance was resumed, and on the 25th the English, much to their astonishment, all but collided with a Russian column marching at right angles to their front. Menschikoff, the Russian commander, believing that the Allies would attack Sevastopol from the north side, was moving the bulk of his army out of the fortress towards Bakshiserai, in order to keep open his communications with the mainland. The Allies had no maps of the

Crimea, and those in the possession of the Russians were so indifferent that one regiment, after marching steadily for the whole of the 20th, finally found itself back in front of Sevastopol . . .

'The horror, misery and suffering of that winter are, as regards the British, too well known . . . The French lost even more men from disease, but . . . the plight of the Russians was the worst of all . . .

'The spring, however, brought its own rather different trials—if not to the armies, at least to their leaders—in the form of an electric cable which reduced the time of transit of correspondence between the head-quarters in the field and their respective capitals from ten days to twenty-four hours. The uses to which either nation put this new faculty of intercommunication were significantly different; Napoleon III . . . showered advice, instructions and suggestions upon his com-mander-in-chief; the British War Office on the other hand concerned itself more with enquiries as to the health of Captain Jarvis, believed to have been bitten by a centipede, and a heated discussion as to whether beards were an aid to desertion. It was small wonder that General Simpson, Raglan's successor, was kept at work answering corre-spondence from 4 a.m. to 6 p.m. daily, or that he expressed the view that the telegraph had "upset everything".' [14]

I sometimes wonder why it is that "The Charge of the Light Brigade", which I think is a very long way from being among the best of Tennyson's poems, is still among his most famous, and why "The Charge of the Heavy Brigade", which took place immediately before that of the Light Brigade, and, if it was no more effectual (which it wasn't) was certainly no less gallant, hardly ever seems to be quoted. If it is not stretching analogy too far, I would say that in certain phases Tennyson's poetry reminds one of the paintings of Manet and of Courbet. At other times, with inspiration working at a lower level, it calls to mind the pictures of the Pre-Raphaelites, and when it comes down to the more obvious blood-and-thunder mechanics of his battle poems the sort of comparison it evokes is with the laborious illustra-tions of Caton Woodville or that improbably competent craftswoman, Lady Butler. Lines such as,

> '. . . he turn'd half round, and bad his trumpeter sound
> To the charge . . .' [15]

or

> '. . . they rode like Victors and Lords
> Thro' the forest of lances and swords
> In the heart of the Russian hordes,

> They rode, or they stood at bay—
> Struck with the sword-hand and slew,
> Down with the bridle-hand drew
> The foe from the saddle and threw
> Underfoot there in the fray—' [16]

are the very stuff of the old *Illustrated London News* on which my imagination fed itself when, as a small boy, I lay with its large bound volumes on the floor of my grandfather's library.

I think it must have been in the same contemplative pose that I first came across the work of Gustave Doré, to whose uneven genius I have been devoted ever since. To me at that age he was the ideal illustrator of the heroic scene and I still remember the chaotic violence of his battle pictures. With the magical imagination of youth, and more conscious of the sound than of the sense, it was almost as though I could hear for myself

> '. . . . *Michael bid sound*
> *The archangel trumpet. Through the vast of Heaven*
> *It sounded, and the faithful armies rung*
> *Hosanna to the Highest: nor stood at gaze*
> *The adverse legions, nor less hideous joined*
> *The horrid shock. Now storming fury rose,*
> *And clamour, such as heard in heaven till now*
> *Was never; arms on armour clashing brayed*
> *Horrible discord, and the madding wheels*
> *Of brazen chariots raged; dire was the noise*
> *Of conflict; overhead the dismal hiss*
> *Of fiery darts in flaming volleys flew,*
> *And flying vaulted either host with fire.*
> *So under fiery cope together rushed*
> *Both battles main, with ruinous assault*
> *And inextinguishable rage . . .*
> *Long time in even scale*
> *The battle hung; till Satan, who that day*
> *Prodigious power had shown, and met in arms*
> *No equal, ranging through the dire attack*
> *Of fighting seraphim confused, at length*
> *Saw where the sword of Michael smote, and felled*
> *Squadrons at once; with huge two-handed sway*
> *Brandished aloft, the horrid edge came down*

> *Wide-wasting. Such destruction to withstand*
> *He hasted, and opposed the rocky orb*
> *Of tenfold adamant, his ample shield*
> *A vast circumference.'* [17]

'The dismal hiss of fiery darts' is not a sound that I ever want to hear again. As a fireman during the blitz I had more than enough of fire bombs, as well as others larger and more frightening. Although in retrospect I feel glad that I went through the experience, I know that this is really only a sort of false pride. What I mean, I suppose, is that I am thankful that I survived. The truth is that I hated the whole thing, and when I was not being bored stiff by the monotony of it all, I was terrified, of fire and smoke and all the horrible hazards of the job, of being electrocuted or drowned or buried alive. Of course, one was thought a hero at the time, but as everyone else was being equally heroic this was not much of a compensation. Besides, 'the fireman was taught to avoid heroics. Only the prospect of saving another life justified risking his own. But he found what seemed to him many good reasons for forgetting to calculate chances. He always knew that he was working in the foremost of danger, for fires were the enemy's normal targets.

'Sometimes he stood firmly on a flame-lit roadway, as the pictures so often show him, knees a little bent and body braced against the thrust of water through his hose. Sometimes he sank to his chin in oily mud, waded through hot rivers of paint, or leapt to dodge fiery streams of petrol. He was not always "on the branch", holding the nozzle at the point of attack. Often he stood to serve his pump for hours at a time as it relayed water from a distance, until so deafened by its never-ending roar that he could hardly hear the bomb explosions.

'He worked at times in heat that blistered the paint on the pump, and turned to steam the water of his jet before it reached its mark. He was taught to "get at it", to close in with his head held down near the branch where the jet's draught made a channel through the smoke, inching forward until he could pour water on the fire's red roots. This might mean perching a ladder on the steep slope of a roof and climbing fifty feet. It might mean taking a quick chance under burning rafters, or in a corridor roofed with stone cracking in the heat. Having got into a building, he might find himself lost in utter darkness, unable even to find his hose and trace his way back.

'He saw the broken bodies of comrades tossed high in the air with their pump by the direct hit of a bomb. He saw walls fall on them, roofs crash through buildings where they were at work.

'He fought in churches where the water steamed in the font and the big bell crashed to earth behind him. Many a time he saw a building that he had quenched by hours of toil re-ignited in an instant by the fall of another bomb.

'While he had water he had hope, for who knew what great skyscraper of flame might not be mastered by dogged patience? But the water sometimes failed. The jet would die away, the hose go limp. Oddly enough, when it did he always looked back along its length with instinctive expectation; but he knew it sometimes meant defeat. That really depressed him—watching a great blaze burn itself out with the mains broken, the emergency basins empty, and every line of access to distant supplies cut off. On those nights he would go back to the station with no songs or joking.' [18]

As a dramatic scene the blitz at close quarters was terrific and in a curious way sometimes exhilarating. Now and then you forgot the danger you were in, and the waste and the carnage and the futility of it all in the enormous excitement of the spectacle. Yet never once did I go on leave without wishing fervently that I need never go back. Once, when I fell down some steps (three, to be exact—it was a peaceful afternoon and I was taking the watchroom attendant a cup of tea), I sprained my ankle and had to spend a few blissful days recovering in the country. While I was there I went one morning to Salisbury Market and on a barrow I found a little book called *A Voice from Waterloo*. On the half-title, in a spidery Victorian hand, was written: 'Purchased on the field of Waterloo and presented to H. W. Tayler by his Uncle—W. A. Poole. Dec'r 1858'.

The author was Sergeant-Major Edward Cotton, late 7th Hussars, who was present throughout the battle and afterwards devoted his life, fourteen years of which he spent as a guide on the battlefield, to investigating and recording exactly what took place. This involved a great deal of patient research, of which the old soldier very sensibly gives full details. His description of the last phases of the battle is a first-rate piece of war-reporting:

'The sanguinary drama was now . . . fast drawing to a close. The Emperor's guards, their country's pride, they who had never turned their backs on foe or fled the battle field, were, for the first time, about to attack men who, like themselves, acknowledged no victor . . . The Imperial guard, led by the undaunted Ney, *"le brave des braves,"* advanced towards a point occupied by the first brigade of British foot-guards, and 5th or Halkett's British brigade. The guards were lying down, for cover from the shower of round and grape-shot and shells thrown amongst them by the French batteries ... As the leading column of the Imperial guard began to ascend the tongue of ground leading to the spot where the Lion [monument] now stands, it suffered most severely from the destructive fire of our right batteries, of which, from being ranged on echelons, every efficient gun played into the exposed long flank of the Imperial column. By this murderous fire the French ranks were most awfully ravaged, and they appeared to wave like high standing corn blown by sudden gusts of wind ... Ney had his horse killed under him, and gallantly led along on foot; at his side General Friant was wounded severely, and General Michel mortally. To men enthusiastic, who felt certain they were advancing to a glorious victory, this was no check, and the Imperial guard pursued its onward course with a firm step ...

'When the head of the column neared the line of the allies, it escaped the terrific fire of our right batteries, while at the same moment their own batteries ceased firing ... The front of the enemy appeared to stand still, from the men being mowed down as they laboured up the slopes, while their rear seemed pressing on. The Imperial guard at length succeeded in crowning the ridge, upon which the French saw nothing but the batteries; they descried through the smoke some cocked hats, but little imagined that one of them covered the head of the illustrious Duke, who was shortly to acquire a last and crowning laurel ...

'The enemy pressed on until within about fifty yards of Halkett's brigade, and the British foot-guards, who were lying down, quietly awaiting the band of veteran heroes. Wellington then gave the words, "Up, guards, make ready" and ordered General Maitland to attack. They rose in line four deep, and appeared to the French as if they had sprung out of the earth; whilst the French grenadiers, with their high bear's-skin caps and red plumes, looked like giants bearing down upon them. Our guards and Halkett's right, the 29th and 33rd, the gallant Halkett waving the latter regiment's colour in their front, advanced a few paces and threw in a tremendous volley, that was followed up by independent file-firing, rapidly and steadily delivered ... The French officers, waving their swords, and with shouts and words of encouragement, attempted to deploy and extend their front. But for this it was too late, the continued cross-fire which assailed them drove the fore-most of the enemy back on their mass ...

'Our adversary's desperate situation being instantly perceived by the Duke, his Grace ordered the charge: Lord Saltoun, who had joined from Hougoumont, called out, "Now's the time, my boys". Our guards and Halkett's left advanced with a loud cheer to the charge, the latter against a column which ... advanced with a noble and admirable bearing; officers in front, arms sloped, drums beating the pas de charge, and between them and on their flanks their brass guns loaded with grape. When within ninety yards of Halkett's left, they halted, carried arms as if to salute, and round-wheeled their guns, down went their port-fires, and crash came the grape, accompanied by a volley, into the 30th and 73rd regiments, who instantly returned the fire and came to the charge ...

'Our guards were pursuing the discomfited enemy into the valley, when the left or second attacking column of the Imperial guard was observed closely pressing on, undismayed by the defeat of their first column. To avoid being taken in flank, orders were given to the British guards to go about and resume their original position, but the word was misunderstood, and they fell into confusion; however notwithstanding the two battalions were mixed pell-mell together, getting the command on recrossing the ridge, "Halt, front, form!" they instantly fronted and formed four deep ...

'The Duke having seen the guards placed in their position, rode a little to the right, and observing the 52nd in a favourable situation, sent to Sir Henry Clinton to move forward the rest of Adam's brigade to charge the Imperial guard, that, with drums beating and deafening shouts of "Vive L'Empereur!" now crowned the summit of the position ... The fate of the battle seemed to quiver on the beam, when the 52nd ... previously screened from the enemy's view by the crest of our ridge, moved down in the most compact order upon the left flank of the Imperial column ... and poured a most deadly fire into their ranks ... The French column seemed now to reel to and fro under the heavy fire and the confusion and disorder which had been increasing, at last became uncontrollable and ... The enemy's troops retired in the greatest confusion, which caused an unsteadiness and panic throughout the remainder of the French army ... All these things combined, convinced the Duke that the favourable moment for making a general attack, was arrived. Closing his telescope with an air of triumph, he ordered the advance of the whole line. This order was received by the eager remains of the army with loud and tremendous cheers.

'The Duke stood on the rise ... with his hat raised in the air, as a signal to advance. The last parting rays of the beautiful setting sun at this moment (a quarter after eight) shone most resplendently, as if to enliven the scene . . . Were I to live to the age of Methuselah, never shall I forget that evening. In front might be seen the retiring columns of the enemy, broken and mingled with crowds of fugitives of all arms, mounted and dismounted, mixed pell-mell together. In the right front was a dense smoke, curling upwards, from the smouldering ruins of Hougomount. Far in the distance to the left front might also be dimly seen the dark columns of the Prussians, many of whom had arrived just in time to witness the overthrow of the French . . .

'About a hundred yards on the allied left . . . a broken column of French infantry was in the act of debouching with some guns, and making a hasty retreat, when the 52nd regiment in its advance came right upon them. The infantry tried to escape, and at the same time to defend themselves as best they could. The artillery turned to their left and attempted to get up the bank, but their horses were immediately shot by the 52nd. A young officer of the battery surrendered; but the commander, a veteran who wore upon his breast the decoration of the Legion of Honour, stood, sword in hand, in the midst of his guns, and in an attitude of bold defiance. A soldier started from the 52nd ranks and made a thrust at him, which the officer parried; a scuffle ensued, the man closed with him, threw him on the ground, and keeping him down with his foot, reversed his musket to bayonet him. The repugnance to the shedding of human blood unnecessarily, (a feeling which we may proudly claim as belonging to British soldiers,) burst forth in a groan of displeasure from his comrades. It came too late; the fatal thrust had passed, and the life of the deserving member of the honoured Legion was extinct. The battery and many prisoners were captured . . .

★ ★ ★

'During this time Plancenoit had been the scene of a most dreadful struggle; the French in the churchyard held out, and the Prussians, finding it of no avail to continue the attack in front, turned the village on both flanks, driving the Imperial guard before them; the latter, finding that they should be cut off from all retreat, fell in disorder, and mixed with the general mass of fugitives, who were flying in all directions towards Rossomme and La Maison-du-Roi, followed by the Prussians, who made a dash at the eagle of the Imperial guard. General Pelet called out, "A moi, chasseurs! sauvons l'aigle ou mourrons autour d'elle!" ("Rally round me, chasseurs! let us save the eagle,

or die protecting it!") Upon this they formed square, and saved the
eagle and the honour of the regiment . . .

'An arrangement had been previously made by Wellington and
Blücher, that the allied army should halt here, and . . . the Duke,
after clearing the high-road and its left of the allied troops, in order
to give full scope to the advancing Prussians, to whom he relinquished
the further pursuit of the flying enemy, remained for some time with
his advanced troops on the right of Rossomme in conversation with
General Vivian, Colonel Colborne and others; after which, promising
to send the provisions up, his Grace turned his horse round and rode
away. On returning leisurely towards Waterloo, about ten o'clock,
at a short distance before reaching La Belle-Alliance, he, aided by a
clouded moon, descried a group of mounted officers making towards
the Genappe high-road from the direction of Frischermont; the Duke
turned off to meet them: it proved to be Blücher and his staff: they
most heartily congratulated each other on the glorious result of the
contest in which they had been so intensely engaged. The conference
lasted about ten minutes, when the veteran Blücher, promising to
leave his inveterate foe rallying time on this side of the frontier, shook
hands with his Grace and proceeded to Genappe . . .

'Thus closed upon us the glorious 18th of June.' [19]

War remains one of the few diseases of which we know the causes
but for which we have not yet the least idea of a cure. Conscience may
sometimes make us cowards, but not always. Yet can one blame the
wife, the mother or the mistress to whom war has meant the sacrifice
of a husband, a son, or a lover if she should echo the sentiments of
'A Soldier's Death'?

> 'Trail all your pikes, dispirit every drum,
> March in a slow procession from afar,
> Ye silent, ye dejected men of war!
> Be still the hautboys, and the flute be dumb!
> Display no more, in vain, the lofty banner.
> For see! where on the bier before ye lies
> The pale, the fall'n, th' untimely sacrifice
> To your mistaken shrine, to your false idol Honour.' [20]

SOURCES

1 J. B. Morton, *By the Way.*
2 Edward Gibbon, *The Decline and Fall of the Roman Empire.*

3 Robert Harling, *Amateur Sailor*.
4 'Yorkist', letter in *The Times*, July 6, 1944.
5 Thomas Campbell, *Hohenlinden*.
6 Lieut.-Col. A. J. L. Fremantle, *The Fremantle Diary*.
7 Ibid.
8 E. R. Beavan, 'Alexander the Great', in *Encyclopaedia Britannica* (1937).
9 William Bolitho, *Twelve Against the Gods*.
10 Rudyard Kipling, *The Beginnings*.
11 The Rt Hon. Sir Winston S. Churchill, *My Early Life*.
12 Alvin Sapinsley, (quoted) *Time*, January 28, 1957.
13 Michael Howard, *The Sunday Times*, November 3, 1957.
14 F. J. Hudlestone and E. W. Sheppard, 'The Crimean War' in *Encyclopaedia
   Britannica* (1937).
15 Alfred, Lord Tennyson, *The Charge of the Heavy Brigade*.
16 Ibid.
17 John Milton, *Paradise Lost*, Book VI
18 Anonymous, *Front Line, 1940–41*.
19 Sergeant-Major Edward Cotton, *A Voice from Waterloo*.
20 Anne, Countess of Winchelsea, *The Soldier's Death*.

Journeys

★

I should like to spend the whole of my life travelling if I
could anywhere borrow another life to spend at home.

WILLIAM HAZLITT, Table-Talk

NEXT to biography and history, books about travelling are my favourite reading. I do not necessarily mean about travelling abroad. The journey from the east end of Piccadilly to the west may be made to seem as interesting as an arctic voyage or as exciting as a trip up the Amazon. Likewise it is possible to cross the Gobi Desert and find nothing more remarkable to say about it than about crossing the Round Pond. What counts is not the geography or the climate or the flora, it is the traveller's attitude of mind. I do not know how far it is from Folkestone to Pekin, but to Philip Jordan, a resourceful and imaginative traveller, even at the age of twelve, distance was no object, nor the means to get where he wanted to go. One day in 1915, it was round about Christmas time, the first Christmas of that war, he stood with his father 'on the cliff top to the east of Folkestone and stared across the empty sea as far as China. Make no mistake: substantial and serene, that remote country lay but thirty miles from where the wind was smacking my bare knees and rattling up the sleeves of my macintosh.

'When we stopped in our walk and turned towards the sea, the sky was dark with ungraded cloud: indeed, the whole world, except that part of it which lay immediately at our feet, was uniformly grey and devoid of hope. Both sea and sky were covered with the same dark stain and there seemed to be no life in the grass on which we stood. From that altitude, visibility extended for about fifteen miles, and we could see across the still waters of the channel until they became indistinguishable from the sky . . .

'It was at that moment that the vision came to us.

'Far over the sea the waters, which until then had not seemed fluid, stirred beneath a sudden, gentle wind which must have blown a highway through the clouds, for a beam of light, sharp and geometrically accurate as a blade, descended from the sky above and seemed, I remember, to cut away the darkness that lay on the waters for a space several miles in breadth.

'But it did more than that: it increased the range of our vision, and from the far darkness emerged a luminous coast line which, by some trick of perspective, came towards us a short way, so that it seemed then as though I had but to stretch my neck to peer into the windows of France.

'For perhaps as long as two minutes the sun illuminated the coast of Europe; but if for the majority of those who shared our vision that day, it did no more than that, for me it shone on distant realms also, and lifted the world from the atlas in which it had always dwelt, giving three dimensions to it, and colour and reality as well.

'Probably all those others who then saw France have not remembered, but the miracle of that day . . . is still, for the small human creature who then witnessed it, a sustaining memory whose details are far clearer than those of almost any subsequent experience.

'What was then made manifest was not only the coast of France, but what lay beyond it; for the cliffs across the sea, ragged with buildings, were only the foreshore of vision. Behind—as clear as that reality on which the eye rested—lay immensity; the sweep of Europe, sundered by the great rivers of history, Rhine and Vistula; the marshlands of the east; and beyond them, solid and permanent, the golden onions with which the summits of the Kremlin's campanili challenged the imagination of the world.

'Nor was that all: in the far distance, no more substantial than a cloud, the spine of the Ural Mountains rose into the pallid skies of Asia.

'In their turn those mountains became solid and passed beneath my feet, yielding to what at first seemed illimitable desert, although, silhouetted upon its far edges, could be seen the water towers of Harbin and, beyond, the bright pavilions of Pekin. When the waters of Pacific seas lapped the fringes of my munificent imagination, the vision closed and darkness came again upon the land. Behind a sudden cloud France trembled and withdrew.

'But I was no longer upon a complacent island: never again could I be insulated from the world of which my country could now be no more than a unit: the gateway of immeasurable knowledge had swung open for a moment, and I had been allowed to cherish what lay beyond its threshold.

'"Look!" Conrad's inextinguishable Marlow says somewhere in *Chance*: "Look! Even a small child lives, plays and suffers in terms of its conception of its own existence. Imagine, if you can, a fact coming in suddenly with a force capable of shattering that very conception of its own existence."

'Well, that was it: that vision of mine was Conrad's "fact". For that reason I have no doubt my journey was the longest and most impressive ever undertaken by a human being: nothing can ever persuade the traveller who made it so suddenly that its wonder has been eclipsed. All the resounding names of men who have done honour to the world by exposing its mysteries to those who had neither the inclination nor the means to discover new roads for themselves, conjure up smaller visions than that which I first saw some twenty years ago . . .

'The curious who follow that long track around the world will find it worn with a constant repetition of my footsteps, bigger now than when they first trod it, but no less eager. Since the age which produced Marco Polo, men no less splendid than he have mapped the world and rolled back from its surface the obscurity with which those who dwell in unknown regions cloak their ways of life: but to none of them can the traveller who then lived within my heart yield pride of place . . .

'He then learned and has not forgotten a great deal of useful information: to travel light: to travel alone; and never to forget that the people who dwell upon his path pluck any journey, however short and unadventurous, from the commonplace and invest it with a magic and an excitement that can never stale.' [1]

To travel alone—I am not sure about that, although freedom from the obligations of friendship are sometimes an advantage in travelling— but for most travellers solitude carries penalties of its own, among them ennui which may lead all too easily to self-reproach. When Dr Alain Bombard set out in 1952 from the Canaries to cross the Atlantic in a small rubber dinghy, he knew that solitude as complete and utter as any castaway had ever known would be one of the hazards against which no precautions could be taken. His journey took him sixty-five days, about two weeks longer than he had calculated, and all through his account of it there shines the clear light of his modesty, his passionate enthusiasm (the purpose of the trip being to prove scientific theories) his unfailing good-humour and his disinterested heroism. Except for a small radio, which eventually gave out, and about half a dozen books, among them Molière, Aeschylus, Montaigne, Rabelais and scores by Bach and Beethoven, he took no more than a man might expect to find himself with if he were suddenly to be cast adrift in an open boat. It was part of the experiment that the only food he would allow himself was to be whatever he could catch, and although he had with him a small stock of emergency rations, these remained in their sealed cannisters throughout the voyage.

Bombard left Las Palmas in his dinghy *L'Hérétique* on October 19: 'The evening was completely clear, the wind blew steadily from the north-north-east and the dinghy forged ahead at a good three and a half knots towards the Grand Canary . . . I had decided against setting a westerly course straight away in order to avoid the Sargasso Sea which, with the Doldrums, was one of the two major dangers of which I had to steer clear.

'North of the route I had chosen, the Northern Equatorial Current

and the Gulf Stream formed between them a gigantic eddy some five
thousand miles in circumference, containing a great mass of seaweed,
the origin of which has always been a mystery: this is the Sargasso Sea,
a great dead expanse ... The whole area has always been a major
navigational hazard, a terrible trap where plant filaments and seaweed
grip vessels in an unbreakable net. To the north it was the sea that spelt
danger. To the south the winds were the menace. Here the two powerful trade winds, one blowing north-east from Portugal, and the other
south-east from the Congo, met in a tremendous conflict in a no-man's
land of violent storms, unpredictable turbulence and disquieting calms,
a sort of buffer state between the northern and southern hemispheres.
It is called the Doldrums, a region of anarchic violence of the elements
... from which I knew I would not be able to free myself if I were
caught there.'
    'The stiff breeze which had sped me on my way did not last for
long; it abandoned me during the evening ...
    'The next day, and the day following, there was still no wind ...
but during the afternoon a breeze sprang up and I was able to set
course ...
    'That night my situation was really brought home to me. It was all
very different from the dummy run I had made across the Mediterranean, a busy, civilized lake, criss-crossed by ships. Now I was in a
boundless ocean with little likelihood of meeting any vessels. The
Atlantic would really put my theories to the test ...
    'The trade wind sprang up again. Soon it approached gale strength.
Carrying me first on the crests and then in their troughs, the waves
either protected me from or exposed me to its blast. Their tops were
breaking all around me. I wondered what would happen if *L'Hérétique*
came just under one of these on-rushing waterfalls ...
    'There is no entry in my log for Thursday, 23rd, because I was too
busy all day with my needle and thread. The wind had blown up fresh
and strong from the right direction; the faithful trade wind from the
north-east which was to carry me to my destination. But fate had its
own ironies; hardly had I trimmed the sail to the wind when it tore
right across at its broadest part ... I threw out my sea anchor, lowered
the sail and rigged the new one to the yard. Half an hour later a sudden
violent gust wrenched it off and sent it flying away like a kite ...' [2]
    Against some such emergency as this Bombard had luckily taken
with him an old torn sail, and now he started 'laboriously to sew it
together again. All I had was a reel of black thread and a few darning
needles. I had to work inch by inch, as the lack of space prevented me

from laying the sail out . . . By the time evening came I had just about finished . . .

'During the whole of the rest of the voyage I always had a pang of fear when I looked at the black darn right across the sail, rather like a piece of scar tissue that threatens to burst. But above all I was afraid of the fear it engendered, because increasing tiredness and exhaustion led me to expect the worst, and this in its turn made me weak and cowardly. From this moment on I was a prey to an inner conflict of morale, quite as vital as that with the elements. When things were going badly I managed to cope with it, but when there was some slight improvement I began to fear the worst again. I began to have doubts about the ability of my equipment to last the course. My low spirits that night are perhaps explained by the fact that I was frozen, chattering with cold, soaked to the skin and encrusted with salt. Never had I waited so desperately for the sun to rise, it seemed that it would be my only salvation . . .' [3]

For ten days Bombard continued his journey steadily south-east-wards. 'The afternoon was the longest and most difficult part of the day, with no way of hiding from the pitiless sun. I devoted the time to reading, writing and my medical studies. At two o'clock I gave myself a complete physical check-up; blood pressure, temperature, state of the skin, nails and hair, condition of the mucous membranes; noting the sea and air temperatures, humidity and weather conditions. Then I subjected myself to a sort of examination of my state of mind and morale and tried to exercise my memory, after which I read the books and music scores I had with me . . .

'When the sun had passed behind my sail, giving me some respite from its rays, I carried out my evening medical examination; measure-ment of urine, muscular strength, stools passed, plus a resumé of the day's activities; the day's haul of fish, its quantity and quality and the use I had made of it, a note of the day's plankton catch, its nature, quantity and taste, and a description of the sea birds I had seen. Dusk brought the night's sleep and I allowed myself the luxury of an hour or two listening to the radio , . .

'On 28th October [the ninth day] I noted: "I am not dreaming about food: a good sign. Indeed, it was the best proof that I was not hungry, because hunger is above all an obsession. I had no cravings of any sort.

'The next day I was suddenly overwhelmed by the thought of the grave situation I was in. Apart from its length, this part of my voyage had an inexorable quality absent from the previous laps [in the Mediter-ranean]. It was impossible for me to stop or turn round, there was not the slightest possibility of any help. I was just a drop in the ocean, part of a world not to be measured in human terms . . , and I had not sighted a ship for some time. The previous day I had seen my first shark since leaving the Canaries, but it passed quickly by. The dolphins, on the other hand, had become familiar acquaintances, I even talked to them at times, as the only friends in sight. When I woke up during the night I was always struck by the beauty of these creatures, swimming parallel to me, leaving phosphorescent wakes like some shooting star.

'From sheer curiosity I thought I would see what effect the beam of an electric torch would have. As soon as I switched it on, all the fish concentrated in its circle of light. I was still lost in admiration of their intricate evolutions, which I could direct more or less at will, when a sudden buffet forced me to clutch the side of the boat. It was a large shark . . . all its teeth flashed in the light of the torch, and its upperside gleamed pure white . . . For a moment or two its tail continued to beat around me like the cracks of a whip, splashing me with sea-water from head to foot. Its white stomach appeared from time to time amidst the phosphorescence, but then, presumably bored by my inactivity, it made off . . .'

Gradually 'relations with my marine neighbours assumed a definite pattern. They became almost like family friends. There were five or six dolphins and a petrel, which paid me a flying visit every day at four o'clock. It was a little black bird, its tail feathers tipped with white, about as large as a Paris sparrow. It baffled me how it managed to cover such distances to seek its sustenance in the middle of the ocean. It approached me from astern every day, sometimes settling down in the sea after four little steps on the water, and disappeared the moment the sun set. The dolphins were much more faithful and stayed with me twenty-four hours a day. They were quite easy to recognize. In trying to catch them with my bent knife the first day, I had wounded them, and the marks still showed. I had noted with interest that fish, like human beings, seem to heal slowly in sea-water. One of my dolphins had an open space about the size of a half crown towards the end of its back and another had been hurt on one of its fins. There were five or six I recognized in the same manner.' 4

On November 5, after being afloat eighteen days, Bombard's physical condition was beginning to cause him discomfort, though not yet serious anxiety. 'Things could be worse,' he noted, 'but I am starting to become obsessed with the idea of food . . . I am sick of eating raw fish, but even more tired of drinking its juice. If only it would rain for a change . . .

'I could still hear the radio at night, but it had become little more than a whisper . . . I could no longer make any check on the time in order to plot my position, and I had not learnt to make use of the Pole Star . . . I was now completely out of touch with the land, was deprived of news, and even started to forget what a human voice sounded like. The only voice and tangible presence was my own, and my life started to resemble more and more that of the animals around me. I began to share their sensations and reactions, eating the same food and catching the same flying fish. My little petrel still kept up his four o'clock rendezvous, while the dolphins had become my protégés. We all tried to hide from the same sun, they in the shadow cast by the dinghy and I behind the sail during the afternoon. Like the fish, my point of reference became the wave, instead of the familiar path or row of trees by which the landsman finds his way.' [5]

On the twenty-fourth day 'the surface of the sea had become strangely calm, exactly as if it were sleeked down with oil, and I suddenly realised why: "Rain! Here comes the rain," I cried aloud . . .

'Like the sound of a soda syphon, monstrously magnified, I heard advancing from far away the noise of water beating on water. I must have waited nearly twenty minutes, watching the slow approach of this manna from heaven. The waves were flattened under the weight of the rain and the wind buffetted me as the squall hit the boat. The cloud passed over slowly, writhing with the vertical turbulence of a small cyclone . . .

'This pleasant interlude was succeeded at about two o'clock in the afternoon by twelve hours of terror. Just as I was peacefully reading Aeschylus, there was a violent blow on the rudder: "That's another shark," I thought, and looked up. What I saw was a large swordfish of undeniably menacing aspect. He was following the dinghy at a distance of about twenty feet, seemingly in a rage, his dorsal fin raised like hackles . . .

'This intolerable anxiety lasted twelve long hours . . . He never approached from ahead, and every time he came at me he changed course at the last moment before striking the floats. I came to believe he was frightened, probably as frightened as I was . . . In the early hours of the morning his wake disappeared, but I spent a sleepless night.' [6]

This was only one of several alarming encounters with sea beasts, among them a whale and a giant ray, but growing weakness and debility gradually decreased Bombard's resistance and each successive challenge was as much a tax on his will power as it was on his physical

strength. But worse was yet to come. After weathering another violent
storm in which, with the main sheet wrapped round his wrist, he tore
through the water so fast that his hand bled from the friction of the
rope, the wind dropped and for nearly a fortnight he moved sluggishly
across the ocean in blistering heat.

On his fifty-third day at sea his reckoning showed that he had a
little over a hundred miles to go. On that day he saw a large cargo
boat and hailed it. 'Imagine how proud I was when the ship, as it drew
near, ran up a Union Jack to the peak and then dipped it three times:
the salute given to warships met on the high seas.' The captain asked
over his loud hailer whether Bombard needed any assistance.

'"Just the time, please, and my exact longitude," I replied.

'"49°50'."

'I was exactly ten degrees, that is to say six hundred miles from my
estimated position.' [7]

Bombard's physical condition by this time was precarious and the
discovery of the grave miscalculation he had made in his position
came as a very severe shock. Nevertheless, after spending an hour or
two on board the cargo boat, and in spite of the captain's earnest
entreaties, he insisted on resuming his solitary journey and climbed
unsteadily back into the dinghy. It was December 10. Not until twelve
days later did he sight land, and on that day he beached *L'Hérétique*
on the coast of Barbados.

I sincerely hope that I shall never have to make a journey like
Bombard's, for if I were ever to be shipwrecked and cast adrift I should
not have his invincible hope to sustain me, nor his patience, his
philosophic bearing or his plain cold courage. Nor am I interested in
travel for its own sake, much less for purposes of scientific research,
I regard it merely as a necessary procedure for getting from one place
to another. Not that I don't appreciate what I see *en route*, but the
tedium of continuous motion, and one's physical subjection to remote
control from a ship's bridge, a flight deck or a footplate, produce a
state of tension in me which neither experience nor the beguiling
euphemisms of travel advertisements seem able to overcome.

A trip that I made many times in my youth was the brief journey
from Parliament Hill Fields to the fringes of Kentish Town, as dingy
a district as any to be found in north London. Although I did not
discover it until much later, it is quite likely that among other little
boys making that same dusty journey at the same time was John
Betjeman. Now, there is a disposition in orthodox circles—meaning
such as have South Kensington, Haslemere, Cheltenham or other

islands of well-bred vacuity for their axis—to regard John Betjeman's poetry as 'funny'—which some of it is—because he tends to write about things that are not usually dealt with by poets, ribbon development, cafés, suburban life in the Home Counties, incandescent lighting, and the cast-iron and fretwork fantasies of mid-Victorian architecture. Yet is there any reason why one should not feel just as strongly about gas lamps as about fluorescent lighting?—the indiscriminate use of which I regard with feelings of firm disapproval. Why, then, should Betjeman's sincerity be doubted when he protests an affection for something such as lighting by gas, which reminds him of his own happy childhood? He may not be a great poet, though I believe that time will cherish his reputation at least as long as Hood's or Calverley's, but he is almost the only serious poet whose Muse concerns herself with what is dingy, vulgar, meaningless and meritricious in our every-day surroundings. This is a theme that might well keep anyone's muse in permanent employment, but part of the charm of Betjeman's is that she knows just how often to show herself and how to keep one wishing she would do so a little more frequently.

'Parliament Hill Fields' appeals to me not only for its beauty—I defy anyone to find a more poignant couplet than that with which the poem ends—but because it describes more with pity than with irony, which would have been easier to invoke, the sunlit squalor of evening descending on a neighbourhood as familiar to me in my childhood as it was to Betjeman in his:

Rumbling under blackened girders, Midland, bound for Cricklewood,
Puffed its sulphur to the sunset where that Land of Laundries stood,
Rumble under, thunder over, rain and tram alternate go,
Shake the floor and smudge the ledger, Charrington, Sells, Dale & Co.,
Nuts and nuggets in the window, trucks along the lines below.

When the Bon Marché was shuttered, when the feet were hot and
                                                              tired,
Outside Charrington's we waited, by the 'STOP HERE IF REQUIRED',
Launched aboard the shopping basket, sat precipitately down,
Rocked past Zwanziger the Baker's, and the terrace blackish brown,
And the Anglo, Anglo-Norman Parish Church of Kentish Town.

Till the tram went over thirty, sighting terminus again,
Past municipal lawn tennis and the bobble-hanging plane;
Soft the light suburban evening caught our ashlar-speckled spire,

Eighteen-sixty Early English, as the mighty elms retire
Either side of Brookfield Mansions flashing fine French-window fire.

Oh the after tram ride quiet, when we heard a mile beyond,
Silver music from the bandstand, barking dogs by Highgate Pond;
Up the hill where stucco houses in Virginia creeper drown;
And my childish wave of pity, seeing children carrying down
Sheaves of drooping dandelions to the courts of Kentish Town.[8]

A friend of Betjeman's was Robert Byron, as enterprising and as
enthusiastic a traveller as any that I have ever come across, to say
nothing of his enormous erudition, his scholarship and the qualities
that distinguished him as a companion and a friend. In 1933 he made
a journey through Persia into regions of Afghanistan which were then
little known. Characteristically, the main items with which he equipped
himself were a sleeping-bag, a sheepskin coat, a handful of introductions
to persons likely to be useful to him on the way, and indefatigable
determination. The discomforts of the journey, if not as acute as those
that Alain Bombard had to endure, were occasionally almost as
dangerous and certainly more varied. In Teheran he decided to buy
a Morris car which he found going for £30 (and which, after doing
sixty miles, became a total loss when the back axle broke). Byron's
description of this transaction must fill anyone who remembers Harry
Tate with a nostalgia for the inspired imbecility of his efforts to buy
a car:
'The sequence . . . of getting possession of the car, getting a licence
to drive it with, getting a permit to stay in Persia at all, getting a
permit to go to Meshed, getting a letter to the Governor of Meshed,
and getting other letters to the governors en route, obliterated four
days. I was said to be "recalcitrant de la loi" for having no identity
card. To obtain one, I furnished the state archives with the secret of
my mother's birthplace, in triplicate. Meanwhile, the owner of the
car had left Teheran, confiding his power of attorney to a very old
lawyer in a pink tweed frock-coat. A bargain was struck; signatures
were officially witnessed; but the police refused to register the transaction because, although the lawyer's power of attorney extended to
all his employer's worldly goods, a Morris car was not mentioned in the
list of those goods. This decision was reversed, on appeal to a higher
police official, who telephoned the fact to his subordinate. But when
we returned to the other department, three hundred yards away, they
knew nothing of it. Neighbouring departments were asked if they had

had the message. At last someone remembered that the person who must have answered the telephone had gone out. Heaven favoured us; we met him in the street, and followed him to his desk. This annoyed him. He would do nothing, he said, without a copy of the power of attorney. Till it was ready, perhaps we would be good enough to leave him in peace. The lawyer hobbled off to buy a clean sheet of paper. We, the owner's son, the garage proprietor and myself, sought asylum on the pavement of the main square, squatting round the crabbed old scribe while his spectacles fell off his nose, and his pen harpooned the paper till it looked like a stencil. A sentence was not finished before the police moved us on; another scarcely begun, before they did so again. Like a colony of disturbed toads, we scuttled round and round the square, jabbing down a word here and there, while dusk deepened into night. When the copy was presented, it had again to be copied, in the office. The square had been better than this; for the office electricity had failed, and matches had to be struck in such quantities that our fingers were burned to the quick. I laughed; the others laughed; the police laughed like madmen; but suddenly became serious, said the certificate of ownership could not after all be ready for three days. An hour's argument evoked a promise of next morning. Next morning I went in search of it; again they said three days. But now, being alone, I had the advantage, speaking enough Persian to say what I wanted, but not enough to understand a refusal. Once more we trooped off to the officer across the street. Men rushed from room to room. The telephone spluttered. The document was born. And all this, let me add, was only a tithe, a mere sample, of my fate during these last four days.' [9]

In due course Byron reached Meshed, whence he set out by bus for Nishapur, ninety miles away. The 'vehicle was carrying twice its proper number of passengers, and their luggage as well. Exhilarated at the prospect of his journey's end, the driver tore downhill at forty miles an hour, lurched across a stream-bed, and had just rebounded against the opposite slope, when to my great surprise the off front wheel ran backwards towards me, buckling the running board with a crunch, and escaped into the desert. "Are you English?" the driver asked in disgust. "Look at that." An inch of British steel had broken clean through.

'It took an hour and a half to fit another joint. The pilgrims huddled down with their backs to the wind, men beneath their yellow sheep-skins, women veiled in black shrouds ... When we started again the driver was seized with a palsy of caution. He proceeded at five miles an hour, stopping at every caravanserai to refresh his nerves with tea; till at last we reached a small pass and a new view.

'Tiers of firelit mountains encircled the horizon. Night, and a surf of clouds, were rolling in from the east. Down in the plain, a blur of smoke, trees, and houses announced Meshed, the holy city of the Shiahs. A gold dome flashed, a blue dome loomed, out of the cold autumnal haze . . .

'A number of cairns marked the sacred vantage. The male pilgrims descended to pray, their backs turned on Meshed in favour of Mecca. The driver descended to collect his dues, and since the husbands were engaged, perforce approached their wives. A screech of protest, rising to a furious and sustained crescendo, blasted the moment of thanksgiving. On prayed the pious husbands, bashing their foreheads on the cairns, lacerating their stockinged feet, heaving sighs and rolling eyes to heaven, in their resolve to postpone the inevitable reckoning. Round the bus danced the driver and his assistant, repulsed by the hooded harpies in their wire cage. One by one the husbands tried to dodge back to their places unseen. One by one the chauffeurs caught them. Each protested for a separate quarter of an hour. But only three refused to pay in the end, and these, snarling and cursing, were ejected from the company with blows and kicks. Led by a whining pharisee, the most active of the devotees, who had been my neighbour on the front seat of the bus, they started away down the hill at a lolloping trot.

'The bus had hardly begun to follow them, before the women at the back set up a threefold clamour. With their fists and household implements they would soon have demolished the thin wooden partition that separated them from the driver and myself. Once more we stopped. Letting fall their veils, the foaming viragos appealed to me to retrieve their men. But now I had no interest save to reach a hotel before dark. "Either take the men back," I told the driver, "or go on. You'll lose my fare too, if we stay here any longer." This argument prevailed. He caught up the men, who were still tearing down the road, and invited them to return. They refused. Backing into the gutter, they refused point-blank thus to favour the monster who had defiled the most hallowed moment of their lives. Again the women shrieked and battered. Again the partition cracked. The whole bus began to creak. "GO ON!" I yelled, stamping till the floorboards were entangled with the brake. Jumping out, the driver seized the deserters, belaboured them till they groaned for mercy, and dragged them back into the bus. The pharisee sought his old place in front, by me. But now it was my turn to go mad. I would not have him near me, I said. In reply, he seized my hand, and pressing it to his prickly, saliva-trickling beard, sprayed it with kisses. A shove sent him sprawling, while I leapt out on the other side, declaring to the now befogged, exhausted, and unhappy driver that rather than suffer further contact with the man, I would walk into Meshed on my own feet and keep what I owed him in my own pocket. At this, the women turned their abuse to the pharisee. The cringing brute was hoisted into the back. And we set off for the holy city at a pace fit to smash a gun-carriage.' [10]

The approach to most cities of the Near East, however uncomfortable the means by which one travels, is probably preferable to approaching London from almost any direction, except via the river. The haphazard hideousness of London's outer suburbs, and the sort of life typified by the poverty of their conception, is one of the most depressing things I know about returning to London from a holiday abroad. Take Greenstead, for example: 'Greenstead is the kind of suburb in which one street is distinguishable from another only if you have to live there. Acres of semi-detached two-storied homesteads sprout like a rash along both sides of the arterial road. The shopping centre, with the chain-store grocers and the cash chemist and the neo-Lutyens bank on the corner, has a block of neat and nasty flats on top of it and a deep stretch of asphalt in front, with cycle racks for the housewives who live off the bus route. In summer the gardens of Waveny Avenue are bright with standard roses as pink as peppermint rock, in winter as empty as the little minds poring over the pools forecasts indoors. The TV aerials are thick above the rooftops and the sky drones with the sound of aircraft leaving or landing on the airport a couple of miles further out. Beyond Princess Parade, where the shops begin, there are the factories, light and bright and airy, like new hyginic jails. But the prisoners in them are not making mail bags; they're turning out toothpaste and tinned beans and cereals and deodorants and razor blades, so that you'll have something to cut your wrists with when you can't stand life in Greenstead a moment longer.' [11]

Yet Greenstead was, within my own memory, a place as pleasant as Hemel Hempstead in Hertfordshire used to be (now it too is almost an outer suburb of London) in the days when Cobbett could say that its 'fields . . . like those in the rich parts of Devonshire, will bear perpetual grass. Any of them will become upland meadows. The land is, in short, excellent, and it is a real corn-country. The *trees* from Redbourne to Hempstead are very fine; oaks, ashes, and beeches. Some of the finest of each sort, and the very finest ashes I ever saw in my life. No villainous things of the *fir-tribe* offend the eye here. The custom is in this part of Hertfordshire . . . to leave a *border* round the ploughed parts of the field to bear grass, and to make hay from, so that, the grass being now made into hay, every corn field has a closely mowed grass walk about ten feet wide all round it, between the corn and the hedge. This is most beautiful! The hedges are now full of the shepherd's rose, honeysuckles, and all sort of wild flowers; so that you are upon a grass walk, with the most beautiful of all flower gardens and shrubberies on your one hand, and with the corn on the other. And thus you go from field to field . . . the sort of corn, the sort of underwood and timber, the shape and size of the fields, the height of the hedge-rows, the height of the trees, all continually varying. Talk of *pleasure-grounds* indeed! What, that man ever invented, under the name of pleasure-grounds, can equal these fields in Hertfordshire?' [12]

Thinking of the Festival Gardens, which with a little taste and imagination might so easily have been transformed into a contemporary Ranelagh, instead of the seedy, vulgar racket that they have become, one can only agree wholeheartedly with Cobbett. *Mais chacun à son goût.* Those who enjoy Blackpool, that dismal and anaemic imitation of Coney Island's mammoth vulgarity, would probably have been bored to find themselves in Xanadu, and devotees of Monte Carlo or Las Vegas would find it hard to understand the pleasure that I get from Farringdon Market, where, rootling among the second-hand book barrows, I have found a number of treasures, as well as some curiosities. One of these, which cost me 2d., is a little book, privately printed, called *Log of a Tour Round the World*, by H. and H. C. Wrigley. Its title page bears the dates 1883-84-85, but beyond this there is no clue to its origin. The identity of the authors, the characters they write about, and their purpose in keeping a log at all, since they travelled by the ordinary steamship lines, are wrapped in mystery. The book is written colloquially without any attempt at style and shows the authors as being observant, suitably impressed by whatever was meant to impress them, and wholly unoriginal in their reactions. For me the fascination of the book is the strength of its period flavour. Whatever else they may have been, the Messrs Wrigley were obviously out-and-out mashers. They remind one, even when they have got as far away as the Antipodes, of characters from Binstead or Phil May come to life, of Romano's in its heyday and the crush bar at the Empire. The following entries refer to their stop at Melbourne and their departure for Tasmania:

Monday, May 5th

'Went to the Criterion at 11 a.m., where we met Will and Fairy ready to go out. So off we went to Brighton by train. Fairy had to be back at the Criterion by 5, but wasn't there till 5.30. Fairy, being a wee bit tight, kicked up a row with her "boss"; so she got the "sack", and when we came in after dining at Menzies' we found she was in tears. So Will immediately melted, and we all went up to Menzies', the leading hotel, and got the fair barmaid a room. Played billiards till late; had some oysters. Fawnes, a fellow from Launceston, N.Z., came up tonight. He is a great friend of Will's, but we don't like him. He was awfully shocked at Will for being spooney on Fairy; said it was awfully wicked and preached like fun ... Before we turned in, Will, Fawnes, Harry, Fairy and myself drove in a cab right down to St Kilda, and had very good fun. Had supper and went to bed.

Tuesday, May 6th

'Breakfasted with Fairy at 9.15 a.m. Left her to put on her gloves and bonnet, which takes her an hour, and went driving about, doing business, getting photos., etc. When we came back to Menzies' it was 11 a.m., and Will and Fairy were waiting for us, so we got our luggage on one cab and drove in another down to the Tasmania Steamship Co.'s Wharf; s.s. *Flinders* with steam up ready to start. Left Melbourne at 1 p.m., after saying "Goodbye" to Will and Fairy. Will was kind enough to give me a kangaroo hide girth, a beauty, as a parting gift. Will has been awfully kind to us while we have been here, and I hope we shall do the same for him when he comes to England. Had a good view of the river Yarrow as we steamed down; passed the P. and O. s.s. *Rome* at Williamstown, getting under weigh for London. Had a jolly quick run down the bay, passed through the Port Phillip heads at 4.30 p.m., had a good view of Queen's Cliff and Sorento, the quarantine station, and got fairly out to sea by dinner time, 5.30, ship rolling a little. She is a very nice steamer, something like the *Hilda*. Two drunken sharpers on board, also two rather decent commercial travellers, who gave us some good hints about Tasmania and New Zealand. Nice little smoking room on board. Lovely night.' [13]

And so, impregnated by their optimism and insularity against the frustrations, the fatigues and the inconveniences of their immense journey, the Wrigley brothers went on their way. If it was lack of imagination that eased their path, excess of it on one occasion was nearly fatal to a traveller as inveterate and as determined as themselves. When Hilaire Belloc set out to walk in a straight line from Toul, in the valley of the Moselle, to Rome, he could hardly have been under any illusion about the difficulties that his route would impose. *The*

Path to Rome, in spite of its pseudo-Rabelaisian affectations of style and its dogmatic overtones, still strikes me as one of the best of all travel books. Belloc, with characteristic determination, refused to be put off when at one point he was told that the Gries Pass could not be got over because of the weather. Against his better judgement, a local guide, who happily for Belloc was as experienced as he was courageous, let himself be talked into making the attempt with him:

'At three o'clock the guide knocked at my door, and I rose and came out to him. We drank coffee and ate bread. We put into our sacks ham and bread, and he white wine and I brandy. Then we set out. The rain had dropped to a drizzle, and there was no wind. The sky was obscured for the most part, but here and there was a star. The hills hung awfully above us as we crossed the spongy valley ... We went on in the uneasy dawn. The woods began to show, and there was a cross where a man had slipped that very April and been killed. Then, most ominous and disturbing, the drizzle changed to a rain, and the guide shook his head and said it would be snowing higher up ... it could not be done, but I said we must attempt it. I was eager, and had not yet felt the awful grip of the cold. For half an hour we plunged on through snow above our knees, and my thin cotton clothes were soaked. So far the guide knew we were more or less on the path, and he went on and I panted after him. Neither of us spoke, but occasionally he looked back to make sure I had not dropped out.

'The snow began to fall more thickly, and the wind had risen somewhat ... I was chattering a little with the cold; but as he did not propose a return, I followed him. The surface was alternately slabs of frozen snow and patches of soft new snow. In the first he cut steps, in the second we plunged, and once I went right in and a mass of snow broke off beneath me and went careering down the slope. He showed me how to hold my staff backwards as he did his alpenstock, and use it as a kind of break in case I slipped.

'We had been about twenty minutes crawling over that wall of snow and ice; and it was more and more apparent that we were in for danger. Before we had quite reached the far side, the wind was blowing a very full gale and roared past our ears. The surface snow was whirring furiously like dust before it ... the rocks on the far side of the slope, rocks which had been our goal when we set out to cross it, had long ago disappeared in the increasing rush of the blizzard.

'Suddenly as we were still painfully moving on, stooping against the mad wind, these rocks loomed up over us as large as houses, and we saw them through the swarming snow-flakes as great hulls are seen

through a fog at sea. The guide crouched under the lea of the nearest;
I came up close to him and he put his hand close to my ear and shouted
to me that nothing further could be done . . . I asked how far we were
from the summit. He said he did not know where we were exactly,
but that we could not be more than eight hundred feet from it . . . I
offered him all I had to go on, but it was folly in me, because if I had
had enough to tempt him and if he had yielded we should both have
died. Luckily it was but a little sum. He shook his head.

'. . . I understood his wisdom, for in a little while the cold began to
seize me in my thin clothes. My hands were numb, my face already
gave me intolerable pain, and my legs suffered and felt heavy . . . The
guide was hesitating whether to stay in this rough shelter, or to face
the chances of the descent. This terror had not crossed my mind, and I
thought as little of it as I could, needing my courage, and being near
to breaking down from he intensity of the cold . . .

'After a little he decided for a return, but he told me honestly what
the chances were, and my suffering from cold mercifully mitigated my
fear . . .

'Well, we returned. Twice the guide rubbed my hands with brandy,
and once I had to halt and recover for a moment, failing and losing
my hold. Believe it or not, the deep footsteps of our ascent were
already quite lost and covered by the new snow since our halt, and
even had they been visible, the guide would not have retraced them.
He did what I did not at first understand, but what I soon saw to be
wise. He took a steep slant downward over the snow-slope, and though
such a pitch of descent a little unnerved me, it was well in the end.
For when we had gone down perhaps nine hundred feet, or a thousand,
in perpendicular distance, even I, half numb and fainting, could feel
that the storm was less violent. Another two hundred, and the flakes
could be seen not driving in flashes past, but separately falling. Then
in some few minutes we could see the slope for a very long way
downwards quite clearly; then, soon after, we saw far below us the
place where the mountain-side merged easily into the plain . . .

'When we saw this, the guide said to me, "Hold your stick thus, if
you are strong enough, and let yourself slide". I could just hold it,
in spite of the cold. Life was returning to me with intolerable pain.
We shot down the slope almost as quickly as falling, but it was
evidently safe to do so, as the end was clearly visible, and had no
break or rock in it.

'So we reached the plain below . . .' [14]

I do not know what it is about travelling among mountains that induces in me a vague feeling of oppression. Perhaps in a former incarnation I belonged to some subterranean species that had its habitat in the bowels of the earth. At any rate, the answer is decidedly in the negative when I put to myself the question—

Are not the mountains, waves and skies a part
Of me and of my soul, as I of them?
Is not the love of these deep in my heart
With a pure passion? [15]

When I remember my delight as a small child in travelling on top of a horse drawn omnibus, and still more when I think of modern conditions of road travel, I often wish that we could revert to the stage coach. I am seldom in such a hurry to get from one place to another that I would not gladly make a sacrifice of time for the pleasure of travelling as the Pickwickians did:

'The portmanteaus and carpet-bags have been stowed away ... the coachman mounts to the box, Mr Weller jumps up behind, the Pickwickians pull their coats around their legs, and their shawls over their noses; the helpers pull the horse-cloths off, the coachman shouts out a cheery "All right," and away they go.

'They have rumbled through the streets, and jolted over the stones, and at length reach the wide and open country. The wheels skim over the hard and frosty ground; and the horses bursting into a canter at a smart crack of the whip, step along the road, as if the load behind them ... were but a feather at their heels. They have descended a gentle slope, and enter upon a level, as compact and dry as a solid block of marble, two miles long. Another crack of the whip, and on they speed, at a smart gallop; the horses tossing their heads and rattling the harness, as if in exhilaration at the rapidity of the motion: while the coachman, holding whip and reins in one hand, takes off his hat with the other, and resting it on his knees, pulls out his handkerchief and wipes his forehead: partly because he has a habit of doing it, and partly because it's as well to show the passengers how cool he is, and what an easy thing it is to drive four-in-hand, when you have had as much practice as he has. Having done this very leisurely (otherwise the effect would be materially impaired), he replaces his handkerchief, pulls on his hat, adjusts his gloves, squares his elbows, cracks the whip again, and on they speed, more merrily than before.

'A few small houses scattered on either side of the road, betoken the entrance to some town or village. The lively notes of the guard's key-bugle vibrate in the clear cold air, and wake up the old gentleman inside, who, carefully letting down the window-sash half-way, and standing sentry over the air, takes a short peep out, and then carefully pulling it up again, informs the other inside that they're going to change directly; on which the other inside wakes himself up, and determines to postpone his next nap until after the stoppage . . .

'And now the bugle plays a lively air as the coach rattles through the ill-paved streets of a country town; and the coachman, undoing the buckle which keeps his ribands together, prepares to throw them off, the moment he stops. Mr Pickwick emerges from his coat collar, and looks about him with great curiosity; perceiving which, the coachman informs Mr Pickwick of the name of the town, and tells him it was market-day yesterday, both of which pieces of information Mr Pickwick retails to his fellow-passengers; whereupon they emerge from their coat collars too, and look about them also. Mr Winkle, who sits at the extreme edge, with one leg dangling in the air, is nearly precipitated into the street, as the coach twists around the sharp corner by the cheese-monger's shop, and turns into the market-place; and before Mr Snodgrass, who sits next to him, has recovered from his alarm, they pull up at the inn yard, where the fresh horses, with cloths on, are already waiting. The coachman throws down the reins and gets down himself, and the other outside passengers drop down also: except those who have no great confidence in their ability to get up again: and they remain where they are, and stamp their feet against the coach to warm them—looking, with longing eyes and red noses, at the bright fire in the inn bar, and the sprigs of holly with red berries which ornament the window.

'But, the guard has delivered at the corn-dealer's shop, the brown paper packet he took out of the little pouch, which hangs over his shoulder by a leather strap; and has seen the horses carefully put to; and has thrown on the pavement the saddle which was brought from London on the coach-roof; and has assisted in the conference between the coachman and the hostler about the grey mare that hurt her off-fore-leg last Tuesday; and he and Mr Weller are all right behind, and the coachman is all right in front, and the old gentleman inside, who has kept the window down full two inches all this time, has pulled it up again, and the cloths are off, and they are all ready for starting, except the "two stout gentlemen," whom the coachman inquires after with some impatience. Hereupon the coachman, and the guard, and Sam Weller, and Mr Winkle, Mr Snodgrass, and all the hostlers, and every one of the idlers, who are more in number than all the others put together, shout for the missing gentlemen as loud as

they can bawl. A distant response is heard from the yard, and Mr
Pickwick and Mr Tupman come running down it, quite out of breath,
for they have been having a glass of ale a-piece, and Mr Pickwick's
fingers are so cold that he has been full five minutes before he could
find the sixpence to pay for it. The coachman shouts an admonitory
"Now then, gen'lm'n!" the guard re-echoes it; the old gentleman
inside, thinks it a very extraordinary thing that people *will* get down
when they know there isn't time for it; Mr Pickwick struggles up on
one side; Mr Tupman on the other; Mr Winkle cries "All right"; and
off they start. Shawls are pulled up, coat collars are re-adjusted, the
pavement ceases, the houses disappear; and they are once again dashing
along the open road, with the fresh clear air blowing in their faces. . .' [16]

Now let us move further afield, from the pale sunshine of a crisp
winter's morning in the Kentish countryside to its antithesis, Bermuda,
which E. B. White once apostrophized in a book given to a friend as
'matchless soil, from coral won! O ring on England's finger! [17]

James Thurber, happening to come upon this inscription on a day
when Bermuda was in the grip of a storm, added his own impression
of the island:

> *I, too, like Mr E. B. White,*
> *Though I am not a singer,*
> *Admire this island, slim and bright*
> *This ring on England's finger;*
> *But memories of rain and blow,*
> *And darker weather rankle,*
> *O aching corn on England's toe!*
> *O sore on England's ankle!* [18]

The fate of Bermuda, like that of many other places whose attraction
once lay in their isolation as well as in their climate, seems to have been
sealed by the expanding tentacles of air travel. Were it my misfortune
to have to earn my living on Wall Street, even such a living as might
enable me to visit Bermuda regularly, I do not think I should want to
see there the same *angst*-ridden faces behind the same cigars, the same
calculating and preoccupied glances, even though mercifully dimmed
by sun-glasses, the same backsides incongruously clad in brightly
patterned beach shorts.

I suppose it is because no enterprising shark has yet hit on the way
to make the 'rose-red city half as old as time' a paying proposition that
Petra has remained to this day a place of such impressive if awe-

inspiring beauty. It is certainly difficult to get at, as Elizabeth Hamilton found when she made the journey from Amman. Because of the heat during the day she had been advised to travel at night, and having found a driver who was willing to make the long and lonely journey, she set off:

'The road went on and on, with on either side a landscape that reached away mysteriously, and overhead, the white ball of the moon. I became sleepy, yet fought against sleep for fear of missing anything. Even so, I slept soundly but intermittently. Each time I awoke we were crossing one of the *wadis* over which the road runs between Amman and Petra . . .

'The moon . . . shone down on mountains that leapt skywards, then dropped into unfathomable valleys. The mountains had a ghastly pallor, like faces under neon lighting. They were creased and gashed with shadows; every ravine and gully was visible. There seemed no end to the mountains . . .

'There was no vegetation except squills, pale and ghostly as the cliffs on which, as if by a miracle, they had taken root. Sometimes the moon hid its face behind the mountains, and then stared at us anew. I closed my eyes in terror, then opened them, rebuking myself for missing anything of this macabre scene. It was like a Blake picture.

'The lights of a car flashed from across the valley, vanished and then were upon us, suddenly, round a bend, dazzlingly bright. It was a road made long years ago for caravans and camels. There was scarcely room to pass. Again, I closed my eyes. When I opened them, the car had gone and I saw a camel ridden by a figure swathed in white. The animal looked pale and huge. I could see the tassels on its head. Its eyes glinted green, and its underlip protruded arrogantly.

'I slept again . . .

'It was day when I woke. The sun was shining, and the sky a clear bright blue. The moon was still there, but it had a shrunken look, like a withered magnolia. Near at hand the landscape was reddish-brown and flat. Then it rolled away in undulating stony hills that overlapped one another or dipped into purple-shadowed hollows. In the far distance there were mountains pencilled against the sky. They were claret-coloured but splashed with deep violet and sapphire; after the pallor of the mountains the colours were breath-taking. On either side of the road camels were feeding—more camels than I had ever seen . . .'

Soon after this, at about eight o'clock, a halt was made for breakfast at a police post where the guides were to be picked up for the last stage of the journey.

'Below us, in the distance were the mountains that I had seen earlier that morning. I knew that beyond them was Petra.

'We walked down a dusty slope to where two boys were waiting with a horse. It was flea-bitten grey, with a long mane and tail. It had a high saddle, an embroidered black and red saddle-cloth, and a bridle decorated with white shells . . . One of the police made a sign for me to get up . . . and so, accompanied by the boys on foot, I set out on the last lap of the journey.

'The elder boy, who was my guide, wore jodphurs and a red and white *keffiyeh*. He had a cartridge belt round his waist, and a rifle slung over his shoulder . . . His lean, brown face was shrewd and full of mischief. He spoke English fairly well. The younger boy, who was carrying bottles of water and a knapsack full of bread, kept up a conversation in Arabic, addressing himself now to his companion, now to me . . .

'We continued downhill, and out onto an open plain. Here so weird a sight met my eyes that I wanted, for a moment, to go not a yard further. At the other edges of the plain there were sinister formations of sandstone—pale and bleached , . . Some were square and flat-topped; others rounded; like lumps of dough that had been fossilized. Some, again, were hollowed into natural caves or cut into tombs that looked like eye-sockets in a skull. Others were carved into towers decorated with a vertical or horizontal groove. In front of me stood massive obelisks. The heat came down, mercilessly, from the hard blue sky, and up from the dazzling chalk-white ground: it was flung back, wave upon wave of it, from the blinding death-pale rocks . . .

'Suddenly a mountain wall blocked our path: violet-coloured but streaked with blue and crimson and green, and dappled with shadows. The colour was restful to the eyes after the white glaring plain. And, again, suddenly, as if by magic . . . we were in the ravine which is called Siq.

'It was cool, almost cold. Cliffs rose on either side, vast and terrible, so close overhead as almost to hide the sky. They were red sandstone, a red that changed with every flicker of light, every shadow. Sometimes it was a pale clear red, then again a deep rose that darkened to purple or blazed into orange. Trees and shrubs grew out from the rocks, junipers, oleanders and figs, broom and the trailing blue-leaved caper plant. The Siq is a dried-up river bed, its floor deep in pebbles. It was also the highway into Petra. Through it caravans from the east used to come, laden with silks and ivories and spices, on their way to Gaza and Alexandria and the world of Greece and Rome.

'Its intense silence was accentuated by every sound: the scrunch of the horses' hooves, the jingle of the bit, the clap of a pigeon's wings. Suddenly, too, there was a sweet, shrill cry from a flight of small black-plumaged birds that now clustered on a boulder, now rose, now settled again . . .

'We went on, the pebbles scrunching, the gorge now widening, now narrowing, and overhead a strip of sky startlingly blue above the red towering rocks. In one place a six-branched candlestick was carved on the face of the cliff. There were niches as though for statues, and what looked little shrines with a classical pillar on either side and a pediment above; or a flight of steps would suddenly appear, going nowhere, coming from nowhere. The atmosphere was strange; it was secretive and empty—utterly empty, except for the boys and myself, the horse, and the birds. Yet it seemed to be possessed by invisible beings, by unseen watching eyes, so that I was thankful for the boys and for the flea-bitten grey, clinking her bit and snuffing the air.

'The Siq ended in a burst of light. There in front of me, cut into the rose-red cliff and seeming to rise out of a tangle of oleanders, was the tomb that has come to be called the *Khazneh*, or the treasury of Pharoah. Four classical pillars, two on either side, supported an architrave with over it a pediment, and above this, so as to form a second story, more pillars and in the centre a lantern upholding an urn . . .'

'To the west there was a huge Roman theatre, to the east a cliff cut into tombs with carved fronts.

'Petra is a place of wonder. Elsewhere there are ruins of temples, palaces and tombs. The difference is that here they are cut into natural rock; have no existence apart from it: so that, in a real sense, Petra is a rock city, not a city built of stone quarried from rock. Most of the buildings are in the classical style. But there are others that go back to an earlier Assyrian tradition . . .

'Another wonder is the colour of the sandstone which ranges from dark earth-red to rose, rose to lurid flame, flame to the red of blood. Engrained in it are surprising shades of violet, china blue, yellow, ivory, indigo, raspberry and coral. Sometimes these merge into one another, like paints on a palette; or they remain distinct, forming clear-cut rings or twirling sugar-stick patterns, each adding a fresh brightness. . .

'The younger boy stayed with the horse, while with the elder I clambered up rocks, pushing my way through tamarisks and figtrees and oleanders, stopping from time to time to take breath or to marvel at the precipice still reaching above me. My companion went ahead, moving at a fine pace, nimble as a goat. I would lose sight of him,

then, in the silence, hear his voice calling back to me: it had a shrill
wild note, like the cry of a bird, ringing out from the cliffs. Each time
I lost sight of him, I was afraid. Then he would come back, leaping
down, careless yet sure-footed, holding out to me a thin brown hand.
He carried my bag for me and, snatching off my straw hat he replaced
it by his own *keffiyeh*, fastening it with the camelhair strings: the rest
of the trip he wore my hat and was mighty pleased with it . . .

'In the heat of the afternoon I sat near the Roman theatre on a
boulder with a fig tree reaching out of its shade. The boys were with
me and the horse tethered nearby . . .

'We had sat, perhaps, half an hour, when the elder leapt to his feet.
"I fetch water," he said. Before I realized what had happened the pair
of them were astride the horse and out of sight. I heard their voices
coming from a distance, faint and unreal. I was alone with the empty
theatre and the tombs. My guide was gone, the horse was gone. So,
too, I remembered, was my bag which the boy was still carrying, and
in it my passport and money . . .

'The boys had been away perhaps ten minutes, but it seemed an hour.
I called out, hoping that I might hear that strange, bird-like voice in
answer. But it was my own voice that came back, flung at me from
the rocks.

'I clambered down from where I was sitting, then up a slope to a
tomb with a front carved from rainbow-streaked stone. Its pillars had
an almost liquid quality, as though they were melting into the rock
from which they had been hewn: they made me think of gutted
candles. I laid my hand on one of them: the sandstone crumbled under
my touch. Then, I went into the darkness, feeling almost an intruder
as I did so. A bird flew out, nearly brushing my face. The roof of
natural rock was black with streaks of white and coral pink; there was
a smell of goats and the air was dank. I came out into the sun beating
down onto the rocks. Overhead a golden-brown eagle soared. It was
then I heard a voice. I strained my ears to listen. It came again. Then
I saw the flea-bitten grey and the boys on her back; the terror was gone:
the terror of the silence, and of a past that was always present. And yet
not wholly gone—rather, kept at bay by companionship both of
human and animal.' [19]

To Miss Hamilton's youthful guides the sand and scrub of the
Jordanian plain and the rocky defiles of its mountains were probably
as familiar as the banks of the Mississipi to Huck Finn. I can never read
of his trip down the river with Jim, the negro who was his friend and
whom he helped to escape from slavery, without wishing that I could

have been with them. Part of the book's charm, and much of Mark Twain's unobtrusive skill, lies in the style, innocent, colloquial, and yet as the same time curiously poetic, of Huck's descriptive patter:

'It was a monstrous big river down there—sometimes a mile and a half wide; we run nights, and laid up and hid day-times; soon as night was most gone, we stopped navigating and tied up—nearly always in the dead water under a two-head; and then cut young cotton-woods and willows and hid the raft with them. Then we set out the lines. Next we slid into the river and had a swim, so as to freshen up and cool off; then we set down on the sandy bottom where the water was about knee-deep, and watched the daylight come. Not a sound anywheres —perfectly still—just like the whole world was asleep, only sometimes the bull-frogs a-clattering, maybe. The first thing to see, looking away over the water, was a kind of dull line—that was the woods on t'other side—you couldn't make nothing else out; then a pale place in the sky; then more paleness, spreading around; then the river softened up, away off, and warn't black any more, but grey; you could see little dark spots drifting along, ever so far away—trading scows, and such things; and long black streaks—rafts; sometimes you could hear a sweep screaking; or jumbled up voices, it was so still, and sounds come so far; and by-and-by you could see a streak on the water which you know by the look of the streak that there's a snag there in a swift current which breaks on it and makes that streak look that way; and you see the mist curl up off of the water, and the east reddens up, and the river, and you make out a log cabin in the edge of the woods, away on the bank on t'other side of the river, being a wood-yard, likely, and piled by them cheats so you can throw a dog through it anywheres; then the nice breeze springs up, and comes fanning you from over there, so cool and fresh, and sweet to smell, on account of the woods and the flowers; but sometimes not that way, because they've left dead fish laying around, gars, and such, and they do get pretty rank; and next you've got the full day, and everything smiling in the sun, and the song-birds just going it!

'A little smoke couldn't be noticed, now, so we would take some fish off of the lines and cook up a hot breakfast. And afterwards we would watch the lonesomeness of the river, and kind of lazy along, and by-and-by lazy off to sleep. Wake up, by-and-by, and look to see what done it, and maybe see a steamboat, coughing along up stream, so far off towards the other side, you couldn't tell nothing about her only whether she was stern-wheel or side-wheel; then for about an hour there wouldn't be nothing to hear nor nothing to see—just solid lonesomeness. Next you'd see a raft sliding by, away off yonder, and maybe a galoot on it chopping, because they're most always doing it on a raft; you'd see the axe flash, and come down—you don't hear nothing; you see that axe go up again, and by the time it's above the man's head, then you hear the *k'chunk!*—it had took all that time to come over the water. So we would put in the day, lazying around, listening to the stillness. Once there was a thick fog, and the rafts and things that went by was beating tin pans so the steamboats wouldn't run over them. A scow or a raft went by so close we could hear them talking and cussing and laughing—heard them plain; but we couldn't see no sign of them; it made you feel crawly, it was like spirits carrying on that way in the air. Jim said he believed it was spirits; but I says:

'"No, spirits wouldn't say, 'dern the dern fog'."

'Soon as it was night, out we shoved; when we got her out to about the middle, we let her alone, and let her float wherever the current wanted her to; then we lit the pipes, and dangled our legs in the water and talked about all kinds of things—we was always naked, day and night, whenever the mosquitoes would let us.

'Sometimes we'd have that whole river all to ourselves for the longest time. Yonder was the banks and the islands, across the water; and maybe a spark—which was a candle in a cabin window—and sometimes on the water you could see a spark or two—on a raft or a scow, you know; and maybe you could hear a fiddle or a song coming over from one of them crafts. It's lovely to live on a raft. We had the sky, up there, all speckled with stars, and we used to lay on our backs and look up at them, and discuss about whether they was made, or only just happened—Jim allowed they was made, but I allowed they happened; I judged it would have took too long to *make* so many. Jim said the moon could a *laid* them; well, that looked kind of reasonable, so I didn't say nothing against it, because I've seen a frog lay most as many, so of course it could be done. We used to watch the stars that fell, too, and see them streak down. Jim allowed they'd got spoiled and was hove out of the nest.

'Once or twice of a night we would see a steamboat slipping along in the dark, and now and then she would belch a whole world of sparks up out of her chimbleys, and they would rain down in the river and look awful pretty; then she would turn a corner and her lights would wink out and her pow-wow shut off and leave the river still again; and by-and-by her waves would get to us, a long time after she was gone, and joggle the raft a bit, and after that you wouldn't hear nothing for you couldn't tell how long, except maybe frogs or something.

'After midnight the people on shore went to bed, and then for two or three hours the shores was blank—no more sparks in the cabin windows. These sparks was our clock—the first one that showed again meant morning was coming, so we hunted a place to hide and tie up, right away.' [20]

The possibilities of making such a journey as Huck's are now, I suppose, pretty remote, though as a waterway the Mississippi has no doubt changed less than the aspect of its banks, for the waters of the world are tamed less easily than the land. Even Venice, in spite of its tourists, which, after all, could hardly be accounted a new industry, remains by the very nature of its situation, more or less inviolate. Municipal tradition, however shrewdly based on commercial instinct, has seen to it that progress in Venice, when it cannot fail to be obvious to the eye, shall at the same time be harmonious and discreet. May it always be so, for whether one be 'a Roman, a Florentine, a Parisian in the secret heart' (or, I would add, an Englishman)'. . . one must also be a Venetian, for there is nothing like it, nothing, anywhere else on earth . . . to sail from Venice to return to Venice: there's richness for you. I watched it float away into a watery grave as I left for Greece . . . I watched it rise hazy from the sea on my return. I sat stupefied as the sun beat down from the blue Italian sky, and we slipped quietly past Schiavoni, the great Piazza, the long, sweet line of honey-coloured houses, the walls thick-plastered red and gold and rust, the terraces entangled carelessly with vine leaves and geraniums.

'Even the docks, when we came to them, had known the touch of magic, even the warehouses gleamed golden as we passed them by; so the voyage ended, and I trod once more the stones of Venice.' [21]

Whether you approach Venice by air, by land or by sea, the magic of the experience never fails.

> *I rode one evening with Count Maddalo*
> *Upon the bank of land which breaks the flow*
> *Of Adria towards Venice: a bare strand*
> *Of hillocks, heaped from ever-shifting sand,*
> *Matted with thistles and amphibious weeds,*
> *Such as from Earth's entrance the salt ooze breeds,*
> *Is this; an uninhabited sea-side,*
> *Which the lone fisher, when his nets are dried,*
> *Abandons; and no other object breaks*

The waste, but one dwarf tree and some few stakes
Broken and unrepaired, and the tide makes
A narrow space of level sand thereon,
Where 'twas our wont to ride while day went down . . .
As those who pause on some delightful way
Tho' bent on pleasant pilgrimage, we stood
Looking upon the evening and the flood
Which lay between the city and the shore
Paved with the image of the sky . . . the hoar
And aery Alps towards the North appeared
Thro' mist, an heaven-sustaining bulwark reared
Between the East and West; and half the sky
Was roofed with clouds of rich emblazonry
Dark purple at the zenith, which still grew
Down the steep West into a wondrous hue
Brighter than burning gold, even to the rent
Where the swift sun yet paused in his descent
Among the many folded hills; they were
Those famous Euganean hills, which bear,
As seen from Lido thro' the harbour piles,
The likeness of a clump of peaked isles—
And then—as if the Earth and Sea had been
Dissolved into one lake of fire, were seen
Those mountains towering as from waves of flame
Around the vaporous sun, from which there came
The inmost purple spirit of light, and made
Their very peaks transparent. 'Ere it fade,'
Said my companion, 'I will show you soon
A better station'—so, o'er the lagune
We glided, and from that funereal bark
I leaned, and saw the city, and could mark
How from their many isles in evening's gleam
Its temples and its palaces did seem
Like fabrics of enchantment piled to heaven.[22]

SOURCES

1   Philip Jordan, *There Is No Return.*
2   Alain Bombard, *The Bombard Story.*

3 Ibid.
4 Ibid.
5 Ibid.
6 Ibid.
7 Ibid.
8 John Betjeman, *Parliament Hill Fields*.
9 Robert Byron, *The Road to Oxiana*.
10 Ibid.
11 Nicolas Bentley, *The Floating Dutchman*.
12 William Cobbett, *Rural Rides*.
13 H. and H. C. Wrigley, *Log of a Tour Round the World, 1883–84-85*.
14 Hilaire Belloc, *The Path to Rome*.
15 Lord Byron, *Childe Harold*.
16 Charles Dickens, *The Pickwick Papers*.
17 E. B. White, reprinted from *The Bermudian*.
18 James Thurber, reprinted from *The Bermudian*.
19 Elizabeth Hamilton, *Put Off Thy Shoes*.
20 Mark Twain, *The Adventures of Huckleberry Finn*.
21 Elizabeth Nicholas, *The Sunday Times*, September 28, 1958.
22 Percy Bysshe Shelley, *Julian and Maddalo*.

A Choice of Creeds

★

For modes of faith let graceless zealots fight;
He can't be wrong whose life is in the right.
ALEXANDER POPE, Essay on Man

'Is there any religion whose followers can be pointed to as distinctly more amiable and trustworthy than those of any other? If so, this should be enough. I find the nicest and best people generally profess no religion at all, but are ready to like the best men of all religions.' [1] Indeed, I am always rather suspicious of people who, not being among the appointed leaders of their faith, make public pronouncements about their religious beliefs. It seems impossible, even for the most well-meaning, not to appear either self-righteous or defiant. And those who are readiest to confess that they are atheists are usually the ones whose motives I suspect most. I can understand that a man may wish publicly to proclaim his faith, even though his doing so, as in the manner of an Oxford Grouper or of Father Divine, may seem distasteful: one's relations with one's conscience are, or it seems to me should be, a private matter. But I find it hard to sympathize with anyone who makes a point of asserting his lack of faith. If your conscience impels you to deny the existence of God, it should be possible to do so without deliberately flying in the face of other people's susceptibilities.

Having said this, it ill becomes me to admit that I have no religion in the accepted sense. But without making this clear there would seem to be no reason for my choice of the passages that follow, nor for my comments on them. I prefer to call myself a sceptic rather than an atheist, for I know of no creed that may be said to be superior to any other, though there are some that seem rather worse. This may sound a sweeping and possibly a foolish assertion for someone whose study of comparative religions is restricted to a single reading of James's *Varieties of Religious Experience*, but that reading was in itself enough to suggest that a bare knowledge of the essential tenets of any religious faith should show whether it is a faith of which one could be worthy, or that is likely to be worthy of oneself. So far this experience has eluded me. As a child I was taken to church fairly regularly, not because either of my parents had more than a perfunctory interest in my going, or in going themselves, but because an uncle of mine was the vicar of a nearby church. He was also, as we later discovered, a hypocrite, a blackguard and a liar, and this discovery went a long way to severing the adolescent tentacles of faith, never very strong in my case, that had sprouted in early childhood.

Even without this disillusioning experience I doubt whether my faith would long have survived the scrutiny of adult reasons, for there are two things that I find especially hard to swallow about the Christian religion. One is the so-called omnipotence of God; the other is the importance attached in varying degrees by both Anglicans and Catholics to the outward trappings of worship. I cannot believe that Christ, who was by all accounts a person of infinite charity and wisdom and common sense, would have approved any expenditure on the glorification of the Church while multitudes of the faithful (and of the unfaithful too, for that matter) have for centuries been condemned to grinding poverty. Nor can I believe that schismatic bickering between High and Low church would have had his approval, or that he would have attached the slightest importance to the placing of communion tables, the lighting of candles, the thumbing of beads, and so on. It seems to me much more likely that he would have condemned all such ritualistic flapdoodle as being entirely out of keeping with the aim and the spirit of his teaching.

One of the great weaknesses, it seems to me, in the argument in favour of the Christian faith is that 'God moves in a mysterious way his wonders to perform'.[2] Why in the world should he do so? And what is the authority for this assertion? As far as I know, God never indicated either directly or indirectly his intention of performing his wonders by stealth or in such a way as to obscure responsibility for his actions. And this, of course, touches very closely on the question of his omnipotence. To my mind, an omnipotent god must be above all omnipotently just, but I can see no omnipotent justice in war or slavery or famine or endemic disease or economic chaos or the recurrent brutalities of nature. Yet these things persist. I am not saying that from God's point of view, and hence from the theologian's, there are not sound reasons for this state of affairs, just as there may have been for Belsen and Buchenwald, or that babies suffering from hereditary syphilis are sometimes born blind, and small girls sometimes raped by lunatics: I am only saying that so far no one has been able to explain to my satisfaction why God, if he be truly omnipotent, allows such things to occur.

The first thing that I require of anyone whom I am to cherish and respect is that I should feel able to trust them implicitly. God's record in matters such as these, if, indeed, he has a hand in them at all, does not inspire me with confidence. I am prepared to believe in my muddled way—and looking at the differences of opinion on the same subject that exist between, for example, Baptists and Roman Catholics, there are some grounds for feeling confused—I am prepared to believe that I have got hold of the wrong end of the stick, that God is not always

omnipotent, nor invariably just. But if that is so, it only complicates my
dilemma. For what is one to make of a god who seems as foolish and as
fallible as man? And yet, to take another aspect of the same problem,
'apart from a religious view of life there seems to be no adequate
answer to the questions raised by human suffering. Philosophy may
and does help men in some degree to reconcile themselves to it, and to
show some of its values. But today its very magnitude is making
suffering for many almost unbearable, and is raising the old dilemma,
"either God is not omnipotent, or he is not good" . . . It can indeed
be said that suffering is one of the conditions of progress; that it keeps
alive tenderness and compassion; and that it helps, if rightly accepted,
to enrich and strengthen character. But the problem remains.

'Much suffering is due to human ignorance, and will be progressively
banished as man's knowledge increases—the conquest of disease and
pain goes on. But much more is the result of man's misuse of his
freedom . . . Nations need not, for example, make war upon each
other. True, the responsibility for war is not shared equally by all who
are involved in it, but the evil or stupidity of some is bound to involve
others; and to fight against evil may be more of a Christian duty than
to submit to it, even though the struggle must increase the sum of
immediate suffering . . . Many are willingly accepting suffering in order
to free the world from tyranny and to win human freedom. Others
suffer with no consciousness of the vicarious nature of their suffering.' [3]

That seems to me as fair and reasonable a summary of the Christian
dilemma as one could hope for. But 'the problem remains'; and the
more one examines its historic details, the more inexplicable it becomes.
'When I consider, for example, the history of religion, I find no warrant
for affirming that its services have outweighed its disservices. Jesus
Christ . . . lit the fires of the Inquisition and set up the Pope at Rome.
Mahomet deluged the earth with blood, and planted the Turk on the
Bosphorus. Saint Francis created a horde of sturdy beggars. Luther
declared the Thirty Years' War.' [4]

One need not go as far back as Luther for a taste of the tyranny
that is sometimes imposed in God's name. No doubt there are to this
day Calvinistic households where the bleak and inhuman regimen that
overshadowed Edmund Gosse's childhood is inflicted on other little
boys as powerless to defend themselves as he was:

'We came down to breakfast,' he says, in his autobiography, 'at the
usual time. My father prayed briefly before we began the meal; after
it, the bell was rung, and, before the breakfast was cleared away, we
had a lengthy service of exposition and prayer with the servants. If the

weather was fine, we then walked about the garden, doing nothing, for about half an hour. We then sat, each in a separate room, with our Bibles open and some commentary on the text beside us, and prepared our minds for the morning service. A little before 11 a.m. we sallied forth, carrying our Bibles and hymn-books, and went through the morning service of two hours;... this was the central event of Sunday.

'We then came back to dinner,—curiously enough to a hot dinner, always, with a joint, vegetables and puddings, so that the cook at least must have been busily at work,—and after it my Father and my stepmother took a nap, each in a different room, while I slipped out into the garden for a little while, but never venturing further afield. In the middle of the afternoon, my stepmother and I proceeded up the village to Sunday School, where I was early promoted to the tuition of a few very little boys. We returned in time for tea, immediately after which we all marched forth, again armed as in the morning, with Bibles and hymn-books, and we went through the evening service, at which my Father preached. The hour was now already past my week-day bedtime, but we had another service to attend, the Believers' Prayer Meeting, which commonly occupied forty minutes more. Then we used to creep home, I often so tired that the weariness was like physical pain, and I was permitted, without further "worship", to slip upstairs to bed.

'What made these Sundays, the observance of which was absolutely uniform, so peculiarly trying was that I was not permitted the in-dulgence of any secular respite. I might not open a scientific book, nor make a drawing, nor examine a specimen. I was not allowed to go into the road ... nor to discuss worldly subjects at meals, nor to enter the little chamber where I kept my treasures. I was hotly and tightly dressed in black, all day long, as though ready at any moment to attend a funeral with decorum. Sometimes, towards evening, I used to feel the monotony and weariness of my position to be almost unendurable, but at this time I was meek, and I bowed to what I supposed to be the order of the universe.' [5]

Had little Gosse's fanatical father allowed himself the advantages of a slightly more liberal education it is possible that he might have come to realize that 'the highest good is to live happily, and not through a life of mortification to expect a happy death. Should we attain felicity in life, death will be easy, as it will be natural and in due season. Whereas by the present system of religious teaching, men are enjoined to value chiefly happiness at the end of life, which, if they were implicitly to follow, they would, by neglecting the first great duty, that of innocent enjoyment during existence, effectually preclude themselves from attaining.' 6

The trouble with any form of dogmatic religion is that it must lead, if practised dogmatically, to some degree of hypocrisy. For although dogma is man-made, it takes account primarily of the spirit, not of the flesh, whereas man's instinct is to do the opposite. 'Honest man or scamp, what did it matter,' said Rousseau, 'provided I went to mass? One must not, however, believe that this way of thinking is peculiar to Catholics; it is common to all dogmatic religions in which faith, not works, is considered the principle thing.' 7

The dangers of exploiting faith as an end in itself, rather than employing it as a means of improving the human lot, have been made unpleasantly obvious by the political gangsters of our own time. Among their forerunners, though one who operated on a much more limited scale, was the Mahdi, the Sudanese ruler who slew General Gordon. Not only did he combine personal ambition with neurotic fervour, but also had the advantage, markedly lacking in most of the priests and prelates of our day, of a daring and romantic aura:

'There is an ancient tradition in the Mahommedan world, telling of a mysterious being, the last in succession of the twelve holy Imams, who, untouched by death and withdrawn into the recesses of a mountain, was destined, at the appointed hour, to come forth again among men. His title was the Mahdi, the guide; some believed that he would be the forerunner of the Messiah; others that he would be Christ himself. Already various Mahdis had made their appearance; several had been highly successful, and two, in mediaeval times, had founded dynasties in Egypt. But who could tell whether all these were not impostors? Might not the twelfth Imam be still waiting, in mystical concealment, ready to emerge, at any moment, at the bidding of God? There were signs by which the true Mahdi might be recognised—unmistakable signs, if one could but read them aright. He must be of the family of the prophet; he must possess miraculous powers of no common kind; and his person must be overflowing with a peculiar sanctity. The pious dwellers beside those distant waters, where holy men by dint of a constant repetition of one of the ninety-nine names of God, secured the protection of guardian angels, and where groups of devotees, shaking their heads with a violence which would unseat the reason of less athletic worshippers, attained to an extraordinary beatitude, heard with awe of the young preacher whose saintliness was almost more than mortal and whose miracles brought amazement to the mind. Was he not also of the family of the prophet? He himself had said so; and who would disbelieve the holy man? When he appeared in person, every doubt was swept away. There was a strange splendour in his presence, an over-powering passion in the torrent of his speech ... A band of enthusiastic disciples gathered round him, eagerly waiting, for the revelation which would crown their hopes. At last, the moment came. One evening, at Abba Island, taking aside the foremost of his followers, the Master whispered the portentous news. He was the Mahdi ...

'The country, groaning under alien misgovernment and vibrating with religious excitement, suddenly found in this rebellious prophet a rallying point, a hero, a deliverer. And now another element was added to the forces of insurrection. The Baggara tribes of Kordofan, cattle-owners and slave-traders, the most warlike and vigorous of the inhabitants of the Sudan, threw in their lot with the Mahdi. Their powerful emirs, still smarting from the blows of Gordon, saw that the opportunity for revenge had come. A holy war was proclaimed against the Egyptian misbelievers. The followers of the Mahdi, dressed, in token of a new austerity of living, in the "jibbeh", or white smock of coarse cloth, patched with variously shaped and coloured patches, were rapidly organised into a formidable army. Several attacks from Khartoum were repulsed; and at last the Mahdi felt strong enough to advance against the enemy. While his lieutenants led detachments into the vast provinces lying to the west and the south—Darfour and Bahr-el-Ghazal—he himself marched upon El Obeid, the capital of Kordofan. It was in vain that reinforcements were hurried from Khartoum to the assistance of the garrison: there was some severe fighting; the town was completely cut off; and after a six months' siege, it surrendered. A great quantity of guns and ammunition and £100,000 in specie fell into the hands of the Mahdi. He was master of Kordofan; he was at the head of a great army; he was rich; he was worshipped. A dazzling future opened before him. No possibility seemed too remote, no fortune too magnificent. A vision of universal empire hovered before his eyes. Allah, whose servant he was, who had led him thus far, would lead him onward still, to the glorious end.

'For some months he remained at El Obeid, consolidating his dominion. In a series of circular letters, he described his colloquies with the Almighty and laid down the rule of living which his followers were to pursue. The faithful, under pain of severe punishment, were to return to the ascetic simplicity of ancient times. A criminal code was drawn up with a barbaric zeal. The blasphemer was to be instantly hanged, the adulterer was to be scourged with whips of rhinoceros hide, the thief was to have his right hand and his left foot hacked off in the market-place. No more were marriages to be celebrated with pomp and feasting, no more was the youthful warrior to swagger with flowing hair: henceforth the believer must banquet on dates and milk, and his head must be kept shaved. Minor transgressions were punished by confiscation of property, or by imprisonment and chains. But the rhinoceros whip was the favourite instrument of chastisement. Men were flogged for drinking a glass of wine, they were flogged for smoking; if they swore, they received eighty lashes for every expletive; and after eighty lashes it was a common thing to die. Before long, flogging grew to be so everyday an incident that the young men made a game of it, as a test of their endurance of pain. With this Spartan ferocity there was mingled the glamour and the mystery of the East. The Mahdi himself, his four Khalifas, and the principal emirs, masters of sudden riches, surrounded themselves with slaves and women, with trains of horses and asses, with bodyguards and glittering arms. There were rumours of debaucheries in high places; of the Mahdi, forgetful of his own ordinances, revelling in the recesses of his harem, and quaffing date syrup mixed with ginger out of the silver cups looted from the church of the Christians. But that imposing figure had only to show itself for the tongue of scandal to be stilled. The tall, broad-shouldered, majestic man, with the dark face and black beard and great eyes—who could doubt that he was the embodiment of a superhuman power? Fascination dwelt in every movement, every glance. The eyes, painted with antimony, flashed extraordinary fires; the exquisite smile revealed, beneath the vigorous lips, white upper teeth with a V-shaped space between them—the certain sign of fortune. His turban was folded with faultless art, his jibbeh, speckless, was perfumed with sandalwood, musk, and attar of roses. He was at once all courtesy and all command. Thousands followed him, thousands prostrated themselves before him; thousands, when he lifted up his voice in solemn worship, knew that the heavens were opened and that they had come near to God. Then all at once the onbeia—the elephant's tusk trumpet—would give out its enormous sound. The nahas—the brazen war-drums—would summon, with their weird rolling, the whole host to arms. The green flag and the red flag and the black flag would rise over the multitude. The great army would move forward, coloured, glistening, dark, violent, proud, beautiful. The drunkenness, the madness of religion would blaze on every face; and the Mahdi, immovable on his charger, would let the scene grow under his eyes in silence.' [8]

The drunkenness and the madness of religion are painful but palpable truths which emphasize the words of the cynic who remarked that the fact 'that God has managed to survive the inanities of the religions that do him homage is truly a miraculous proof of his existence'. [9]

A lady to whom I once repeated this told me not to be blasphemous. I said that if God was as I imagined he would be, he would have appreciated the remark, for 'I have never understood why it should be considered derogatory to the Creator to suppose that He has a sense of humour'. [10] Perhaps the reason is that so many people, particularly, it would seem, those who hold Low Church views, themselves suffer from a severe attrition of the sense of humour. It is difficult to imagine either a Calvinist or a Lutheran rolling about with laughter. Or take the Salvation Army. I am well aware that it has done an enormous amount of practical good, and by its example of piety and self-sacrifice must have inspired good in hosts of others. Yet how anyone with the vestige of a sense of humour could fail to see that the 'Army', with its particular brand of tambourine evangelism, its mock-martial spirit (so wildly at variance with the sedate airs of its soldiery) its antiquated and often unbecoming uniform—how anyone could fail to see that these things have their funny side is something that I in my irreverence cannot understand.

For that matter, the faithful, both High and Low, seem to find no unconscious humour even in that part of the Prayer Book which says: 'It is a thing plainly repugnant to the Word of God, and the custom of the Primitive Church, to have publick Prayer in the Church, or to minister the Sacraments in a tongue not understanded of the people.' [11]

If one glances at other passages in the Prayer Book, this, the twenty-third of the 39 Articles, seems to be almost deliberately ironic. How many factory workers, farm hands, shop assistants, bus conductors, clerks, typists or children of school leaving age, could explain the significance of these words from the Athanasian Creed:

'... The Father uncreate, the Son uncreate: and the Holy Ghost uncreate.

The Father Incomprehensible, the Son incomprehensible: and the Holy Ghost incomprehensible.

The Father eternal, the Son eternal; and the Holy Ghost eternal.

And yet there are not three eternals: but one eternal.

As also there are not three incomprehensibles, nor three uncreated: but one uncreated, and one incomprehensible.' [12]

Those who feel an inclination to criticise the allusive obscurities of some forms of contemporary writing might profitably turn their attention to the Prayer Book. So also might the authorities of the Church, though there are other reforms, more urgently needed, with which they might also busy themselves, such as in the stipends of the clergy, where gross disparities are still tolerated. However, the Church of England is not alone in the need to overhaul its ideas. I daresay the Buddhists, the Mormons, and others are just as far behind the times, as are those who advocate an attitude of passive resistance to the troubles of their fellow men. A life of abnegation may have been all very well in the Middle Ages, but in the vastly different social and economic conditions of our time it seems to me that the deliberate withdrawal of one's abilities and one's energies from the life of the community cannot be justified except on the grounds of self-indulgence of the spirit. It is the coward's way out of an admittedly grave dilemma, this refusal to face the responsibilities of existence in a world one may have grown to detest; this giving up the struggle, if you see it that way, for man's soul, which will not be saved, if at all, by prayer and fasting but by honest toil and the brotherhood of man being brought to reality. And it will not bring it an inch nearer for one man to shave the top of his head or another to foreswear the gift of speech. That it is possible for such things still to be done, ostensibly in God's name, in what are supposed to be reasonably enlightened communities shows how far we have yet to go before we can attain the simplicity of mind and faith that were Christ's. The argument has been put less generously by Samuel Butler but in words that mean the same thing: 'Christ was crucified once and for a few hours. Think of the hundreds of thousands whom Christ has been crucifying in a quiet way ever since.' [13] However, let us be fair. Let us consider those to whom the experiences of religion are a happier reality than the facts of existence. Seeing what has happened to the Russians since they got rid of God, one cannot help thinking that even at the price they paid for their beliefs they were in several important respects better off in the days of which it could be said that 'there is a church almost in every street, and the Kremlin is a citadel of cathedrals. During Holy Week, towards the end of which the evidences of the fasting season grow more and more obvious by the closing of restaurants and the impossibility of buying any wine and spirits, there were, of course, services every day. During the first three days of Holy Week there was a curious ceremony to be seen in the Kremlin, which was held every two years. This was the preparation of the chrism of holy oil. While it was slowly stirred and churned in

great cauldrons, filling the room with hot fragrance, a deacon read
the Gospel without ceasing (he was relieved at intervals by others),
and this lasted day and night for three days. On Maundy Thursday the
chrism was removed in silver vessels to the Cathedral . . . The morning
service in the Cathedral of the Assumption on Maundy Thursday . . .
was crowded to suffocation. Everybody stood up, as there was no room
to kneel. The church was lit with countless small wax tapers. The
priests were clothed in white and silver. The singing of the noble
plain chant without any accompaniment ebbed and flowed in perfect
discipline; the bass voices were unequalled in the world. Every class of
the population was represented in the church. There were no seats,
no pews, no precedence nor privilege. There was a smell of incense
and a still stronger smell of poor people, without which, someone said,
a church is not a church. On Good Friday there was the service of the
Holy Shroud, and besides this a later service in which the Gospel was
read out in fourteen different languages, and finally a service beginning
at one o'clock in the morning, and ending at four, to commemorate
the Burial of Our Lord. How the priests endured the strain of these
many and exceedingly long services was a thing to be wondered at;
or the fast, which was kept strictly during all this period, precluded
utter, eggs and milk, in addition to all the more solid forms of
nourishment, and the services were about six times as long as those of
the Catholic or other churches.' [14]

Christianity is curiously adhesive. How is one to stop people believing in God? It is forty years since the communists, brimming with
confidence, set out to tackle this problem in Russia: they have not
solved it yet. 'In the heyday of Comrade Yaroslavsky and his League
of the Godless, nothing seemed easier. All that had to be done was to
put the clergy out of business, close the churches, expose the inconsis-
tancies of the biblical narrative, identify the Hierarchy with the oppressive ruling classes, and, at top speed, build heaven on earth. All these
things were done except the last, and this turned out to be a fundamental omission.' [15]

I wonder if heaven on earth seems any nearer to the emancipated
Soviet citizen, living in his police state under the shadow of atomic
annihilation, than it did to his ancestors of little more than a generation
ago? No doubt they were backward, no doubt they oppressed and
exploited, poor, degraded and often wretched in the extreme, but at
least some comfort was afforded them by their religion and even the
most rebellious of them could hardly have denied, if he were honest,
that the vulgar, aspiring, treacherous and brutal little Khrushchev

hardly offers a favourable comparison in terms of human behaviour with the example set by Christ. It was probably one of the communists most serious psychological mistakes to attempt the overthrow of a religion as deeply established as that of the Orthodox Church in Russia without first making sure, instead of proceeding on a hopeful assumption, that a belief in materialism could be successfully substituted for a belief in God. I should have thought it would not have taken a particularly shrewd observer to understand the significance attached to religion in pre-Revolutionary Russia and the hold that I imagine it must have had on the hearts and imagination of most of the people. The celebration of Easter in Moscow, as described by Maurice Baring, gives some indication of this:

'The most solemn service of the year took place at midnight on Saturday in Easter week. From eight until ten o'clock the town, which during the day had been crowded with people buying provisions and presents and Easter eggs, seemed to be asleep and dead. At about ten people began to stream towards the Kremlin. At eleven o'clock there was already a dense crowd, many of the people holding lighted tapers, waiting outside in the square, between the Cathedral of the Assumption and that of Ivan Veliki. A little before twelve the cathedrals and palaces on the Kremlin were all lighted up with ribbons of various coloured lights. Twelve o'clock struck, and then the bell of Ivan Veliki began to boom: a beautiful, full-voiced, immense volume of sound—a sound which Clara Schumann said was the most beautiful she had ever heard. It was answered by other bells, and a little later all the bells of all the churches in Moscow were ringing together. Then from the Cathedral came the procession: first, the singers in crimson and gold; the bearers of the gilt banners; the Metropolitan, also in stiff vestments of crimson and gold; and after him the officials in their uniforms. They walked round the Cathedral to look for the Body of Our Lord, and returned to the Cathedral to tell the news that He was risen. The guns went off, rockets were fired, and illuminations were seen across the river, lighting up the distant cupola of the great Church of the Saviour with a cloud of fire.

'The crowd began to disperse and to pour into the various churches. I went to the Manège—an enormous riding school, in which the Ekaterinoslav Regiment had its church. Half the building looked like a fair. Long tables, twinkling with hundreds of wax tapers, were loaded with the three articles of food which were eaten at Easter—a huge cake called *kulich;* a kind of sweet cream made of curds and eggs, cream and sugar, called *Paskha* (Easter); and Easter eggs, dipped and dyed in many colours. They were waiting to be blessed. The church itself was a tiny little recess on one side of the building. There the priests were officiating, and down below in the centre of the building the whole regiment was drawn up. There were two services—a service which began at midnight and lasted about half an hour; and Mass, which followed immediately after it, lasting till about three in the morning. At the end of the first service, when the words "Christ is risen", were sung, the priest kissed the deacon three times, and then the members of the congregation kissed each other, one person saying, "Christ is risen", and the other answering, "He is risen, indeed". The colonel kissed the sergeant; the sergeant kissed all the men one after another. While this ceremony was proceeding, I left and went to the Church of the Saviour, where the first service was not yet over. Here the crowd was so dense that it was almost impossible to get into the church, although it was immense. The singing in this church was ineffable. I waited until the end of the first service, and then I was borne by the crowd to one of the narrow entrances and hurled through the doorway outside. The crowd was not rough; they were not jostling one another, but with cheerful carelessness people dived into it as you dive into a scrimmage at football, and propelled the unresisting herd towards the entrance, the result being, of course, that a mass of people got wedged into the doorway, and the process of getting out took longer than it need have done; and had there been a panic, nothing could have prevented people being crushed to death. After this I went to a friend's house to break the fast and eat *kulich*, *Paskha*, and Easter eggs, and finally returned home when the dawn was faintly shining on the dark waters of the Moscow River, whence the ice had only lately disappeared.' [16]

Without necessarily implying approval of episcopal splendour or endorsing the need for it—though I see no reason why the Pope should not eventually come as close to Jesus as the humblest Quaker— I should be sorry, on purely aesthetic grounds, to see all of it done away with. Whether in the church of Greek Orthodoxy or in the temple of some oriental faith, the ceremonial element deserves a place simply by virtue of its intrinsic beauty, however shabby, makeshift or incongruous it may be seen to be on closer inspection. Could anything be more disillusioning, for instance, than the haphazard, disorganized and noisy ceremony at the shrine in the palace at Mau where Professor Narayan Godbole found himself in the presence of God?

'God is not born yet—that will occur at midnight—but He has also been born centuries ago, nor can He ever be born, because He is the

Lord of the Universe, who transcends human processes. He is, was not, is not, was. He and Professor Godbole stood at opposite ends of the same strip of carpet.

> "*Tukaram, Tukaram,*
> *Thou art my father and mother and everybody.*
> *Tukaram, Tukaram,*
> *Thou art my father and mother and everybody* . . ."

'This corridor in the palace at Mau opened through other corridors into a courtyard. It was of beautiful hard white stucco, but its pillars and vaultings could scarcely be seen behind coloured rags, iridescent balls, chandeliers of opaque pink glass, and murky photographs framed crookedly. At the end was the small but famous shrine of the dynastic cult, and the God to be born was largely a silver image the size of a teaspoon. Hindus sat on either side of the carpet where they could find room, or overflowed into the adjoining corridors and the court-yard—Hindus, Hindus only, mild-featured men, mostly villagers, for whom anything outside their villages passed in a dream. They were the toiling ryot, whom some call the real India. Mixed with them sat a few tradesmen out of the little town, officials, courtiers, scions of the ruling house. Schoolboys kept inefficient order. The assembly was in a tender, happy state unknown to an English crowd, it seethed like a beneficient potion. When the villagers broke cordon for a glimpse of the silver image, a most beautiful and radiant expression came into their faces, a beauty in which there was nothing personal, for it caused them all to resemble one another during the moment of its indwelling, and only when it was withdrawn did they revert to individual clods. And so with the music. Music there was, but from so many sources that the sum-total was untrammelled. The braying, banging, crooning, melted into a single mass which trailed round the palace before joining the thunder. Rain fell at intervals throughout the night.

'It was the turn of Professor Godbole's choir. As Minister of Educa-tion, he gained this special honour. When the previous group of singers dispersed into the crowd, he pressed forward from the back, already in full voice, that the chain of sacred sounds might be uninterrupted. He was barefoot and in white, he wore a pale blue turban; his gold pince-nez had caught in a jasmine garland, and lay sideways down his nose. He and the six colleagues who supported him clashed their cymbals, hit small drums, droned upon a portable harmonium, and sang:

> *"Tukaram, Tukaram,*
> *Thou art my father and mother and everybody*
> *Tukaram, Tukaram,*
> *Thou art my father and mother and everybody*
> *Tukaram, Tukaram . . ."*

They sang not even to the God who confronted them, but to a saint; they did not one thing which the non-Hindu would feel dramatically correct; this approaching triumph of India was a muddle (as we call it), a frustration of reason and form. Where was the God Himself, in whose honour the congregation had gathered? Indistinguishable in the jumble of His own altar, huddled out of sight amid images of inferior descent, smothered under rose-leaves, overhung by oleographs, out-blazed by golden tablets representing the Rajah's ancestors, and entirely obscured, when the wind blew, by the tattered foliage of a banana. Hundreds of electric lights had been lit in His honour (worked by an engine whose thumps destroyed the rhythm of the hymn). Yet His face could not be seen. Hundreds of His silver dishes were piled around Him with the minimum of effect. The inscription which the poets of the State had composed were hung where they could not be read, or had twitched their drawing-pins out of the stucco, and one of them (composed in English to indicate His universality) consisted, by an unfortunate slip of the draughtsman, of the words,

> *'"God si Love."*
> *'"God si Love"*. . .
> *'"Tukaram, Tukaram . . ."*

continued the choir, reinforced by a squabble behind the purdah curtain, where two mothers tried to push their children at the same moment to the front. A little girl's leg shot out like an eel. In the courtyard, drenched by the rain, the small Europeanized band stumbled off into a waltz. *Nights of Gladness* they were playing. The singers were not perturbed by this rival, they lived beyond competition. It was long before the tiny fragment of Professor Godbole that attended to outside things decided that his pince-nez was in trouble, and that until it was adjusted he could not choose a new hymn. He laid down one cymbal, with the other he clashed the air, and with his free hand he fumbled at the flowers round his neck. A colleague assisted him. Singing into one another's grey moustaches, they disentangled the chain from the tinsel into which it had sunk. Godbole consulted the music-book, said word to the drummer, who broke rhythm, made a thick little blur of sound, and produced a new rhythm. This was more exciting, the inner images it evoked more definite, and the singers' expressions became fatuous and languid. They loved all men, the whole universe, and scraps of their past, tiny splinters of detail, emerged for a moment to melt into the universal warmth. Thus Godbole, though she was not important to him, remembered an old woman he had met in Chandrapore days. Chance brought her into his mind while it was in this heated state, he did not select her, she happened to occur among the throng of soliciting images, a tiny splinter, and he impelled her by his spiritual force to that place where completeness can be found. Completeness, not reconstruction. His senses grew thinner, he remembered a wasp seen he forgot where, perhaps on a stone. He loved the wasp equally, he impelled it likewise, he was imitating God. And the stone where the wasp clung—could he . . . no, he could not, he had been wrong to attempt the stone, logic and conscious effort had seduced, he came back to the strip of red carpet and discovered that he was dancing upon it. Up and down, a third of the way to the altar and back again, clashing his cymbals, his little legs twinkling, his companions dancing with him and each other. Noise, noise, the Europeanized band louder, incense on the altar, sweat, the blaze of lights, wind in the bananas, noise, thunder, eleven-fifty by his wristwatch, seen as he threw up his hands and detached the tiny reverberation that was his soul. Louder shouts in the crowd. He danced on. The boys and men who were squatting in the aisles were lifted forcibly and dropped without changing their shapes into the laps of their neighbours. Down the path thus cleared advanced a litter.

'It was the aged ruler of the state, brought against the advice of his physicians to witness the Birth ceremony.

'No one greeted the Rajah, nor did he wish it; this was no moment for human glory. Nor could the litter be set down, lest it defiled the temple by becoming a throne. He was lifted out of it while its feet remained in the air, and deposited on the carpet close to the altar, his immense beard was straightened, his legs tucked under him, a paper containing red powder was placed in his hand. There he sat, leaning against a pillar, exhausted with illness, his eyes magnified by many unshed tears.

'He had not to wait long. In a land where all else was unpunctual, the hour of the Birth was chronometrically observed. Three minutes before it was due, a Brahman brought forth a model of the village of Gokul (the Bethlehem in that nebulous story) and placed it in front of the altar. The model was on a wooden tray about a yard square; it was of clay, and was gaily blue and white with streamers and paint. Here, upon a chair too small for him and with a head too large, sat King Kansa, who is Herod, directing the murder of some Innocents, and in a corner, similarly proportioned, stood the father and mother of the Lord, warned to depart in a dream. The model was not holy, but more than a decoration, for it diverted men from the actual image of the God, and increased their sacred bewilderment. Some of the villagers thought the Birth had occurred, saying with truth that the Lord must have been born, or they could not see Him. But the clock struck midnight, and simultaneously the rending note of the conch broke forth, followed by the trumpeting of elephants; all who had packets of powder threw them at the altar, and in the rosy dust and incense, and clanging and shouts, Infinite Love took upon itself the form of SHRI KRISHNA, and saved the world. All sorrow was annihilated, not only for Indians, but for foreigners, birds, caves, railways, and the stars; all became joy, all laughter; there had never been disease nor doubt, misunderstanding, cruelty, fear. Some jumped in the air, others flung themselves prone and embraced the bare feet of the universal lover; the women behind the purdah slapped and shrieked; the little girl slipped and danced by herself, her black pigtails flying. Not an orgy of the body; the tradition of that shrine forbade it. But the human spirit had tried by a desperate contortion to ravish the unknown, flinging down science and history in the struggle, yes, beauty herself. Did it succeed? Books written afterwards say "Yes". But how, if there is such an event, can it be remembered afterwards? How can it be expressed in anything but itself? Not only from the unbeliever are mysteries hid, but the adept himself cannot retain them. He may think, if he chooses, that he has been with God, but as soon as he thinks it, it becomes history, and falls under the rules of time.

'A cobra of papier-maché now appeared on the carpet, also a wooden cradle swinging from a frame. Professor Godbole approached the latter with a red silk napkin in his arms. The napkin was God, not that it was, and the image remained in the blur of the altar. It was just a napkin, folded into a shape which indicated a baby's. The Professor dandled it and gave it to the Rajah, who, making a great effort, said, "I name this child Shri Krishna," and tumbled it into the cradle. Tears poured from his eyes, because he had seen the Lord's salvation. He was too weak to exhibit the silk baby to his people, his privilege in former years. His attendants lifted him up, a new path was cleared through the crowd, and he was carried away to a less sacred part of the palace . . .

'Down in the sacred corridors, joy had seethed to jollity. It was their duty to play various games to amuse the newly-born God, and to simulate his sports with the wanton dairy-maids of Brindaban. Butter played a prominent part in these. When the cradle had been removed, the principle nobles of the state gathered together for an innocent frolic. They removed their turbans, and one put a lump of butter on his forehead, and waited for it to slide down his nose into his mouth. Before it could arrive, another stole up behind him, snatched the melting morsel, and swallowed it himself. All laughed exultantly at discovering that the divine sense of humour coincided with their own. "God is Love!" There is fun in heaven ... All spirit as well as all matter must participate in salvation, and if practical jokes are banned, the circle is incomplete. Having swallowed the butter, they played another game which chanced to be graceful: the fondling of Shri Krishna under the similitude of a child. A pretty red and gold ball is thrown, and he who catches it chooses a child from the crowd, raises it in his arms, and carries it round to be caressed. All stroke the darling creature for the Creator's sake, and murmur happy words. The child is restored to his parents, the ball thrown on, and another child becomes for a moment the World's Desire. And the Lord bounds hither and thither through the aisles, chance and the sport of chance, irradiating little mortals with His immortality ... When they had played this long enough—and being exempt from boredom, they played it again and again—they took many sticks and hit them together, whack smack, as though they fought the Pandava wars, and threshed and churned with them, and later on they hung from the roof of the temple, in a net, a great black earthenware jar, which was painted here and there with red, and wreathed with dried figs. Now came a rousing sport. Springing up, they struck at the jar with their sticks. It cracked, broke, and a mass of greasy rice and milk poured on to their faces. They ate and smeared one another's mouths, and dived between each other's legs for what had been pashed upon the carpet. This way and that spread the divine mess, until the line of schoolboys, who had somewhat fended off the crowd, broke for their share. The corridors, the court-yard, were filled with benign confusion. Also the flies awoke and claimed their share of God's bounty. There was no quarrelling, owing to the nature of the gift, for blessed is the man who confers it on another, he imitates God. And those "imitations", those "substitutes", continued to flicker through the assembly for many hours, awaking in each man, according to his capacity, an emotion that he would not have had otherwise. No definite image survived; at the Birth it was questionable whether a silver doll or a mud village, or a silk napkin, or an intangible spirit, or a pious resolution, had been born. Perhaps all these things! Perhaps none! Perhaps all birth is an allegory! Still, it was the main event of the religious year.' [17]

Except that no mess is made and the climax of the ceremony is less abandoned, the celebration of mass in St Peter's still offers sights and sounds that must be as gorgeous, as incomprehensible, and as diverting to the senses of a sceptic like myself as any that the Hindu religion can provide. I say 'still' because change, in the sense of emancipation of thought and scientific progress, must always be repugnant to those who adhere closely to a dogmatic faith, for religious dogma invariably breaks down if you apply the test of common sense to it or make a practical analysis of its claims. Things in the Catholic church, for instance, are not so very different to what they were in 1830 when Charles Greville visited Rome. What one chiefly notices in his description of the ceremonies he attended is not so much that the ritual has changed, however slightly, as the behaviour of the worshippers:

'Yesterday morning to the Sistine again; prodigious crowd, music moderate. As soon as it was over we set off to see the benediction; and after fighting, jostling, and squeezing through an enormous crowd, we reached the loggia over one side of the colonnade. The piazza of St Peter's is so magnificent that the sight was of necessity fine, but not near so much as I had fancied. The people below were not numerous or full of reverence. Till the Pope appears the bands play and the bells ring, when suddenly there is a profound silence; the feathers are seen waving in the balcony, and he is borne in on his throne; he rises, stretches out his hands, blesses the people—URBI ET ORBI—and is borne out again. A couple of indulgences were tossed out, for which there is a scramble, and so it ends.

'Off we scampered, and by dint of tremendous exertions, reached the hall in which the feet of the pilgrims are washed. The Pope could not attend, so the Cardinal Deacon officiated. No ceremony can be less imposing, but none more clean. Thirteen men are ranged on a bench —the thirteenth represents the angel who once jointed the party— dressed in new white caps, gowns, and shoes; each holds out his foot in succession; an attendant pours a few drops of water on it from a golden jug which another receives in a golden basin; the cardinal wipes it with a towel, kisses the foot, and then gives the towel, a nosegay, and a piece of money to the pilgrim—the whole thing takes up about five minutes—certain prayers are said, and it is over.

'Then off we scampered again through the long galleries of the

Vatican to another hall where the pilgrims dine. The arrangements for the accommodation of the Ambassadors and strangers were so bad that all these passages were successive scenes of uproar, scrambling, screaming, confusion, and danger, and, considering that the ceremonies were all religious, really disgraceful. We got with infinite difficulty to another box, raised aloft in the hall, and saw a long table at which the thirteen pilgrims seated themselves; a cardinal in the corner read some prayers, which nobody listened to, and another handed the dishes to the pilgrims, who looked neither to the right nor the left, but applied themselves with becoming gravity to the enjoyment of a very substantial dinner. The whole hall was filled with people, all with their hats on, chattering and jostling, and more like a ring of blacklegs and blackguards at Tattersall's than respectable company at a religious ceremony in the palace of the Pope. There remained the cardinals' dinner, but I had had more than enough, and came away hot, jaded, and disgusted with the whole affair.

'In the evening I went to St Peter's ... the church was crowded; there was a Miserere in the chapel, which was divine, far more beautiful than anything I have heard in the Sistine, and it was the more effective because at the close it really was night. The lamps were extinguished at the shrine of the Apostle, but one altar—the altar of the Holy Sepulchre—was brilliantly illuminated. Presently the Grand Penetentiary, Cardinal Gregorio, with his train entered, went and paid his devotions at this shrine, and then seated himself on the chair of the Great Confessional, took a golden wand, and touched all those who knelt before him. Then came a procession of pilgrims bearing muffled crosses; penitents with faces covered, in white, with tapers and crosses; and one long procession of men headed by these muffled figures, and another of women accompanied by ladies, a lady walking between every two pilgrims ... They attended them to the church (the Trinità della Pellegrine) and washed their feet and fed them. A real washing of dirty feet. Both the men and the women seemed of the lowest class but their appearances and dresses were very picturesque. These processions entered St Peter's, walked all round the church, knelt at the altars, and retired in the same order, filing along the piazza till they were lost behind the arches of the colonnades. As the shades of night fell upon the vast expanse of this wonderful building it became really sublime; "the dim religious light" glimmering from a distant altar, or cast by the passing torches of the procession, the voices of the choir as they sang the Miserere swelling from the chapel, which was veiled in dusk, and with no light but that of the high taper half hid behind the altar,

with the crowds of figures assembled round the chapel moving about
in the obscurity of the aisles and columns, produced the most striking
effect I ever beheld.' [18]

But what, after all, do such ceremonies signify, whether performed
in the East or in the West? Religion, if it counts for anything, surely
counts as an attitude of mind, not merely as a way of thinking and
acting on predetermined occasions. 'It is well said, in every sense, that
a man's religion is the chief fact with regard to him A man's, or a
nation of men's. By religion I do not mean here the church-creed which
he professes, the articles of faith which he will sign, and, in words or
otherwise, assert . . . This is not what I call religion . . . But the thing a
man does practically believe (and this is often enough *without* asserting
it even to himself, much less to others); the thing a man does practically
lay to heart, and know for certain, concerning his vital relations to this
mysterious Universe, and his duty and destiny there . . . That is his
religion; or, it may be, his mere scepticism and *no-religion:* the manner
it is in which he feels himself to be spiritually related to the Unseen
World or No-World. . . . Of a man or of a nation we inquire, therefore, first of all, what religion they had? Was it Heathenism,—plurality
of gods, mere sensuous representation of this Mystery of Life, and for
chief element therein Physical Force? Was it Christianism; faith in an
Invisible, not as real only, but as the only reality? . . . Was it Scepticism,
uncertainty and inquiry whether there was an Unseen World, any
Mystery of Life except a mad one;—doubt as to all this, or perhaps
unbelief and flat denial? Answering of this question is giving us the
soul of the history of the man or nation.' [19]

SOURCES

1   *The Notebooks of Samuel Butler.*
2   William Cowper, *Light Shining out of Darkness.*
3   Anonymous, *The Times,* April 10, 1943.
4   G. Lowes Dickinson, *A Modern Symposium.*
5   Sir Edmund Gosse, *Father and Son.*
6   Samuel Taylor Coleridge, *Table-Talk.*
7   *The Confessions of Jean-Jacques Rousseau.*
8   Lytton Strachey, *Eminent Victorians.*
9   Ben Hecht, *A Child of the Century.*
10 The Very Rev. Dean Inge, *A Rustic Moralist.*
11 *The Book of Common Prayer.*

12   Ibid.
13   See 1.
14   Maurice Baring, *The Puppet Show of Memory.*
15   Edward Crankshaw, *The Observer,* January 1, 1957.
16   See 14.
17   E. M. Forster, *A Passage to India.*
18   Charles C. F. Greville, *The Greville Memoirs,* vol. i.
19   Thomas Carlyle, *On Heroes.*

Art and Architecture

*

In art as well as in life it must be given us sometimes to judge as lovers, and not with the chill impartiality of mere intimate acquaintance.

THE EARL OF BALFOUR, *Essays and Addresses*

WHEN I was a small boy I had three ambitions: one was to be a clown in a circus, another was to be a fireman, and the third was to be an artist. I do not think I ever seriously imagined that some day I might achieve one of these ambitions, or if I did that it would turn out to be all that I had expected. So I count myself lucky not only to have realized all three, but to have found that on the whole they were just as interesting and as exciting as they had seemed when I viewed them deceptively enriched through the prism of childhood's vision.

When it came to being an artist I knew without any doubt what sort I wanted to be. I never had the least ambition—until it was too late to fulfil it—to be a painter. From the first I wanted to be an illustrator. My father's study, and my grandfather's too, were full of picture books and bound copies of illustrated magazines and I suppose it was from looking at these that I first got the idea of wanting to draw. I spent a great deal of time poring over these volumes and in doing so I no doubt absorbed unconsciously much that was to be useful to me later on.

I soon grew to know the work of the *Punch* artists of the period and could distinguish their styles even before I could understand the significance, such as it was, of their jokes. My father often had copies of *Le Rire* and of *Simplicissimus* sent to him by friends abroad and also of *Les Lundis de Caran d'Ache*. These last gave me even greater pleasure.

Caran d'Ache is an artist to whom my own debt is immeasurable. His dexterity, his vigour, his simplicity and the intensity of his observation are to my mind unsurpassed by any other comic artist, nor did his hasty and prodigious output seem to affect the standard of his draughtsmanship or the authority of his line. The traditions of English comic illustration, however, are founded upon works that are very different in style and feeling from his. They are founded on the talents of artists such as Rowlandson, Cruikshank, Doyle and Leech, by all of whom, either directly or indirectly, my own work has also been influenced; but it is to Caran d'Ache's satiric approach as well as to the discipline and economy of his methods that I feel I owe most.

My appetite for illustration was as insatiable in those days, and as indiscriminate, as it was for books; and artists as different as Flaxman,

Doré, Beardsley, Rackham, Steinlen, Fuseli, the Beggarstaffs, Bewick
and Tenniel appealed equally to my imagination.

My father's taste in art was catholic without being very enterprising,
and I think that it probably influenced my own. His taste was also
quite untutored (although for an amateur he was no mean draughtsman) and he had an instinctive appreciation of what it was that gave
the work of certain artists its distinction and what made that of others
seem meritricious or vulgar.

Considering how intense is the pleasure that I have always got
from looking at pictures, it may seem surprising that I seldom get
much enjoyment from reading about art. With the exception of
Ruskin and Sir Kenneth Clark, who can write of abstractions with a
lucidity that makes most other critics seem turgid and verbose, as a
good many of them are, there are few authorities of whom I can
truthfully say that they have taught me more, except in the historical
sense, than I have learnt from using my own eyes. For some people
the enjoyment of looking at pictures is genuinely enhanced by a
knowledge of aesthetics, but for myself I cannot imagine that anything
I might read about Giorgione or El Greco or Degas would add to the
pure contemplative pleasure that I get from looking at their paintings.

I am not suggesting—and it would be stupid as well as impertinent
to do so—that criticism has not an important and occasionally even a
noble function to perform in awakening and keeping alert our appreciative instincts and in helping us to acquire standards of taste and
judgement which, without some such assistance, most of us might
never achieve, and so would as readily remain content with the bad
and the indifferent as with the good. But I do not need to be told what
to look for in a picture in order to appreciate the beauties of this or
that work of art—supposing it to be concerned with beauty, but that
is another matter. Criticism of this kind, however well intentioned,
destroys for me the excitement of discovery and blunts the power of
observation, which are among the most rewarding pleasures of looking
at paintings.

When the National Gallery reopened some of the rooms that had
been damaged during the war, I found in one of them a portrait by
Gainsborough of his daughter Mary. I did not remember having seen
it before and to my inexpert eye it looked as though it had been over-
cleaned and therefore had probably lost something of its original
character. Yet here, caught for all time, was the very essence of Mary
Gainsborough's being, so that her disposition, her understanding and
her appearance are apprehended as clearly as the tones of her father's

voice were once heard in the rooms of that double-fronted pink brick
house off the market square at Sudbury, where he lived in the days
before fame had overtaken him.

Not one word of all that has been written about Gainsborough, who
has come in for a pretty large share of critical as well as uncritical
admiration, could have added to the fullness or the immediacy of the
impression I had as I stood and gazed at this picture of his Mary.
Oblivion descended on me; it was as though I knew with intimate
certainty the sensations that must have been aroused by her voice and
by her glance, by the scent of her, by hearing her footsteps and the
rustle of her dress, by the fleeting touch of her hand against mine on
the banisters . . . That magic was Gainsborough's and his alone. To
attempt analysis or explanation of such a painting would be not merely
superfluous, it would be an insult to Gainsborough's transcendent gifts.

To experience such sensations when looking at paintings is not
unique. The deep-felt piety of Giotto, the pastoral melancholy of
Claude, the domesticity of Terborch, the neo-classical dreamscapes of
Ernst and Dali, all of them must surely find an echoing chord in
the imagination of this or that beholder, as on an easier level of understanding the Pre-Raphaelites have powers to transport the adolescent
dreamer to regions rich, romantic, glowing and meticulous in authentic
detail. 'It seems to me that the object and intention of all the Arts
is . . . to gratify the mind by realising and embodying what never
existed but in the imagination . . . facts, and events, however they may
bind the historian, have no dominion over the poet or the painter . . .
And why? Because those arts, in their highest province, are not
addressed to the gross senses; but to the desires of the mind, to that
spark of divinity which we have within, impatient of being circumscribed and pent up by the world which is about us. Just so much as
our art has of this, just so much of dignity, I had almost said of divinity,
it exhibits; and those of our artists who possessed this mark of distinction
in the highest degree, acquired from thence the glorious appellation
of Divine.' [1]

In his *apologia pro vita sua* Shaw's Dubedat says: 'I believe in Michael
Angelo, Velasquez and Rembrandt; in the might of design, the
mystery of colour, the redemption of all things by Beauty everlasting,
and the message of Art . . .' [2] It was easier then perhaps than it is now
to adopt such a creed and live up to it, but 'a world lacerated by wars
. . . is hardly calculated to produce idyllic painting. It is the fault
not of the artists but of their environment that they can no longer offer
us the delicious visions of a Giorgione, a Watteau or a Renoir.' [3]

When I hear or read thundering denunciations of 'modern art' by self-confident Philistines (in any case, 'there is no such thing as modern art. There is no such thing as ancient art. The antithisis is as senseless as would be division of history into centuries. History is one unbroken stream. If we knew Degas, Degas knew Ingres, and so on, *ad infinitum*' [4])—whenever I chance to hear the Philistines' mock-modest bleatings, mock-modesty being a favourite weapon in their armoury: it is supposed to be the deadliest form of cynicism—or when I come across their intolerant pronouncements I wonder why the simple truth is not apparent to them that the environment of the age in which they live is not merely unsuitable but is actually hostile to the production of idyllic painting. I suppose it is because truth and simplicity are things that a really hard-boiled Philistine cannot bear to face. Without the protection of a battery of half-baked rules of thought the world of the imagination grows too alarming. He becomes trapped in a jungle of ideas and forms and abstractions that he does not understand and, because they demand an effort of imagination, does not want to understand. The more modest philistine—and how few of them there are—is content to admit his ignorance and subside into the undergrowth, happy to escape to his TV, his pools and his Sunday newsrag. Whereas the more aggressive type implies that what he does not understand must be *ipso facto* rubbish. To please this type of Yahoo painting, and literature too, of course, should be life-like, though preferably not too like life.

Writing should be jolly and above all straightforward, so that one does not have to think too much about what one is reading. There are exceptions, of course. Dickens, being a moralist as well as a humorist, can get away with a certain amount of dirt and gloom; but Dostoievsky, who is neither—a moralist who is not also an optimist doesn't count—is not to be taken seriously and can be regarded as a legitimate butt for facetiousness, even though one may not have read anything that he has written. In painting, realism must be the keynote, though a certain amount of distortion is permitted to the antique. Thus Breughel, in his less fanciful and more jocular mood, is acceptable, and though his occasional lapses into indecency are to be regretted, such as someone showing his bare bottom, Breughel has been dead long enough for such indiscretions scarcely to count. Really, of course, we prefer Annigoni. It is always a comfort when 'we can turn art back upon itself so that it reflects life no longer, and we can judge it for the fidelity with which it repeats its own past achievements. It now *looks* like art. What a relief!' [5]

If that sounds cynical, I do not think it is entirely so. The philistine is to be blamed for a good many faults; indifference, obstinacy and conceit are often among them, but an instinctive preference for what is familiar is common to most of us. It is when the weight of that preference is allowed to become so heavy that it inhibits the use of one's eyes and one's imagination that the rot sets in. That the philistine's vision should approximate more closely to that of Van Eyck than to that of, say, Manet is understandable, because most people judge an artist by the degree of his success in representing external realities. 'Van Eyck, when he painted a brocade mantle, subordinated himself, with an objective interest in things, to an existing object: and he created something that produces the same impression as a real brocade mantle, whereas a Manet contents himself with the appearance . . . Van Eyck's work is productive of illusion if we stand at a distance of one foot, three feet or two yards, whereas the work of Manet is tied in its effect to a definite point of vision—the very one from which the painter has given his rendering of the subject.' [6] A simple, not to say obvious, truth, which incidentally might well serve as a ready-to-wear definition of impressionism.

Hostility towards movements in art, like hostility towards other manifestations of the human spirit, is usually based on some sort of misconception. In the case of art it is that it has a duty to fulfil, irrespective of any functional purpose, that duty being to offer a direct representation of the physical world. This is a neat and convenient theory for those in whom imagination has failed to tick, if it ever started to do so, though most of us are born with some degree of imagination. But this theory leaves out of account one important consideration: art is not concerned merely with what we see but 'with our whole being—our knowledge, our memories, our associations. To confine painting to purely visual sensations is to touch only the surface of our spirits.' [7]

I suppose that in its time, and for a long while after its beginnings, no movement in the history of painting aroused more controversy than impressionism. Man is by nature a conservative animal—at least I have yet to come across one of the species who was born a radical— and no move towards emancipating the mind can ever be made without arousing furious opposition from those who are content to dwell all their lives in the intellectual climate into which they were born; so the hostility with which impressionism had to contend for so long is perhaps less surprising than its triumph, particularly when we consider how unpropitious was the soil from which the movement sprang. For 'the magic of impressionist painting has spread the illusion in England that the late nineteenth and early twentieth centuries in France were a golden age. They were, in fact, a period of defeat and humiliation and of the blackest and most cynical materialism.' [8] Perhaps it was this fact that caused Ruskin, as percipient as he was sometimes erratic in his criticism, and biased as much by morality as by aesthetics, completely to ignore the impressionist movement in his *Modern Painters*. When the last volume was published, in 1860, Corot (not an impressionist in the accepted sense of the term but deeply influential on the movement) was sixty-four, Boudin thirty-six, Pissarro thirty, Manet twenty-eight, and Degas an already precocious twenty-six. Yet not one of these painters is mentioned; nor for that matter are Delacroix, Daumier or Courbet (at forty-one the youngest of these three in 1860) whose influence upon the impressionists can hardly have been unrecognized by Ruskin. Knowing his opinion of Whistler, it is not difficult to imagine what he probably thought of them. But it is hard to understand how anyone deeply appreciative of painting can fail to recognize the genius of a painter such as Renoir, who although he was too young in 1860 to have merited Ruskin's attention was past middle-age when Ruskin died, without, so far as I know, having made the slightest acknowledgement of his genius. Yet I feel sure that few people nowadays with even the slightest appreciation of painting would deny that 'Renoir at his best . . . has all the qualities that constitute a great painter, pressed down and running over . . . It is not surprising that the great landscapes, the great still lifes, the great flower paintings . . . have been done by the great figure-painters. "The proper study of mankind is man", and it is the anthropomorphic spirit that informs the landscapes, still lifes and flower paintings of the great figure painters, that lifts these things to an altogether higher plane than the performances of specialists. It was Renoir's education in the severe experience of a painter on china, where no correction is possible, that placed him above the vulgar temptation of seeing alone in oil-paint what Cennino Cennini called "its great convenience"; a convenience in which decadent votaries have seen but an unlimited permit to bungle. Forms the most precise and delicate, complications of bulk, perspective and light and shade, were solved by this miraculous brush as if in play.' [9]

Renoir happens to be a favourite of mine among the impressionists and perhaps this blinds me to the merits of some of the others, Cézanne for instance, whose importance is probably greater but whom I appreciate less, partly because of my laziness in observation, partly because I seem to have had more opportunities of seeing Renoirs than Cézannes.

Appreciation, I am convinced, is two thirds curiosity, the *desire* to know, and one third observation. You need not be an expert, for instance, to discover for yourself that 'in Italian painting the space between the eyes marks the period of the picture. Between Cimabue and the Renaissance, from master to master, the eyes are set successively farther away from the nose, leaving off their Byzantine characteristic and moving towards the temples, until finally, in Correggio and Andrea del Sarto, they are back where they were placed by the art and beauty of antiquity.' [10]

In the same way, there is no substitute for observation in considering the significance of colours. 'We speak of warm and cold colours, as in music of the minor and major key. Where colours are concerned it is a question not of absolute differentiation but of something more or less. Red stands at one end of the scale, blue at the other. Among the red colours there are some which are warmer and others which are colder. The red of strawberries, scarlet and crimson, are warmer than red lake and vermilion. Ice is white and blue, fire glows red. The sense of feel has given the sense of sight the terms. We say "cold" of the appearance of the sky, of infinity, of distance, of everything bald and torpid; warmth is suggested by that which is near, which grows organically, which is filled with sap, which is alive.

'Colours, according as to whether they belong to the cold or warm category, act as symbols, and indeed direct upon emotion, nor according to convention. The cool colours express remoteness, distance, transfiguration—also reserved dignity; the warm colours express nearness, intimacy, earthly narrowness. That which is seen in the distance contains cooler colours than that which is seen in the vicinity. The impressionists, who carried out their observations in the open air, favour the cool colours. In the choice of this or that key, race and individuality reveal themselves." [11]

Perhaps it is stretching a point to say that the Pre-Raphaelites could not have occurred in any other country except England, but what seems certain is that the almost vulgar exuberance of their palettes would have been considerably toned down if, for instance, the members of the Brotherhood had all been Frenchmen. Considering the impact that their first appearance made on public taste it may seem odd that the influence of the Pre-Raphaelites on English painting turned out to be as brief and superficial as it was. I think the reason probably lies in the fact that 'all forms of expression have within them the seeds of their own destruction, and just as classicism tends to emptiness and lack of vitality, so materialism tends to vulgarity'.[12] In spite of their desire and determination to achieve the ethereal, nothing in the work of the Pre-Raphaelites is more evident than their materialistic outlook, as is shown by their fervid preoccupation with detail and their fondness for the interpretation of sentimental ideas and emotions. Carried to its laborious extremes by artists such as Frith and Martineau, Pre-Raphaelite painting evaporated through sheer sterility.

To find an example of a similar form of hara-kiri in our own time, we have only to look at the surrealists. 'The subconscious, the unconscious, the dream-world does offer a rich almost limitless panorama for the explorations of art; but . . . the limitation which circumscribed surrealist art arose from its effort to reveal the subconscious. For in that effort control and intention were increasingly relinquished . . . The subconscious may greatly shape one's art; undoubtedly it does so. But the subconscious cannot create art. The very act of making a painting is an intending one; thus to intend and at the same time to relinquish intention is a hopeless contradiction.' [13]

This does not mean that all forms of experimental art must eventually lead into the same sort of sheepfold as the one in which the surrealists have penned themselves. 'Painters are now, as indeed they always were, bent upon projecting their imaginative vision'; but one of the difficulties, from the public's point of view, of appreciating the results is that this vision has become much more subjective, much more remote from the vision of other people. Or shall we say that they leave the representation of pleasing objects to the camera, and concentrate upon expression through design, colour and handling? These formal elements in painting can be made gay or tragic or serene, no less than the analogous elements in a symphony. Neglecting description, painting has become less and less like literature, more and more like music.

'Disturbing as this is to our habits, the painter cannot be blamed. It is a characteristic of our civilization that not only all the arts but all the sciences have become vastly more unapproachable by those without expert training. Every educated Victorian could understand the arguments of Darwin. How few of us can begin to understand Einstein, or even Darwin's successors in biology?' [14]

Even if art has become more unapproachable, this does not alter what seems to me its fundamental purpose, but merely indicates a change—admittedly in some cases a radical one—in methods of achieving that purpose, which is 'to help us to understand the object presented as if from within, so that we may enter into real sympathy with it . . . share its actual mode of being and understand it; whereas science deals with it from without and considers its relation to its setting in its context and analyses it into its own component parts . . . It is that kind of intimate appreciation which art is always concerned to create, and it does this by concentrating our attention upon the object in such a way that it will not wander. That is why pictures are put into frames. It helps you to avoid looking at anything except the picture.[15]

'A good picture is usually the result of a love-affair. The artist's eye is captured by something—a mountain or an old man or a bunch of flowers; and his imagination crystallises upon it, often burning it into something very different from what it would appear to other people. In much the same way, when we fall in love, it is not so much with a person as with our ideas of that person. We endow the beloved with all sorts of excellences, to the bewilderment of our friends. The painter, for his part, tells us what he has seen in the mountain or the old man or the vase: Cézanne paints his Montagne Ste-Victoire, Rembrandt his Rabbi, Van Gogh his sunflowers. At first the public is bewildered: "It isn't like that. Why does he pretend to see it like that?" The artist is called incompetent or insane, because he has depicted what he sees with his imagination, instead of what we see with our eyes. Time passes; if the artist is a great artist, his vision of the world gradually imposes itself: we learn to see through his eyes; and the derided picture may appear in reproduction upon the walls of ten thousand homes. Forty years ago, Van Gogh's *Sunflowers*, for instance, excited contemptuous guffaws: now it has replaced *The Monarch of the Glen* in popular esteem. It is only good art, usually, that survives, one may notice.'[16]

II

To say that one knows nothing about art but knows what one likes has come to be regarded as fatuous, partly because it is a cliché, and clichés have a way of sounding fatuous even when they contain a grain of truth. But in this case illogical would surely be nearer the mark. Understanding certainly enhances appreciation, but—forgive the cliché—*ars longa, vita brevis*. Few people, unless they are interested professionally in the study of art, can afford the time and application that is needed to acquire even an elementary understanding of the problems involved, but that does not prevent their enjoyment of a work of art. There are a great many things I know nothing about but concerning which I know very well what I like. Architecture is one of them. Having very little knowledge by which to judge the merits or defects of a piece of architecture my taste is catholic, which means that it embraces all sorts of things which someone more knowledgeable might disapprove of, and with good reason; the Royal Opera House, for instance, Grand Central Station, Fredensborg Slot, West Wycombe parish church, Rockefeller Centre and the music school at Avignon, which not one in a thousand who goes to gape at the Palais des Papes notices, though it stands at right angles to it. To my mind, no pleasure equals in its own quiet way that of looking with an untutored eye at some piece of architecture and making one's own discovery of its beauty, though of course there are certain sorts of building to which everyone's reaction is probably more or less the same. For example, 'anyone who enters a Gothic cathedral must be aware that he is walking back into the primeval forest of existance, with birds, beasts, monsters and angels looking through the foliage. But with classical building man was giving expression to that upper part of his consciousness which would cut itself more and more from its background to live in the Ionic temple of the intellect.' [17]

'We require from buildings, as from men, two kinds of goodness: first, the doing their practical duty well; then that they be graceful and pleasing in doing it; which last is itself another form of duty.' [18]

I would add to these criteria, which are Ruskin's, a third kind of goodness that we require and a more intangible one than either of his: if the building is, or is intended to be, one of historic significance, it then requires something that supersedes mere gracefulness: it requires nobility, which in itself may not be inconsistant even with a certain lack of grace. When I first went to Venice I was surprised and, let me confess it, a fraction disappointed that St Mark's did not seem, feature for feature, as beautiful as some other churches I have seen. In the richness and conglomerate ornamentation of both the outside and the inside there is an effect that sometimes borders on vulgarity and which if it were copied today would almost certainly be condemned as being so. Yet surely no other church in the world symbolizes more eloquently the ecstasy of the Christian religion:

'There opens before us a huge cave, hewn out into the form of a Cross, and divided into shadowy isles by many pillars. Round the domes of its roof the light enters only through narrow apertures like large stars; and here and there a ray or two from some far-away casement wanders into the darkness, and casts a narrow phosphoric stream upon the waves of marble that heave and fall in a thousand colours along the floor. What else there is of light is from torches, or silver lamps, burning ceaselessly in the recesses of the chapels; the roof sheeted with gold, and the polished walls covered with alabaster, give back at every curve and angle some feeble gleaming to the flames; and the glories round the heads of the sculptured saints flash out upon us as we pass them, and sink again into the gloom. Under foot and over head, a continual succession of crowded imagery, one picture passing into another, as in a dream; forms beautiful and terrible mixed together; dragons and serpents, and ravening beasts of prey, and graceful birds that in the midst of them drink from running fountains and feed from vases of crystal; the passions and pleasures of human life symbolized together, and the mystery of its redemption; for the mazes of interwoven lines and changeful pictures lead always at last to the Cross, lifted and carved in every place and upon every stone; sometimes with the serpent of eternity wrapped round it, sometimes with doves beneath its arms, and sweet herbage growing forth from its feet, but conspicuous most of all on the great rood that crosses the church before the altar, raised in bright blazonry against the shadow of the apse.' [19]

I wonder what Ruskin, stuffed with the bread of piety and drunk with the wine of medievalism, would have had to say about the skyscrapers of New York. In their capacity to exalt the human spirit perhaps they are not as different from the stones of Venice as one might at first suppose. My guess is that after due reflection, and with certain reservations about their lack of ornament, he would have approved.

'The morning following my arrival in New York formed an effervescent contrast to the evening's mood. I had slept on a thirtieth floor, with my bed beneath a window and I opened my eyes to see the gilt-encrusted cupola of a skyscraper sparkling in a clear blue sky. Everything sparkled and flashed that morning as I wandered in the streets: the windows up and down the skyscrapers shone like crystal, the bright particles of granite in the pavements glittered. Out on Fifth Avenue the chill unerring wind of New York cut up from the harbour and made the great banners over the shop-fronts sway lazily and heavily in the sun . . . More and more I had the feeling of being in a legendary medieval city, some magnified version of one of those white-spired, turretted towns painted in fifteenth century France to illustrate the chronicles of Froissart. I attempted to analyse the elation that I felt . . . It did not seem to me compact merely of the sun and the crisp electric air of the city, nor due to the sights of pagan luxury on every hand. It was, I decided, basically the effect of the skyscrapers, of those tall aspiring walls of granite which evoke such feelings of awe and excitement as those we gain from standing in the nave of some great European cathedral: for example Chartres. Then too there was the intellectual satisfaction which New York offers. For unlike London this city is a creation of the mind. It is an intellectual or mathematical solution, not an organic growth. New York did not happen: it was made. It was made to fit on to its narrow island, and along its river banks. The relation of the buildings to the streets, or of the streets to the harbour, of the harbour to the sea give an illusion of precision quite foreign to the sprawling effect of the splendid city of London. New York gives one the supreme satisfaction usually found only in a taut and perfect prose style.' [20]

If the precision of New York really is an illusion—and I find it difficult to believe that this impression, perhaps as marked as any that a reasonably observant foreigner will carry away, is accidental—the precision of the Parthenon leaves nothing to chance.

'An Architect once pointed out to me that one of the most striking instances of the Greek fastidiousness in matters of art is to be found in the pavement of the Parthenon, which is not quite flat, but which is made on a slight curved incline, so that the effect of perfect flatness to the eye should be complete. The curve cannot be detected unless the measurements are taken, showing, as the architect said to me, that the Greeks aimed at the maximum of effect with the minimum of advertisement' [21]; an aspiration far from sympathetic nowadays to many architects, and I should say to most builders.

'The dormitory housing estates on the outskirts of cities are a limbo created by the combination of meanness with theoretical good intentions. The little gardens that man's incurable love of earth has obliged the council or the speculative builder to provide, soon make a ragged wilderness of broken fences and sheds. The streets wander aimlessly about, representing either simple chaos or the whimsy notions of a planning officer. Nothing has grown; nothing is inevitable. All over England the houses are the same; for they are built of materials that are not local but cheap. A house at Bradford, a house at Dagenham, will show the same silly stucco, the same paltry composition roof. Since 1945 there has been an improvement, and the sight of these better houses, flats, schools, is the most hopeful thing to be seen in Britain.' [22]

Yet it is still far too often true that the 'average English house combines all the curses of civilization with the vicissitudes of life in the open'. [23]

'It is strange that a people which had to its credit the architecture of the Georgian age, and which created the most beautiful villages in the world, should have built Leeds and Manchester and Sheffield. Here is the explanation. They are the creation of a new class. We are still under the shadow of its insensitiveness. A visit to Oxford will show what injury has been done in the last twenty-five years to the beauty of one of the world's most beautiful cities. For evil as well as for good the middle class stamped itself on the century which it made.' [24]

As Bulwer-Lytton remarked with characteristic pomposity, yet with a good deal of truth, 'in nothing . . . is the material and unelevated character which belongs generally to the intellectual spirit of our times more developed than in our national architecture. A stranger in our streets is struck with the wealth, the gaud, the comfort, the bustle, the animation. But how rarely is he impressed with the vast and august simplicity, that is the result in architecture, as in letters, of a lofty taste, and the witness of a people penetrated with a passion for the *great!* The first thing that strikes us in England is the lowness of all the public buildings—they appear uncompleted; you would imagine a scythe had been drawn across them in the middle: they seem dedicated to St Denis, after he had lost his head. The next thing that strikes you in them is the want of originality—they are odd, but unoriginal. Now, wherever an architecture is not original, it is sure to be inappropriate: we transplant what belongs to one climate to another wholly distinct from it—what is associated with one history or religion, to a site in which the history and religion are ludicrously opposed to it.' [25]

I suppose that very few people read Lytton nowadays, and with good reason: his writings have become a bore. All the same, there is something in what he has to say about the want of originality in our architecture, particularly that of our public buildings. There are plenty of examples of our native genius from which to evolve a contemporary idiom suitable to public architecture, rather than go on making slavish imitations of continental styles. There is the Horse Guards, for instance, and Regent's Park and Somerset House; there is Kenwood, and Sion House and Hampton Court, all within a stone's throw of London, and many more besides. Yet it is depressing to see some of the effects that have been achieved through rigidity of mind, poverty of imagination and fear of public opinion.

Some of the happiest examples of public as well as domestic architecture that I know of are in the American Colonial style. The campus at Harvard is a beautiful example of the one, and though I have not seen Monticello, the house in Virginia where Thomas Jefferson lived, it is as clearly a delightful example of the other.

'Monticello, on its windswept hilltop, overlooking Charlottesville and surrounded by cedar trees, is an intensely individual house. Where Mount Vernon is merely the place where George Washington lived from the age of fifteen, Monticello is a house constructed by Thomas Jefferson for his own comfort and amusement. It embodies all those elements of proportion and elegance, of experiment and enterprise which make the third President of the United States so sympathetic a figure among his prosy and loquacious contemporaries. Monticello, its high rooms echoing to the clanking of the great hall clock telling the day of the week, could not have been devised by anybody else. Each room is an architectural experiment, reaching its climax in the designer's bed, fitted into the thickness of the wall, between his study and his dressing-room so that on waking he could get out of bed into whichever room he wished. The noble beauty of the dining-room (which was characteristically fitted with a lift for getting up wine from the cellar) evidences Jefferson's enthusiasm for classicism, while the small staircase, crushed in between a bedroom and a passage, betrays the carefree hand of the amateur architect. At Monticello, and in the University of Virginia which, with its collonades and porticoes, and its circular domed library, he designed, you can gain a direct apprehension of this civilized and astounding personality. The countryside round Charlottesville contains numerous exemplars of his civilizing influence. By designing for his friends houses with domes, pillars, porticoes, long herbaceous borders and well-planted trees, variations in fact of his own home at Monticello, Thomas Jefferson changed the visual aspect of this portion of Virginia, replacing the practical by the beautiful, the banal by the effective.

'The afternoon was getting on towards four o'clock and we began to leave ... We got into the car and bumped away over the coarse grass of the lane for one final visit before returning home. This was to a house as uninhabited as Monticello, but more logically so. It was in fact the house at Barboursville, probably designed by Thomas Jefferson and certainly burned down after the Civil War. This ruin, lying near the little village of Barboursville, is hard to find for those who do not know it. The car turned into a deserted drive, and we went some way along beneath aged oak and elm trees which met overhead. Leaving the car in this tunnel we got out and advanced towards a high and sombre wall of box. These box hedges, the most famous in Virginia, are from eight to nine feet high, and they shield the ruins of Barboursville as effectually as the thorn hedges of Rackham's imagination protect the Sleeping Beauty. Behind the hedges, in utter silence, stood the ruin, entangled in a grove of dark and mournful trees, themselves shrouded in poison ivy and creeping plants. So closely do the shrubs and trees and creepers envelop this burned-out house that it too gives an illusion of growth: it seems rooted in the soil, and subject like the vegetation round it, to a seasonal change. We were seeing, I felt, its summer aspect, the ruin in fullest bloom, white and luscious. At first you were aware chiefly of four tall, round, smooth plaster pillars, the remnants of the portico, which rise into the air to end abruptly in broken and useless capitals. Then, entering through a hole in the brick wall where a door once hung, you find again the pattern of Monticello: the circular hall, the long drawing-room, the dining room. But in this dining room, a walnut grows, and in this rotunda no clocks clank. Underfoot was the soft and feathery foliage of summer. The lower portions of the wall were padded with wild myrtle. Here and there over the ruins languid laburnums drooped their lemon-coloured sprays. These flowers, and the white pillars, and the sunshine almost gave an air of gaiety to this melancholy scene.

'Looking round the ruins with relish, I knew that I enjoyed this more than Monticello or anything we had seen that day. Was it mere natural morbidity or romanticism? Or was it that this decay, this natural solution for the old age of a house, seemed more true and honourable than the artificial preservation, the glass showcases and the white explanatory labels, of Monticello? The world of Jefferson, its ideals and interests and pastimes, have substantially passed away. At Monticello the hands of later generations have piously conserved the shell in which this world was lived. The result is brittle and lifeless. At Barboursville Nature has done its own preservation, making of this ruined eighteenth century mansion a spectacle of wild and immediate beauty. I know quite well which of the two solutions I preferred.' [20]

SOURCES

1   Sir Joshua Reynolds, *Discourses delivered to the Students of the Royal Academy.*
2   George Bernard Shaw, *The Doctor's Dilemma.*
3   Raymond Mortimer, on Graham Sutherland's paintings, *Harper's Bazaar*, April, 1948.
4   Walter Richard Sickert. *A Free House!*
5   Lynton Lamb, 'Predicaments of Illustration', *Signature*, No. 4, 1947.
6   Max J. Friedlander, *Art and Connoisseurship.*
7   Sir Kenneth Clark, *Landscape into Art.*
8   Patrick Leigh Fermor, *The Sunday Times*, March 21, 1954.

9 See 4.
10 Edmond and Jules de Goncourt, *Journals*.
11 See 6.
12 See 7.
13 Ben Shahn, *The Shape of Content*.
14 See 3.
15 Archbishop Temple, *The Resources and Influences of English Literature*.
16 See 3.
17 Jacquetta Hawkes, *A Land*.
18 John Ruskin, *The Stones of Venice*.
19 Ibid.
20 James Pope-Hennessy, *America is an Atmosphere*.
21 Maurice Baring, *The Puppet Show of Memory*.
22 See 17.
23 George Mikes, *How to Be an Alien*.
24 Sir Richard Livingstone, 'Where Do We Go From Here?' *Evening Standard*, May 13, 1947.
25 Edward Bulwer-Lytton, *England and the English*.
26 See 20.

Philosophic Doubt

★

A man of words and not of deeds,
Is like a garden full of weeds.
ANONYMOUS, from *Gammer Gurton's Garland*

I AM not a great reader of philosophy. It seems to me a subject that needs more leisure and concentration for its profitable understanding than do most subjects, and as time almost as much as inclination governs the choice of what I read, philosophy somehow tends to get over-looked and only dipped into at odd moments. As a result, I have never consciously accepted or digested any philosophic system of thought or conduct as a guiding principle of my existence and through not doing so have probably missed a lot in life. When I was young enough to take life seriously I was always trying to impose some sort of system on my reading. I would resolve, for instance, to read a certain number of books on a chosen subject and to read them in a certain order, I suppose with some vague idea that this would inculcate a systematic appreciation of the subject. But it never worked. I have not got that sort of mind, and having an eager rather than a discriminating appetite for the printed word made it the more difficult to apply such a system.

One thing I have learnt from the little philosophy that I have read is the difficulty that faces one, especially a casual reader like myself, in trying to arrive at fixed conclusions on the subject. How, for instance, does one square Montaigne's opinion that 'Philosophy is doubt' [1] with Bacon's, that it is the 'great Mother of the sciences' ? [2] Or Plato's, that 'Philosophy is the highest music' [3] with Keats's complaint that it

> ... will clip an Angel's wings
> Conquer all mysteries by rule and line,
> Empty the haunted air, the gnomèd mine—
> Unweave a rainbow'? [4]

You see, then, why I have called this section Philosophic Doubt. It won't take you long, however, if you are an academic philosopher, or even an amateur of the subject, to pick holes in some of the examples I have chosen to illustrate my attitude of uncertainty. But as nothing gives a don greater pleasure than picking holes in other people's opinions, I am thus set to please the academic enthusiast as well, I hope, as the less critical reader. In justice to the few dons of my acquaintance —some I may even call friends—in justice to them I should add that my opinion of the species is not based upon the ones I know personally. There is a conceit about a certain type of don, however, that is to me infinitely more repellent than the simple nit-witted conceit of certain types of actors or men of letters, or that portentious conceit that is an occupational disease of politicians, or the mock-modest conceit of the jolly good sportsman, or the bland conceit that titles or inherited wealth often lend to those with an uncertain sense of their own dignity. The intellectual arrogance of the type of don that I mean, which is often coupled with a loud, rapid and effusive utterance, a tendency to lose interest in the sound of other people's voices and a keen, dogmatic manner, the implicit contempt for anything frivolous, low-brow or commonplace, are characteristics of this type which now and again would make it a pleasure to kick his teeth in.

But this is by the way. My conception of philosophic doubt embraces dubiety on a far wider scale than is implied by the existence of differing philosophic systems. To begin with there is the question of existence itself ... Do we, in fact, exist? The weight of affirmative evidence in G. K. Chesterton's case might have been thought to be conclusive, but even he was not quite sure:

'Bowing down in blind credulity,' he said, 'as is my custom, before mere authority and the tradition of the elders, superstitiously swallowing a story I could not test at the time by the experiment of private judgment, I am firmly of the opinion that I was born on the 29th of May, 1874. Of course what many call hearsay evidence might be questioned in theory, as in the Baconian controversy or a good deal of the Higher Criticism. The story of my birth might be untrue. I might be the long-lost heir of the Holy Roman Empire, or an infant left by ruffians from Limehouse on a door-step in Kensington, to develop in later life a hideous criminal heredity. Some of the sceptical methods applied to the world's origin might be applied to my origin, and a grave and earnest enquirer come to the conclusion that I was never born at all.' [5]

Having had the happiness and good fortune to have seen—or at any rate to have believed I was seeing—a good deal of Chesterton during the first fifteen years or so of my life, I am emphatically on the side of those who claim that he *did* exist. Furthermore, he often recommended to me books that he thought I would enjoy, and although time has altered my opinions about some of them, in general his recommendations still hold good.

One of the authors he brought to my notice for the first time was Hazlitt. As this coincided with the idea that was beginning just then to take hold of me, that I might eventually become an artist, it was rather discouraging to realize that 'it is the mischief of the regular study of all art and science, that it proportionably unfits a man for those pursuits or emergencies in life, which require mere courage and promptitude. To anyone who has found how difficult it is to arrive at truth or beauty, with all the pains and time he can bestow upon them, everything seems worthless that can be obtained by a mere assumption of the question, or putting a good face upon the matter. Let a man try to produce a fine picture, or to solve an abstruse problem by giving himself airs of self-importance, and see what he will make of it. But in the common intercourse of life, too much depends on this sort of assurance and quackery. This is the reason why scholars and other eminent men so often fail in what personally concerns themselves. They cannot take advantage of the follies of mankind; nor submit to arrive at the end they have in view by unworthy means.' [6]

In earlier and in some ways happier times the position of the artist in society was very different to that which Hazlitt implies. He was not necessarily looked upon as either a freak or a charlatan, which is usually the fate nowadays of the artist who tries to express his ideas in terms that are not immediately intelligible to the majority. This change in the popular attitude towards artists, and in fact, towards the arts in general, got its impetus, I suspect, from the materialistic trend of thought that began to gain ground about the time of the industrial revolution. Mysticism, imagination and poetry have never made much appeal to the sort of man who believes first and foremost in materialistic values. Yet 'once men were concerned with the quality of life as a whole and with their relation to the universe; they could assume, for example, that the ritual and revelry of the Twelve Days of Christmas were of infinitely greater value that the small material gains to be won by working for those twelve days. Now a man who makes a comparable choice must be called an absentee and seen as a traitor.' [7]

This passion for conformity, sometimes at the expense of far older and more justly cherished beliefs, sometimes even at the expense of reason or justice, strikes me as one of the most undesirable as well as most unwise developments in the society of our age. I am far from being an advocate of the Chestertonian heresy of a return to medievalism as a panacea for some of materialism's worst effects on society. You cannot put the clock back and hope that by so doing you will alter only those things that you want to see altered. There can be no progress, no forward movement of thought, in a society that places the importance of conformity for political ends above the freedom to act according to one's beliefs.

It is this instinctive and popular veneration of the conformer and the suspicion of the individualist in the United States that sometimes makes one wonder whether the American people will eventually be capable of rising to the heights towards which the current of history seems to be directing them. With a prescience that occurs surprisingly often in their *Journals*, the Goncourts remarked that they thought 'the day will come when all the modern nations will adore a sort of American god, a god who will have been a man that lived on earth and about whom much will have been written in the popular press; and images of this god will be set up in the churches, not as the imagination of each individual painter may fancy him, not floating on a Veronica kerchief, but established, fixed once and for all by photography. Yes, I foresee a photographed god, wearing spectacles. On that day civilization will have reached its peak and there will be steam-propelled gondolas in Venice.' [8]

Allowing that atomic-powered *vaporetti* are more likely, there is more than a grain of truth in the unpleasing possibilities envisaged by the Goncourts. Is it any wonder therefore if 'instinctively, man does not love the truth, and . . . is right not to love it? Falsehood and myth show a much pleasanter face. It is always more agreeable to imagine genius in the form of a tongue of fire than in the image of a neurotic.' [9] Likewise, 'if we make an examination of what is generally understood by happiness . . . we shall find all its properties and adjuncts will herd under this short definition: that it is a perpetual possession of being well deceived . . . 'tis manifest, what mighty advantages fiction has over truth; and the reason is just at our elbow; because imagination can build nobler scenes, and produce more powerful revolutions than fortune or nature will be at expense to furnish.' [10]

Whether one derives greater happiness through the exercise of one's imagination than by pleasure to be got through physical realities depends upon the quality of one's mind. For myself, I have never been able to decide about this; I only know that 'both my happiness and my unhappiness I owe to the love of pleasure'.[11] Perhaps the simplicity of this conclusion may lead one into thinking it less profound than consideration would show it to be, for I think that no one who can bear to be honest with himself would deny that it is usually true. It also shows, incidentally, that in giving expression to a philosophic conclusion there is a half-way house between the guileless platitudes of Wilhelmina Stitch and an assertion such as, 'that if statements about sense-data are taken, as properly they should be, to refer not to quasi-objective constituents of material things but to immediate subjective appearances, their certainty is established by linguistic guarantees'.[12] Being, as I have said, an ignoramus in the field of philosophy, I am unable to make head or tail of this sort of thing except by the most prodigious mental efforts, and even then am sometimes left in doubt as to whether I have got hold of the writer's proper meaning. I realize, of course, that the study of philosophy is an extraordinarily difficult business and that its terms are far less susceptible of precise definition than those of the physical sciences; but I also feel pretty sure that a remark such as the one I have just quoted could have been put more intelligibly, even if at greater length, by someone like Sir Kenneth Clark, for example, a writer whose discipline of thought and expression makes it possible to explain highly complicated ideas in language that is invariably of the plainest. Heaven preserve us from the sabbatarian philosopher whose syndicated column of homely wisdom sluices the pool-soaked, TV-ridden minds of millions of readers each week, but must one go to the other extreme? One may not always agree with Plato, or with Hume or Bergsen or Whitehead, who are among the few philosophers whose works I have now and again dipped into, but at least one can usually get the drift of their ideas without having to hack one's way through a jungle of verbiage. Swift, who I am sure would have found the right rejoinder to assertions about sense-data being established by linguistic guarantees, in considering one of the fundamental problems of existence, did not find it necessary to wrap up his meaning in similar jargon and yet is able to make an idea which I take to be a no less complicated one clear to an intelligence as simple as my own. 'The question is only this,' says he, 'whether things that have place in the imagination may not as properly be said to exist, as those that are seated in the memory which may be justly held in the affirmative, and very much to the advantage of the former, since this is acknowledged to be the womb of things, and the other allowed to be no more than the grave.' [13]

There seems to be something here akin to the meaning of Dunne's *Experiment With Time*, not that I would be so rash as to think that I have grasped more than an inkling of the theory which that remarkable book was written to expound. Can one say that what evolves from the process of imagination has existence? May it not more truthfully be said to exist in time, though not in substance? I might have believed so if Gertrude Stein had not confused me about this: 'So then there was the Keysers counting money and the Steins counting money and they all like to spend money, unless you can really have the pleasure of being a miser there is no pleasure like the spending of money, and it is hard to be a miser, a real miser they are as rare as geniuses it takes the same kind of thing to make one, that is time must not exist for them. *There must be a reality that has nothing to do with the passage of time* and it is very hard for anyone to have that in them, not hard almost impossible, but there is no way of having it unless you have it, I have it and so had Hetty Green. Oh yes.' 14

So there you are. If you are lucky enough, it seems, or rich enough, there is a reality that has nothing to do with the passage of time. And of course what Gertrude says about time and genius is right undoubtedly right I mean about a reality that has nothing to do with time, the italics were mine incidentally, I mean even if you are incidentally only a genius at ping pong ping pong must mean more to you when you are actually playing ping pong than the fact that whole minutes of your allotted span are incidentally clicking away like the balls on the table and as she says, being a miser calls for genius in a kind of way but it is just one kind of genius I have not got. How I envy Hetty Green whoever she may be but I shall never have it. Oh no.

I do not know what Gertrude's definition of genius may have been, but I cannot imagine she would have had much patience with Ruskin's theory, which related it to an infinite capacity for taking pains. But then I do not imagine she would have had much patience with Ruskin in any case; still less that he would have had any with her. All the same, I would give a lot to see them confronted with each other in some place hereafter.

Ruskin, for whom I have in some respects enormous admiration, was unfortunately a prig of a very high order. But what is priggish in an Englishman may well be all right in someone who is not, for instance, in someone who is Chinese. In China, 'to the question, "How do you do?" the commonest reply, "Very well, thanks" is not really very satisfactory, because there is about it an obvious smack of complacency, and when human beings encounter complacency their natural reaction is to try to disturb it. It is in recognition of this that wise men hurry past their personal boasting and immediately return the ball by adding, "How are you?" and then he who has opened the gambit is at a disadvantage, and if he says that he too is very well he is left high and dry in his self-satisfaction.

'The best answer I know comes from those great masters of social intercourse, the classical Chinese. Following them you should reply, "I am trying to diminish the number of my failings, but I have not so far been successful".' 15

In my own case it is not for want of trying. But the trouble is that such a lot of my failings, extravagance, for instance, carelessness in reading and writing, procrastination, staying up late and eating too fast, are often due to the realization that Time is breathing down my neck. To me not a single one of man's inventions would be worth a farthing beside that of a twenty-five hour day. 'The present,' said Gibbon, 'is a fleeting moment, the past is no more; and our prospect of futurity is dark and doubtful. This day may *possibly* be my last. But the laws of probability, so true in general, so fallacious in particular, still allow about fifteen years. I shall soon enter into the period which, as the most agreeable of his long life, was selected by the judgement and experience of the sage Fontanelle. His choice is approved by the eloquent historian of nature, [Buffon] who fixes our moral happiness to the mature season in which our passions are supposed to be calmed, our duties fulfilled, our ambition satisfied, our fame and our fortune established on a solid basis. In private conversation, that great and amiable man added the weight of his own experience; and this autumnal felicity might be exemplified in the lives of Voltaire, Hume, and many other men of letters. I am far more inclined to embrace than to dispute this comfortable doctrine. I will not suppose any premature decay of the mind or body; but I must reluctantly observe that two causes, the abbreviation of time, and the failure of hope, will always tinge with a browner shade the evening of life.' [16]

All the same, I do not think of Gibbon as a pessimist, but rather as a realist. But perhaps in 1789 it was not so hard as it seems nowadays to be the second without being the first. The gentle melancholy of his conclusion is reflected in that spotted mirror wherein Logan Pearsall Smith often looked for truth:

'Oh dear, this living and eating and growing old; these doubts and aches in the back and want of interest in the Moon and Roses . . .

'Am I the person who used to wake in the middle of the night and laugh with the joy of living? Who worried about the existence of God, and danced with young ladies till long after daybreak? Who sang "Auld Lang Syne" and howled with sentiment, and more than once gazed at the stars through a blur of great, romantic tears?' [17]

Addison, in rather the same frame of mind, describes how one evening when he was strolling in his garden, 'surveying the moon walking in her brightness, and taking her progress among the constellations, a thought rose in me which I believe very often perplexes and disturbs men of serious and contemplative natures. David himself fell into it in that reflection, "When I consider the heavens, the works of thy fingers, the moon and the stars which thou hast ordained; what is man that thou art mindful of him, and the son of man that thou regardest him?" In the same manner, when I had considered that infinite host of stars, or, to speak more philosophically, of suns, which were then shining upon me, with those innumerable sets of planets of worlds, which were moving round their respective suns; when I still enlarged the idea, and supposed another heaven of suns and worlds rising still above this which we discovered, and these still enlightened by a superior firmament of luminaries, which are planted at so great a distance that they may appear to the inhabitants of the former as the stars do to us;—in short, whilst I pursued this thought, I could not but reflect on that little insignificant figure which I myself bore amid the immensity of God's works.

'Were the sun, which enlightens this part of the creation, with all the host of planetary worlds that move about him, utterly extinguished and annihilated, they would not be missed more than a grain of sand upon the seashore. The space they possess is so exceedingly little in comparison of the whole, that it would scarce make a blank in the creation. The chasm would be imperceptible to an eye, that could take in the whole compass of nature, and pass from one end of the creation to the other, as it is possible there may be such a sense in ourselves hereafter, or in creatures which are at present more exalted than ourselves. We may see many stars by the help of glasses, which we do not discover with our naked eyes; and the finer our telescopes are, the more still are our discoveries. Huygenius carries thought so far, that he does not think it impossible there may be stars whose light is not yet travelled down to us, since their first creation. There is no question but the universe has certain bounds set to it; but when we consider it is the work of infinite power, prompted by infinite goodness, with an infinite space to exert itself in, how can our imagination set any bounds to it?

'To return therefore to my first thought, I could not but look upon myself with secret horror, as a being that was not worth the smallest regard of one who had so great a work under his care and superintendency. I was afraid of being overlooked in the immensity of nature, and lost among that infinite variety of creatures, which in all probability swarm through all these immeasurable regions of matter.

'In order to recover myself this mortifying thought, I considered that it took rise from those narrow conceptions, which we are apt to entertain of the divine nature. We ourselves cannot attend to many different objects at the same time. If we are careful to inspect some things, we must of course neglect others. This imperfection that cleaves in some degree to creatures of the highest capacities, as they are creatures, that is, beings of finite and limited natures. The presence of every created being is confined to a certain measure of space, and consequently his observation is stinted to a certain number of objects. The sphere in which we move and act and understand, is of a wider circumference to one creature than another, according as we rise one above another in the scale of existence. But the widest of these our spheres has its circumference. When therefore we reflect on the divine nature, we are so used and accustomed to this imperfection in ourselves, that we cannot forbear in some measure ascribing it to him in whom there is no shadow of imperfection. Our reason indeed assures us that his attributes are infinite, but the poorness of our conceptions is such, that it cannot forbear setting bounds to everything it contemplates, till our reason comes again to our succour, and throws down all those little prejudices which rise in us unawares, and are natural to the kind of man.' [18]

To the comforts of his religion Addison was able to add those of the eighteenth century's scientific ignorance. I wonder whether his piety and detachment would have withstood the knowledge that such a thing as the hydrogen bomb existed. To scientists the progress of science must sometimes seem maddeningly slow, but perhaps the hand of providence is at work here, for if it were faster the probability is that most of us would rapidly be driven into lunatic asylums. Imagine the effect it would have had on men's minds if Rutherford had discovered in two weeks all that his disciples discovered in the two decades after his death. We should have leapt from apprehension of the Maxim gun to the realization that the snuffing out of the human race overnight had become a practical possibility. It can hardly be said that distance lends enchantment to the view that science reveals, but at least we are allowed to get our breath back between the twitchings of the curtain. Already in 1879, Berthelot, the French chemist was predicting that in 'a hundred years from now, thanks to physical and chemical science, men would know of what the atom is constituted, and would be able, at will, to moderate, extinguish and light up again the sun as if it were a gas lamp. Claude Bernard, for his part, had apparently declared that in a hundred years of physiological science man would be so completely the master of organic law that he would create life in competition with God.' [19]

The Goncourts, who recorded these remarks as part of a dinner-table conversation, 'raised no objection', but added, 'we have the feeling that when this time comes in science, God with his white beard will come down to earth, swinging a bunch of keys, and will say to humanity, the way they say at five o'clock at the Salon, "Closing time, gentlemen"'. [20]

SOURCES

1 Michel de Montaigne, *Essays*, Book II.
2 Francis Bacon, *De Argumentis Scientarum*, Book I.
3 Plato, *Phædo*.
4 John Keats, *Lamia*.
5 G. K. Chesterton, *Autobiography*.
6 William Hazlitt, *Characteristics*.
7 Jacquetta Hawkes, *A Land*.
8 Edmond and Jules de Goncourt, *Journals*.
9 Ibid.
10 Jonathan Swift, *The Tale of a Tub*.
11 Palinurus, *The Unquiet Grave*.
12 *The Times Literary Supplement*, date unknown, *circa* 1955.
13 See 10.
14 Gertrude Stein, *Everybody's Autobiography*.
15 Douglas Woodruff, *Still Talking at Random*.
16 Edward Gibbon, *Memoirs of my Life and Writing*.
17 Logan Pearsall Smith, *Trivia*.
18 Joseph Addison, *Essays*.
19 See 8.
20 Ibid.

Tableaux Vivants

★

To behold a battle fought, like that of Cressy, or Agincourt, or Poictiers (saith Froissart) than which I doubt if antiquity can show any more glorious; to see one of Caesar's triumphs in old Rome revived, or the like; to be present at an interview, as that famous of Henry the Eighth and Francis the First, so much renowned all over Europe where the two kings, with their wives, met with such state and pomp that no age ever saw the like: so infinitely pleasant are such shows, to the sight of which oftentimes they will come hundreds of miles, give any money for a place, and remember many years after with singular delight.

ROBERT BURTON, *The Anatomy of Melancholy*

THE man who is nothing of a kibitzer is no friend of mine. With indiscriminate curiosity, sometimes even with interest, the kibitzer will watch whatever is going on—road-menders at work, scaffolders, housebreakers, processions, parades, fiestas, fires, riot and civil commotion, all are temptations to his idle gaze. Being a kibitzer is all wrong, of course; a man should be up and doing, not hanging around watching other people going about their business. The moralist content to live in a tub has some excuse for being indolent. By his passive example he at least is attempting to influence the course of human affairs for what he hopes will be the general good. But I, watching the Guards troop their colour, or some splendid building burning down, have no interest except in the spectacle itself and no motive but the excitement it arouses in me; not a commendable attitude, I admit, and perhaps one that I should be ashamed of, but organized indolence has become so much a part of contemporary life that the kibitzer's occasional indulgence hardly seems to call for apology.

Before the trades unions outgrew their strength and, as sometimes happens in such cases, became slightly feeble-minded as a result, the British were not afraid of work and England was a dignified and consequently a respected nation. I think it was Shaw who said that the dignity of man is in proportion to the contribution he makes to society, and it is true that since we became one of the laziest communities in Europe a good deal of our dignity has evaporated and the respect that we still enjoy is either for our past achievements or for such intangibles as moral leadership, the concept of the British Commonwealth and so on. In the nineteenth century we were an enterprising nation, but now, like the Italians and the Spaniards (although significantly unlike the Germans and the Japanese) we seldom put our backs into it unless self-interest points to the advantages of our working really hard. Also, since those advantages have become more evenly distributed among us they are less easy to recognize and in the absence of obvious incentives we tend to relapse too easily into being lazy.

It is partly the fatal ease with which we decline into this attitude that makes so many of us good kibitzers, ready to stand and watch rather than to take part. Of course, the golden age of the kibitzer is over. It was the Industrial Revolution that finished it off, with its encouragement of standardization and a materialistic outlook. When steam came in, pagantry went out, and with it a great deal that must have been fine to watch. The opening of the Crystal Palace, the apotheosis of the Revolution, was no doubt a splendid occasion, but I would much prefer to have seen the opening of one of the great fairs held in the Low Countries during the Middle Ages. Whether, if I had lived in earlier times, I should have shared the popular taste for sadistic spectacles, the bear pits, the prize fights, the public executions and so on, I don't know. The mere idea of such things seems revolting nowadays, yet those who watched them were, as we know, not always the most callous or the most debased. Pepys, and Dickens too I believe, witnessed public hangings without apparently feeling unduly squeamish and I have an idea that the Goncourts also described an execution. If so, it can hardly have been more vividly described at first-hand than Arnold Bennett's entirely imaginary account in *The Old Wives' Tale*. Sophia Bains had eloped to Paris with Gerald Scales who, on the morning of the execution, left her alone in the bedroom of their seedy hotel and went off with his friend Chirac to see what was going on:

'The cool, grey beginnings of dawn were in the sky, and every detail of the square was visible. Without exception all the windows were wide open and filled with sightseers. In the background of many windows were burning candles or lamps that the far distant approach of the sun was already killing. In front of these, on the frontier of two mingling lights, the attentive figures of the watchers were curiously silhouetted. On the red-tiled roofs, too, was a squatted population. Below, a troop of gendarmes, mounted on caracoling horses stretched in line across the square, was gradually sweeping the entire square of a packed, gesticulating, cursing crowd. The operation of this immense besom was very slow. As the spaces of the square were cleared they began to be dotted by privileged persons, journalists or law officers or their friends, who walked to and fro in conscious pride; among them Sophia descried Gerald and Chirac, strolling arm-in-arm and talking to two elaborately clad girls, who were also arm-in-arm.

'Then she saw a red reflection coming from one of the side streets of which she had a vista; it was the swinging lantern of a waggon drawn by a gaunt grey horse. The vehicle stopped at the end of the square from which the besom had started, and it was immediately surrounded by the privileged, who, however, were soon persuaded to stand away. The crowd, amassed now at the principal inlets of the square, gave a formidable cry and burst into the refrain—

> *Le voilà!*
> *Nicolas!*
> *Ah! Ah! Ah!*

'The clamour became furious as a group of workmen in blue blouses drew piece by piece all the components of the guillotine from the wagon and laid them carefully on the ground, under the superintendence of a man in a black frock-coat and a silk hat with broad flat brims; a little fussy man of nervous gestures. And presently the red columns had risen upright from the ground and were joined at the top by an acrobatic climber. As each part was bolted and screwed to the growing machine the man in the high hat carefully tested it. In a short time that seemed very long, the guillotine was finished save for the triangular steel blade which lay shining on the ground, a cynosure. The executioner pointed to it, and two men picked it up and slipped it into its groove, and hoised it to the summit of the machine. The executioner peered at it interminably amid a universal silence. Then he actuated the mechanism, and the mass of metal fell with a muffled, reverberating thud. There were a few faint shrieks, blended together, and then an overpowering racket of cheers, shouts, hootings, and fragments of song. The blade was again lifted, instantly reproducing silence, and again it fell, liberating a new bedlam. The executioner made a movement of satisfaction. Many women at the windows clapped enthusiastically, and the gendarmes had to fight brutally against the fierce pressure of the crowd. The workmen doffed their blouses and put on coats, and Sophia was disturbed to see them coming in single file towards the hotel, followed by the executioner in the silk hat . . .

'Her eye caught the guillotine again, and was held by it. Guarded by gendarmes, that tall and simple object did most menacingly dominate the square with its crude red columns. Tools and a large open box lay on the ground beside it. The enfeebled horse in the waggon had an air of dozing on his twisted legs. Then the first rays of the sun shot lengthwise across the square at the level of the chimneys; and Sophia noticed that nearly all the lamps and candles had been extinguished. Many people at the windows were yawning; they laughed foolishly after they had yawned. Some were eating and drinking. Some were shouting conversations from one house to another. The mounted gendarmes were still pressing back the feverish crowds that growled at all the inlets to the square . . .

'At intervals the crowd would burst out in a violent staccato—

Le voilà!
Nicolas!
Ah! Ah! Ah!

And the final 'Ah' was devilish.

'Then a gigantic passionate roar, the culmination of the mob's fierce savagery, crashed against the skies. The line of maddened horses swerved and reared, and seemed to fall on the furious multitude while the statue-like gendarmes rocked over them. It was a last effort to break the cordon, and it failed.

'From the little street at the rear of the guillotine appeared a priest, walking backwards, and holding a crucifix high in his right hand, and behind him came the handsome hero, his body all crossed with cords, between two warders, who pressed against him and supported him on either side. He was certainly very young. He lifted his chin gallantly, but his face was incredibly white. Sophia discerned that the priest was trying to hide the sight of the guillotine from the prisoner with his body . . .

'Except the voice of the priest, indistinctly rising and falling in prayer for the dying, there was no sound in the square or its environs. The windows were now occupied by groups turned to stone with distended eyes fixed on the little procession. Sophia had a tightening of the throat, and the hand trembled by which she held the curtain. The central figure did not seem to her to be alive; but rather a doll, a marionette wound up to imitate the action of a tragedy. She saw the priest offer the crucifix to the mouth of the marionette, which with a clumsy unhuman shoving of its corded shoulders butted the thing away. And as the procession turned and stopped she could plainly see that the marionette's nape and shoulders were bare, his shirt having been slit. It was horrible. "Why do I stay here?" she asked herself hysterically. But she did not stir. The victim had disappeared now in the midst of a group of men. Then she perceived him prone under the red column, between the grooves. The silence was now broken only by the tinkling of the horses' bits in the corners of the square. The line of gendarmes in front of the scaffold held their swords tightly and looked over their noses, ignoring the privileged groups that peered almost between their shoulders . . .

'The distant bell boomed once. Then a monosyllabic voice sounded, sharp, low, nervous . . . There was a clicking noise . . .

'She shrank down to the floor in terror and loathing, and hid her face and shuddered. Shriek after shriek, from various windows, rang on her ears in a fusillade; and then the mad yell of the penned crowd, which, like herself, had not seen but had heard, extinguished all other noise. Justice was done.' [1]

Let us now turn to a very different kind of spectacle in which justice was done to appetites as hungry for sensation, but of a less morbid kind. During a visit to Rome in 1830, Charles Greville went to see the procession of the Corpus Domini: 'The magnificence of ceremonies and processions here depends upon the locality, and the awnings and flowers round the piazza spoilt it all. It was long and rather tiresome— all the monks and religious orders in Rome, the cardinals and the Pope, plenty of waxlights, banners, and crosses, the crosses of Constantine and Charlemagne ... the Pope looks as if he was huddled into a short bed, and his throne, or whatever it is called, is ill managed. He is supposed to be in the act of adoration of the Host, which is raised before him, but as he cannot kneel for such a length of time, he sits covered with drapery, and with a pair of false legs stuck out behind him to give his figure the appearance of kneeling. Before him are borne the triple crown and other Pontifical ornaments. The Guardia Nobile, commanded by Prince Barberini, looked very handsome, and all the troops *en très-belle tenue*. All the Ambassadors and foreigners were in this palace, and from it we flocked to St Peter's, which is always a curious sight on these occasions from the multitudes in it and the variety of their appearance and occupation—cardinals, princes, princesses, mixed up with footmen, pilgrims, and peasants. Here, Mass going on at an altar, and crowds kneeling round it; there, the Host deposited amidst a peal of music at another; in several corners, cardinals dressing or undressing, for they all take off the costume they wore in the procession and resume their scarlet robes in the church; men hurrying about with feathers, banners, and other paraphernalia of the day, the peasantry in their holiday attire, and crowds of curious idlers staring about. All this is wonderfully amusing, and is a scene which presents itself in continual variety.' [2]

Much the same could probably have been said of the Great Frost in 1620, which was, 'historians tell us, the most severe that has ever visited these islands. Birds froze in mid-air and fell like stones to the ground. At Norwich a young countrywoman started to cross the road in her usual robust health and was seen by the onlookers to turn visibly to powder and be blown in a puff of dust over the roofs as the icy blast struck her at the street corner. The mortality among sheep and cattle was enormous. Corpses froze and could not be drawn from the sheets. It was no uncommon sight to come upon a whole herd of swine frozen immovable upon the road. The fields were full of shepherds, ploughmen, teams of horses, and little bird-scaring boys all struck stark in the act of the moment, one with his hand to his nose, another with the bottle to his lips, a third with a stone raised to throw at the raven who sat, as if stuffed, upon the hedge within a yard of him. The severity of the frost was so extraordinary that a kind of petrifaction sometimes ensued; and it was commonly supposed that the great increase of rocks in some parts of Derbyshire was due to no eruption, for there was none, but to the solidification of unfortunate wayfarers who had been literally turned to stone where they stood. The Church could give little help in the matter, and though some landowners had these relics blessed, the most part preferred to use them either as landmarks, scratching posts for sheep, or, when the form of the stone allowed, drinking troughs for cattle, which purposes they serve, admirably for the most part, to this day.

'But while the country people suffered the extremity of want, and the trade of the country was at a standstill, London enjoyed a carnival of the utmost brilliancy. The Court was at Greenwich, and the new King seized the opportunity that his coronation gave him to curry favour with the citizens. He directed that the river, which was frozen to a depth of twenty feet and more for six or seven miles on either side, should be swept, decorated and given all the semblance of a park or pleasure ground, with arbours, mazes, alleys, drinking booths, etc., at his expense. For himself and the courtiers, he reserved a certain space immediately opposite the Palace gates; which, railed off from the public only by a silken rope, became at once the centre of the most brilliant society in England. Great statesmen, in their beards and ruffs, despatched affairs of state under the crimson awning of the Royal Pagoda. Soldiers planned the conquest of the Moor and the downfall of the Turk in striped aroburs surmounted by plumes of ostrich feathers. Admirals strode up and down the narrow pathways, glass in hand, sweeping the horizon and telling stories of the north-west passage and the Spanish Armada. Lovers dallied upon divans spread with sables. Frozen roses fell in showers when the Queen and her ladies walked abroad. Coloured ballons hovered motionless in the air. Here and there burnt vast bonfires of cedar and oak wood, lavishly salted, so that the flames were of green, orange and purple fire. But however fiercely they burnt, the heat was not enough to melt the ice which, though of singular transparency, was yet of the hardness of steel. So clear indeed was it that there could be seen, congealed at a depth of several feet, here a porpoise, there a flounder. Shoals of eels lay motionless in a trance, but whether their state was one of death or merely of suspended animation which the warmth would revive puzzled the philosophers. Near London Bridge, where the river had frozen to a depth of some twenty fathoms, a wrecked wherry boat was plainly visible, lying on the bed of the river where it had sunk last autumn, overladen with apples. The old bumboat woman, who was carrying her fruit to market on the Surrey side, sat there in her plaids and farthingales with her lap full of apples, for all the world as if she were about to serve a customer, though a certain blueness about the lips hinted the truth. 'Twas a sight King James specially liked to look upon, and he would bring a troupe of courtiers to gaze with him. In short, nothing could exceed the brilliancy and gaiety of the scene by day. But it was at night that the carnival was at its merriest. For the frost continued unbroken; the nights were of perfect stillness; the moon and stars blazed with the hard fixity of diamonds, and to the fine music of flute and trumpet the courtiers danced.' ³

From the ice-bound Thames in the seventeenth century your imagination must now bound forward in time and space to modern Tripolitania, to the fort of Mizda, 'isolated in the empty plain. Around its massive towers a group of huts, built of earthen bricks, straw and dung, formed a village ... Mizda is reputed to be a country of sorcerers, weavers of spells, and holy men ... the Arabs called Mizda *blād el asrar*, the land of mysteries. This is probably due in part to the presence of the Senussite *zāwiya* and to the presence of Negro families who brought with them superstitions and tribal practices from equatorial Africa.' ⁴ Few Europeans can have got to know the shy Senussi as well as the Duc di Pirajno, a Sicilian nobleman who became a doctor and spent most of his working life among the native tribes of Italian North Africa. It was Mahdi, the fort's medical orderly, who first told him about Fusúda, the scorpion-charmer. 'Mahdi could read and write and he talked to me about the scorpions with something of the air of a specialist. However, he was inclined sometimes to get a little out of his depth, and it was obvious that he was repeating fragments he had heard from someone else who had studied the subject.

'In any case, it was from Mahdi that I learned that although many fanatical Moslems condemn the use of magic because it involves the use of diabolical intervention, nevertheless the Prophet himself permits the use of spells to protect the faithful against the stings of scorpions—on condition that the spell, the *roquia*, is pronounced in comprehensible language and contains the sacred name of Allah.

'When I expressed some doubt about the existance of magicians nowadays, Mahdi assured me that they did exist. He told me about Fusúda, a negress who handled the most poisonous scorpions as though they were harmless crickets. When therefore he offered one evening to take me to see Fusúda, so that I might witness her extraordinary powers for myself, curiosity got the better of me and I agreed to go.

'The *zāwiya* is in the lower Gontar district and behind it, hidden in a labyrinth of narrow, earth-coloured walls, under a few ragged palm trees battered by unceasing winds, we came upon a hovel with crumbling walls, discoloured by smoke.

'The only light in the interior, which was without windows, came from a brazier; people and objects were only vaguely discernible, and the darkness magnified the sound of whispering and the shuffling of bare feet on mats, so that when an invisible hand lit a lamp in a niche on the wall I was surprised to find that there were only four of us: Mahdi, two old black women from the Fezzan, and myself.

'The negresses were perfectly aware of the object of my visit, but they insisted on Mahdi's explaining all over again that the *tebīb* had come because he wanted to see Fusúda. The sly smile of the brothelkeeper sat firmly on each wrinkled, ape-like countenance; they pressed around me and seized me by the arms to force me to sit down. Tea had to be taken with solemn ritual before Fusúda appeared before us.

'The hut had a low roof made of palm trunks; the wind whistled outside, and from a distance came the sound of boys chanting in the *zāwiya*—young voices which trailed off into a confused murmur when the teacher began in a nasal voice to intone a new verse.

'The teapot was now singing on the brazier and the tea was poured first into the cups and then back again into the pot to obtain the right infusion of bitter tea and sugar. I was required to drink three cups—the first only slightly sweetened, the second flavoured with mint, and the third full of roasted peanuts . . .

'When I had emptied the third cup the old woman threw some *bhur*, dear to the nostrils of negroes, on the fire, and as its perfume began to fill the hut Fusúda entered like a shadow, enveloped from head to foot in a *hāik* so dark in colour that it was almost invisible.

'She sat herself in front of me and looked me over with the one eye which the *hāik*, twisted over her head and drawn across the face, left uncovered.

'"God save you. You are the *tebīb?*"

'The chanting from the *zāwiya* rose and fell, and Fusúda swayed to and fro to the obsessive rhythm.

'"You have come to see the scorpions?"

'Her voice was slow and a little husky, and she spoke with an accent that distorted the words.

'"Do you know the spell that charms the scorpions?" she asked.

'"No."

'A malicious smile played round her mouth, and there was a passing light of mischief in the one visible eye.

'"You know many things, *tebīb*, yet you do not know how to charm scorpions?"

'She shook her head and continued musing.

'"I think you wish to see the scorpions because you do not know the medicine for them."

'She became silent and relaxed her posture, closing her eyes; she seemed to fall asleep, but her shoulders continued to move to the rhythm of the distant chanting. On the brazier the *bhur* continued to burn and made a slight sizzling sound. Suddenly, the girl shook herself and with a slow movement of head, breast and hips, threw off her *hāik*. Seated cross-legged, erect from the hips, she remained covered by the *suriya*, the sleeveless, low-cut Arab shift.

'She was a young negress with thick, purplish lips and a short, only slightly flattened, nose . . . Her forehead was strongly convex, her eyes coffee-coloured with yellowish whites; her tight black curls clung closely to her head and left her ringless ears uncovered; her arms and hands were bare of bracelets or rings. Beside her the ugliness of the two old Fezzanese women was repulsive.

'She took a wicker basket which they handed to her and lifted the multi-coloured lid. In the bottom of the basket a large scorpion was lashing about in a fury, its tail erect like a sword.

'Fusúda looked at it, her lips half open, her eyes half closed, and then took it between two fingers and placed in on her shoulder. The creature stumbled there, scrabbling upon the buckle of her chemise, then lost its foothold and slipped down into the hollow of her collar-bone. She threw back her head and the scorpion climbed up her neck, across her lower jaw and made its way slowly across her cheek. She closed an eye and it passed over her eyelid onto her forehead and attached itself to her woolly hair.

'Fusúda took it in her hand again, stroked it, murmured some words I could not catch, tickled its belly and suddenly popped it into her mouth. Only its tail, quivering and lashing out in every direction, protruded from between her thick lips, its poisonous sting striking the girl's chin and nostrils. A moment later the scorpion, covered in saliva, was frantically twisting about, wild with excitement, in the palm of her hand; she smiled at the little monster, and laid it in her armpit. Then with a swift movement she unfastened her shoulder buckle and let fall her suriya so that she was naked to the thighs. She thrust the scorpion between her legs, leaving only the tail obscenely protruding.

'Fusúda threw back her head and laughed—with silent, ghoulish laughter, her mouth wide open, her glazed eyes nearly closed. Meanwhile she started playing with another, yellow striped scorpion, smaller but more poisonous than the other. She poked it with her finger-nail and blew on its head, and when it lashed out in fury she put out her tongue and used it to fence with the deadly tail, which struck but did not wound her. Both scorpions were now on Fusúda's crossed arms. She watched them. Antediluvian monsters in miniature, they faced each other with all their weapons and members ready. Slowly and clumsily they approached each other; they grappled each other by the legs, their tails lashing and quivering in a frenzy which communicated itself to the girl, who shivered as if she were suffering from a tertian fever. Her lips were drawn back from her teeth and her eyes converged on the combatants in a ferocious squint.

'Suddenly she emitted the shrill, piercing notes of the *zaghārīt*, the war-cry which excites men to battle, and the two monsters in miniature seemed to understand and to respond. Locked together, they wrestled and struggled clawing at each other, their arched tails waving, seeking the adversary's vulnerable spot; their stings beat against each other's backs as they had beaten against Fusúda's face and tongue and lips. All at once they were still. The thrusts had gone home; the poison had struck them motionless. There was a spasm or two in the tails still inserted in the wounds; a pincer let go, slowly, painfully; a leg stretched out in a last spasm, and the two reptiles, still interlocked, rolled dead on to the mat.

'Fusúda's body slumped forward, and she clasped her hands round her knees, shuddering; she was foaming at the mouth, and her breasts and belly were running with sweat . . . she remained motionless with closed eyes. The only sign of life was a quiver that now and then mounted across her abdomen. I touched her arm; it was cold, like that of a corpse.

'"Truly this woman knows the Koran", said Mahdi, this being apparently the only conclusion he had been able to arrive at. For myself, I could draw no conclusion at all.' [5]

I wonder what the good ducal doctor would have made of the empirical approach to a no less mysterious problem of pathology (or was it gastronomy?) made by two seekers after truth who examined the tomb of Dean Colet?

'After the conflagration his monument being broken, his coffin, which was lead, was full of liquour which conserved the body. Mr

Wyld and Ralph Greatorex tasted it and 'twas of a kind of insipid tast, something of an ironish tast. The body felt, to the probe of a stick which they thrust into a chinke, like brawne,' [6] though still preferable perhaps to a meal that was once served to those indefatigable travellers, so reminiscent of the Goons, the brothers Wrigley. On September 27, 1884, in the course of their circumnavigation of the globe from Liverpool, they arrived at Kioto in southern Japan.

'On entering the house, the first thing we did was to take off our boots. We then went upstairs to a large room, very nicely got up, where there were five dancing girls, all of them very pretty, and with splendid dresses. The orchestra consisted of two wretched old women, with a sort of banjo with three strings, on which they make most discordant noises. We then proceeded to have "chow", which consisted of several courses of raw fish, rotten fish, dried fish and stinking fish, with plenty of saki to wash it down with. But, however, having just finished dinner we did not partake. Then the dancing began. A girl got up with a fan in her hand, made a bow, puckered up her mouth, put on a squint, and began to dance. It was very graceful, but they utterly spoilt it by the expression they put on. After her, a girl, with an umbrella, got up and danced very well. Then they danced together, a sort of minuet, very prettily. Next a solo from the smallest girl, sounding like a cat crying. Then R. T. Younger gave them a "Highland Fling", which was thoroughly enjoyed by all present.' [7]

A few months later the brothers Wrigley were in India:

'Got up at 6.30 a.m. to go to Amber, the old town. Started at 7.30 and first passed through Jeypore, in which we saw a dead Hindu going to be burnt. As it was early morning the natives were feeding the pigeons in the town: they are sacred and are never killed. It is a wonderful sight, myriads of them in dense masses on the roofs and in the street circling round the carriage. The way to Amber, which is six-and-a-half miles off, lies through the country, the road lined with tombs and cactus hedges. We saw numbers of wild peacocks, doves and parrots of all descriptions. At one-and-a-half miles from Amber we were met at the foot of the hill by one of the Maharajah's elephants, which he had sent down for us—very kind of him—as the hills are too steep for carriage. So we mounted the elephant and rode up the hill. The town is very interesting, though mostly in ruins. There is a tank full of crocodiles in the middle. We went to the top of the hill where there is a palace built entirely of marble, very beautiful. The elephant was a very good one; knelt down for us to ascend and descend. We returned the same way. In the afternoon we visited the Crocodile

Pond in Jeypore; they came when called by their keeper, and we fed them with pieces of goat flesh. Went over the Maharajah's stables, very dilapidated lot of carriages. Grand fete in honour of Spring. Maharajah on a huge elephant, with thirty accompanying. First came the bullocks (Hindoo) drawing the gun carriages, then a regiment of camels with swivel guns (small ones) fixed on to their backs. After these a regiment of Lancers, and then the elephants, on the largest of which sat the Maharajah. The men on the other elephants were throwing a red powder about by the ton, which caused the air to appear quite pink; it had a most splendid effect. Afterwards came more troops. Altogether a most striking and never-to-be-forgotten scene. We saw the whole affair very well. In the temple of the Marble Palace at Amber was an Hindoo goddess, whom of course we were not allowed to go near, and in her temple was one of the largest diamonds I ever saw. She was covered all over with jewels and gold; must have been worth a million. They had just sacrificed a goat. Went to bed early.' [8]

There was practically nothing in the course of their journey that the Wrigleys, with their simple, candid and curiously observant, though utterly humourless gaze, did not seem to look upon with either interest or amusement. Though not everyone would have found them ideal travelling companions, and irritating though their ineffable bonhomie and their philistinism must have been, one has to hand it to them for their curiosity and enterprise. Beckford, for a certainty, would have been driven mad by them. They, on the other hand, would obviously have been delighted to have kept him company on his visit to the Escurial with his friend Roxas: 'There is something most severely impressive in the facade of this regal convent, which, like the palace of Persepolis, is overshadowed by the adjoining mountain; nor did I pass through a vaulted cloister into the court before the church, solid as if hewn out of a rock, without experiencing a sort of shudder . . . The sun being again overcast, the porches of the church, surmounted by grim statues, appeared so dark and cavern-like, that I thought myself about to enter a subterraneous temple set apart for the service of some mysterious and terrible religion. And when I saw the high altar, in all its pomp and jasper-steps, ranks of columns one above the other, and paintings filling up every interstice, full before me, I felt completely awed.

'The sides of the recess, in which this imposing pile is placed, are formed by lofty chapels, almost entirely occupied by catafalques of gilt enamelled bronze. Here, with their crowns and sceptres humbly prostrate at their feet, bare-headed and unhelmed, kneel the figures, large as life, of the Emperor Charles the Fifth, and his imperious son, the second Philip, accompanied by those of their unhappy consorts and ill-fated children. My sensations of dread and dreariness were not diminished upon finding myself alone in such company; for Roxas had left me to deliver some letters to his right reverence the prior, which were to open to us all the arcana of this terrific edifice, at once a temple, a palace, a convent, and a tomb.

'Presently my amiable friend returned, and with him a tall old monk, with an ash-coloured, forbidding countenance, and staring eyes, the expression of which was the farthest removed possible from anything like cordiality. This was the mystagogue of the place—the prior *in propria persona*, the representative of St Jerome, as far as this monastery and its domain was concerned, and a disciplinarian of celebrated rigidness . . .

'First we visited some apartments with vaulted roofs, painted in arabesque, in the finest style of the sixteenth century; and then a vast hall, which had been used for the celebration of mass, whilst the great church was building, where I saw the Perla in all its purity, the most delicately-finished work of Raphael, the Pesce, with its divine angel, graceful infant, and devout young Tobit, breathing the very soul of pious, unaffected simplicity. My attention was next attracted by that most profoundly pathetic of pictures, Jacob weeping over the bloody garment of his son; the loftiest proof in existence of the extraordinary powers of Velasquez in the noblest work of art.

'These three pictures so absorbed my admiration, that I had little left for a host of glorious performances by Titian and the highest masters, which cover the plain, massive walls of these conventual rooms with a paradise of glowing colours; so I passed along almost as rapidly as my grumbling cicerone could desire, and followed him up several flights of stairs, and through many and many an arched passage and vestibule, all of the sternest doric, into the choir, which is placed over the grand western entrance, right opposite, at the distance of more than two hundred feet, to the high altar and its solemn accompaniments. No regal chamber I ever beheld can be compared, in point of sober harmonious majesty, to this apartment, which looks more as if it belonged to a palace than to a church. The series of stalls, designed in a severer taste than was common in the sixteenth century, are carved out of the most precious woods the Indies could furnish. At the extremity of this striking perspective of onyx-coloured seats, columns, and canopies, appears suspended upon a black velvet pall that revered image of the crucified Saviour, formed of the purest ivory, which Cellini seem to have sculptured in moments of devout rapture and inspiration . . .

'We went down from the choir, I can scarcely tell whither, such is the extent and intricacy of this stupendous edifice. We passed, I believe, through some of the lateral chapels at the great church, into several quadrangles, one in particular, with a fountain under a cupola in the centre, surrounded by doric arcades, equal in justness of proportion and architectural terseness to Palladio's court in the convent of S. Giorgio Maggiore.

'My lord the prior, not favouring a prolonged survey, I reluctantly left this beautiful court, and was led into a low gallery, roofed and wainscoted with cedar, lined on both sides by ranges of small doors of different-coloured Brazil-wood, looking in appearance, at least, as solid as marble. Four sacristans, and as many lay-brothers, with large lighted flambeaux of yellow wax in their hands, and who, by the by, never quitted us more the remainder of our peregrinations, stood silent as death ready to unlock those mysterious entrances.

'The first they opened exhibited a buffet, or *credence*, three stories high, set out with many a row of grinning skulls, looking as pretty as gold and diamonds could make them; the second, every possible and impossible variety of odds and ends, culled from the carcasses of martyrs; the third, enormous ebony presses, the secrets of which I begged for pity's sake might not be intruded upon for my recreation, as I began to be heartily wearied of sight-seeing; but when my conductors opened the fourth mysterious door, I absolutely shrank back, almost sickened by a perfume of musk and ambergris . . .

'The prior who is not easily pleased, seemed to have suspicions that the seriousness of my demeanour was not entirely orthodox; I overheard him saying to Roxas, "Shall I show him the Angel's feather? You know we do not display this our most-valued, incomparable relic to everybody, nor unless upon special occasions."—"The occasion is sufficiently special," answered my partial friend; "the letters I brought to you are your warrant, and I beseech your reverence to let us look at this gift of heaven, which I am extremely anxious myself to adore and venerate."

'Forth stalked the prior, and drawing out from a remarkably large cabinet an equally capacious sliding shelf—(the source, I conjecture, of the potent odour I complained of)—displayed lying stretched out upon a quilted silken mattress, the most glorious specimen of plumage ever beheld in terrestrial regions—a feather from the wing of the Archangel Gabriel, full three feet long, and of a blushing hue more soft and delicate than that of the loveliest rose. I longed to ask at what precise moment this treasure beyond price had been dropped—whether from the air—on the open ground, or within the walls of the humble tenement at Nazareth; but I repressed all questions of an indiscreet tendency—the why and wherefore, the when and how, for what and to whom such a palpable manifestation of archangelic beauty and wingedness had been vouchsafed.

'We all knelt in silence, and when we rose up after the holy feather had been again deposited in its perfumed lurking-place . . . he led the way through a labyrinth of cloisters, gloomy as the grave; till ordering a grated door to be thrown open, the light of our flambeaux fell upon a flight of most beautiful marble steps, polished as a mirror, leading down between walls of the rarest jaspers to a portal of no great size, but enriched with balusters of rich bronze, sculptured architraves, and tablets of inscriptions, in a style of the greatest magnificence.

'As I descended the steps, a gurgling sound, like that of a rivulet, caught my ear. "What means this?" said I. "It means," answered the monk, "that the sepulchral cave on the left of the stairs, where repose the bodies of many of our queens and infantas, is properly ventilated, running water being excellent for that purpose". I went on, not lulled by these rippling murmurs, but chilled when I reflected through what precincts flows this river of death.

'Arrived at the bottom of the stairs, we passed through the portal just mentioned, and entered a circular saloon, not more than five-and-thirty feet in diameter, characterized by extreme elegance, not stern solemnity. The regal sarcophagi, rich in golden ornaments, ranged one above the other, forming panels of the most decorative kind; the lustre of exquisitely sculptured bronze, the pavement of mottled alabaster; in short, this graceful dome, covered with scrolls of the most delicate foliage, appeared to the eye of my imagination more like a subterranean boudoir, prepared by some gallant young magician for the reception of an enchanted and enchanting princess, than a temple consecrated to the king of terrors.

'My conductor's visage growing longer and longer every minute, and looking pretty nearly as grim as that of the last-mentioned sovereign, I whispered Roxas it was full time to take our leave; which we did immediately after my intimating that express desire, to the no small satisfaction, I am perfectly convinced, of my lord the prior.

'Cold and hungry, for we had not been offered a morsel of refreshment, we repaired to a warm opulent-looking habitation belonging to one of my kind companion's most particular friends, a much favoured attendant of his catholic Majesty's; here we were received with open arms and generous hospitality; and it grew pitch dark before we quitted this comfortable shelter from the piercing winds, which blow almost perpetually over the Escurial, and returned to Madrid.' 9

Little more than a hundred years earlier, Sir Richard Fanshawe, on his appointment as Ambassador to the Court of Spain, had also entered Madrid, travelling in state. His wife Anne, to whose charming, sometimes ingenuous, yet often deeply touching memoirs we are indebted for a remarkable picture of life in the seventeenth century, describes Sir Richard's triumphant progress:

'On Wednesday, the 18th of June, my husband had his audience of his Catholic Majesty; who sent the Marquis de Malpica to conduct him, and brought with him a horse of his Majesty's for my husband to ride on, and thirty more for his gentlemen, and his Majesty's coach with the guard that he was captain of . . .

'About eleven o'clock set forth out of his lodgings my husband thus: first went all those gentlemen of the town and palace that came to accompany him, then went twenty footmen all in new liveries of the same colour that we used to give, which is a dark green cloth with a frost upon green lace, then went my husband's gentlemen, and next before himself his cameradoes two and two:

Mr Wycherley and Mr Lorim,
Mr Godolphin,   Sir Edward Turner,
Sir Andrew King,   Sir Benjamin Wright,
Mr Newport and Mr Bertie.

Then my husband, in a very rich suite of clothes of a dark fillemonte brocade laced with silver and gold lace, nine laces, every one as broad as my hand, and a little silver and gold lace laid between them, both of very curious workmanship; his suit was trimmed with scarlet taffety ribbon; his stockings of white silk upon long scarlet ones; his shoes black, with scarlet shoe-strings and garters; his linen very fine, laced with very rich Flanders lace; a black beaver, buttoned on the left side, with a jewel of twelve hundred pounds value. A rich curious wrought gold chain, made in the Indies, at which hung the King his Majesty's picture, richly set with diamonds, cost £300. which his Majesty, in great grace and favour, had been pleased to give him at his coming home from Portugal. On his fingers he wore two rich rings; his gloves trimmed with the same ribbon as his clothes. All his whole family were very richly clothed, according to their several qualities. Upon my husband's left rode the Marquis of Malpica, Captain of the German guard, and the Major-domo to his Majesty, being that week in waiting: by him went all the German guard, and by them my husband's eight pages, clothed all in velvet, the same colour as our liveries; next them followed his Catholic Majesty's coach, and my husband's coach of state, with four black horses, the finest that ever came out of England, none going in the Court [sic] but the King himself. The coach was of rich crimson velvet, laced with a broad silver and gold lace, fringed round with a massy silver and gold fringe, and the falls of the boot so rich that they hung almost down to the ground: the very fringe cost almost four hundred pounds. The coach was very richly gilt on the outside, and very richly adorned with brass work, with rich tassels of gold and silver, hanging round the top of the curtains round about the coach. The curtains were of rich damask, fringed with silver and gold; the harness for six horses was richly embossed with brass work; the reins and tassels for the horses of crimson silk, silver and gold. This coach is said to be the finest that ever entered Madrid with any Ambassador whatsoever. Next to this followed the French Ambassador's coach, then my husband's second coach, which was of green figured velvet, with green damask curtains, handsomely gilt, adorned on the outside, with harness for six horses, suitable to the same . . .

'Thus they rode through the greatest streets of Madrid . . .' [10]

A few years earlier, in May 1660, Sir Richard, who had supported the King's cause and was imprisoned for doing so, had been sent for by Charles to accompany him on his return from France to England.

'Upon the King's restoration, the Duke of York, then made Admiral, appointed ships to carry over the company and servants of the King, who were very great. His Highness appointed for my husband and his family a third-rate frigate, called the Speedwell; but his Majesty commanded my husband to wait on him in his own ship. We had by the States' order sent on board to the King's most eminent servants, great store of provisions: for our family, we had sent on board the Speedwell, a tierce of claret, a hogshead of Rhenish wine, six dozen of fowls, a dozen of gammons of bacon, a great basket of bread, and six sheep, two dozen of neat's tongues, and a great box of sweetmeats . . . we went on board upon the 23rd of May, about two o'clock in the afternoon. The King embarked at four of the clock, upon which we set sail, the shore being covered with people, and shouts from all places of a good voyage, which was seconded with many volleys of shot interchanged: so favourable was the wind, that the ships' wherries went from ship to ship to visit their friends all night long. But who can sufficiently express the joy and gallantry of that voyage, to see so many great ships, the best in the world, to hear the trumpets and all other music, to see near a hundred brave ships sail before the wind with the vast cloths and streamers, the neatness and cleanness of the ships, the strength and jollity of the mariners, the gallantry of the commanders, the vast plenty of all sorts of provisions; but above all the glorious Majesties of the King and his two brothers, were so beyond man's expectation and expression.' [11]

Anne Fanshawe's *Memoirs* would be among my favourite bedside books if I had such a collection, but the trouble about bedside books is where to keep them. If I were to put beside my bed all those that I constantly enjoy dipping into, not even the great bed of Ware, that commodious and uncomfortable relic, would be large enough for the purpose. I have never actually got as far as making a list of the books that I should like to keep beside me, but I know that along with Anne Fanshawe's *Memoirs* I should put the Diary of a very different sort of woman, Fanny Burney. In spite of her egoism, her hypochondria, and her attitude of long-suffering—and one way or another she had a good deal to put up with—her *Diary* is as entertaining, and in its way quite as acute, as any kept by some of her more gifted and better-informed contemporaries. For five years she lived at Court as Assistant Keeper of the Robes to Queen Charlotte. It was during this period, in 1788, that the King began to show signs of madness. In what seems to have been one of his spells of mental twilight there occurred the incident, both alarming and pathetic, that Fanny here relates:

'What an adventure had I this morning! One that has occasioned me the severest personal terror I ever experienced in my life.

'Sir Lucas Pepys persisting that exercise and air were absolutely necessary to save me from illness, I have continued my walks, varying my gardens from Richmond to Kew, according to the accounts I received of the movements of the King . . .

'This morning, when I received my intelligence of the King from Dr John Willis, I begged to know where I might walk in safety. "In Kew Gardens," he said, "as the King would be in Richmond".

'"Should any unfortunate circumstance," I cried, "at any time, occasion my being seen by his Majesty, do not mention my name, but let me run off without call or notice". This he promised . . .

'Taking, therefore, the time I had most at command, I strolled into the gardens. I had proceeded, in my quick way, nearly half the round, when I suddenly perceived, through some trees, two or three figures. Relying on the instructions of Dr John, I concluded them to be workmen and gardeners; yet tried to look sharp and in so doing, as they were less shaded, I thought I saw the person of his Majesty!

'Alarmed past all possible expression, I waited not to know more, but turning back, ran off with all my might. But what was my terror to hear myself pursued!—to hear the voice of the King himself loudly and hoarsely calling after me: "Miss Burney! Miss Burney!"

'I protest I was ready to die. I knew not in what state he might be at the time; I only knew the orders to keep out of his way were universal; that the Queen would highly disapprove of any unauthorized meeting, and that the very action of my running away might deeply, in his present irritable state, offend him. Nevertheless, on I ran, too terrified to stop . . .

'The steps still pursued me, and still the poor hoarse and altered voice rang in my ears—more and more footsteps resounded frightfully behind me—the attendants all running, to catch their eager master, and the voices of the two Doctor Willises loudly exhorting him not to heat himself so unmercifully . . .

'Soon after, I heard other voices, shriller, though less nervous, call out: "Stop! stop! stop!"

'I could by no means consent; I knew not what was purposed, but I recollected fully my agreement with Dr John that very morning, that I should decamp if surprised, and not be named . . .

'On I flew; and such was my speed, so almost incredible to relate or recollect, that I fairly believe no one in the whole party could have overtaken me, if these words, from one of the attendants, had not reached me: "Doctor Willis begs you to stop!"

'"I cannot! I cannot!" I answered, still flying on, when he called out: "You must, ma'am; it hurts the King to run."

'Then, indeed, I stopped—in a state of fear really amounting to agony. I turned round, I saw the two Doctors had got the King between them, and three attendants of Dr Willis's were hovering about. They all slackened their pace, as they saw me stand still; but such was the excess of my alarm, that I was wholly insensible to the effects of a race which, at any other time, would have required an hour's recruit.

'As they approached, some little presence of mind happily came to my command: it occurred to me that, to appease the wrath of my flight, I must now show some confidence: I therefore faced them as undauntedly as I was able, only charging the nearest of the attendants to stand by my side.

'When they were within a few yards of me, the King called out: "Why did you run away?"

'Shocked at a question impossible to answer, yet a little assured by the mild tone of his voice, I instantly forced myself forward, to meet him, though the internal sensation, which satisfied me this was a step the most proper to appease his suspicions and displeasure, was so violently combated by the tremor of my nerves, that I fairly think I may reckon it the greatest effort of personal courage I have ever made.

'The effort answered: I looked up, and met all his wonted benignity of countenance, though something still of wildness in his eyes. Think, however, of my surprise, to feel him put both his hands round my two shoulders and then kiss my cheek!

'I wonder I did not really sink, so exquisite was my affright when I saw him spread out his arms! Involuntarily, I concluded he meant to crush me: but the Willises, who have never seen him till this fatal illness, not knowing how very extraordinary an action this was from him, simply smiled and looked pleased, supposing, perhaps, it was his customary salutation!

'He now spoke in such terms of his pleasure in seeing me, that I soon lost the whole of my terror; astonishment to find him so nearly well, and gratification to see him so pleased, removed every uneasy feeling, and the joy that succeeded, in my conviction of his recovery, made me ready to throw myself at his feet to express it.

'What a conversation followed! When he saw me fearless, he grew more and more alive, and made me walk close by his side, away from the attendants, and even the Willises, themselves, who, to indulge him, retreated. I own myself not completely composed, but alarm I could entertain no more.

'Everything that came uppermost in his mind he mentioned; he seemed to have just such remains of his flightiness as heated his imagination without deranging his reason, and robbed him of all control over his speech, though nearly in his perfect state of mind as to his opinions.

'What did he not say! He opened his whole heart to me—expounded all his sentiments, and acquainted me with all his intentions.

'He assured me he was quite well—as well as he had ever been in his life; and then inquired how I did, and how I went on? and whether I was more comfortable?

'If these questions, in their implication, surprised me, imagine how that surprise must increase when he proceeded to explain them! He asked after the coadjutrix [the Queen], laughing, and saying: "Never mind her—don't be oppressed—I am your friend! Don't let her cast you down! I know you have a hard time of it—but don't mind her!" . .

and putting his hand on his breast, in the most solemn manner, he gravely and slowly said: "I will protect you!—I promise you that—and therefore depend upon me!"

'I thanked him; and the Willises, thinking him rather too elevated, came to propose my walking on. "No, no, no!" he cried, a hundred times in a breath; and their good humour prevailed, and they let him again walk on with his new companion . . .

'Then he asked me some questions that very greatly distressed me, relating to information given him in his illness, from various motives, but which he suspected to be false, and which I knew he had reason to suspect: yet was it most dangerous to set anything right, as I was not aware what might be the views of their having been stated wrong. I was as discreet as I knew how to be, and I hope I did no mischief; but this was the worst part of the dialogue.

'He next talked to me a great deal of my dear father, and made a thousand inquiries concerning his *History of Music*. This brought him to his favourite theme, Handel . . .

'Then he ran over most of his oratorios, attempting to sing the subjects of several airs and choruses, but so dreadfully hoarse that the sound was terrible.

"Dr Willis, quite alarmed at this exertion, feared he would do himself harm, and again proposed a separation. "No! no! no!" he exclaimed, "not yet; I have something I must just mention first."

'Dr Willis, delighted to comply, even when uneasy at compliance, again gave way.

'The good King then greatly affected me. He began upon my revered old friend, Mrs Delany; and he spoke of her with such warmth—such kindness! "She was my friend!" he cried, "and I loved her as a friend! I have made a memorandum when I lost her—I will show it you."

'He pulled out a pocket-book, and rummaged some time, but to no purpose.

The tears stood in his eyes—he wiped them, and Dr Willis again became very anxious. "Come, sir," he cried, "now do you come in and let the lady go on her walk—come, now, you have talked a long while—so we'll go in—if your Majesty pleases."

'"No, no!" he cried, "I want to ask her a few questions; I have lived so long out of the world, I know nothing!"

'He then told me he was very much dissatisfied with several of his state officers, and meant to form an entire new establishment. He took a paper out of his pocket-book, and showed me his new list.

'This was the wildest thing that passed; and Dr John Willis now seriously urged our separating; but he would not consent; he had only three more words to say, he declared, and again he conquered.

'He now spoke of my father, with still more kindness, and told me he ought to have had the post of Master of the Band, and not that little poor musician Parsons, who was not fit for it: "But Lord Salisbury," he cried, "used your father very ill in that business, and so he did me! However, I have dashed out his name, and I shall put your father's in—as soon as I get loose again!"

'This again—how affecting was this!

'"And what," cried he, "has your father got, at last? Nothing but that poor thing at Chelsea? O, fie! fie! fie! But never mind! I will take care of him! I will do it myself."

'Then presently he added: "As to Lord Salisbury, he is out already, as this memorandum will show you, and so are many more. I shall be much better served; and when once I get away, I shall rule with a rod of iron!"

'This was very unlike himself, and startled the two good doctors, who could not bear to cross him, and were exulting at my seeing his great amendment, but yet grew quite uneasy at his earnestness and volubility.

'Finding we must now part, he stopped to take leave, and renewed again his charges about the coadjutrix. "Never mind her!" he cried, "depend upon me! I will be your friend as long as I live!—I here pledge myself to be your friend!" And then he saluted me again just as at the meeting, and suffered me to go on.' [12]

Part of youth's pathos lies in its acute susceptibility to embarrassment, and Roger Lowe's discomfort in the predicaments with which life seemed systematically to face him arouse one's sympathy as much as one's amusement. Lowe was a mercer's apprentice in the small Lancashire town of Ashton-in-Makerfield, and he had the unusual accomplishment for a poor youth in the seventeenth century of being able to read and write, and for several years he kept a diary. He was much troubled by problems of morality and by his own conscience, and seemed perpetually to be stumbling into situations which, though miserably embarrassing to him, might well have struck a young man of happier disposition as something to laugh at. Such was his encounter with an obstinate ram: On 'Tusday,' says Lowe, 'I sat in shop all day. Onely I went up Greene to old parson Lee's and John Haselden and Thomas Rosbothom and we alltogether jesting. Thomas Rosbothom and John Haselden attempted with either of them a good kibbow [cudgel] to suprize poor parson and I in parson's shop, but we defended our selves awhile, but in Conclusion I was glad to creepe up into a loft to secure my selfe, but was taken att last and sufferd efliction. I made them to laugh in telling them how once I was hurried with a Tupp [ram] in a Rope, who comeing towards Leigh with Tupp in fielde, the Tupp sett upon poor Hodge and so geper knowd [?] me that in the conclusion I cryd out. But none heard me, and I, being onecqueinted how to act with tuppe in Rope, let hime have the length of rope, and tuppe rann all wayes backewards and fell one me, so that I was put in a terrible fright what to doe to save my shinnes. I was almost in a . . . [?] condition. I layd me down with my head opon my leggs, and he gave me such a patt on the head [as] made me turne up white eyes. I thought and was halfe efraid lest I had gotten old Nicke on the Rope. I prayed to God to deliver me from the tuppe and Rope, but in the conclusion my bones ware sore, braines sicke, and heart dead with feare what to do with tupp. I looked at tupp with an angry countenance, but could not tell how to be revenged. Kill hime I durst not—then I should have had the labour to have caryd hime, which I could not. Faire words would not pacifie hime nor angry countenances efright hime, but att last I resolved upon a manly resolution thus: "What, Hodge, art in a streite? What's the reason of thes feare and greege? A tupp. A tupp? does that daunt thee? Stand upon they leggs and fight manfully in answer ther unto!" I did, and gat a kibbow out of the hedge, and tupp and I fell to it, but the tupp orecame me. I could do no good, but downe on my knees againe. I get hold of tupps hornes and of one of his feet, and cast hime. "So now, tupp, I intend to be revenged on thee," and smote him on the head. But with great difficultie I gat hime to Leigh, but nere was in such a puzle in all my life as I was with that tupp.' [13]

At least there was no one to witness this rather undignified encounter, unlike one that occurred between an alderman and his horse when Queen Victoria drove in state to the City of London in the year of her accession:

'At Temple Bar the procession was joined by the Lord Mayor, aldermen, Common Councilmen and other civic authorities, who, while awaiting the Queen's arrival had been afforded accommodation in the old banking house of Child & Co.; their steeds, which had been borrowed from the artillery barracks at Woolwich, were stationed in Middle Temple Lane. The soldier to which each horse belonged attended as squire, holding the bridle rein of each equestrian alderman. A contemporary account says—"How the respected fathers of the City performed the exploit of mounting is perhaps not exactly matter of history. However, with much care and pains bestowed by the troopers, their assistant squires, they were at last placed on horseback and formed into procession. We believe only one fell off, and that accident happened through a laudable desire to perform an obeisance to a fair lady at a window. The worthy alderman fell flat upon the ground, and his horse walked over him. Since the days of John Gilpin no feat of a citizen of London on horseback has excited so much masculine laughter and feminine sympathy.

"Several brother aldermen rushed to the assistance of the fallen cavalier, who was hoisted into his saddle amidst general cheers and laughter".' [14]

The Queen's accession took place in 1837, three years before the birth of a writer who was to become one of the most famous and at the same time most contentious novelists of her reign, and whom I regard, in spite of what seems like his temporary eclipse, as one of the greatest of all English novelists—Thomas Hardy. Except for the assertion that there is 'almost no passion' in Hardy's work, I would recommend Lascelles Abercrombie's analysis of it in the *Encyclopaedia Britannica* to anyone who feels himself daunted by Hardy's now remote and almost monolithic reputation. Professor Abercrombie, while preserving the detachment proper to a critic, still manages to suggest that if one is unfamiliar with Hardy, the first plunge into his novels will come as a literary adventure. In almost any of them one can choose a passage at random and be pretty sure to find in it something to appeal to one's interest or sentiment. Both the romanticist in me and the man of action (admittedly a dwarf), as well as the botanist and the Pre-Raphaelite, respond to the account of Sergeant Troy showing off to Bathsheba in *Far From the Madding Crowd*. They had met in secret on a summer's evening in a pit hidden by ferns on the common near Bathsheba's house. Troy had promised to give her a display of sword drill:

'At eight o'clock this midsummer evening, whilst the bristling ball of gold in the west still swept the tips of the ferns with its long, luxuriant rays, a soft brushing-by of garments might have been heard among them, and Bathsheba appeared in their midst, their soft, feathery arms caressing her up to her shoulders . . .

'She reached the verge in the middle of the ferns. Troy stood on the bottom, looking up towards her.

'"I heard you rustling through the fern before I saw you," he said, coming up and giving her his hand to help her down the slope.

'The pit was a saucer-shaped concave, naturally formed, with a diameter of about thirty feet, and shallow enough to allow the sunshine to reach their heads. Standing in the centre, the sky overhead was met by a circular horizon of fern: this grew nearly to the bottom of the slope and then abruptly ceased. The middle within the belt of verdure was floored with a thick flossy carpet of moss and grass intermingled, so yielding that the foot was half-buried in it.

'"Now," said Troy, producing the sword, which, as he raised it into the sunlight, gleamed a sort of greeting, like a living thing, "first we have four right and four left cuts. Infantry cuts and guards are more interesting than ours, to my mind; but they are not so swashing . . . Now I'll let you see some loose play, giving all the cuts and points, cavalry and infantry, quicker than lightning . . . You are my antagonist, with this difference from real warfare, that I shall miss you every time by one hair's breadth, or perhaps two. Mind you don't flinch, whatever you do . . ."

'He flourished the sword by way of introduction number two, and the next thing of which she was conscious was that the point and blade of the sword were darting with a gleam towards her left side, just above her hip; then of their appearance on her right side, emerging as it were from between her ribs, having apparently passed through her body. The third item of consciousness was that of seeing the same sword, perfectly clean and free from blood held vertically in Troy's hand . . .

'"Oh!" she cried out in affright, pressing her hand to her side. "Have you run me through?—no, you have not! Whatever have you done?"

'"I have not touched you," Troy said quietly . . . "Now you are not afraid, are you? Because if you are I can't perform. I give my word that I will not only not hurt you, but not once touch you . . . only stand still as a statue. Now!"

'In an instant the atmosphere was transformed to Bathsheba's eyes. Beams of light caught from the low sun's rays, above, around, in front of her, well-nigh shut out earth and heaven—all emitted in the marvellous evolutions of Troy's reflecting blade, which seemed everywhere at once, and yet nowhere specially. These circling gleams were accompanied by a keen rush that was almost a whistling—also springing from all sides of her at once. In short, she was enclosed in a firmament of light, and of sharp hisses, resembling a sky-full of meteors close at hand . . .

'Behind the luminous stream of this *aurora militaris*, she could see the hue of Troy's sword arm, spread in a scarlet haze over the space covered by its motions, like a twanged harpstring, and behind all Troy himself, mostly facing her; sometimes, to show the rear cuts, half turned away, his eye nevertheless always keenly measuring her breadth and outline, and his lips tightly closed in sustained effort. Next, his movements lapsed slower and she could see them individually. The hissing of the sword had ceased, and he stopped entirely.

'"That outer loose lock of hair wants tidying," he said, before she had moved or spoken. "Wait: I'll do it for you."

'An arc of silver shone on her right side: the sword had descended. The lock dropped to the ground . . .

'"But how could you chop off a curl of my hair with a sword that has no edge?"

'"No edge! This sword will shave like a razor. Look here."

'He touched the palm of his hand with the blade, and then, lifting it, showed her a thin shaving of scarf-skin dangling therefrom.

'"But you said before beginning that it was blunt and couldn't cut me!"

'"That was to get you to stand still . . .

'She shuddered. "I have been within an inch of my life, and didn't know it!"' [15]

To come within an inch of one's life at some moment in its course is an experience that a good many people go through, and having done so are not likely to forget it. To *live* within an inch of it indicates a fortitude or an indifference to the continuation of life that few of us possess. A professional gun-man cannot afford the anxiety or the civilizing scruples that the workings of imagination involve. That is why most professional men of violence are usually found to be men of limited intelligence. In the early twenties one of the most powerful figures in Chicago's underworld, not excepting Al Capone, was Dion O'Banion. Ostensibly he was a florist; in fact he was a bootlegger operating on a prodigious scale. He was also, at that time, the only gangster in Chicago who carried three guns—and he was ambidextrous. His suits were made with three gun pouches, 'one in the right front trousers pocket; one under the left armpit of the coat, and one in the left outside coat pocket . . . he went gunning where and when he pleased, and for reasons as quixotic as the snubbing of a friend.' [16] At noon on November 4, 1924, he was in his shop getting ready some flowers that were to be collected for the funeral of Mike Merlo, a rival gangster who through some mishap had died a natural death:

'O'Banion was in the rear of the shop, which was divided by a partition, clipping the stems of a bunch of chrysanthemums. With him was William Crutchfield, a negro porter.

'A blue Jewett sedan, headed south, stopped with engine idling, at the curb, directly opposite the entrance. It contained four men. One stayed at the wheel. Three alighted. Once in the shop they walked abreast. The man in the centre was tall, wearing a brown overcoat and a brown fedora hat. The other two were short and stocky.

'O'Banion was saying to Crutchfield, "The floor is littered with leaves and petals, Bill. Better brush them up." He heard the customers enter and went to the front of the shop.

'"Hello, boys, you from Mike Merlo's?" was his greeting. In his left hand he held his florist's shears. His right was extended.

'"Yes," replied the centre man, grasping the extended right.

'This much Crutchfield witnessed, having swept up the litter and passing the swinging door, then partly open, at that moment. The rest he heard . . .

'Six times the gun spoke—two bullets in the right breast; a third through the larynx; a fourth to the left of it a bit; a fifth in the right cheek. The five were fired within as many seconds. There was a pause before the sixth. It was the finish shot, to make certain of the job. It was fired into the left cheek as O'Banion lay sprawled among his flowers. The revolver was held so close that the skin was powder-burned.

'The centre man had held O'Banion's right in a vice-like grip while the man on his left did the shooting. The man on his right, presumably, had imprisoned O'Banion's left to prevent his drawing his emergency revolver . . . Thus was the handshake murder introduced to Chicago.'[17]

O'Banion was no doubt given as splendid a funeral as Mike Merlo, though let us hope that for the sake of the mourners it was better organized, and for the sake of the victim more decorous, than that of George II, of which Walpole sent this account to his friend George Montagu:

'I had the curiosity to go to the burying t'other night; I had never seen a royal funeral; nay, I walked as a rag of quality, which I found would be, and so it was, the easiest way of seeing it. It is absolutely a noble sight. The prince's chamber, hung with purple, and a quantity of silver lamps, the coffin under a canopy of purple velvet, and six vast chandeliers of silver on high stands, had a very good effect. The ambassador from Tripoli and his son were carried to see that chamber. The procession, through a line of foot-guards, every seventh man bearing a torch, the horse-guards lining the outside, their officers with

drawn sabres and crape sashes on horseback, the drums muffled, the
fifes, bells tolling, and minute guns,—all this was very solemn. But the
charm was the entrance of the abbey, where we were received by the
dean and chapter in rich robes, the choir and almsmen bearing torches;
the whole abbey so illuminated, that one saw it to greater advantage
than by day; the tombs, long aisles, and frettled roof, all appearing quite
distinctly, and with the happiest chiaro scuro. There wanted nothing
but incense, and little chapels here and there, with priests saying mass
for the repose of the defunct; yet one could not complain of its not
being catholic enough . . , When we came to the chapel of Henry the
Seventh, all solemnity and decorum ceased; no order was observed,
people sat or stood where they could or would; the yeomen of the
guard were crying out for help, oppressed by the immense weight of
the coffin; the bishop read sadly, and blundered in the prayers; the
fine chapter, *man that is born of woman*, was chaunted, not read; and
the anthem, besides being immeasurably tedious, would have served
as well for a nuptial. The real serious part was the figure of the Duke of
Cumberland, heightened by a thousand melancholy circumstances. He
had a dark brown adonis, and a cloak of black cloth, with a train of
five yards. Attending the funeral of a father could not be pleasant:
his leg extremely bad, yet forced to stand upon it near two hours;
his face bloated and distorted with his late paralytic stroke, which has
affected too one of his eyes, and placed over the mouth of the vault,
into which, in all probability, he must himself so soon descend; think
how unpleasant a situation! He bore it all with a firm and unaffected
countenance. This grave scene was fully contrasted by the burlesque
Duke of N—. He fell into a fit of crying the moment he came into the
chapel, and flung himself back in a stall, the archbishop hovering over
him with a smelling-bottle; but in two minutes his curiosity got the
better of his hypocrasy, and he ran about the chapel with his glass
to spy who was or was not there, spying with one hand and mopping
his eyes with the other. Then returned the fear of catching cold; and
the Duke of Cumberland, who was sinking with heat, felt himself
weighed down, and turning round, found it was the Duke of N—
standing upon his train, to avoid the chill of the marble. It was very
theatric to look down into the vault, where the coffin lay, attended by
mourners with lights.' [18]

A hundred years before this melancholy scene was enacted a very
different one took place in the Abbey when, on April 23, 1661,
Charles II was crowned. Pepys, needless to say, was on the spot:
'About four I rose and got to the Abbey, where I followed Sir J.

Denham, the Surveyor, with some company that he was leading in. And with much ado, by the favour of Mr Cooper, his man, did get up into a great scaffold across the North end of the Abbey, where with a great deal of patience I sat from past four till eleven before the King come in. And a great pleasure it was to see the Abbey raised in the middle, all covered with red, and a throne (that is a chaire) and footstoole on the top of it; and all the officers of all kinds, so much as the very fidlers, in red vests. At last comes in the Dean and Prebends of Westminster, with the Bishops, (many of them in cloth of gold copes,) and after them the Nobility, all in their Parliament robes, which was a most magnificent sight. Then the Duke, and the King with a scepter (carried by my Lord Sandwich) and sword and wand before him, and the crowne too. The King in his robes, bare-headed, which was very fine. And after all had placed themselves, there was a sermon and the service; and then in the Quire at the high altar, the King passed through all the ceremonies of the Coronacon, which to my great grief I and most in the Abbey could not see. The crowne being put upon his head, a great shout begun, and he come forth to the throne, and there passed through more ceremonies: as taking the oath, and having things read to him by the Bishopp; and his Lords (who put on their caps as soon as the King put on his crowne) and bishops come, and kneeled before him. And three times the King at Armes went to the three open spaces on the scaffold, and proclaimed, that if any one could show any reason why Charles Stewart should not be King of England, that now he should come and speak. And a General Pardon also was read by the Lord Chancellor, and meddalls flung up and down by my Lord Cornwallis, of silver, but I could not come by any. But so great a noise that I could make but little of the musique; and indeed it was lost to every body. I went out a little while before the King had done all his ceremonies, and went round the Abbey to Westminster Hall, all the way within rayles, and 10,000 people with the ground covered with blue cloth; and scaffolds all the way. Into the Hall I got, where it was very fine with hangings and scaffolds one upon another full of brave ladies; and my wife in one little one, on the right hand. Here I stayd walking up and down, and at last upon one of the side stalls I stood and saw the King come in with all the persons (but the soldiers) that were yesterday in the cavalcade; and a most pleasant sight it was to see them in their several robes. And the King come in with his crowne on, and his sceptre in his hand, under a canopy borne up by six silver staves, carried by Barons of the Cinque Ports, and little bells at every end. And after a long time, he got up to the farther end, and all set them-

selves down at their several tables; and that was also a brave sight:
and the King's first course carried up by the Knights of the Bath.
And many fine ceremonies there was of the Heralds leading up people
before him, and bowing; and my Lord of Albemarle's going to the
kitchen and eating a bit of the first dish that was to go to the King's
table. But above all, was these three Lords, Northumberland, and
Suffolke, and the Duke of Ormond, coming before the courses on
horseback, and staying so all dinner-time, and at last bringing up
(Dymock) the King's Champion, all in armour on horseback, with his
speare and targett carried before him. And a Herald proclaims "That
if any dare deny Charles Stewart to be lawful King of England, here
was a Champion that would fight;" and with these words, the Champion flings down his gauntlet, and all this he do three times in his going
up towards the King's table. To which when he is come, the King
drinks to him, and then sends him the cup which is of gold, and he
drinks it off, and then rides back again with the cup in his hand. I went
from table to table to see the Bishops and all others at their dinner, and
was infinitely pleased with it. And at the Lords' table, I met with
William Howe, and he spoke to my Lord for me, and he did give him
four rabbits and a pullet, and so Mr Creed and I got Mr Minshell to
give us some bread, and so we at a stall eat it, as every body else did
what they could get. I took a great deal of pleasure to go up and down,
and look upon the ladies, and to hear the musique of all sorts, but
above all, the 24 violins. About six at night they had dined, and I
went up to my wife. And strange it is to think, that these two days
have held up fair till now that all is done, and the King gone out of the
Hall; and then it fell a-raining and thundering and lightening as I have
not seen it do for some years: which people did take great notice of;
God's blessing of the work of these two days, which is a foolery
to take too much notice of such things. I observed little disorder in all
this, only the King's footmen had got hold of the canopy, and would
keep it from the Barons of the Cinque Ports, which they endeavoured
to force from them again, but could not do it till my Lord Duke of
Albemarle caused it to be put into Sir R. Pye's hand till tomorrow to
be decided. At Mr Bowyer's; a great deal of company, some I knew,
others I did not. Here we staid upon the leads and below till it was late,
expecting to see the fire-works, but they were not performed tonight:
only the City had a light like a glory round about it with bonfires.
At last I went to King-Streete, and there sent Crockford to my father's
and my house, to tell them that I could not come home tonight,
because of the dirt, and a coach could not be had. And so I took my

wife and Mrs Frankleyn (who I profered the civility of lying with my wife at Mrs Hunt's to-night) to Axe-yard, in which at the further end there were three great bonfires and a great many great gallants, men and women; and they laid hold of us, and would have us drink the King's health upon our knees, kneeling upon a faggot, which we all did, they drinking to us one after another. Which we thought a strange frolique; but these gallants continued there a great while; and I wondered to see how the ladies did tipple. At last I sent my wife and her bedfellow to bed, and Mr Hunt and I went in with Mr Thornbury (who did give the company all their wine, he being yeoman of the wine-cellar to the King); and there, with his wife and two of his sisters, and some gallant sparks that were there, we drank the King's health, and nothing else, till one of the gentlemen fell down stark drunk, and there lay; and I went to my Lord's pretty well. Thus did the day end with joy everywhere.' [19]

It is not often that those in close touch with affairs of state are as observant, still less as communicative, even in private, as Pepys, and generally speaking they are right to err on the side of discretion. Whatever may be said against secret diplomacy, it is pretty obvious from attempts that have been made in recent years to conduct diplomatic negotiations with the maximum of publicity, that this does not work as well as when such negotiations—involving, as sometimes they must, loss of face, opportunity or initiative, or the admission that the results of expediency may be preferable to those of sticking to a principle —when such things as these are involved, surely discussions held in private are likely to be more fruitful than when they are conducted to the accompaniment of a barrage of publicity. But it is a good thing, if sometimes chastening in its effects, that now and again a Pepys, a Greville or a Harry Hopkins is on hand to draw in the background against which the politicians are called on to perform their *coups de théâtre*, their *mariages de convenance*, or perhaps their *felo de se*. Among those who served President Lincoln, both John G. Nicolay, his secretary, and Gideon Welles, Secretary of the Navy in his last administration, kept confidential diaries in which they recorded their observation of events that have gone to the making of American history, of which none was perhaps more significant for the future than Lincoln's murder by the actor, John Wilkes Booth:

'It was only about noon . . . that Booth learned that the President was to go to Ford's Theatre that night to see the play *Our American Cousin* . . . Booth was perfectly at home in Ford's Theatre. Either by himself, or with the aid of friends, he arranged his whole plan of attack and escape during the afternoon. He counted upon address and audacity to gain access to the small passage behind the President's box . . .

'A few minutes before ten o'clock, leaving his horse at the rear of the theatre in charge of a call-boy, he went into a neighbouring saloon, took a drink of brandy, and, entering the theatre, passed rapidly to the little hallway leading to the President's box. Showing a card to the servant in attendance, he was allowed to enter, closed the door noiselessly, and secured it with the wooden bar he had previously made ready without disturbing any of the occupants of the box . . . Holding a pistol in one hand and a knife in the other, he opened the box door, put the pistol to the President's head, and fired. Major Rathbone sprang to grapple with him, and received a savage knife wound in the arm. Then, rushing forward, Booth placed his hand on the railing of the box and vaulted to the stage. It was a high leap, but nothing to such an athlete. He would have got safely away but for his spur catching in the flag that draped the front of the box. He fell, the torn flag trailing on his spur; but, though the fall had broken his leg, he rose instantly, and brandishing the knife and shouting, "*Sic semper tyrannis!*" fled rapidly across the stage and out of sight. Major Rathbone called, "Stop him!" The cry rang out, "He has shot the President!" and from the audience, stupid at first with surprise, and wild afterward with excitement and horror, two or three men jumped upon the stage in pursuit of the assassin. But he ran through the familiar passages, leaped upon his horse, rewarding with a kick and a curse the boy who held him, and escaped into the night.

'The President scarcely moved; his head drooped forward slightly, his eyes closed. Major Rathbone, not regarding his own grievous hurt, rushed to the door of the box to summon aid. He found it barred, and someone on the outside beating and clamouring for admittance. It was at once seen that the President's wound was mortal. A large derringer bullet had entered the back of the head, on the left side, and, passing through the brain, lodged just behind the left eye. He was carried to a house across the street and laid upon a bed in a small room at the rear of the hall on the ground floor.' [20]

Gideon Welles was called from his bed and went to the house, where he found the President 'extended diagonally across the bed, which was not long enough for him. He had been stripped of his clothes. His large arms, which were occasionally exposed, were of a size which one would scarce have expected from his spare appearance. His slow, full respiration lifted the clothes with each breath that he took. His features were calm and striking. I had never seen them appear to better advantage than for the first hour, perhaps, that I was there. After that his right eye began to swell and that part of his face became discoloured.

'. . . a double guard was stationed at the door and on the sidewalk to repress the crowd, which was of course highly excited and anxious. The room was small and overcrowded. The surgeons and members of the Cabinet were as many as should have been in the room, but there were many more, and the hall and the other rooms in the front or main house were full . . .

'A door which opened upon a porch or gallery, and also all the windows, were kept open for fresh air. The night was dark, cloudy, and damp and about six it began to rain. I remained in the room until then without sitting or leaving it, when, there being a vacant chair which someone left at the foot of the bed, I occupied it for nearly two hours, listening to the heavy groans, and witnessing the wasting life of the good and great man who was expiring before me.

'About 6 a.m. I experienced a feeling of faintness and for the first time after entering the room, a little past eleven, I left it and the house, and took a short walk in the open air. It was a dark and gloomy morning, and rain set in before I returned to the house, some fifteen minutes later. Large groups of people were gathered every few rods, all anxious and solicitous. Some one or more from each group stepped forward as I passed, to inquire into the condition of the President, and to ask if there was no hope. Intense grief was on every countenance when I replied that the President could survive but a short time. The coloured people especially—and there were at this time more of them, perhaps, than of whites—were overwhelmed with grief.

'Returning to the house, I seated myself in the back parlour, where the Attorney General and others had been engaged in taking evidence concerning the assassination . . .

'A little before seven, I went into the room where the dying President was rapidly drawing near the closing moments. His wife soon after made her last visit to him. The death-struggle had begun. Robert, his son, stood with several others at the head of the bed. He bore himself well, but on two occasions gave way to overpowering grief and sobbed aloud, turning his head and leaning on the shoulder of Senator Sumner. The respiration of the President became suspended at intervals, and at last entirely ceased at twenty-two minutes past seven.'[21]

At what point in the continual inheritance of knowledge does reason overtake sentiment? When the honour that we still do to

Lincoln's memory becomes submerged, as it must, in indifference to his death, as we are now indifferent to the murder of Caesar, it will be possible to regard it in a manner as free from the passions aroused by principle and by a sense of outrage, as the manner in which we regard the presence of an Egyptian mummy. That the object in front of us was once a creature of flesh and blood, of warmth and feeling, perhaps of beauty and intelligence, is something that we realize yet cannot fully comprehend. Death and transfiguration are but two phases of the same process—that of time's effect upon the body which, from the moment of death, lessens the intensity with which we have loved or hated. Not even the over-exquisite sensibilities of the Goncourts extended beyond polite 'dejection'—and even that, I suspect, was a euphemism for 'distaste'—at the sight of a corpse two thousand years old:

'We are in a vast room . . . The sunlight filters in through the lacelike design of the Arabic shutters at the windows and falls in luminous rose patterns upon the mummy boxes and sarcophagi. Each of them has tacked to it a bit of paper bearing the Egyptian name of its inhabitant and the geneological line. All about us, on plain wooden shelves, are dried heads, skulls tied with bits of rag and of every colour, some green with the patina of bronze, others oozing bitumen and naphtha in the sunlight; still others black and stuck over with little squares of gold leaf, and yet others with the beautiful ivory pallor of old bones, and great hollows of shadow in the empty eye sockets. In the heap, amidst all these receding foreheads, a brow swollen with thought and wisdom, a nobly Socratic head, and beside it a fleshless skull of a woman whom one imagines to have been beautiful, covered with a luxuriant mass of hair, reddened and carmined as is the hair of the others, a great braid, half crumbling, blinding her eyes.

'Thrown crosswise on a table is the mummy about to be *debanded*. All round the table stand frock coats with decorations in their button-holes. Soon begins the interminable unwinding of the cloth in which this stiff package is swaddled. This is a woman who was once alive —two thousand four hundred years ago—and the redoubtable and distant past of a being upon whose form we are about to gaze, and whose infinite slumber we, in our curiosity about history, are about to violate, seems to put the whole roomful of people, and their avidity to see what is before them, into a kind of religious state.

'They unwind, unwind, and still unwind, with no apparent diminution in the size of the package and no feeling, as it were, of approaching the body. The band seems to grow as they work and to threaten never to come to an end, while the attendants continue their interminable unwinding. At one moment, in order to get along faster and to hasten the stripping of the creature, the mummy is set up on its feet, which knock as if at the end of a pair of wooden legs, and the thing begins to twirl and gyrate and waltz horribly, in the hurrying arms of the attendants: the package stands up, Death in a bundle.

'The thing is laid down again and the unwinding continues. The yards and yards of cloth pile up, rise mountain high, cover the table with the charming rusted-saffron tone of this never-bleached stuff, and strange smells begin to rise, warm and spicy emanations of funereal myrrh and aromatics—the odours of black voluptuousness of the bed of the antique corpse.

'At last, with this persistent unwinding, a vaguely human outline begins to be discernible. "Berthelot! Robin! Look here!" cries Mariette; and with the help of a knife he digs out of the armpit something that is passed round and seems to be a flower with a pleasant odour; a little bouquet planted by Egypt in the moist armpit of its dead.

'The last of the band has been unwound, the cloth is at its end, and here is a bit of flesh—black! A fact almost astonishing, so far had one been on the way to expect that beneath a band so well preserved there must live a corpse guarded through eternity in its original state. Du Camp rushed forward with a sort of frantic nervousness as the neck and head were unwound. Suddenly, in the blackness of the bitumen coagulated at the base of the throat, there gleamed a little gold. "A necklace!" someone exclaimed. And with a chisel, digging into the stony flesh, Du Camp brought up a small gold plaque bearing an inscription written with a *calamus*, a reed, and cut out in the shape of a sparrowhawk. Thereafter a little Horus and a large green scarab were detached. Mariette, who took charge of the bit of gold, said that it bore a prayer by this woman for the coming together of her heart and entrails with her body on the Day of Eternity.

'Feverishly, pincers and knives went down the length of this desiccated corpse, which gave off the sound of paste-board, denuding the deformed, sexless chest and belly whose blackened surface was furrowed with red clots of dried blood. They stripped the arms that were stuck to the torso, and the hands which, in a gesture of stiffened modesty—the very gesture of the Medici Venus—were lowered over the pubis with the gilded nails of their fingers.

'A last band stripped away from the face disclosed suddenly an enamel eye in which the pupil had run over into the white, an eye at once alive and sick, so that it was frightening. Then the nose appeared, flattened, broken and clogged by the embalmer, and the smile of a gold leaf appeared on the lips of the tiny head on which were ravellings of short hair that seemed still to bear the moisture and sweat of the hour of death.

'There she was this woman who had once been alive—two thousand four hundred years ago—there she was, lying in full view on a table, stricken and outraged by the light of day, all her modesty bared to the sun and the glances of men. We stood about chatting, laughing, smoking. The poor profaned corpse, so well veiled and buried, once so secure in the promise of repose and of a secret and eternal inviolability, which the hazard of archaeology had flung here like a pauper's corpse on a dissecting table—there it lay, and not a soul, except the two of us, feeling the slightest dejection about it!' [22]

There is to my mind a nightmarish quality about this episode. It induces something of that sense of revulsion that you might expect in a story by Le Fanu or Ambrose Bierce, a revulsion from inchoate forces, from the eyes of antiquity slowly lifting their lids and staring back at one through the mists of two thousand years. This is the stuff of an opium-eater's dream, although, as de Quincey tells us, such impressions are far from being the most alarming that the diet induces:

'The opium-eater loses none of his moral sensibilities or aspirations; he wishes and longs as earnestly as ever to realize what he believes possible, and feels to be exacted by duty; but his intellectual apprehension of what is possible infinitely outruns his power, not of execution only, but even of proposing or willing. He lies under a world's weight of incubus and nightmare; he lies in sight of all that he would fain perform, just as a man forceably confined to his bed by the mortal languour of paralysis, who is compelled to witness injury or outrage offered to some object of his tenderest love;—he would lay down his life if he might but rise and walk; but he is powerless as an infant, and cannot so much as make an effort to move . . .

'My dreams were accompanied by deep-seated anxiety and funereal melancholy, such as are wholly incommunicable by words . . . the sense of space, and in the end the sense of time, were both powerfully affected. Buildings, landscapes, etc., were exhibited in proportions so vast as the bodily eye is not fitted to receive. Space swelled and was amplified to an extent of unutterable and self-repeating infinity. This disturbed me very much less than the vast expansion of time. Sometimes I seemed to have lived for seventy or a hundred years in one night; nay, sometimes had feelings representative of a duration far beyond the limits of any human experience . . .

'Many years ago, when I was looking over Piranesi's *Antiquities of Rome*, Coleridge, then standing by, described to me a set of plates from that artist, called his "Dreams", and which recorded the scenery of his own visions during the delirium of a fever. Some of these (I describe only from memory of Coleridge's account) represented vast Gothic halls; on the floor of which stood mighty engines and machinery, wheels, cables, catapults, etc., expressive of enormous power put forth or resistance overcome. Creeping along the sides of the walls, you perceived a staircase; and upon this, groping his way upwards, was Piranesi himself. Follow the stairs a little farther, and you perceive them reaching an abrupt termination, without any balustrade and allowing no onwards to him who should reach the extremity, except into the depths below. Whatever is to become of poor Piranesi, at least you suppose that his labours must now in some way terminate. But raise your eyes, and behold a second flight of stairs still higher, on which again Piranesi is perceived, by this time standing on the very brink of the abyss. Once again elevate your eye, and a still more aerial flight of stairs is descried; and there again is the delirious Piranesi, busy on his aspiring labours: and so on, until the unfinished stairs and the hopeless Piranesi both are lost in the upper gloom of the hall. With the same power of growth and endless reproduction did my architecture proceed in dreams. In the early stage of the malady, the splendours of my dreams were indeed chiefly architectural; and I beheld such pomp of cities and palaces as never yet was beheld by the waking eye, unless in the clouds. From a great modern poet I cite the part of a passage which describes, as an appearance actually beheld in the clouds, what in many of its circumstances I saw frequently in sleep:[23]

> "*The appearance instantaneously disclosed,*
> *Was of a mighty city—boldly say*
> *A wilderness of building, sinking far*
> *And self-withdrawn into a wondrous depth,*
> *Far sinking into splendour without end!*
> *Fabric it seemed of diamond and gold,*
> *With alabaster domes and silver spires,*
> *And blazing terrace upon terrace, high*
> *Uplifted; here, serene pavilions bright,*
> *In avenues disposed; there, towers begirt*
> *With battlements that on their restless fronts*
> *Bore stars—illumination of all gems!*

By earthly nature had the effect been wrought
Upon the dark materials of the storm
Nor pacified; on them, and on the coves,
And mountain-steeps and summits whereunto
The vapours had receded, taking there
Their stations under a cerulean sky." [24]

' ... To my architecture succeeded dreams of lakes and silvery expanses of water: these haunted me so much that I feared lest some dropsical state or tendency of the brain might thus be making itself (to use a metaphysical word) *objective*, and that the sentient organ might be projecting itself as its own object ... The waters gradually changed their character—from translucent lakes, shining like mirrors, they became seas and oceans. And now came a tremendous change, which, unfolding itself slowly like a scroll, through many months, promised an abiding torment; and, in fact, it never left me, though recurring more or less intermittingly. Hitherto the human face had often mixed in my dreams, but not despotically, nor with any special power of tormenting. But now that affection which I have called the tyranny of the human face began to unfold itself ... now it was that upon the rocking waters of the ocean the human face began to reveal itself; the sea appeared paved with innumerable faces, upturned to the heavens; faces, imploring, wrathful, despairing; faces that surged upwards by thousands, by myriads, by generations: infinite was my agitation; my mind tossed, as it seemed, upon the billowy ocean, and weltered upon the weltering waves.

'The Malay has been a fearful enemy for months. Every night, through my dreams, I have been transported into Asiatic scenery. I know not whether others share in my feelings on this point; but I have often thought that if I were compelled to forego England, and to live in China, among Chinese manners and modes of life and scenery, I should go mad. The causes of my horror lie deep, and some of them must be common to others. Southern Asia, in general, is the seat of awful images and associations ... Man is a weed in those regions. The vast empires, also, into which the enormous population of Asia has always been cast, give a further sublimity to the feelings associated with all Oriental names or images. In China, over and above what it has in common with the rest of Southern Asia, I am terrified by the modes of life, by the manners, by the utter abhorrence placed between myself and *them*, ... I could sooner live with lunatics, with vermin, with crocodiles or snakes. All this, and much more than I can say, the reader must enter into before he can comprehend the unimaginable horror which these dreams of Oriental imagery and mythological tortures impressed upon me. Under the connecting feeling of tropical heat and vertical sunlights, I brought together all creatures, birds, beasts, reptiles, all trees and plants, usages and appearances, that are found in all tropical regions, and assembled them together in China or Hindostan. From kindred feelings, I soon brought Egypt and her gods under the same law. I was stared at, hooted at, grinned at, chattered at, by monkeys, by paroquets, by cockatoos. I ran into pagodas, and was fixed for centuries at the summit, or in secret rooms; I was the idol; I was the priest; I was worshipped; I was sacrificed. I fled from the wrath of Brama through all the forests of Asia; Vishnu hated me; Seeva lay in wait for me. I came suddenly upon Isis and Osiris; I had done a deed, they said, which the ibis and the crocodile trembled at. Thousands of years I lived and was buried in stone coffins, with mummies and sphynxes, in narrow chambers at the heart of eternal pyramids. I was kissed, with cancerous kisses, by crocodiles, and was laid, surrounded with all unutterable abortions, amongst reeds and Nilotic mud . . .

'Over every form, and threat, and punishment, and dim sightless incarceration, brooded a killing sense of eternity and infinity. Into these dreams only it was, with one or two slight exceptions, that any circumstances of physical horror entered. All before had been moral and spiritual terrors. But here the main agents were ugly birds, or snakes, or crocodiles, especially the last. The cursed crocodile became to me the object of more horror than all the rest. I was compelled to live with him; and as was always the case in my dreams, for centuries. Sometimes I escaped and found myself in Chinese houses. All the feet of the tables, sofas, etc., soon became instinct with life; the abominable head of the crocodile, and his leering eyes, looked out at me, multiplied into ten thousand repetitions; and I stood loathing and fascinated. So often did this hideous reptile haunt my dreams that many times the very same dream was broken up in the very same way: I heard gentle voices speaking to me (I hear everything when I am sleeping) and instantly I awoke; it was broad noon, and my children were standing, hand in hand, at my bedside, come to show me their coloured shoes, or new frocks, or to let me see them dressed for going out. No experience was so awful to me, and at the same time so pathetic, as this abrupt translation from the darkness of the infinite to the gaudy summer air of the highest noon, and from the unutterable abortions of miscreated gigantic vermin to the sight of infancy and innocent *human* natures.'[25]

De Quincey's Autobiography is one of those indispensable experiences in reading, some of which nevertheless do not prove as rewarding as others generally considered less worthy—I much prefer Binstead, for instance, to Rabelais—that I came upon rather late in life. It was during the war and as an antidote to the news nothing could have acted better. Not that the news just then—it was in 1942—was bad; but still it was war news and the horrors of De Quincey's imagination came as a relief from the horrors of actuality. North Africa had been cleared of the Axis armies and General de Gaulle had gone to Tunis to visit the Bey:

'The palace, hardly bigger than a decent country rectory, is the private residence of the Beys, to which the new Bey has withdrawn as a measure of war austerity. His mounted guards, on magnificent sleek horses, and with red pennants on their lances, escorted General de Gaulle and General Maste to the gates, where they found awaiting them foot guards in uniforms of the Ottoman Empire, the officers wearing black frock-coats with pleated skirts over madder-red trousers, their breasts gleaming with decorations and their swords flashing under the African sun. On the steps were standing the Bey's ministers, the second of whom has the title of Minister of the Pen, their long black coats embroidered with golden oak leaves.

'The Ministers greeted the two generals and led them to the Bey. The procession crossed the small interior courtyard, from the upper floor of which could be seen the dark eyes of the womenfolk of the royal household, eager with curiosity as they peeped through the lattice windows, daring to be seen in order to catch a glimpse of the visitors.

'The throne room was hardly bigger than a boudoir: but delightfully built in the usual North African style, with tiled walls and small stained-glass windows high up.

'On a gilt throne set on a dais too high for him sat the Bey, his legs dangling, a spare, quiet old man in a white frock coat.

'At first one's eyes were distracted from this scene and rivetted on the decoration of the setting. The tiles were covered with photographs and etchings of former Beys, like family portraits in a Victorian nursery. Monstrous chandeliers like those of the Paris Opera House hung from the ceiling; but on the walls were gas brackets with the rose-tinted shades of a suburban boarding-house at the turn of the century. While one gazed dumb, the band struck up the *Marseillaise*, which was followed by the Bey's hymn, a strange, winding tune, oriental yet Europeanized, as baffling to the ear in its incongruity as the whole scene was to the eyes.

'For a moment one wanted to smile. But the gentle voice of the Bey giving his rhythmical Arab greetings and the deep, warm tones of General de Gaulle's reply, while attendants handed round glasses of almond syrup and dishes of sweetmeats, were so genuine in their dignity that laughter was disarmed. The Bey placed over General de Gaulle's shoulder the collar of the Order of the Blood Royal, a special distinction making the general a brother of the Bey; as all other existing collars of the Order had been awarded, the Bey had given his guest that kept for the palace museum. General de Gaulle stooped down to receive the embrace, and the visit was over.' [26]

It might be Greville reporting the scene (in fact it was *The Times*), so observant is the writer of those little details that bring the scene to life and which a more pedestrian journalist would ignore as insignificant. Take this entry, for instance, from Greville's diary, on February 16, 1830:

'Last night the English Opera House was burnt down—a magnificent fire. I was playing whist at the Travellers' with Lord Granville, Lord Auckland and Lord Ross, when we saw the whole sky illuminated and a volume of fire rising in the air. We thought it was Covent Garden, and directly set off to the spot. We found the Opera House and several houses in Catherine Street on fire (sixteen houses), and, though it was three in the morning, the streets filled by an immense multitude. Nothing could be more picturesque than the scene, for the flames made it as light as day and threw a glare upon the strange and motley figures moving about. All the gentility of London was there from Princess Esterhazy's ball and all the clubs; gentlemen in their fur cloaks, pumps and velvet waistcoat mixed with objects like the *sans-culottes* in the French Revolution—men and women half dressed, covered with rags and dirt, some with nightcaps or handkerchiefs round their heads—then the soldiers, the firemen, and the engines, and the new police running and bustling, and clearing the way, and clattering along, and all with that intense interest and restless curiosity produced by the event, and which received fresh stimulus at every new burst of the flames as they rose in a shower of sparks like gold dust.' [27]

From a distance the sight must have been not unlike one that Walpole saw one evening in June from Strawberry Hill:

'I am just come out of the garden in the most oriental of all evenings, and from breathing odours beyond those of Araby. The acacias, which the Arabians have the sense to worship, are covered with blossoms, the honey-suckles dangle from every tree in festoons, the seringas are thickets of sweets, and the new cut hay in the field tempers the balmy gales with simple freshness, while a thousand sky rockets launched into the air at Ranelagh or Marybone illuminate the scene, and give it an air of Haroun Alraschid's paradise.' [28]

SOURCES

1   Arnold Bennett, *The Old Wives' Tale*.
2   Charles C. F. Greville, *The Greville Memoirs*, vol. i.
3   Virginia Woolf, *Orlando*.
4   Alberto Denti di Pirajno, *A Cure for Serpents*.
5   Ibid.
6   John Aubrey, *Brief Lives*.
7   H. and H. C. Wrigley, *Log of a Tour Round the World, 1883–84–85*.
8   Ibid.
9   *The Travel-Diaries of William Beckford*.
10 *The Memoirs of Anne, Lady Fanshawe*.
11 Ibid.
12 *The Diary of Fanny Burney*.
13 *The Diary of Roger Lowe*.
14 Andrew W. Tuer and Chas. E. Fagan, *The First Year of a Silken Reign*.
15 Thomas Hardy, *Far from the Madding Crowd*.
16 Fred D. Pasley, *Al Capone*.
17 Ibid.
18 Horace Walpole, letter to The Hon. George Montagu, November 13, 1760.
19 *The Diary of Samuel Pepys*.
20 John G. Nicolay and John Hay, *Abraham Lincoln*.
21 *Diary of Gideon Welles*.
22 Edmond and Jules de Goncourt, *Journals*.
23 Thomas de Quincey, *Confessions of an Opium-Eater*.
24 William Wordsworth, The Excursion, Book II.
25 See 23.
26 Anonymous, *The Times*, June 28, 1943.
27 See 2.
28 See 18, June 10, 1765.

The Companionship of Sound

*

The kingdom of music is not the kingdom of this world;
it will accept those whom breeding and intellect and culture
have alike rejected.

E. M. FORSTER, *A Room with a View*

Orpheus with his lute made trees,
And the mountain tops that freeze,
  Bow themselves when he did sing
To his music, plants and flowers
Ever sprung; as sun and showers
  There had made a lasting spring.

Everything that heard him play,
Even the billows of the sea,
  Hung their heads, and then lay by.
In sweet music is such art,
Killing care, and grief of heart
  Fall asleep, or hearing die.[1]

IN the early thirties I was living in St John's Wood, where I had a small top floor room at the back of a house overlooking an old garden. Here I worked as well as slept, and if I had plenty to do I spent all day there, except when I went downstairs to eat. Like most young people, I enjoyed other company better than my own, so the wireless was then a true friend: truer, as it turned out, than I realized at the time.

As most of my listening was done while I was drawing at my easel, what I listened to was less important than the companionship of sound. There was always some form of dance music, and of course there were innumerable talks and discussions, which I usually listened to with no more than half an ear. But of classical music my choice was usually limited to what I knew fairly well, and that was little enough. This was no doubt because I had inherited from both sides of my family an indifference to music that left me ignorant even of its first principles. Looking back on those days, I am not sure this was not a good thing. It left my mind more open to the subject than it probably would have been if at an early age I had been persuaded against my inclination to learn the piano or some other instrument. My ears were innocent, and so I was ready to listen without prejudice when more or less by chance I began to take notice of the talks on music given by Sir Walford Davies.

How much I and others of my generation owe to that great and good man it is impossible to say. To me it seemed as though up till then my auditory sense had been divided into separate channels, according to the nature of certain sounds, and that the one by which music could be communicated had been stopped up since birth and was now gradually being uncovered. It was the beginning of a process that opened the way to a world of delights entirely different from any that I had ever known. This process, which is sometimes a very difficult one to understand, is a form of pleasure to which there can be no end, though I know there are people, otherwise intelligent, who think of music not as an evolutionary manifestation of the human spirit, but as a distinct artistic process that began and ended somewhere between the fifteenth and nineteenth centuries. I am thinking, for example, of a friend of mine, a man of cultivated tastes and an intelligent listener, to whom Bach and Handel and Mozart afford true and sincere pleasure, but to whom almost every composer since Rossini is anathema. 'Scarlatti I adore,' he once said to me, 'but I cannot be doing with Brahms'. This was no affectation, though the attitude it expressed may have been partly due to laziness.

If I had learnt nothing else from Sir Walford Davies, it would have been that to listen to music with a closed mind is as much a waste of time as to listen to it with cotton wool in your ears. I cannot pretend that I get the same enjoyment from contemporary music as from that of earlier times. In fact, as I grow older I am aware that my instincts tend to favour the past rather than the present or the future. This is a common weakness, and a deplorable one I think, but it is part of the business of growing old, though I don't think it need necessarily be so. At least it is something that I am aware of it, though this doesn't prevent me from having some difficulty in trying to come to grips with certain composers of the present day. Looking back, however, I am encouraged by the recollection of my earlier distaste for some composers whom I now enjoy almost as much, if not quite as easily, as those of the eighteenth century, whose works are among those that give me the greatest delight.

'My pretentions to musical taste are merely a few of Nature's instincts, untaught and untouched by Art.' [2] Though there are some composers, Wagner, for instance, of whom I find a little goes a long way, who defy all my attempts to come to terms with their work, there are few whom I think I could not get to like if I had the opportunity of hearing them often enough.

'People sometimes speak as if all good music were grave and complex—or at any rate as if they believed their opponents to think so: it would be not less absurd to say that all good literature is tragic, to banish from its domain all that company of jest an mirth and honest laughter to which Milton in *L'Allegro* offers a poet's welcome. In music there is abundant room for every mood and we need be at no pains to set one against another. But in music, as in literature, every mood may be nobly or ignobly cultivated—tangled with weeds of illiteracy and impurity or abundant with blossoms of exquisite and entrancing loveliness. It is of high importance to us, both in the conduct of our lives and in the cultivation of our characters, that we should study to discriminate between the various forms of this most potent influence. "True education," says Aristotle, quoting from Plato, "is that we shall learn to form a right judgment about our pains and pleasures"; and of all our pleasures those which are wrought by music are among the most keen and penetrating.' [3]

To anyone who doubts the wisdom of Plato, I would commend Burton's anatomy of music. He must be a hard man to please, and tone deaf as well, who can truthfully say that not one of the aspects of music that Burton discusses makes an appeal to his senses, for music, he says, 'is a roaring-meg against melancholy, to rear and revive the languishing soul; "affecting not only the ears, but the very arteries, the vital and animal spirits, it erects the mind, and makes it humble". This it will effect in the most dull, severe, and sorrowful souls, "expel grief with mirth, and if there be any clouds, dust, or dregs of cares yet lurking in our thoughts, most powerfully it wipes them all away", and that which is more, it will perform all this in an instant: "cheer up the countenance, expel austerity, bring in hilarity", "inform our manners, mitigate anger". Athenaeus calleth it an infinite treasure to such as are endowed with it ... Many other properties Cassidorus reckons up of this our divine music, not only to expel the greatest griefs, but "it doth extenuate fears and furies, appeaseth cruelty, abateth heaviness, and to such as are watchful it causeth quiet rest; it takes away spleen and hatred, be it instrumental, vocal with strings, wind, such as are played with the breath, without any action of the hands, etc; it cures all irksomeness and heaviness of the soul. Labouring men that sing to their work can tell as much, and so can soldiers when they go to fight, whom drum, fife, and such-like music animates; as Censorinus informeth us, the fear of death can be banished by music. "It makes a child quiet," the nurse's song; and many times the sound of a trumpet on a sudden, bells ringing, a carman's whistle, a boy singing some ballad tune early in the street, alters, revives, recreates a restless patient that cannot sleep in the night, etc. In a word, it is so powerful a thing that it ravisheth the soul, the queen of the senses, by sweet pleasure (which is a happy cure), and corporal tunes pacify our incorporeal soul; speaking without a mouth, it exercises domination over the soul and carries it beyond itself, helps, elevates, extends it.' [4]

Herrick invoked 'musique to becalme his fever' with these words

> Charm me asleep, and melt me so
>   With thy Delicious Numbers;
> That being ravisht, hence I goe
>   Away in easy slumbers.
>   Ease my sick head,
>   And make my bed,
>   Thou Power that canst sever
>   From me this ill :
>   And quickly still :
>   Though thou not kill
>   My Fever.
>
> Thou sweetly canst convert the same
>   From a consuming fire,
> Into a gentle-licking flame,
>   And make it thus expire.
>   Then make me weep
>   My paines asleep ;
>   And give me such reposes,
>   That I, poore I,
>   May think, thereby,
>   I live and die
>   'Mongst Roses.
>
> Fall on me like a silent dew,
>   Or like those Maiden showrs,
> Which, by the peepe of day, doe strew
>   A Baptime o're the flowers.
>   Melt, melt my paines,
>   With thy soft straines ;
>   That having ease me given,
>   With full delight,
>   I leave this light;
>   And take my flight
>   For Heaven. [5]

The marvellous economy of Herrick's poetry is a perpetual wonder. With words and forms and images that are of the simplest he evokes sentiments that are among the most difficult to apprehend or to describe, of which the effects of listening to music are perhaps the most elusive. Not even Shakespeare can better express the sensation produced in one's mind by the cadence of a song or the gentle, melancholic strains of a lute. It is an art within an art, this faculty of interpreting one form of experience in terms of another. Ruskin demonstrates it in his analysis of Turner's art, and in a different sphere, Respighi in describing the fountains of Rome. It is instructive in the difficulties of this form of aesthetic interpretation to take the example of a writer of luxuriant imagination and exotic vocabulary who nevertheless fails where Herrick succeeds. Ouida's *belle inconnue* is out to impress Lord Strathmore with her musical gifts:

'"Do you like music, monsieur?" she asked him, with that suddenness which had in it nothing abrupt, but was rather the suddenness of a fawn's or an antelope's swift graces. Then, without awaiting a reply, without apology or prelude, inspired by that caprice which rules all women more or less, and ruled this one at every moment and in every mood, she began to sing one of the sweet, gay, familiar Canzone of Figaro, with a voice at which the nightingales in the linden-leaves might have broken their little throats in envying despair. Then, without pause, she passed on to the sublime harmonies of the *Stabat Mater*—now wailing like the sigh of a vesper hymn from convent walls at evensong, now bursting into passionate prayer like the swell of a Te Deum from Cathedral altar. She sang on without effort, without pause, blending the most incongruous harmonies into one strange, bizarre, weird-like yet entrancing whole, changing the Preghiero from *Masaniello* for one of Verdi's gayest arias, mingling Küken's "Slumber Song" with some reckless Venetian barcarolle, breaking off the solemn cadence of the Pro Peccatis with some mischievous chansonette out of the Quartier Latin, and welding the loftiest melodies of Handel's *Israel* with the laughing refrain of Louis Abadie's ballads. Out on the still night air rose the matchless music of voice, rich, clear, thrilling, a very intoxication of sound; mingling with the ebb and flow of the waters, the tremulous sigh of the leaves, and the rival song of the birds in the boughs. Those sitting within the darkened chamber listened spellbound; the peasantry, laughing and chatting under the low roof of the hostelry, hushed their gossip in enchanted awe; the boatmen in the vessel moored in the shadow below looked up and left off their toil; and, as suddenly as it had rung out on the summer air, the exquisite melody ceased, and died away like the notes of a bell off the silence of the night. She looked up at Strathmore, the starlight shining in the dreamy, smiling depths of her eyes, and saw that he listened eagerly, breathlessly, wonderingly, subdued and intoxicated even despite himself by the marvellous magic, the luxurious richness of this voluptuous charm of song, with a spell which, the moment it ceased, was broken.

'"You like music?" she asked him, softly; "ah, yes, I see it in your face."' [6]

Even Ouida, with her incomparable instinct for anti-climax, can never have plumbed the depths of unconscious humour with richer effect. Another example of the same thing, although tinged with sadness, concerns Beethoven, not a man with whom one would ordinarily associate comic effects. Infirmity is not a thing to be mocked, but occasionally, as in the effect that Beethoven's deafness had on his conducting, it is impossible to resist a private smile at its consequences.

'Beethoven mounted the conductor's desk. The orchestra, which was well aware of his infirmity, was filled with an anxiety which was only too soon justified, for no sooner had the music begun that its composer began to present a bewildering spectacle. At the *piano* passages he lowered himself to a kneeling posture, at the *forte* he sprang up, so that his figure shrank now to the size of a dwarf and vanished under the desk, now towered above it like a giant, his hands and arms gesticulating as if the music had instantly galvanized them into immeasurable energy. At first this did not upset the performance: the vanishing and reappearance of his body synchronised with the shrinking and swelling of the music. But suddenly the great man got ahead of his orchestra and vanished at the *fortes* and rose up at the *pianos*. Disaster was imminent. At the critical moment Capellmeister Unlauf took up the baton and it was somehow conveyed to the orchestra that thenceforward he would direct.' [7]

If Tolstoy had had a sense of humour he might have seen the funny side of Wagner, who himself must be given pretty low marks on this score not to have perceived the inherent bathos of Lohengrin appearing on a stuffed swan, or of Rhine Maidens tipping the scale at about ten stone apiece. As it is, Tolstoy's criticism of *Siegfried* is merely peevish, though not without point:

'When I arrived, an actor in tights was seated before an object intended to represent an anvil; he wore a wig and a false beard; his white, well cared-for hands were not in the least those of the manual worker; his free and easy manner, prominent belly and noticeable absence of muscle at once betrayed the actor. With an unbelievable hammer he was striking, as no one ever yet struck, a sword equally fantastic. One guessed that he was a dwarf because he walked with his legs bent at the knee. He uttered a long cry, holding his mouth strangely

open. The orchestra also emitted strange sounds, beginnings that came
to nothing. Then another actor came on with a horn slung over his
shoulder, leading a man on all fours disguised as a bear. He loosed the
bear at the dwarf who rushed away, forgetting this time to bend his
legs. The actor with the human face represented the hero Siegfried.
For some time he uttered cries and the dwarf replied in a similar fashion.
A pilgrim came on: this was the god Wotan. Wigged like the other,
he planted himself, with his lance, in an absurd attitude and proceeded
to relate to Mime what Mime already knew, but what had to be
somehow conveyed to the public. Then Siegfried seized the fragments
which were supposed to represent the remains of the sword, forged
them, and sang: "Heaho, heaho, hoho! Hoho, hoho, hoho, hoho!
Hoheo, haho, hoheo, hoho!" and that was the end of the first act.
It was all so false, so stupid that I had difficulty in sitting it out. But my
friends implored me to stay, assuring me that the second act would be
better.

'The scene is a forest. Wotan rouses the dragon. At first the dragon
says: "I want to sleep". Then he emerges from the cave. The dragon
is represented by two men covered with a green hide with scales
attached. At one end of the hide they switch the tail, at the other they
open a crocodile mouth from which comes fire. The dragon, whose
job it is to terrify—and doubtless, with children of five, he would
succeed—pronounces certain words in a bass voice. It is so silly, so
puerile, that one is amazed to see various big-wigs in the audience;
and yet thousands of so-called intelligent folk watch, listen and go into
ecstasies.' [8]

Being no Wagnerite, though finding enough pleasure in his music
here and there to prevent me taking quite so dim a view of it as
Tolstoy's, I find the feelings that Vernon Lee had about it much the
same as my own. Writing to Maurice Baring about Bayreuth, she says:
'Although I expected little enjoyment, I have been miserably disappointed . . . What is insufferable to me is the atrocious way in which
Wagner takes himself seriously: the self-complacent (if I may coin an
absurd expression) auto-religion implied in his hateful unbridled long-
windedness and reiteration; the element of degenerate priesthood in
it all, like English people contemplating their hat linings in Church,
their prudery about the name of God . . . Surely all great art of every
sort has a certain coyness which makes it give itself always less than
wanted: look at Mozart, he will give you a whole act of varying
dramatic expression (think of the first act of Don Giovanni) of deepest,
briefest pathos and swift humour, a dozen perfect songs or concerted

pieces, in the time it takes for that old *poseur* Amfortas, to squirm over his Grail, or Kundry to break the ice with Parsifal. Even *Tristan*, so incomparably finer than Wagner's other things, is indecent through its dragging out of situations, its bellowing out of confessions which the natural human being dreads to profane by showing or expressing. With all this goes what to me is the chief psychological explanation of Wagner (and of his hypnotic power over some persons), his *extreme slowness of vital tempo*. Listening to him is like finding oneself in a planet where the Time's unit is bigger than ours: one is on the stretch, devitalised as by the contemplation of a slug ... I had the good fortune (like Nietzsche) of hearing *Carmen* just after the *Ring*. The humanity of it, and the modesty also, are due very much to the incomparable briskness of the rhythm and phrasing; the mind is made to work quickly, the life of the hearer to brace itself to action.' [9]

It was not until long after everyone else had come to regard television as being as indispensable a part of life as electric light that I acquired a set, and at the same time a gramophone. But I still derive as much amusement as I get from either of these by sweeping the air with my radio in search of music. Often I am rewarded by sounds—always apparently the same sounds, or sounds that are much alike—as of a muezzin calling the faithful to prayer, which for all I know may be the case. I have never identified the station from which these sounds come, but I suspect it to be somewhere in North Africa, possibly Algiers. The sound is a wavering chant, which to my untutored ears seems to have no discernible rhythm. It is brisk, though slightly melancholy and now and again is accompanied by the twanging of an instrument that seems to be strung no tauter than a hammock. Sometimes a low drooling noise suggests someone playing a pipe. To most occidental ears such a combination would sound execrable, and yet, though I cannot say why, it has for me a drowsy charm. I believe that if I could learn enough about music I should come to love the music of the East as I love its offspring of the West. Certainly I find it preferable to the twelve tone scale or to *musique concrète*, or in fact to a good deal of Western music composed long before such discoveries as these; and that goes for most English music of the twentieth century, which is dry, folksy, thin, monotonous—or pompous, if one follows the erratic example of Elgar.

The music that comes to me from Algiers, if it be Algiers, must sound in its own small way not unlike that to which T. E. Lawrence listened one night at Jidda with Sir Ronald Storrs and a party of friends:

'In the evening the telephone rang; and the Sherif called Storrs to the instrument. He asked if we would not like to listen to his band. Storrs, in astonishment, asked what band? and congratulated his holiness on having advanced so far towards urbanity. The Sherif explained that the headquarters of the Hejaz Command under the Turks had had a brass band, which played each night to the Governor-General; and when the Governor-General was captured by [Emir] Abdulla at Taif his band was captured with him. The other prisoners were sent to Egypt for internment; but the band was excepted. It was held in Mecca to give music to the victors. Sherif Hussein laid his receiver on the table of his reception hall, and we, called solemnly one by one to the telephone, heard the band in the Palace at Mecca forty-five miles away. Storrs expressed the general gratification; and the Sherif, increasing his bounty, replied that the band should be sent down by forced march to Jidda, to play in our courtyard also, "And," said he, "you may then do me the pleasure of ringing me up from your end, that I may share your satisfaction" . . .

'Next day . . . Abdulla came to dine with Colonel Wilson. We received him in the courtyard on the house steps. Behind him were his brilliant household servants and slaves, and behind them a pale crew of bearded, emaciated men with woe-begone faces, wearing tatters of military uniform, and carrying tarnished brass instruments of music. Abdulla waved his hand towards them and crowed with delight, "My Band". We sat them on benches in the forecourt, and Wilson sent them cigarettes, while we went up to the dining room, where the shuttered balcony was opened right out, hungrily, for a sea breeze. As we sat down, the band, under the guns and swords of Abdulla's retainers, began, each instrument apart, to play heartbroken Turkish airs. Our ears ached with noise; but Abdulla beamed . . .

'We got tired of Turkish music, and asked for German. Aziz stepped out on the balcony and called down to the bandmen in Turkish to play us something foreign. They struck shakily into *Deutschland über Alles* just as the Sherif came to his telephone in Mecca to listen to the music of our feast. We asked for more German music; and they played *Eine feste Burg*. Then in the midst they died away into flabby discords of drums. The parchment had stretched in the damp air of Jidda. They cried for fire; and Wilson's servants and Abdulla's bodyguard brought them piles of straw and packing cases. They warmed the drums, turning them round and round before the blaze, and then broke into what they said was the Hymn of Hate, though no one could recognize a European progression in it all. Sayed Ali turned to Abdulla and said, "It is a death march". Abdulla's eyes widened; but Storrs who spoke in quickly to the rescue turned the moment to laughter; and we sent out rewards with the leavings of the feast to the sorrowful musicians, who could take no pleasure in our praises, but begged to be sent home.' [10]

The music of the Arab countries, like the music of Africa, with its broken rhythms and, as it sometimes sounds to Western ears, cacophonic quality, is a reminder that although jazz, in the accepted sense, originated in the Deep South, round about the turn of the century, its early origins stretch a good deal further back in time and history. And to have an historical sense—that is, a sense of how a composer's music must have sounded to his contemporaries and not how it appears to us in that wisdom after the event which is known as an historical view—is as necessary to the enjoyment and understanding of jazz as it is in any other form of music. 'Jazz being an extremely young art-form, it is possible for the mere middle-aged to recall (all too easily) the original impact of early works which are now seen only as steps in an artistic development and in their general relation to what has happened since.' [11]

A great deal of 'what has happened since', for which jazz may be seen as the starting point, is deplorable. Jazz does not mean the sickly, stereotyped, over-orchestrated and banal arrangements that ooze from dance bands everywhere, but more particularly in England; it does not mean the kind of stuff that is droned into microphones by imitators of Sinatra dressed in jackets two sizes too large for them, or by top-heavy girls who try to disguise, usually with tragic lack of success, the fact that their nearest point of contact with the Deep South has been Bootle; it does not mean the sheet music that forms the staple intellectual diet of these unpleasing characters, and of those who throng the pavements and more appropriately the gutters of Denmark Street: jazz is what began as a form of music expressive of 'the life of common people, white and coloured in many great cities of the United States. It began to be distinctive and recognizable in the Mississippi Delta, round New Orleans, towards the end of the nineteenth century. The common people were, for common people, doing pretty well. Wages were good, so there was money to spare for street parades on Labour Day and Emancipation Day, money for picnics and barbecues out on the lake shore at West End, Bucktown and Milneburg, for baseball games at Carrollton Park, for outdoor dances at Johnson and Lincoln Parks, or for wild all-night parties in the uptown dance-halls. All occasions in New Orleans called for music.

'During the six days of the annual Mardi Gras carnival anyone who played any instrument was sure of good money. People—says Spencer

Williams, the negro composer, who was a boy in New Orleans then—didn't walk about the streets, they danced, and everybody whistled or sang all the time. Vegetable peddlars sang the blues to draw custom. Junkmen, waffle-sellers and piemen played the blues: as another coloured musician, Jelly Roll Morton, recalled: "They could take a ten-cent toy trumpet, take the wooden mouthpiece off, having only the metal for mouthpiece, and play more blues with that instrument than any trumpeter I have met throughout the country. Without valves in their horns, they could play all the notes of the scale, simply by the use of their lips; and they could be heard three blocks away."

'Then there were the spasm bands. They played along the sidewalks outside the saloons and theatres, usually with an equipment of freak instruments—bass viols with bodies made out of sugar barrels, cigar-box fiddles, cowbells, old kettles and lengths of gas-piping. The most famous of these bands consisted of boys aged from twelve to fifteen, known by such names as Stalebread Charley, Warm Gravy, Chinee and Whisky.

'The saloons and sidewalks where spasm music and street singers found their most receptive audiences were those of the French quarter. Jelly Roll Morton has registered a vivid snapshot of the district. "The streets were crowded with men walking in both directions; police were always in sight, never less than two abreast, this always guaranteed the safety of all concerned. Lights of all colours were glittering and glaring, music was pouring into the streets from every house. Women were standing in the doorways, singing or chanting some kind of blues, some very happy, some very sad, some with a desire to end it all by poison, some planning a big outing, a dance or some other kind of enjoyment. Some were real ladies in spite of their downfall, and some were habitual drunkards, and some were dope fiends as follows: opium, crown, heroin, cocaine, laudanum, morphine. All these drugs could be had, sometimes at the nearest pharmacy; without disappointment at any hour of the year, Chinatown would be waiting."

'Undoubtedly a great deal of jazz has been produced in surroundings for which "underworld" is almost an understatement. But the underworld did not create jazz, which grew out of the whole life of the people, their working hours as well as their pleasures: *Washerwomen's Blues* and *Coal Cart Blues* are as representative as *Streetwalker Blues* and *Ginhouse Blues*. The new idiom was formed not only by the dance orchestras in the sporting houses, but also by brass bands playing for such innocent occasions as brotherhood parades, athletic gatherings and picnics; it was formed by the ten-cent horn-players peddling pies, and in the barbershops, where a guitar or mandolin for the use of waiting customers was as much standard equipment as the virginals in a barber's in Elizabethan London—a lucky and bizarre improvisation on the guitar is still called a barber-shop chord. Buddy Bolden, the earliest jazz musician about whom anything substantial is known, was equally famous for his cornet-playing with the Eagle Band on parades, at picnics and open-air dances, and in tough night haunts; and he was a barber who rehearsed his band in the back room of his shop on Franklin Street. Basic jazz still comes from everyday life.' [12]

I feel sure that Pepys would have enjoyed jazz. Even though the snob in him creeps out now and again, as it creeps out sometimes in all but the least complicated of us, he was a creature of democratic instincts; which means being something more than merely a good mixer, since feelings as well as appearances are involved. The democratic origins of jazz—how highfalutin that sounds. But it means what it says: the origins of jazz were democratic, just as folk dancing, glee singing, ha'penny shoving, whist driving, and other innocuous ways of wasting time are democratic in their origins. Pepys loved music, and although those who love music often hate jazz and rightly assert that you can enjoy jazz without loving music, I believe Pepys's love would have been of the sort that leads one to accept jazz, not to sneer at it. On February 27, 1667 he went with his wife 'to the King's House to see *The Virgin Martyr*, the first time it hath been acted a great while: and it is mighty pleasant; not that the play is worth much, but it is finely acted by Beck Marshall. But that which did please me beyond anything in the whole world, was the wind-musique when the angel comes down; which is so sweet that it ravished me, and indeed, in a word, did wrap up my soul so that it made me really sick, just as I have formerly been when in love with my wife; that neither then, nor all the evening going home, and at home, I was able to think of any thing, but remained all night transported, so as I could not believe that ever any musique hath that real command over the soul of a man as this did upon me; and makes me resolve to practice wind-musique, and to make my wife do the like.' [13]

Some years before the war I was on holiday in France and at the end of a long day's driving I came late in the evening to Bergerac. I did not care much for the look of the town, probably because I was feeling tired and stiff and hungry. Slowly, under a copper-coloured sky streaked with ragged shafts of violet and pink, we drove across the bridge over the Dordogne and towards the rue Gambetta where, according to Michelin, we should find beds and *confit de canard*. The further we went the less I liked the look of the place. Then suddenly, round a corner, with short and inconvenient steps, came a little brass band, *la bande des pompiers*. It was like something out of a René Clair film, with music that might have been, and was for all I know, by one of *Les Six*, shrill, brisk, a little off key and a long way out of date. I have loved the memory of Bergerac ever since and over the years have treasured the impression of those musical *pompiers*. I am reminded of them by the description that Sir Osbert Sitwell has given of the village band of Montegufoni, though the sounds and circumstances of their performance are rather different from those of the band at Bergerac:

'The cellars, replacing medieval dungeons—though some of these still existed—reached to a great depth . . . and one of the dark, vaulted rooms, lit by a grating and the light from an open foor, offered music as well as wine . . . The very first letter I had received addressed to me at the Castle came from La Società di Montegufoni—in other words, the village band . . . The letter contained a warmly-phrased request to me to become patron and president, and I was delighted with it . . . I would sometimes, of an afternoon or evening, attend a rehearsal, and it must be admitted that those hours offered some of the strongest and strangest physical sensations of a lifetime.

'From above, from the courtyard, or the room adjoining it, only a little muffled rhythm, a bumping and squeaking, could be distinguished, but once you entered the inmost and deepest stone chamber in which the band was playing, the sound conquered and prevailed over every other feeling. The effect, I think, owed its resonance to the fact that the cellar was surrounded, at each side and above and below, by similar echoing apartments, and that there were several storeys or depths of them. Be the cause what it may, the volume of droning and buzzing and clattering was so tremendous as to seem to add an element to Nature herself, as you breathed the sound, inhaled it, drew it in through the very pores of the skin, lived in it, as fish in water. The music might not be good, but you were plunged and immersed in it. The sound vibrated through every cell in the body, so that you felt a part of it and that it was a part of you. The tunes, exclamatory, dramatic, old-fashioned, possessed a rusticity, both in their kind and in the playing of them, that I have nowhere else encountered, yet it cannot be denied that they were powerful, and rendered with power . . . The scene, too, was memorable: the gracefully-vaulted, rather low room, with walls stained by age, draped with cobwebs, as though it were a hall in the Palace of the Sleeping Beauty, and lit, for the daylight scarcely entered through door and narrow window, by a single acetylene flare, which threw into one corner the huge distorted cylinders of shadow cast by the vats. Moreover, the solemnity and intentness with which the Società Filarmonica played, was worthy of a more notable body: these men, at other times vivacious, cared for nothing now but the score in front of them. The conductor, with gleaming, bead-like eyes, wore an elegantly cut dark suit and a cap with a patent-leather peak. Standing on a box in the middle of the cellar, with resolution he beat the air, and round him, as near as their instruments allowed, were clustered the members of the band, the majority of them blowing and writhing in the grip of enormous brazen serpents, now extinct save in the most remote and secluded Latin communities. Some of the coils showed signs of the perpetual Laocoön-like struggle, by large dents, but, notwithstanding, the huge gold mouths bellowed.

'What, the reader may enquire, was the reason for this constant, arduous practice? . . . The answer is: it led, for one thing, to the most enjoyable band contests, when on a fine evening the crest of every knoll in the broad valley would rise up, crowned by its own din and brazen blare; for another; and more important, it was necessary as prelude for the supreme event of the year, at Montegufoni itself, the festa in the Great Court on the day of the Patron Saint of the Castle, late in the autumn.' 14

I suppose it would be sacrilegious to regard Dryden's *Song for Saint Cecilia's Day* as a hymn, otherwise it must surely have become one of the happier ones included in that dreariest of symposia, *Hymns Ancient and Modern,* of which the bulk is characterized by a poverty of musical invention and a mediocrity of poetic expression seldom found anywhere outside the realms of pre-war musical comedy. How ingenious is Dryden in the use of onomatopaeia and associative phrases—'the double double double beat of the thundering drum', and 'the trumpet's loud clangour', and what milk-and-water this makes of such a dirge as 'O God, our help in ages past'.

> From harmony, from heavenly harmony
> This universal Frame began:
> When nature underneath a heap
> Of jarring atoms lay,
> And could not heave her head,
> The tuneful voice was heard from high,
> 'Arise, ye more than dead!'

The cold, and hot, and moist, and dry,
In order to their stations leap,
And Music's power obey.
From harmony, from heavenly harmony
This universal frame began:
From harmony to harmony
Through all the compass of the notes it ran,
The diapason closing full in man.

What passion cannot Music raise and quell?
When Jubal struck the corded Shell,
His listening Brethren stood around,
And, wond'ring, on their Faces fell
To worship that celestial sound:
Less than a God they thought there could not dwell
Within the hollow of that shell,
That spoke so sweetly, and so well.
What passion cannot Music raise and quell?

The trumpet's loud clangour
Excites us to arms
With shrill notes of anger,
And mortal alarms.
The double double double beat
Of the thundering drum
Cries, Hark the foes come;
Charge, charge, 'tis too late to retreat!

The soft complaining flute
In dying notes discovers
The woes of hopeless lovers
Whose dirge is whisper'd by the warbling lute.

Sharp violins proclaim
Their jealous pangs and desperation,
Fury, frantic indignation,
Depths of pain and heights of passion,
For the fair, disdainful dame.[15]
But oh! what Art can teach,
What human voice can reach
The sacred organ's praise?
Notes inspiring holy love,

Notes that wing their heavenly ways
To mend the choirs above.

Orpheus could lead the savage race;
And trees uprooted left their place,
    Sequacious of the lyre;
But bright Cecilia rais'd the wonder higher:
When to her organ vocal breath was given,
An angel heard, and straight appear'd
    Mistaking Earth for Heaven.

GRAND CHORUS

As from the power of sacred lays
    The spheres began to move,
And sung the great Creator's praise
    To all the blest above;
So when the last and dreadful hour
This crumbling pagent shall devour
The trumpet shall be heard on high,
The dead shall live, the living die,
And Music shall untune the sky.

Harking back now to opera, the thing that bothers me about it
is its fundamental absurdity. This is a dilemma that is common
enough, I daresay, among the musically uneducated. However hard I
try I cannot reconcile my appreciation of the music, intense though
that appreciation often is, with my realization that the action is more
often than not absurd. But, as Professor Dent has pointed out, there
are some kinds of music that seem 'to make these stories credible, or if
not credible as records of actual fact, at any rate credible as expressions
of human emotion.' [15] By this definition *Der Rosenkavalier* gets by
with me, and so does *Alceste*, but not *Madame Butterfly*, nor *Lucia di
Lammermoor*. But in *Alceste* no one is called upon to do or say anything
that appears to be particularly ludicrous. Yet if, for example, the
famous sextette in *Lucia* were spoken instead of being sung, the effect,
as everybody on the stage has something different to say, would be
extremely odd. In one of his revues André Charlot made the experiment
of seeing how this would work out and I have never forgotten how
funny it was. But *Lucia*, with its improbable fusion of Scotch heroics
and Latin passion, lends itself readily to sacrilege. Even so sophisticated
a critic as E. M. Forster is not unsusceptible to its comic possibilities.

Philip Herriton, the hero, if that is the right word for him, of *Where Angels Fear to Tread*, goes with a couple of friends to hear a performance of the opera in the theatre of a small Italian town:

'He had been to this theatre many years before, on the occasion of a performance of *La Zia di Carlo*. Since then it had been thoroughly done up, in the tints of the beetroot and the tomato, and was in many other ways a credit to the little town. The orchestra had been enlarged, some of the boxes had terra-cotta draperies, and over each box was now suspended an enormous tablet, neatly framed, bearing upon it the number of that box. There was also a drop-scene, representing a pink and purple landscape, wherein sported many a lady lightly clad, and two more ladies lay along the top of the proscenium to steady a large and pallid clock. So rich and so appalling was the effect, that Philip could scarcely suppress a cry. There is something majestic in the bad taste of Italy; it is not the bad taste of a country that knows no better; it has not the nervous vulgarity of England, or the blinded vulgarity of Germany. It observes beauty, and chooses to pass it by. But it attains to beauty's confidence. This tiny theatre of Monteriano spraddled and swaggered with the best of them, and these ladies with their clock would have nodded to the young men on the ceiling of the Sistine.

'Philip had tried for a box, but all the best were taken: it was rather a grand performance, and he had to be content with stalls. Harriet was fretful and insular. Miss Abbott was pleasant, and insisted on praising everything: her only regret was that she had no pretty clothes with her.

'"We do all right," said Philip, amused at her unwonted vanity.

'"Yes, I know; but . . . we had no need to come to Italy like guys..."

'This time he did not reply . . . for he saw a charming picture, as charming a picture as he had seen for years—the hot red theatre; outside the theatre, towers and dark gates and mediaeval walls; beyond the walls olive-trees in the starlight and white winding roads and fireflies and untroubled dust; and here in the middle of it all, Miss Abott, wishing she had not come looking like a guy . . .

'"Don't you like it at all?" he asked her.

'"Most awfully." And by this bald interchange they convinced each other that Romance was here.

'Harriet, meanwhile, had been coughing ominously at the drop-scene, which presently rose on the grounds of Ravenswood, and the chorus of Scotch retainers burst into cry. The audience accompanied with tappings and drummings, swaying in the melody like corn in the wind. Harriet, though she did not care for music, knew how to listen to it. She uttered an acid "Shish!"

'"Shut it," whispered her brother.

'"We must make a stand from the beginning. They're talking."

'"It is tiresome," murmured Miss Abbott; "but perhaps it isn't for us to interfere".

'Harriet shook her head and shished again. The people were quiet, not because it is wrong to talk during a chorus, but because it is natural to be civil to a visitor. For a little time she kept the whole house in order, and could smile at her brother complacently.

'Her success annoyed him. He had grasped the principle of opera in Italy—it aims not at illusion but at entertainment—and he did not want this great evening party to turn into a prayer-meeting. But soon the boxes began to fill, and Harriet's power was over. Families greeted each other across the auditorium. People in the pit hailed their brothers and sons in the chorus, and told them how well they were singing. When Lucia appeared by the fountain there was loud applause, and cries of "Welcome to Monteriano!" . . .

'Lucia began to sing, and there was a moment's silence. She was stout and ugly; but her voice was still beautiful, and as she sang the theatre murmured like a hive of happy bees. All through the coloratura she was accompanied by sighs, and its top note was crowned in a shout of universal joy.

'So the opera proceeded. The singers drew inspiration from the audience, and the two great sextettes were rendered not unworthily. Miss Abbott fell into the spirit of the thing. She, too, chatted and laughed and applauded and encored, and rejoiced in the existence of beauty . . .

'Harriet, like M. Bovary on a more famous occasion, was trying to follow the plot. Occasionally she nudged her companions, and asked them what had become of Walter Scott. She looked round grimly. The audience sounded drunk . . . Violent waves of excitement, all arising from very little went sweeping round the theatre. The climax was reached in the mad scene. Lucia clad in white, as befitted her malady, suddenly gathered up her streaming hair and bowed her acknowledgements to the audience. Then from the back of the stage —she feigned not to see it—there advanced a kind of bamboo clothes-horse, stuck all over with bouquets. It was very ugly, and most of the flowers in it were false. Lucia knew this, and so did the audience; and they all knew that the clothes-horse was a piece of stage property, brought in to make the performance go year after year. None the less did it unloose the great deeps. With a scream of amazement and joy she embraced the animal, pulled out one or two practicable blossoms, pressed them to her lips, and flung them to her admirers. They flung them back, with loud melodious cries, and a little boy in one of the stage-boxes snatched up his sister's carnations and offered them. "Che carino!" exclaimed the singer. She darted at the little boy and kissed him. Now the noise became tremendous. "Silence! silence!" shouted many old gentlemen behind. "Let the divine creature continue!" But the young men in the adjacent box were imploring Lucia to extend her civility to them. She refused, with a humorous expressive gesture. One of them hurled a bouquet at her. She spurned it with her foot. Then, encouraged by the roars of the audience, she picked it up and tossed it to them. Harriet was always unfortunate. The bouquet struck her full in the chest, and a little *billet-doux* fell out of it into her lap.

'"Call this classical?" she cried, rising from her seat. "It's not even respectable! Philip! take me out at once."

'"Whose is it?" shouted her brother, holding up the bouquet in one hand and the *billet-doux* in the other. "Whose is it?"

'The house exploded, and one of the boxes was violently agitated, as if someone was being hauled to the front. Harriet moved down the gangway, and compelled Miss Abott to follow her. Philip, still laughing and calling "Whose is it?" brought up the rear. He was drunk with excitement . . .

'"To the left!" the people cried. "The innamorato is to the left."

'He deserted his ladies and plunged towards the box. A young man was flung stomach downwards across the balustrade. Philip handed him the bouquet and the note. Then his own hands were seized affectionately. It all seemed quite natural . . .

'"Silence! silence!" cried the audience, who were beginning to have enough. "Let the divine creature continue." Miss Abbott and Harriet had disappeared . . . "No! no!" cried the young man. "You don't escape me now." For Philip was trying feebly to disengage his hands. Amiable youths bent out of the box and invited him to enter it . . . The next moment he was swinging by his arms. The moment after he shot over the balustrade into the box. Then the conductor, seeing the incident was over raised his baton. The house was hushed, and Lucia di Lammermoor resumed her song of madness and death.' [17]

I have had the good luck to have heard some truly memorable performances of opera, but none that I have enjoyed more than I would have enjoyed that performance of *Lucia*. I do not ask for perfection in opera; the element of improbability is too strong as a rule to allow for that—at a concert I feel entitled to be more critical—and light music too, meaning, for example, that of Chabrier or Offenbach, need not be performed with quite the precision and delicacy that Mozart requires for it to sound tolerable. 'Give me books, fruit, French wine and fine weather and a little music out of doors, played by somebody I do not know,' [18] and I would ask for nothing more. Indeed, music of the kind to suit one's mood, at night and in the open air, is as felicitous a pleasure as any that I know of.

Pepys, too, found enjoyment in this sort of entertainment. 'So I to White Hall,' he records, 'and there all the evening by the Queene's side; and it being a most summer-like day, and a fine warm evening, the Italians came in a barge under the leads before the Queene's drawing-room; and so the Queene and ladies went out and heard them for almost an hour.' [19]

A slight transition in time and space gives us Beckford in place of Pepys and Venice instead of Whitehall: 'I passed to a balcony which impends over the canal, and is twined round with plants forming a green festoon springing from two large vases of orange trees placed at each end. Here I established myself to enjoy the cool, and observe, as well as the dusk would permit, the variety of figures shooting by in their gondolas. As night approached, innumerable tapers glimmered through the awnings before the windows. Every boat had its lantern, and the gondolas moving rapidly along were followed by tracks of light, which gleamed and played upon the waters. I was gazing at these dancing fires when the sounds of music were wafted along the canals, and as they grew louder and louder, an illuminated barge, filled with musicians, issued from the Rialto, and stopping under one of the palaces, began a serenade, which stilled every clamour and suspended all conversation in the galleries and porticos; till, rowing slowly away, it was heard no more. The gondoliers, catching the air, imitated its cadences, and were answered by others at a distance, whose voices, echoed by the arch of the bridge, acquired a plaintive and interesting tone. I retired to rest, full of the sound; and long after I was asleep, the melody seemed to vibrate in my ear.' [20]

We do not know, unfortunately, what music it was that was played at Claremont on the night that Walpole listened to an impromptu concert there, but that it continued to vibrate in the ear long afterward is more than likely, for although his musical appreciation was not very highly developed, the occasion was one that gave him great pleasure. He had been invited over from Strawberry Hill by Miss Pelman:

'The day was delightful, the scene transporting . . . at twelve we made a tour of the farm in eight chaises and calashes, horsemen and footmen, setting out like a picture of Wouverman's . . . we had a magnificent dinner, cloaked in the modesty of earthen ware; French horns and hautboys on the lawn. We walked to the Belvedere on the summit of the hill, where a theatrical storm only served to heighten the beauty of the landscape, a rainbow on a dark cloud falling precisely behind the tower of a neighbouring church ... From thence we passed into the wood, and the ladies formed a circle on chairs before the mouth of the cave, which was overhung to a vast height with woodbines, lilacs and laburnums, and dignified by the tall, shapely cypresses. On the descent of the hill were placed the French horns; the abigails, servants, and neighbours wandering below by the river; in short, it was Parnassus, as Watteau would have painted it. Here we had a rural syllabub, and part of the company returned to town; but were replaced by Giardini and Onofrio, who with Nivernois on the violin, and Lord Pembroke on the base, accompanied Miss Pelham, Lady Rockingham, and the Duchess of Grafton, who sang. This little concert lasted till past ten, then there were minuets, and as we had seven couple left, it concluded with a country dance ... A quarter after twelve they sat down to supper, and I came home by a charming moonlight.' [21]

SOURCES

1   William Shakespeare, *Henry the Eighth*.
2   Robert Burns, Letter to George Thomson, August 30, 1739.
3   Sir William Henry Hadow, *Collected Essays*.
4   Robert Burton, *The Anatomy of Melancholy*.
5   Robert Herrick, *To Musique, to Becalme his Fever*.
6   Ouida, *Strathmore*.
7   A. W. Thayer, *The Life of Ludwig von Beethoven*.
8   Leo Tolstoy, *What is Art?*
9   Vernon Lee, letter to Maurice Baring, *The Puppet Show of Memory*.
10 T. E. Lawrence, *Seven Pillars of Wisdom*.
11 Anonymous, 'One of the Most Original Men in Jazz History,' *The Times*, May 16, 1959.
12 Iain Lang, *Jazz in Perspective*.
13 *The Diary of Samuel Pepys*.
14 Sir Osbert Sitwell, *Great Morning*.
15 John Dryden, *Song for Saint Cecilia's Day*.
16 Professor Edward J. Dent, *Opera*.
17 E. M. Forster, *Where Angels Fear to Tread*.
18 Source unknown.
19 See 13.
20 William Beckford, *Dreams, Night Thoughts and Incidents*.
21 Horace Walpole, letter to The Hon. George Montagu, May 19, 1763.

Love

*

Love is a voluntary affection, and desire to enjoy that which is good. Desire wisheth, love enjoys; the end of the one is the beginning of the other; that which we love is present: that which we desire is absent. 'It is worth the labour,' saith Plotinus, 'to consider well of love, whether it be a god or a devil, or passion of the mind, or partly god, partly devil, partly passion'. He concludes love to participate of all three, to arise from desire of that which is beautiful and fair, and defines it to be 'an action of the mind desiring that which is good'.

ROBERT BURTON, *The Anatomy of Melancholy*

THE natural apprehension that one might feel in disagreeing with Doctor Johnson being mitigated by the barrier of time, there now being almost two hundred years between us, I feel it safe to say that of a good many foolish things said by him, in the intervals between many more that were wise, surely nothing could have been further from the truth than that 'love has no great influence on the sum of life'.[1] This sounds the more surprising in a man so well loved as Johnson, in spite of his imperfections, which must often have been hard to bear, and who was himself capable of deep and generous affection. One would have thought that history, if not experience, would clearly have shown the power, whether for good or evil, that is exerted by love. To dismiss it as of no great influence seems to argue that those on whom the destiny of the world has depended have been either indifferent or impervious to its effect upon the senses, as upon character, ambition, circumstance and all that governs the human lot. Love, in whatever relationship it appears, whether between different sexes or the same sex, is the only emotion besides hate that is not in some degree amenable to reason, 'and therefore there are no common principles upon which one can persuade another concerning it. Every man feels for himself, and knows how he is affected by particular qualities in the person he admires, the impressions are too minute and delicate to be substantiated in language.' [2]

I am not a great reader of romances and would as soon spend a night with Clio as with Aphrodite. Consequently there are great tracts of romantic literature that I have never even tried to explore, nor have my occasional forays into the field of contemporary romance led me to suppose that I am missing much by not doing so. The painstaking analysis of complex relationships and the introspective reasoning, however subtle, of writers preoccupied with charting the ins and outs of love, leave me for the most part untouched, and to read of love without its having some sort of effect on one's imagination seems to me as dreary a way of spending time with a book as reading the early (or late) works of the Sidney Webbs.

I am not particular as to the kind of love with which an author deals; I ask only that it shall not be taken to pieces and prodded, or soaked in psychological sauce. *Don Quixote*, as tedious a novel to my mind as was ever indifferently translated (if there is a good translation, I have never come across it) is here and there relieved by some rather touching accounts of Sancho Panza's love for his donkey. I am not a particular lover of animals, but there is something of Sancho's simple and authentic feeling in Sterne's account of meeting the owner of the dead ass that he found on the road between Montreul and Namport. When he arrived at the post-house there with his servant, La Fleur, a sorrowful looking man was sitting outside:

'And this, said he, putting the remains of a crust into his wallet, and this should have been thy portion, said he, hadst thou been alive to have shared it with me. I thought by the accent, it had been an apostrophe to his child; but 'twas to his ass . . . The man seemed to lament it much; and it instantly brought into my mind Sancho's lamentation for his; but he did it with more true touches of nature.

'The mourner was sitting upon a stone-bench at the door, with the ass's pannel and its bridle on one side, which he took up from time to time, then laid them down, look'd at them and shook his head. He then took his crust of bread out of his wallet again, as if to eat it; held it some time in his hand, then laid it upon the bit of his ass's bridle, looked wistfully at the little arrangement he had made, and then gave a sigh.

'The simplicity of his grief drew numbers about him, and La Fleur among the rest, whilst the horses were getting ready; as I continued sitting in the post-chaise, I could see and hear over their heads.

'He said he had come from Spain, where he had been from the furthest borders of Franconia; and had got so far on his return home, when his ass died. Every one seemed desirous to know what business could have taken so old and poor a man so far a journey from his own home.

'It had pleased Heaven, he said, to bless him with three sons, the finest lads in all Germany; but having in one week lost two of the eldest of them by the smallpox, and the youngest falling ill of the same distemper, he was afraid of being bereft of them all; and made a vow, if Heaven would not take him from him also, he would go in gratitude to St Iago in Spain.

'When the mourner got thus far on his story, he stopp'd to pay nature his tribute and wept bitterly.

'He said, Heaven had accepted the conditions, and that he had set out out from his cottage with this poor creature, who had been a patient partner of his journey, that it had eat the same bread with him all the way, and was unto him as a friend.

'Every body who stood about, heard the poor fellow with concern. La Fleur offered him money. The mourner said, he did not want it—it was not the value of the ass, but the loss of him; and upon this told them a long story of a mischance upon their passage over the Pyrenean mountains, which had separated them from each other three days; during which time the ass had sought him as much as he had sought the ass, and that they had neither scarce eat or drank till they met.

'Thou hast one comfort, friend, said I, at least, in the loss of thy poor beast; I'm sure thou hast been a merciful master to him. Alas! said the mourner, I thought so, when he was alive, but now that he is dead I think otherwise. I fear the weight of myself and my afflictions together have been too much for him—they have shortened the poor creature's days, and I fear I have them to answer for. Shame on the world! said I to myself; did we but love each other as this soul loved his ass, 'twould be something.' [3]

Among the poets of all times, as among the more susceptible fauna of Tin Pan Alley and Sunset Boulevard, there has been no more prolific inspiration than love; which is the reason that I have included more verse here than anywhere else. I have tried to avoid the obvious in favour of poems that I hope are less well known. In any case, the choice is too wide to allow one to do more than make an arbitrary selection. Which to call my favourite love poems I should be hard put to say; probably some of those thrown off so copiously by Herrick, though Quarles's 'Divine Rapture' must come very near the top:

> Ev'n like two little bank-dividing brooks,
>   That wash the pebbles with their wanton streams,
> And having ranged and searched a thousand nooks,
>   Meet both at length in silver-breasted Thames,
>   Where in a greater current they conjoin:
> So I my best-beloved's am; so he is mine.
>
> Ev'n so we met; and after long pursuit,
>   Ev'n so we joyn'd; we both became entire;
> No need for either to renew a suit,
>   For I was flax and he was flames of fire
>   Our firm-united souls did more than twine;
> So I my best-beloved's am; so he is mine.
>
> If all those glittering Monarchs that command
>   The servile quarters of this earthly ball,
> Should tender, in exchange, their shares of land,

I would not change my fortunes for them all:
Their wealth is but a counter to my coin:
The world's but their's; but my beloved's mine.

Nay more; if the fair Thespian ladies all
Should heap together their diviner treasure,
That treasure should be deemed a price too small
To buy a minute's lease of half my pleasure.
'T is not the sacred wealth of all the nine
Can buy my heart from him, or his, from being mine.

Nor Time, nor Place, nor Chance, nor Death can bow
My least desires unto the last remove;
He's firmly mine by oath; I his by word;
He's mine by faith; and I am his by love;
He's mine by water; I am his by wine;
Thus I my best-beloved's am; thus he is mine.

He is my Altar; I his Holy Place;
I am his guest; and he, my living food;
I'm his by penetence; he's mine by grace;
I'm his by purchase; he is mine by bloud;
He's my supporting elm; and I his vine:
Thus I my best-beloved's am; thus he is mine.

He gives me wealth, I give him all my vows:
I give him songs; he gives me length of dayes:
With wreaths of grace he crowns my conqu'ring brows:
And I his Temples with a crown of Praise;
Which he accepts as an ev'rlasting signe,
That I my best-beloved's am; that he is mine.[4]

It is agreeably typical of Pepys, himself a highly susceptible character, to find him speaking of 'a new interest I am making, by a match in hand between the eldest son of Sir G. Carteret and Lady Jemimah Montagu,'[5] daughter of the Earl of Sandwich. Shortly after this entry comes the following account of Pepys' part in the marriage festivities, a series of delays en route having prevented his arrival in time for the ceremony itself.

A slightly depressing atmosphere hangs over the proceedings, due no doubt to the extreme timidity of the groom. 'But Lord! what silly discourse we had as to love matters, he being the most awkward man I ever met with in my life as to that business.' [6] And a little later: 'I find Mr Carteret as backward almost in his caresses as he was the first day.' [7] So, it seems, did the bride. However, Pepys was not one to let such an occasion fizzle out in an atmosphere of gloom and it is obvious that he soon became the life and soul of the party:

'Up; and very betimes by six o'clock at Deptford, and there finds Sir G. Carteret, and my Lady ready to go: I being in my new coloured silk suit, and coat trimmed with gold buttons and gold broad lace round my hands, very rich and fine. By water to the ferry, where when we come, no coach there; and tide of ebb so far spent as the horse-boat could not get off on the other side the river to bring away the coach. So we were fain to stay there in the unlucky Isle of Doggs in a chill place, the morning cool, and the wind fresh, above two if not three hours to our great discontent. Yet being upon a pleasant errand, and seeing that it could not be helped, we did bear it very patiently; and it was worth my observing to see how upon these two scores, Sir G. Carteret, the most passionate man in the world, and that was in greatest haste to be gone, did bear with it, and very pleasant all the while, at least not troubled much so as to fret and storm at it.

'Anon the coach comes: in the mean time there coming a news thither with his horse to go over, that told us he did come from Islington this morning; and that Proctor the vintner of the Mitre in Wood-street, and his son, are dead this morning there, of the plague; he having laid out abundance of money there, and was the greatest vintner for some time in London for great entertainments. We, fearing the canonicall hour would be past before we got thither, did with a great deal of unwillingness send away the licence and wedding-ring. So that when we come, though we drove hard with six horses, yet we found them gone from home; and going towards the church, met them coming from church, which troubled us. But, however, that trouble was soon over; hearing it was well done: they being both in their old clothes; my Lord Crewe giving her, there being three coach fulls of them. The young lady mighty sad, which troubled me; but yet I think it was only her gravity in a little greater degree than usual. All saluted her, but I did not till my Lady Sandwich did ask me whether I had saluted her or no.

'So to dinner, and very merry we were; but in such a sober way as never almost any thing was in so great families: but it was much better. After dinner company divided, some to cards, others to talk ... At night to supper ... and which, methought, was the most extra-

ordinary thing, all of us to prayers as usual, and the young bride and
bridegroom too: and so after prayers, soberly to bed; only I got into
the bridegroom's chamber while he undressed himself, and there was
very merry, till he was called to the bride's chamber, and into bed they
went. I kissed the bride in bed, and so the curtaines drawne with the
greatest gravity that could be, and so good night. But the modesty
and gravity of this business was so decent, that it was to me indeed ten
times more delightful than if it had been twenty times more merry
and jovial. Thus I ended this month with the greatest joy that ever I
did any in my life, because I have spent the greatest part of it with
abundance of joy, and honour, and pleasant journeys, and brave
entertainments, and without cost of money; and at last live to see the
business ended with great content on all sides.' [8]

How different and how much less inhibited was Pepys in his attitude
to love than Rousseau, whose disposition, though apparently no less
amorous, made him the sort of campanion that a girl would hardly
think of as the man to give her a gay evening. Except with his faithful
Thérèse he seldom seems to have found the same simple enjoyment or
relative content that Pepys experienced. However, with Thérèse he
did achieve a measure of domestic happiness, though it is typical that
in describing it he should find it necessary to qualify it as 'the most
perfect . . . that human weakness can permit. My Thérèse's heart was
that of an angel; intimacy increased our attachment, and we daily
felt more and more how perfectly we were made for each other. If our
pleasures could be described, their simplicity would appear ridiculous;
our walks, tête-à-tête, outside the city, where I spent my eight or ten
sous magnificently in some beer-house; our little suppers at the open
window, at which we sat opposite each other on two low chairs placed
upon a trunk, which filled up the breadth of the window-niche. In
this position, the window served us as a table, we breathed the fresh
air, we could see the surrounding country and the passers-by, and,
although we were on the fourth storey, we could look down upon the
street while we ate. Who could describe, who could feel the charm of
these meals, at which the dishes consisted of nothing more than a
quartern loaf of bread, a few cherries, a morsel of cheese, and half a
pint of wine, which we shared between us? Friendship, confidence,
intimacy, tranquillity of mind, how delicious are your seasonings.
Sometimes we remained there till midnight, without thinking of it or
suspecting how late it was . . .' [9]

It is a picture that has all the charm of one by Chardin, and speaks as
clearly of Thérèse's devotion to her earnest-minded and humourless

lover as it does of his long fidelity to one so inferior to himself in education and understanding.

Some years ago my friend Fred Bason gave me a present of two small leather-bound books, gilt-tooled and with marbled boards, that smelt agreeably of the past. They turned out to be an early edition of Geoffrey Crayon's (or rather, Washington Irving's) *Sketch Books*, published in Paris in 1824. Included in one of them is this sad little poem, of which I have not been able to discover the author. It is called 'Corydon's Doleful Knell':

A garland shall be framed
By Art and Nature's skill,
Of sundry-coloured flowers,
In token of good-will.

And sundry-coloured ribands
On it I will bestoe;
But chiefly blacke and yellowe
With her to grave shall go.

I'll deck her tomb with flowers,
The rarest ever seen;
And with my tears as showers,
I'll keep them fresh and green.[10]

Flowers, and no doubt tears as well, were a token of love and youthful homage that was once paid to Swinburne:

'On a lovely September day, more years ago than I care to remember, a very young lady disembarked from a ship which had travelled from Bournemouth to the Isle of Wight.

'The very young lady carried an enormous sheaf of red roses. Behind her trailed a captive Handmaiden, dark green in colour from a malady caused by the sea and by disapproval, some ten years older than the very young lady, and looking very cross. She was cross because she had not enjoyed the sea-trip, because she disapproved of the sea, and because she did not feel well. She carried a jug of milk, a honeycomb, a wreath of bayleaves, and the very young lady's coat.

'The very young lady had run away from Bournemouth, and from her grandmother, to whom she was much attached, and from a visiting clergyman, to whom she was decidedly not attached, in order to visit the grave of Algernon Charles Swinburne (with whose poems she had fallen passionately in love) in the little cemetry at Bonchurch, and to place offerings in the Greek manner upon that grave.

'The ladies drove in an open cab, drawn by a horse tattered with age, to Bonchurch, and, when there, the younger lady entered into a furious and protracted battle with the verger (or whatever official was in charge of the cemetry), routed him, and, bending under a fuchsia bush which is almost a tree in size, poured the milk, and placed the bay-wreath, roses and the honeycomb, upon the grave of the poet.

'That is very many years ago, but the no-longer young lady remembers still the excitement of the adventure, the enchanted September day, and the appalling storm which broke over her head on her return to Bournemouth—with her grandmother acting as lightning and the visiting clergyman acting as thunder—for both Swinburne and running away were much disapproved of.' [11]

Since this courageous escapade the young lady has herself achieved fame as a poet: her name is Edith Sitwell, and she has done more than anyone else to stimulate a love of poetry in me, and even to awaken a modest understanding of it. But that she would disapprove of much that I enjoy I have not the slightest doubt, for my poetic tastes are simple and orthodox, which is really the same thing as saying they are timid and conventional. However, there are some poems that are favourites of mine and of which I feel safe in thinking that Dame Edith would approve. One of these is Michael Drayton's 'The Parting':

> Since there's no help, come, let us kiss and part;
> Nay, I have done, you get no more of me;
> And I am glad, yea, glad with all my heart
> That thus so cleanly I myself can free.
>
> Shake hands for ever, cancel all our vows,
> And, when we meet at any time again,
> Be it not seen in either of our brows
> That we one jot of former love retain.
> Now at the last gasp of Love's latest breath,
> When, his pulse failing, Passion speechless lies,
> When Faith is kneeling by his bed of death,
> And Innocence is closing up his eyes—
>   Now if thou wouldst, when all have given him over,
>   From death to life thou might'st him yet recover. [12]

The first time I read this poem it made an instantaneous impression on me, unlike most poetry that I read, which I find it difficult to appreciate until it has become familiar. There is something very moving in the dignity and finality of this poem, with its utter rejection of hope, cancelled by a note of noble resignation; until one comes to the last despairing and pitiful *volte face.*

'Love,' says Dryden, 'is the noblest frailty of the mind'.[13] Or if you prefer a more hard-boiled definition: 'Love is based upon a view of women that is impossible to any man who has had any experience of them.'[14] From a practical as well as a biological point of view I suppose one has to accept the distasteful conclusion 'that there is no true love short of eating and consequent assimilation ... What ... can awaken less consciousness of warm affection than an oyster? Who would press an oyster to his heart? or pat it and want to kiss it? Yet nothing short of its complete absorption into our own being can in the least satisfy us. No merely superficial temporary contact of exterior form to exterior form will serve us. The embrace must be consummate, not achieved by a mocking environment of draped and muffled arms that leaves no lasting trace on organization or consciousness, but by an enfolding in the bare and warm bosom of an open mouth—a grinding out of all differences of opinion by the sweet persuasion of the jaws, and the eloquence of a tongue that now convinces all the more powerfully because it is inarticulate and deals but with the one universal language of agglutination. Then we become made one with what we love—not heart to heart, but protoplasm to protoplasm.'[15]

Not a very romantic attitude, but that, of course, is the trouble with science. It is forced, poor thing, to deal only with realities. It cannot take account of feelings, except in the physiological sense or as the basis of psychological analysis, and therefore human frailty means nothing to it; which is why the only explanation that science can offer of love is the rather boring one of biological attraction. If you have had more of love's pains than of its pleasures, you may be justified perhaps in feeling some sympathy with the suggestion made by Gilbert's Patience, that

If love is a thorn, they show no wit
Who foolishly hug and foster it.
If love is a weed, how simple they
Who gather and gather it day by day!
If love is a nettle that makes you smart,
Why do you wear it next your heart?
And if it be neither of these, say I,
Why do you sit and sob and sigh?[16]

I came to Gilbert and Sullivan in my very early youth (and would have stayed with them if, as my critical faculties awoke, I had not found the acting and production of the operas so intolerably stale and unimaginative). Even before I rightly knew its meaning, I used to sing that song of Patience's, as I sang many of the other songs, for my own amusement. By and large, I think I incline more to Gilbert's view, which is that of the optimist, than to Dryden's, which I suppose is the pessimist's. Oddly enough, Cobbett, who was certainly more of a realist than an optimist, would, I am sure, have supported Gilbert. I find something rather touching, despite its happy ending, in Cobbett's account of his wooing, which began while he was serving as a soldier in Canada:

'When I first saw my wife, she was thirteen years old, and I was within about a month of twenty-one. She was the daughter of a sergeant of artillery, and I was the sergeant major of a regiment of foot, both stationed in forts near the city of St John, in the province of New Brunswick. I sat in the same room with her for about an hour, in company with others, and I made up my mind that she was the very girl for me. That I thought her beautiful is certain, for that I had always said would be an indispensable qualification; but I saw in her what I deemed marks of that sobriety of conduct which . . . has been by far the greatest blessing of my life. It was now dead of winter, and, of course, the snow several feet deep on the ground, and the weather piercing cold. It was my habit, when I had done my mornings writing, to go out at break of day to take a walk on a hill at the foot of which our barracks lay. In about three mornings after I had first seen her, I had, by an invitation to breakfast with me, got up two young men to join me in my walk; and our road lay by the house of her father and mother. It was hardly light, but she was out on the snow, scrubbing out a washing tub. "That's the girl for me," said I, when we had got out of her hearing . . .

'From the day that I first spoke to her, I never had a thought of her being the wife of any other man, more than I had a thought of her being transformed into a chest of drawers; and I formed my resolution at once, to marry her as soon as we could get permission, and to get out of the army as soon as I could. So that this matter was at once settled as firmly as if written in the book of fate. At the end of about six months, my regiment, and I along with it, were removed to Frederickton, a distance of a hundred miles up the river of St John; and, which was worse, the artillery were expected to go off to England a year or two before our regiment! The artillery went, and she along

270   A CHOICE OF ORNAMENTS

with them; and now it was that I acted a part becoming a real and sensible lover. I was aware that, when she got to that gay place Woolwich, the house of her father and mother, necessarily visited by numerous persons not the most select, might become unpleasant to her, and I did not like, besides, that she should continue to work hard. I had saved a hundred and fifty guineas, the earnings of my early hours, in writting for the paymaster, the quarter-master, and others, in addition to the savings of my own pay. I sent her all my money before she sailed, and wrote to her, to beg of her, if she found her home uncomfortable, to hire a lodging with respectable people: and, at any rate, not to spare the money, by any means, but to buy herself good clothes, and to live without hard work, until I arrived in England; and I, in order to induce her to lay out the money, told her that I should get plenty more before I came home.

'As the malignity of the devil would have it, we were kept abroad two years longer than our time, Mr Pitt (England not being so tame then as she is now) having knocked up a dust with Spain about Nootka Sound. Oh how I cursed Nootka Sound, and poor brawling Pitt too, I am afraid! At the end of four years, however, home I came, landed at Portsmouth, and got my discharge from the army ... I found my little girl a servant of all work (and hard work it was), at five pounds a year, in the house of a Captain Brisac; and, without hardly saying a word about the matter, she put into my hands the whole of my hundred and fifty guineas unbroken!' [17]

For more than forty years Cobbett and his Ann lived a life as devoted and as happy as it could be, given that he was one of the partners. I esteem and admire Cobbett both as a man and a writer, but the qualities that made him in his way a great man, the passionate sincerity of his convictions, the vehemence with which he defended them, and the pugnacity with which he often attacked those who held contrary opinions, must have made him difficult to live with. That he and Ann remained happily together until he died is as profound a tribute to their mutual love and common sense as was given to another pair of lovers, unknown this time, who died and were buried together, and for whom Richard Crashaw wrote this epitaph:

To those whom death again did wed
This grave's the second marriage-bed.
For though the hand of Fate could force
'Twixt soul and body a divorce,
It could not sever man and wife,

Because they both lived but one life.
Peace, good reader, do not weep;
Peace; the lovers are asleep.
They, sweet turtles, folded lie
In the last knot that love could tie.
Let them sleep, let them sleep on,
Till the stormy night be gone,
And the eternal morrow dawn;
Then the curtains will be drawn
And they wake into a light
Whose day shall never die in night.[18]

There speaks the voice of a man who must have known love's contentment and, though he may also have known its pains, the intensity of its happiness and the abiding peace of mind that is its reward.

Let me now turn once more to Sterne, who gives us by way of contrast a reminder of how little love has to do with the making of it:

'When you have gain'd the top of Mount Taurira, you run presently down to Lyons: adieu then to all rapid movements! 'Tis a journey of caution; and it fares better with sentiments, not to be in a hurry with them; so I contracted with a voiturin to take his time with a couple of mules, and convey me in my own chaise safe to Turin through Savoy . . .

''Twas a wet and tempestuous night; so that by the delay . . . the voiturin found himself obliged to keep up five miles short of his stage at a little decent kind of an inn by the road-side.

'I forthwith took possession of my bed-chamber, got a good fire, order'd supper; and was thanking Heaven it was no worse, when a voiture arrived with a lady in it and her servant-maid.

'As there was no other bed-chamber in the house, the hostess, without much nicety, led them into mine, telling them, as she usher'd them in, that there was nobody in it but an English gentleman; that there were two good beds in it, and a closet without the room which held another. The accent in which she spoke of this third bed did not say much for it. However, she said there were three beds, and but three people, and she durst say, the gentleman would do anything to accommodate matters. I left not the lady a moment to make a conjecture about it, so instantly made a declaration that I would do any thing in my power.

'As this did not amount to an absolute surrender of my bed-chamber,

I still felt myself so much the proprietor, as to have a right to do the honours of it—so I desired the lady to sit down, pressed her into the warmest seat, call'd for more wood, desired the hostess to enlarge the plan of the supper, and to favour us with the very best wine.

'The lady had scarce warm'd herself five minutes at the fire, before she began to turn her head back, and give a look at the beds; and the oftener she cast her eyes that way, the more they return'd perplex'd. I felt for her—and for myself; for in a few minutes, what by her looks, and the case itself, I found myself as much embarrassed as it was possible the lady could be herself.

'That the beds we were to lie in were in one and the same room, was enough simply by itself to have excited all this, but the position of them, for they stood parallel, and so very close to each other, as only to allow space for a small wicker chair betwixt them, rendered the affair still more oppressive to us. They were fixed up moreover near the fire, and the projection of the chimney on one side, and a large beam which cross'd the room on the other, form'd a kind of recess for them that was no way favourable to the nicety of our sensations. If anything could have added to it, it was that the two beds were both of them so very small, as to cut us off from every idea of the lady and the maid lying together; which in either of them, could it have been feasible, my lying beside them, though a thing not to be wish'd, yet there was nothing in it so terrible which the imagination might not have pass'd over without torment.

'As for the little room within, it offer'd little or no consolation to us; 'twas a damp cold closet, with a half dismantled window-shutter, and with a window which had neither glass or oil paper in it to keep out the tempest of the night. I did not endeavour to stifle my cough when the lady gave a peep into it; so it reduced the case in course to this alternative—that the lady should sacrifice her health to her feelings, and take up with the closet herself, and abandon the bed next to mine to her maid, or that the girl should take the closet, etc., etc.

'The lady was a Piedmontese of about thirty, with a glow of health in her cheeks. The maid was a Lyonoise of twenty, and as brisk and lively a French girl as ever moved. There were difficulties every way—and the obstacle of the stone in the road, which brought us into the distress, great as it appeared whilst the peasants were removing it, was but a pebble to what lay in our ways now. I have only to add, that it did not lessen the weight which hung upon our spirits, that we were both too delicate to communicate what we felt to each other upon the occasion.

'We sat down to supper; and had we not had more generous wine to it than a little inn in Savoy could have furnish'd, our tongues had been tied up till necessity herself had set them at liberty, but the lady having a few bottles of Burgundy in her voiture, sent down her *fille de chambre* for a couple of them; so that by the time supper was over, and we were left alone, we felt ourselves inspired with a strength of mind sufficient to talk, at least, without reserve upon our situation. We turn'd it every way, and debated and considered it in all kinds of lights in the course of a two hours' negotiation; at the end of which the articles were settled finally betwixt us, and stipulated for in form and manner of a treaty of peace—and I believe with as much religion and good faith on both sides, as in any which has yet the honour of being handed down to posterity.

'They were as follows:

'First. As the right of the bed-chamber is in Monsieur, and he thinking the bed next to the fire to be the warmest, he insists upon the concession on the lady's side of taking up with it.

'Granted, on the part of Madame; with a proviso: that as the curtains of that bed are of a flimsey transparent cotton, and appear likewise too scanty to draw close, that the *fille de chambre* shall fasten up the opening, either by corking pins, or needle and thread in such manner as shall be deem'd a sufficient barrier on the side of Monsieur.

'2dly. It is required on the part of Madame, that Monsieur shall lie the whole night through in his *robe de chambre*.

'Rejected: inasmuch as Monsieur is not worth a *robe de chambre;* he having nothing in his portmanteau but six shirts and a black silk pair of breeches.

'The mentioning of the silk pair of breeches made an entire change of article, for the breeches were accepted as an equivalent for the *robe de chambre;* and so it was stipulated and agreed upon, that I should lie in my black silk breeches all night.

'3dly. It was insisted upon, and stipulated for by the lady, that after Monsieur was got to bed, and the candle and fire extinguished, that Monsieur should not speak one single word the whole night.

'Granted; provided Monsieur's saying his prayers might not be deem'd an infraction of the treaty.

'There was but one point forgot in this treaty, and that was the manner in which the lady and myself should be obliged to undress and get to bed. There was one way of doing it, and that I leave to the reader to devise; protesting as I do, that if it is not the most delicate in nature, 'tis the fault of his own imagination—against which this is not my first complaint.

'Now when we were got to bed, whether it was the novelty of the situation, or what it was, I know not; but so it was, I could not shut my eyes; I tried this side and that, and turn'd and turn'd again, till a full hour after midnight; when Nature and patience both wearing out, O my God! said I.

'"You have broke the treaty, Monsieur," said the lady, who had no more sleep than myself. I begg'd a thousand pardons, but insisted it was no more than an ejaculation. She maintain'd 'twas an entire infraction of the treaty. I maintain'd it was provided for in the clause of the third article.

'The lady would by no means give up the point, though she weaken'd her barrier by it; for in the warmth of the dispute, I could hear two or three corking pins fall out of the curtain to the ground.

'"Upon my word and honour, Madame," said I, stretching my arm out of bed by way of asseveration—

'(I was going to have added, that I would not have trespass'd against the remotest idea of decorum for the world)—

'But the *fille de chambre* hearing there were words between us, and fearing that hostilities would ensue in course, had crept silently out of her closet, and it being totally dark, had stolen so close to our beds, that she had got herself into the narrow passage which separated them, and had advanced so far up as to be in a line betwixt her mistress and me.

'So that when I stretched out my hand, I caught hold the *fille de chambre's*—' [19]

I was reminded when I first read this of Johnson's assertion that 'were it not for imagination, Sir, a man would be as happy in the arms of a chambermaid as of a Duchess'.[20] But where women were concerned Johnson was probably a man of more scrupulous honour than Sterne; or perhaps it was that he was more imaginative. Anyway, he was as free from cynicism as any man can be who has risen to fame in the trade of letters and has come up the hard way; but he was also rather lacking in humour, so it is all the more unlikely that he intended that remark to be anything but a statement of truth; which, however distasteful it may be to have to admit it, I suspect it is for most of us.

> Once did my thoughts both ebb and flow,
> As passion did them move;
> Once did I hope, straight fear again,—
> And then I was in love.

Once did I waking spend the night,
And tell how many minutes move;
Once did I wishing waste the day,—
And then I was in love . . .

Once did I breathe another's breath
And in my mistress move;
Once was I not mine own at all,—
And then I was in love . . .[21]

No emotion has inspired more poetry, both good and bad, than love. Unfortunately some of the best of it is so hackneyed that one's enjoyment of it has been blunted. So it says much for the indestructible beauty of Thomas Ford's lines to a lady sweet and kind (which, incidentally, I have seen ascribed to both Herrick and Barnabe Googe, but I prefer to rely on Dame Edith Sitwell's attribution) that they still retain the power to move me, though I am sure no song has been forced more often or with more ludicrous effect through the ill-formed larynxes of British baritones, droning across the carpeted wastes of seaside palm courts. Yet the image once evoked by this poem in my adolescent mind is still as fresh and fair to me as when I first came across it:

There is a lady sweet and kind,
Was never face so please'd my mind;
I did but see her passing by,
And yet I love her till I die.

Her gesture, motion and her smiles
Her wit, her voice, my heart beguiles,
Beguiles my heart, I know not why,
And yet I love her till I die.

Her free behaviour, winning looks,
Will make a Lawyer burn his books.
I touched her not, alas, not I,
And yet I love her till I die.

Cupid is wingèd and doth range,
Her country so my love doth change,
But change she earth, or change she sky,
Yet will I love her till I die.[22]

And now here is love of another kind; a kind familiar to anyone whose susceptibilities were awoken early and who is still sufficiently thin-skinned to be able to remember how sharp are the pangs as well as the pleasures of youth:

'Miss Shepherd is a boarder at the Misses Nettingalls' establishment. I adore Miss Shepherd. She is a little girl, in a spencer, with a round face and curly flaxen hair. The Misses Nettingalls' young ladies come to the Cathedral too. I cannot look upon my book, for I must look upon Miss Shepherd. When the choristers chaunt, I hear Miss Shepherd. In the service I mentally insert Miss Shepherd's name—I put her among the Royal Family. At home, in my own room, I am sometimes moved to cry out, "Oh, Miss Shepherd" in a transport of love.

'For some time, I am doubtful of Miss Shepherd's feelings, but at length, Fate being propitious, we meet at the dancing school. I have Miss Shepherd for my partner. I touch Miss Shepherd's glove, and feel a thrill go up the right arm of my jacket, and come out of my hair. I say nothing tender to Miss Shepherd, but we understand each other. Miss Shepherd and myself live but to be united.

'Why do I secretly give Miss Shepherd twelve Brazil nuts for a present, I wonder? They are not expressive of affection, they are difficult to pack into a parcel of any regular shape, they are hard to crack, even in room doors, and they are oily when cracked; yet I feel that they are appropriate to Miss Shepherd; and oranges inumerable. Once, I kiss Miss Shepherd in the cloak room. Ecstasy. What are my agony and indignation next day, when I hear a flying rumour that the Misses Nettingall have stood Miss Shepherd in the stocks for turning in her toes.

'Miss Shepherd being the one pervading theme and vision of my life, how do I ever come to break with her? I can't conceive. And yet a coolness grows between Miss Shepherd and myself. Whispers reach me of Miss Shepherd having said she wished I wouldn't stare so, and having avowed a preference for Master Jones—for Jones, a boy of no merit whatever. The gulf between me and Miss Shepherd widens. At last, one day, I meet the Misses Nettingalls' establishment out walking. Miss Shepherd makes a face as she goes by, and laughs to her companion. All is over. The devotion of a life—it seems a life, it is all the same—is at an end; Miss Shepherd comes out of the morning service, and the Royal Family knows her no more!' [23]

'The symptoms of the mind in lovers,' says Burton, 'are almost infinite, and so diverse that no art can comprehend them; though they be merry sometimes, and rapt beyond themselves for joy, yet most part, love is a plague, a torture, a hell, a bittersweet passion at last; love abounds with both honey and gall, it hath both sweet and bitter taste . . .

> Its sweetness more than honey doth delight
> Its bitterness doth worse than wormwood spite.

'Like a summer fly or sphinx's wings, or a rainbow of all colours, which, when turned to the sun were golden, and when turned to the clouds dark, like the colours of the rainbow, fair, foul, and full of variation, though most part irksome and bad. For, in a word, the Spanish Inquisition is not comparable to it; "a torment and execution" it is . . . an unquenchable fire, and what not?' [24]

And yet, 'many men, to fetch over a young woman, widows, or whom they love, will not stick to crack, forge, and feign anything comes next, bid his boy fetch his clock, rapier, gloves, jewels, etc., in such a chest, scarlet-golden-tissue breeches, etc., when there is no such matter; or make any scruple to give out . . . that he was master of a ship, kept so many servants; and to personate their part the better, take upon them to be gentlemen of good houses well descended and allied, hire apparel at brokers', some scavenger or pricklouse tailors to attend upon them for the time, swear they have great possessions, bribe, lie, cog, and foist how dearly they love, how bravely they will maintain her, like any lady, countess, duchess, or queen; they shall have gowns, tires, jewels, coaches, and caroches, choice diet,

> The heads of parrots, tongues of nightingales,
> The brains of peacock, and of ostriches,
> Their bath shall be the juice of gilliflowers,
> Spirit of roses and of violets,
> The milk of unicorns, etc.,

as old Volpone courted Celia in the comedy, whenas they are not such men, not worth a groat, but mere sharkers, to make a fortune, to get their desire, or else pretend love to spend their idle hours, to be more welcome and for better entertainment.' [25]

I do not feel that Burton can have had much sympathy with lovers, though God knows there is no state of mind that calls so loudly for understanding. No man who had not been a little soured by experience could be as analytical in his views on love, though he was not, to do him justice, cynical about it, like Thomas Walthoe, a poet of whom I know nothing—except that he wrote this epigram:

> *Belinda has such wond'rous charms,*
> *'Tis* HEAV'N *to lie within her arms:*
> *And she's so charitably giv'n,*
> *She wishes all mankind in* HEAV'N.[26]

When so much appalling sentimentality is introduced into songs and films and novels, to say nothing of life itself, a little cynicism about love now and then is rather refreshing; not that I am always and indubitably sure of what is sentimental and what is not. In most cases it is fairly obvious; in some it may depend on one's mood, in others on the subject. Love of dogs, however sincere, is invariably mawkish when given utterance; and it is difficult to express a strong degree of affection for one's native land without sounding self-conscious. Why then should it not sound equally sentimental—which I maintain it does not—to apostrophise one's love in these terms?

> *Have you seen but a bright lily grow,*
> *Before rude hands have touch'd it?*
> *Have you mark'd but the fall of the snow,*
> *Before the soil hath smutch'd it?*
> *Have you felt the wool of beaver,*
> *Or swan's down ever?*
> *Or have smelt o' the bud o' the brier*
> *Or the nard i' the fire?*
> *Or have tasted the bag o' the bee?*
> *O so white, O so soft, O so sweet is she!* [27]

If that is being sentimental, I am all for it. Allan Cunningham (on what authority I do not know), quotes Walpole as having given this definition of sentimentality:

> *I sit with my toes in a brook,*
> *And if anyone axes forwhy?*
> *I hits them a rap with my crook,*
> *For 'tis sentiment does it, says I.*[28]

That seems to me as good a definition of sentimentality as any that I know. For what other reason, barring accidents, should anyone sit with his toes in a brook? Would it be sentimental to sit with them in a footbath? Of course not, because sentiment has no purpose except the indulgence of romantic feelings for their own sake; not that such a definition makes it easier to decide between what is sentimental and what is not. Was Leigh Hunt being sentimental, for instance, in his description of Mrs Jordan, the actress?

'Nature herself in one of her most genial forms ... was Mrs Jordan; who, though she was neither beautiful, nor handsome, nor even pretty, nor accomplished, nor "a lady", nor anything conventional, or *comme il faut* whatsoever, yet she was so pleasant, so cordial, so natural, so full of spirits, so healthily constituted in mind and body, had such a shapely leg withal, so charming a voice, and such a happy and happy-making expression of countenance, that she appeared something superior to all those requirements of acceptability, and to hold a patent from Nature herself for our delight and good opinion ... The way in which she would take a friend by the cheek and kiss her, or make up a quarrel with a lover, or coax a guardian into good humour, or sing (without accompaniment) the song of "Since thee I'm doomed", or "In the dead of the night", trusting, as she had a right to do, and as the house wished her to do, to the sole effect of her sweet, mellow and loving voice—the reader will pardon me, but tears of pleasure and regret come into my eyes at the recollection, as if she personified whatsoever was happy at that period of life, and which has gone like herself. The very sound of the little familiar word *bud* from her lips (the abbreviation of husband) as she packed it closer, as it were, in the utterance, and pouted it up with fondness in the man's face, taking him at the same time by the chin, was a whole concentrated world of the power of loving.' [29]

Nowhere, to my mind, has that power of loving been more touchingly expressed than in the letter that Sir Walter Raleigh wrote to his wife as he lay in the Tower the night before he was to be beheaded.

'You shall now receive, my dear wife, my last words, in these my last lines, my Love I send you, that you may keep it when I am dead, and my Counsel that you may remember it when I am no more. I would not by my will present you with Sorrows, dear Bess. Let them go into the grave with me, and be buried in the dust. And seeing it is not the will of God that I shall see you any more in this life, bear it patiently and with a heart like thyself.

'First I send you all the thanks which my heart can conceive or my words can express for your many travails and care taken for me, which, though they have not taken effect, as you wished, yet my debt to you is not the less; but pay it I never shall in this world.

'Secondly, I beseech you, for the love you bare me living, do not hide yourself many days after my death, but by your travails seek to help your miserable fortunes, and the right of your poor Child. Thy mournings cannot avail me, I am but dust.

'Thirdly, you shall understand that my land was conveyed *bona fide* to my child. The writings were drawn at Midsummer twelve months, my honest Cousin Brett can testify so much, and Dalberrie, too, can remember somewhat therein. And I trust my Blood will quench their malice that have thus cruelly murthered me; and that they will not seek also to kill thee and thine with extreme poverty.

'To what friend to direct thee, I know not, for all mine have left me in the true time of trial; and I plainly perceive that my death was determined from the first day.

'Most sorry I am, God knows, that being thus surprised with death, I can leave you in no better estate. God is my witness, I meant you all my office of wines, or all that I could have purchased by selling it, half my stuff, and all my jewels; but some on't for the boy. But God hath prevented all my resolutions, and even that great God that ruled all in all. But if you can live free from want, care for no more; the rest is but vanity.

'Love God, and begin betimes, to repose yourself on Him, and therein shall you find true and lasting riches, and endless comfort. For the rest, when you have travailled and wearied all your thoughts over all sorts of worldly cogitations, you shall but sit down by sorrow in the end.

'Teach your son also to love and fear God whilst he is yet young, that the fear of God may grow up with him; and the same God will be a husband to you, and a father to him, husband and a father which cannot be taken from you.

'Baylie oweth me £200 and Adrian Gilbert £600. In Jersey, I have also much money owing me, besides the arrears of the Wines will pay my debts. And howsoever you do, for my soul's sake, pay all poor men.

'When I am gone, no doubt you shall be sought by many; for the world thinks that I was very rich. But take heed of the pretences of men, and their affections; for they last not but in honest, and worthy men; and no greater misery can befall you in this life than to become a prey, and afterwards to be despised. I speak not this, God knows, to dissuade you from marriage, for it will be best for you, both in respect of the world and of God.

'As for me, I am no more yours, nor you mine. Death hath cut us asunder; and God hath divided me from this world, and you from me.

'Remember your poor child, for his father's sake, who chose you, and loved you in his happiest times.

'Get those Letters (if it be possible) which I wrote to the Lords, wherein I sued for my life. God is my witness, it was for you and yours I desired life. But it is true that I desdain myself for begging it; for know it, dear wife, that your son is the son of a true man, and one, who in his own respect, despiseth death and all his mishapen and ugly shapes.

'I cannot write much. God knows how hardly I steal this time, while others sleep; and it is also high time that I should separate my thoughts from this world.

'Beg my dead body, which living was denied thee; and either lay it at Shirbourne (if the land continue) or in Exeter Church by my Father and Mother.

'I can say no more, time and death call me away.

'The everlasting, powerful, infinite and omnipotent God, that Almighty God who is goodness itself, the true life, and true light, keep thee and thine; have mercy on me, and teach me to forgive my persecutors and accusers, and send us to meet in His glorious kingdom.

'My dear wife farewell. Bless my poor Boy, Pray for me, and Let my good God hold you both in his arms.

'Written with the dying hand of sometime thy Husband but now (alas) overthrown.

Wa. Raleigh

Yours that was, But now not my own.

W. R.[30]

That Raleigh was reprieved at the last moment and lived another fifteen years does nothing to diminish the nobility of his words. He would have died, as he lived, with courage and dignity.

You might not expect to find the power of loving so warmly expressed by a poet as facile and, if you like, as frivolous as Hood. But that he felt it just the same is clear from lines that he wrote on seeing his wife and two children asleep:

> And has the earth lost its so spacious round,
> The sky its blue circumference above,
> That in this little chamber there is found
> Both earth and heaven—my universe of love!
> All that my God can give me, or remove,
> Here sleeping, save myself, in mimic death.
> Sweet that in this small compass I behove
> To live their living and to breathe their breath![31]

Another and a greater Victorian, whose poetry I am very fond of, is Browning. But, like his labyrinthine contemporary Hopkins, he seems to me rather a bore when he becomes intoxicated by his own ingenuity, and his technique, instead of being exploited as a means, seems to become an end in itself. Perhaps his experiments with these brisk, unorthodox and convoluted rhythms were simply a way of letting off some of the steam that must have made him such an exhausting character to live with. 'Meeting at Night', shows, however, quite another side of his genius, the side I enjoy most. This poem compares in its sharp intensity with the Pre-Raphaelite vision of Arthur Hughes (who, though he was not a member of the Brotherhood, was a better painter than some who were). It has a sense of compact emotion, of clandestine tension that I find curiously thrilling:

> *The grey sea and the long black land;*
> *And the yellow half moon large and low;*
> *And the startled little waves that leap*
> *In fiery ringlets from their sleep,*
> *As I gain the cove with pushing prow,*
> *And quench its speed in the slushy sand.*
>
> *Then a mile of warm sea-scented beach;*
> *Three fields to cross till a farm appears;*
> *A tap at the pane, the quick sharp scratch*
> *And the blue spurt of a lighted match,*
> *And a voice less loud thro' its joys and fears,*
> *Than the two heats beating each to each!* [32]

A voice in which both the fears and joys of love are echoed with intensity, yet never with sentimentality, is the voice of Lady Anne Fanshawe, which speaks to us from the seventeenth century in tones as warm and as true as her *Memoirs* show her to have been. In 1651, after the Battle of Worcester, her husband, who supported the King's cause, was captured and brought to London, where for ten days he was lodged in custody at Whitehall.

'During this time of his imprisonment,' says Lady Anne, 'I failed not constantly to go, when the clock struck four in the morning, with a dark lantern in my hand, all alone and on foot, from my lodging in Chancery Lane, at my cousin Young's, to Whitehall, at the entry that went out of King's Street into the bowling ground. There I would go under his window and softly call him. He that after the first time expected me, never failed to put out his head at first call. Thus we talked together; and sometimes I was so wet with rain that it went in at my neck and out at my heels.' [33]

How vivid and how touching does she make their meetings seem. One can imagine the damp, whispered colloquies, the brief farewells that left so much of their love unspoken.

It was the experience of the Goncourts that little was left unsaid on the subject of love if ladies were present at meals.

'During a luncheon at Trianon, at which Princesse Mathilde [niece of Napoleon III] was present, the Princess asked each guest what he would best like to possess to remember a woman by. One said a letter, another a lock of hair, a third a flower. I said a child, and was all but thrown out of the cottage;' which one suspects was a victory for truth over hypocrisy. [34]

Of all human emotions none has given rise to more varied definitions than love. To the sophist, those who 'fall in love look for a little haven in the world, where they can be sure of being admired where they are not admirable and praised where they are not praiseworthy'. [35] To the sentimentalist love means moonlight and roses. And to the cynic, 'the magic of first love is our innocence that it can ever end'. [36] But most of us seem to content to believe that

> *Love is not love*
> *Which alters when it alteration finds,*
> *Or bends with the remover to remove.*
> *O no, it is an ever-fixed mark*
> *That looks on tempests and is never shaken;*
> *It is the star to every wand'ring bark,*
> *Whose worth's unknown, although his height be taken.*
> *Love's not Time's fool, though rosy lips and cheeks*
> *Within his bending sickle's compass come.*
> *Love alters not with his brief hours and weeks,*
> *But bears it out even to the edge of doom.*
> *If this be error and upon me proved,*
> *I never writ, nor no man ever loved.* [37]

SOURCES

1   Samuel Johnson, *Lives of the Poets.*
2   Samuel Johnson, Boswell's *Life.*

 3 Laurence Sterne, *A Sentimental Journey through France and Italy.*
 4 Francis Quarles, *Divine Rapture.*
 5 *The Diary of Samuel Pepys.*
 6 Ibid.
 7 Ibid.
 8 Ibid.
 9 *The Confessions of Jean-Jacques Rousseau.*
10 Anonymous, from *The Sketchbooks of Geoffrey Crayon, gent.*
11 Dame Edith Sitwell, *The Pleasures of Poetry.*
12 Michael Drayton, *The Parting.*
13 John Dryden, *The Indian Emperor.*
14 H. L. Mencken, *Prejudices.*
15 *The Notebooks of Samuel Butler.*
16 W. S. Gilbert, *Patience.*
17 William Cobbett, *Advice to a Young Man.*
18 Richard Crashaw, *Epitaph upon a Husband and Wife.*
19 See 3.
20 See 2.
21 Anonymous, from Walter de la Mare's *Love.*
22 Thomas Ford, *There is a Lady Sweet and Kind.*
23 Charles Dickens, *David Copperfield.*
24 Robert Burton, *The Anatomy of Melancholy.*
25 Ibid.
26 Thomas Walthoe, 'Epigram', from *Georgian Love Songs*, ed. John Hadfield.
27 Ben Jonson, *Charis, her Triumph.*
28 Horace Walpole, attributed to: Allan Cunningham's *Life.*
29 Leigh Hunt, *Essays.*
30 Sir Walter Raleigh, letter to his wife, from *The Five Best English Letters*, ed. the Earl of Birkenhead.
31 Thomas Hood, *Lines on seeing my Wife and Children asleep in the same chamber.*
32 Robert Browning, *Meeting at Night.*
33 *The Memoirs of Anne, Lady Fanshawe.*
34 Edmond and Jules de Goncourt, *Journals.*
35 Bertrand Russell, *The Conquest of Happiness.*
36 Benjamin Disraeli, *Henrietta Temple.*
37 William Shakespeare, *Sonnets.*

The Body Politic

★

What this country needs at the present moment is because it
must be manifest to everybody and I say again without fear
of contradiction that if so we must get together only by the
determination to march shoulder to shoulder towards the goal
of nothing but the sternest and most steadfast devotion to and
so I say once more what we need is.

J. B. MORTON, By the Way

'THERE are two great currents in the history of humanity: baseness, which makes conservatives; and envy, which makes revolutionaries.' [1] And there is the trickling stream of pure and undefiled abnegation which bears along the solitaries, the mystics, the screwballs, who sometimes achieve by faith and example miracles which neither power nor violence can bring about. Such characters are rare, unfortunately, on the political scene. Wanting nothing for themselves, they are regarded by those already there as freaks, charlatans or madmen, according to the extent of their influence. Gandhi, through piety and passive resistance, helped directly to achieve for India what years of bloodshed and violence had failed to bring about. There was no place in his philosophy for hatred or contempt or cynicism. Consequently he was mistrusted and derided by those who made the mistake of judging him by standards applicable to men of worldly and ambitious ideas. He was one of the few exceptions—and few indeed they are— who prove the rule that it is 'impossible for a man of squeamish and uncompromising virtue to be a successful politician, and it requires the nicest feeling and soundest judgment to know upon what occasions and to what extent it is allowable and expedient to diverge from the straight line. Statesmen of the greatest power, and with the purest intentions, are perpetually counteracted by prejudices, obstinacy, interest, and ignorance; and in order to be efficient they must turn, and tack, and temporise, sometimes dissemble.' [2] The need for doing all this is sometimes understandable, though to my mind always regrettable. Any occupation, short of an actor's, that requires a man to turn and tack, temporise and dissemble in order to make a success of it seems neither a dignified nor a very worthwhile occupation.

I try to believe, though sometimes it is not easy, that I am fundamentally an optimist, and therefore I detest cynicism, which seems to me the negation of hope. I detest it particularly in public affairs, and that is the reason that I abhor party politics. It seems that they cannot be conducted except in an atmosphere of cynicism, sometimes of open hatred. 'A meditation on the conduct of political societies made old Hobbes imagine that war was the state of nature,' [3] and no wonder. I do not doubt the sincerity of those who hold that party divisions, whether operating for good or evil, are inseparable from good government, but no one has yet been able to convince me—and it is not for want of trying—that any one political party has greater resources of

wisdom or ability or virtue than any other. The aims of good government, as inhabitants of the free world understand them, seem to me
broadly speaking the same for all parties, and I cannot help feeling that
a great deal of bitterness and misdirected effort and waste of time could
be avoided if politicians would agree upon this in times of peace as
they agreed on it in wartime, without apparently any great damage to
their integrity or independence. Given a reasonable amount of good
will on both sides, it should not be beyond the wisdom and ingenuity
even of politicians to find a far larger measure of agreement with their
opponents than they are ordinarily disposed to admit. On the rare
occasions when this is done, it is done largely as a matter of political
expediency, not because the public interest requires that a stop be put
to political intrigues and manoeuvres. Once a politician has tasted the
sweets of office, and so long as they have not made him sick, the
craving for them is hard to overcome.

Allowing, then, that as things are some form of opposition is a
political necessity, the problem remains of persuading your opposition
to admit publicly that self-sacrifice will sometimes do more good than
sticking to a political principle. A Utopian idea perhaps—but why not?
Because it would make a mockery of party politics, and most politicians
are party men first and Utopians second, and at the risk of seeming a
prig, I must confess that 'a man who entertains in his mind any political
doctrine, except as a means of improving the condition of his fellows,
I regard as a political intriguer, a charlatan, and a conjurer—as one who
thinks that, by a certain amount of wire-pulling, he may raise himself
in the estimation of the world.[4]

'I am aware that this theory of politics will seem to many to be . . .
overstrained . . . many will declare that the majority even of those who
call themselves politicians,—perhaps even of those who take an activ-
part in politics,—are stirred by no such feelings as these, and acknowe
ledge no such motives.'[5] Men whose interests incline towards party
politics become what they are 'partly by education,—following their
fathers,—partly by chance, partly as openings come, partly in accordance with the bent of their minds, but still without any far-fetched
reasonings . . . and in the battle of politics, as it goes, men are led
further and further away from first causes till at last a measure is
opposed by one simply because it is advocated by another, and members
of Parliament swarm into lobbies, following the dictation of their
leaders, and not their own individual judgments.'[6]

This question of loyalty versus freedom of conscience must be nearly
as old as parliamentary government itself and is never likely to be

resolved. Only by both sides agreeing to withdraw their Whips for an experimental period, say of six months, could it be decided whether our parliamentary system would be harmed by, or would benefit from, members voting for what they believe to be right rather than for what the Party Whips tell them is the correct course of conduct. Is it any wonder, with things as they are, that the question can seriously be asked, 'Is not the very word "politician" everywhere a term of reproach? Is not a government-office everywhere synonymous with incapacity and sloth? What a miserable position is that of a member of Parliament, compelled to give his vote on innumerable questions of which he does not understand the rudiments, and giving it at the dictation of party chiefs who themselves are controlled by the blind and brainless mechanism of the caucus! The people are the slaves of their representatives, the representative of their chiefs, and the chiefs of a conscienceless machine! And that is the last word of governmental science! Oh, divine spirit of man, in what chains have you bound yourself, and call it liberty, and clap your hands!' [7]

That, perhaps, is taking it rather far, yet I think there is some truth in this view, though in one respect it fails to give credit where it is due, namely to the Civil Service, that often overworked, permanently underpaid, usually thankless and perpetually anonymous benefactor of the public. Having once been a civil servant myself, I do not share the popular antipathy towards the Civil Service, which seems to me on the whole unjustified. In reminding us, as the press is always eager and willing to do, of defects or scandals in the Civil Service, it seldom makes any attempt to remind us also that in spite of its shortcomings, most of them inherent because of its size and complexity, the Service has a pretty high record of integrity and efficiency. If it had not, we should soon begin to get into difficulties. That is why the political independence of the Civil Service is of such very great importance. It 'must not be under the heavy hand of purely political selection or influence. It must not be afraid of . . . spending money for worthy purposes, but it must detest and fear waste and . . . above all else . . . be independent—and this kind of independence means the wisdom, the experience, the courage to identify the special interests and the pressures that are always at work, to see the public interest steadily, to resist its subordination no matter what the political hazards.' [8]

On the other hand, 'to govern mankind,' as Chesterfield said, 'one must not overrate them; and to please an audience as a speaker, one must not over-value it. When I first came into the House of Commons, I respected that assembly as a venerable one, and felt a certain awe upon me; but upon better acquaintance that awe soon vanished, and I discovered that of the five hundred and sixty, not above thirty could understand reason ... that those thirty only required plain common sense, dressed up in good language; and that all the others only required flowing and harmonious periods, whether they conveyed any meaning or not; having ears to hear, but not sense enough to judge.' [9]

Things do not seem to have changed as much since then as one might have expected. Learning history is easy; learning its lessons seems almost impossibly difficult. That 'the rulers of the world still feel things in their effects, and never foresee them in their causes' [10] is unfortunately true of all but a very few individuals, and they, unhappily, are for most of the time prisoners of circumstance. The real rulers of the world are the politicians, which is perhaps one of the causes for our 'terrible state o' chassis'. Somerset Maugham once said that as soon as he began to be successful, he found himself 'often asked to houses where politics were the ruling interest. I could not discover,' he says, 'in the eminent statesmen I met there any marked capacity. I concluded, perhaps rashly, that no great degree of intelligence was needed to rule a nation. Since then I have known in various countries a good many politicians who have attained high office. I have continued to be puzzled by what seemed to me the mediocrity of their minds. I have found them ill-informed upon the ordinary affairs of life and I have not often discovered in them either subtlety of intellect or liveliness of imagination. At one time I was inclined to think that they owed their illustrious position only to their gift of speech, for it must be next door to impossible to rise to power in a democratic community unless you can catch the ears of the public; and the gift of speech, as we know, is not often accompanied by the power of thought. But since I have seen statesmen who did not seem to me very clever conduct public affairs with reasonable success I cannot but think I was wrong: it must be that to govern a nation you need a specific talent, and that this may very well exist without general ability.' [11]

I do not come across many politicians, but of perhaps a score whom I have met or got to know, only one has struck me as being remarkable for his general ability, and he, incidentally, was not very successful as a politician. The type of person who usually makes a success in politics is not of a type that I instinctively admire. 'The people I admire most are those who are sensitive and want to create something or discover something, and do not see life in terms of power ... They found religions, great or small, or they produce literature and art, or they do disinterested scientific research, or they may be what is called "ordinary people", who are creative in their private lives, bring up their children decently, for instance, or help their neighbours.' [12]

Selfish though it may sound, the idea of trying to improve society or adapt it to the needs of a changing world has never had much interest for me. Being intellectually of a timid and rather lazy disposition, I prefer the plodding pace of evolution to the undoubtedly more exciting and energetic march of revolution. Besides, 'you cannot revolutionize classes . . . without revolutionizing culture. It is idle to suppose you can communicate to a democracy the heritage of an aristocracy. You may give them books, show them pictures, offer them examples. In vain! The seed cannot grow in the new soil. The masses will never be educated in the sense that the classes were. You may rejoice in the fact, or you may regret it; but at least it should be recognised.' [13] And if it is your aim to re-educate them, the only way is to start all over again. It was said by the Goncourts that 'every four or five hundred years savagery becomes necessary to revivify the world. The world would die of uninterrupted civilization. There was a time in Europe when, an old population of a pleasant land being reduced to a decent state of anaemia, there would come down from the North, on its back, a horde of six-foot barbarians to remanufacture its race. Now that there are no longer any savages in Europe, the workers will be doing this job in another fifty years. And the job will be called the social revolution.' [14]

Even to the Goncourts in their ivory tower it was obvious that we of the succeeding century were going to be in for a pretty rough time, nor was it illogical for them to assume that Marx's disciples, who would be the ones to give it to us, would try to push the clock forward, not backwards, as things have turned out. Trollope in his *Autobiography* draws the picture of an imaginary Conservative who 'thinks that the preservation of the welfare of the world depends on the maintenance of those distances between the prince and the peasant by which he finds himself to be surrounded.' [15] For 'prince' read 'plutocrat', for 'peasant', 'worker', and the same applies to a good many people who even nowadays regard the word 'democracy' as anathema. What is wrong with the word is its perpetual reiteration, to the point where it has become almost meaningless, by politicians and journalists of every shade and inclination. James Russell Lowell quotes Theodore Parker, the American preacher, as saying that democracy means 'not "I'm as good as you are", but "You're as good as I am",[16] a distinction that implies a humility which experience shows it would be stupid to expect in most politicians, or, for that matter, most journalists. The spirit of democracy, which to me means the peaceful toleration of opposing opinion and acquiesence in the proven will of the majority when it happens to conflict with your own hopes, is exemplified in the conduct of the electorate at Eatanswill:

'The stable yard exhibited unequivocal symptoms of the glory and strength of the Eatanswill Blues. There was a regular army of blue flags, some with one handle, and some with two, exhibiting appropriate devices, in golden characters four feet high, and stout in proportion. There was a grand band of trumpets, bassoons and drums, marshalled four abreast, and earning their money, if ever men did, especially the drum beaters, who were very muscular. There were bodies of constables with blue staves, twenty committeemen with blue scarfs, and a mob of voters with blue cockades. There were electors on horseback, and electors a-foot. There was an open carriage and four, for the honourable Samuel Slumkey; and there were four carriages and pair, for his friends and supporters: and the flags were rustling, and the band was playing, and the constables were swearing, and the twenty committee-men were squabbling, and the mob were shouting, and the horses were backing, and the post-boys perspiring; and everybody, and everything, then and there assembled, was for special use, behoof, honour and renown, of the candidates for the representation of the Borough of Eatanswill, in the Commons House of Parliament of the United Kingdom.

'Loud and long were the cheers, and mighty was the rustling of one of the blue flags, with "Liberty of the Press", inscribed thereon, when the sandy head of Mr Pott was discerned in one of the windows, by the mob beneath; and tremendous was the enthusiasm when the honourable Samuel Slumkey himself, in top boots, and a blue neckerchief, advanced and seized the hand of the said Pott, and melodramatically testified by gestures to the crowd, his ineffaceable obligations to the Eatanswill Gazette.

'"Is everything ready?" said the honourable Samuel Slumkey to Mr Perker.

'"Everything, my dear sir," was the little man's reply.

'"Nothing has been omitted, I hope?" said the honourable Samuel Slumkey.

'"Nothing has been left undone, my dear sir,—nothing whatever. There are twenty washed men at the street door for you to shake hands with; and six children in arms that you're to pat on the head, and inquire the age of; be particular about the children, my dear sir,—it has always a great effect that sort of thing."

'"I'll take care," said the honourable Samuel Slumkey.

'"And, perhaps, my dear sir—" said the cautious little man, "perhaps if you *could*—I don't mean to say it's indispensable—but if you *could* manage to kiss one of 'em, it would produce a very great impression on the crowd."

'"Wouldn't it have as good an effect if the proposer or seconder did that?" said the honourable Samuel Slumkey.

' "Why, I am afraid it wouldn't," replied the agent ...

'"Very well," said the honourable Samuel Slumkey, with a resigned air, "then it must be done. That's all."

'"Arrange the procession," cried the twenty committee-men.

'Amidst the cheers of the assembled throng, the band, and the constables, and the committee-men, and the voters, and the horsemen, and the carriages, took their places—each of the two-horse vehicles being closely packed with as many gentlemen as could manage to stand upright in it; and that assigned to Mr Perker, containing Mr Pickwick, Mr Tupman, Mr Snodgrass, and about half a dozen of the committee beside.

'There was a moment of awful suspense as the procession waited for the honourable Samuel Slumkey to step into his carriage. Suddenly the crowd set up a great cheering.

'"He has come out," said little Mr Perker, greatly excited; the more so as their position did not enable them to see what was going forward.

'Another cheer, much louder.

'"He has shaken hands with the men," cried the little agent.

'Another cheer, far more vehement.

'"He has patted the babies on the head," said Mr Perker, trembling with anxiety.

'A roar of applause that rent the air.

'"He has kissed one of 'em!" exclaimed the delighted little man.

'A second roar.

'"He has kissed another," gasped the excited manager.

'A third roar.

'"He's kissing 'em all!" screamed the enthusiastic little gentleman. And, hailed by the deafening shouts of the multitude, the procession moved on.

'How, or by what means it became mixed up with the other procession, and how it was ever extricated from the confusion consequent thereupon, is more than we can undertake to describe, inasmuch as Mr Pickwick's hat was knocked over his eyes, nose and mouth in the proceedings. He describes himself as being surrounded on every side, when he could catch a glimpse of the scene, by angry and ferocious countenances, by a vast cloud of dust, and by a dense crowd of combatants. He represents himself forced up some wooden steps by the persons from behind: and on removing his hat, found himself surrounded by his friends, in the very front of the left-hand side of the hustings. The right was reserved for the Buff party, and the centre for the mayor and his officers; one of whom—the fat crier of Eatans-will—was ringing an enormous bell, by way of commanding silence, while Mr Horatio Fizkin, and the honourable Samuel Slumkey, with their hands upon their hearts, were bowing with the utmost affability to the troubled sea of heads that inundated the open space in front; and from whence arose a storm of groans, and shouts, and yells, and hootings, that would have done honour to an earthquake.

'"There's Winkle," said Mr Tupman, pulling his friend by the sleeve."

'"Where?" said Mr Pickwick, putting on his spectacles, which he had fortunately kept in his pocket hitherto.

'"There," said Mr Tupman, "on the top of that house". And there, sure enough, in the leaden gutter of a tiled roof, were Mr Winkle and Mrs Pott, comfortably seated in a couple of chairs, waving their handkerchiefs in token of recognition—a compliment which Mr Pickwick returned by kissing his hand to the lady.

'The proceedings had not yet commenced; and as an inactive crowd is generally disposed to be jocose, this very innocent action was sufficient to awaken their facetiousness.

'"Oh you wicked old rascal," cried one voice, "looking arter the girls, are you?"

'"Oh, you wenerable sinner," cried another.

'"Putting on his spectacles to look at a married 'ooman!" said a third.

'"I see him a winkin' at her, with his wicked old eye," shouted a fourth.

'"Look arter your wife, Pott," bellowed a fifth;—and then there was a roar of laughter.

'As these taunts were accompanied with invidious comparisons between Mr Pickwick and an aged ram, and several witticisms of the like nature; and as they moreover rather tended to convey reflections upon the honour of an innocent lady, Mr Pickwick's indignation was excessive; but as silence was proclaimed at the moment, he contented himself by scorching the mob with a look of pity for their misguided minds, at which they laughed more boisterously than ever.' [17]

When you come down to it, it is not on theories or principles that people base their attitude towards government; that attitude is determined largely by simple economic factors, by the cost of living, by how heavily they are taxed, and whether the system of taxation operates fairly. Like most Frenchmen, Sacha Guitry had decided views on politics, particularly on fiscal matters:

'If I were the Government, as my *concierge* says, it would be on the exterior signs of feigned poverty that I would unmercifully tax those persons who do not spend their income.

'I know of people who are in possession of an income of seven or eight thousand francs a year and who do not spend one quarter of that amount. I consider them first of all as imbeciles, and also as crooks. To give a cheque without having the funds to meet it is a banking operation that is provided for in the code of criminal law, and it is but right that it should be severely punished. But I would willingly be just as severe in regard to those who possess money but who do not issue cheques. The man who hoards up money destroys the rhythm of life by interrupting the monetary circulation, and he has no right to do so.'[18]

I suppose that most politicians who take their politics seriously and are in the game not so much for what they can get out of it as for what they can put into it, would say that such a scheme is merely laughable. ('Why, Sir, most schemes of political improvement are very laughable things',[19] and who am I to say that I know better in this matter than Doctor Johnson?) But is such an idea basically any more ridiculous than the spectacle of a so-called responsible government stooping to the encouragement of gambling as a deliberate act of fiscal policy?

Maybe it is foolish of me to resent so strongly the cynicism that seems to infect most politicians sooner or later. But their profession having become what they have made it, cynicism is perhaps the only frame of mind in which it seems tolerable.

No, I am afraid that about 'the worth of political life, I am quite an infidel . . . and shall never be converted.'[20]

SOURCES

1 Edmond and Jules de Goncourt, *Journals*.
2 Edmund Burke, *A Vindication of Natural Society*.
3 Ibid.
4 Anthony Trollope, *An Autobiography*.
5 Ibid.
6 Ibid.
7 G. Lowes Dickinson, *A Modern Symposium*.

8   Adlai Stevenson, speech at Denver, Colorado, September 5, 1952.

9   *The Letters of Lord Chesterfield.*

10 Thomas Love Peacock, preface to *Headlong Hall.*

11 W. Somerset Maugham, *The Summing Up.*

12 E. M. Forster, *What I Believe.*

13 See 1.

14 Ibid.

15 See 4.

16 James Russell Lowell, *Essays.*

17 Charles Dickens, *The Pickwick Papers.*

18 Sacha Guitry, *Memoirs of a Cheat.*

19 Samuel Johnson Boswell's, *Life.*

20 Charles Dickens, *David Copperfield.*

As Large as Life

*

In each human heart are a tiger, a pig, an ass and a nightingale; diversity of character is due to their unequal activity.

AMBROSE BIERCE, *The Devil's Dictionary*

I HAVE an incurable addiction to biography, and as a natural consequence, I suppose, to memoirs, letters and diaries. Even an indifferent biography usually has an advantage for me over the average novel, if such a one exists. And by 'average' what I mean is one that earns or consolidates a wide and popular reputation for its author—because few of the novelists whom I most admire could be considered popular in the broad sense of the word. (And 'Who are the members of this *élite?*' I seem to hear you ask. Well, to begin with there is E. M. Forster; then I would also include François Mauriac, Virginia Woolf, Maurice Baring, John Steinbeck, Carson McCullers, Lawrence Durrell, L. P. Hartley, Iris Murdoch and Joyce Cary. My inability to think of any others off-hand shows either that I am badly read (which is true) in modern fiction or with what a slip-shod and uncritical eye I take in what I do read. Probably it indicates both.

When I say that the biographer sometimes has an advantage for me over the novelist, I do not mean that I prefer a bad biography to a good novel. I mean simply that the positive knowledge of a man's existence, no matter how long ago, predisposes me to take a more lively interest in him than most creatures born of the novelist's imagination. No doubt this has something to do with the fact that the novelists whom I most enjoy—and let me admit that I have never read a novel with any other object than enjoyment—are those who reflect life through the exploration of character rather than in the play of events. That is why Rider Haggard, for instance, whom I recognize as an admirable story-teller, strikes me as something of a bore, while Baring, a novelist of uneven inspiration and one whose stories often move at a snail's pace, seems to me an absorbing writer. There is no straining after effect in his stories, as, for example, with a writer like Conan Doyle, whose efforts to make Sherlock Holmes an unusual character by grafting unlikely eccentricities onto a personality already sufficiently emphatic, merely resulted in his producing a figure of hopeless improbability —but, nevertheless, one whose adventures I thoroughly enjoy.

It is sometimes said of certain writers that they tend to create characters that are larger than life. I doubt that this is possible. I am often reminded when seeing or meeting people for the first time of the saying that truth is stranger than fiction; nor do I think that this is due especially to a lifetime spent in observing humanity through the distorting spectacles of the caricaturist. We have all come across the

298

sort of man whom we imagine to be built in the image of Falstaff, the woman in whom we see, perhaps all too clearly, the likeness of Emma Bovary, or the youth who might be half-brother to Trabb's boy. Conversely, there is no character that I know of in fiction who for sheer extravagance of personality could hold a candle to 'Romeo' Coates, the Gifted Amateur, as celebrated for the elegance of his curricle as for the splendour of his attire, whereon shone diamonds as bright as his hopes, which were to remain tragically unfulfilled, of triumphantly wooing the Thespian muse.

'The first record of Mr Coates' appearance on the stage in England appears in Mr Pryse Gordon's memoirs. He tells us that: "In the year 1809 I was at Bath and stayed at the York House, where I found this gentleman an inmate, and we generally met in the coffee-room at breakfast. He shortly attracted my notice by rehearsing passages from Shakespeare during his morning meal, with a tone and gesture extremely striking both to the eye and the ear; and, though we were strangers to each other, I could not help complimenting him on the beauty of his recitations, although he did *not always stick to his author's text*. On one occasion I took the liberty of correcting a passage from *Romeo and Juliet*. 'Aye,' said he, 'that is the reading, I know, for I have the play by heart, but I think I have improved upon it.' I bowed with submission, acknowledging I was not a profound critic. This led to a dissertation on the merits of this fine tragedy. When he informed me that he had frequently performed the part of 'Romeo' at Antigua, of which island he was a native, adding that he always travelled with the dress of that character amongst his other garments, I lamented that, with the extraordinary talents he seemed to possess, he had not gratified the English public with a specimen of his powers . . . 'I am ready and willing,' replied our Roscius, 'to play Romeo to a Bath audience, if the manager will get up the play and give me a good Juliet—my costume is superb and adorned with diamonds, but I have not the advantage of knowing the manager . . ., I observed that I was acquainted with this gentleman, and would either make the necessary arrangements, or give him a line of introduction, as he preferred." In the end, the performance was arranged, and took place on February the ninth, 1810, without any loss of life, since nothing heavier than orange peel was thrown on this occasion. Nor did the curtain fall until Act V, when Romeo seized a crowbar in order to break into Juliet's tomb. Then the attitude of the audience became so menacing that as nothing but the crowbar stood between Mr Coates and imminent dissolution, it was thought wiser to lower the curtain and declare the play at an end . . .

'But Mr Coates was not to be daunted. He repeated the performance ... at Cheltenham. Here he met with no very serious disaster, for the only untoward event was that just as he had repeated the lines: "Oh, let me hence, I stand on sudden haste." instead of acting according to that urgency, Romeo went down on all fours, and in that position crawled round and round the stage. In vain did the prompter call, "Come off, come off". It was some time before Mr Coates heard him and, when he did, he responded that he would come off as soon as he had found his diamond knee-buckle! This pleased the audience, and they allowed the play to reach its proper conclusion, in the hope that something of the same kind might happen again ...

On the ninth of December, 1811, he appeared at the Haymarket Theatre in the part of the gay Lothario in Rowe's tragedy, *The Fair Penitent*, and in his hands tragedy lost all her gloom. The occasion was that of a benefit performance ... and how huge were the crowds that besieged the doors of the theatre, eager to see the gifted amateur... At least one thousand persons were turned away from the box entrance alone, whilst many people with money to spend besieged the stage-door and offered as much as five pounds for a single admission to go behind the scenes. Not an empty seat could be found ...

'When, at last, the Gifted Amateur appeared ... the noise was cataclysmic. There were catcalls, there was much whistling, and shrieks of cock-a-doodle-doo—this latter expression of condemnation referred to ... Mr Coates' crest. Calm and intrepid, that gentleman faced his traducers, in a dress of the utmost richness, wrought of "a species of silk so woven as to give it the appearance of chased silver; from his shoulders hung a mantle of pink silk; edged with bullion fringe; around his neck was a kind of gorget, richly set with jewels, and at his side was a handsome gold-hilted sword. Coates' head-dress was composed of a Spanish hat surmounted by tall, white plumes, while his feet were encased in shoes of the same material as his dress, and these were fastened with large diamond buckles."

'Unperturbed by the splendour of Mr Coates' costume, the audience would not allow him to reach that final scene which was, as a rule, the joy of all beholders. An eye-witness, describing this pregnant ending of the play, exclaims: "Who shall describe the grotesque agonies of the dark seducer, his plastered hair escaping from the comb that held it, and the dark crineous cordage that flapped upon his shoulders in the convulsions of his dying moments, and the cries of the people for medical aid to accomplish his eternal exit? Thus, when in

his last throes his coronet fell, it was miraculous to see the defunct arise'
and after he had spread a nice handkerchief on the stage, and there
deposited his head-dress, free from all impurity, philosophically resume
his dead condition; but it was not yet over, for the exigent audience,
not content that when the men were dead, why there's an end, insisted
on a repetition of the awful scene, which the highly flattered corpse
executed three separate times, to the gratification of the cruel and
torment-loving audience" . . .

'And now Mr Coates was approaching the summit of his ambition,
the dream which his loyal and innocently snobbish soul had cherished
for so long. For, after many subterranean burrowings, which were
only equalled by his perfectly frank trumpetings for attention, Mr
Coates, on the eleventh of February, 1813, was presented by General
Baker to the Prince Regent, at the Royal levee . . .

'Mr Coates was not in the slightest surprised, therefore, when he
received, on the fourth of February, 1813, "a portentous missive sealed
with the Royal Arms, and left, so the attendants stated, by a gentleman
in a scarlet coat". Mr Coates with a trembling hand broke open the
seal, and read the contents of the letter, which ran thus:

'"The Lord Chamberlain is commanded by His Royal Highness
the Prince Regent to invite Mr Robert Coates to a ball and supper at
Carlton House on Friday evening. The company to appear in the
costume of the manufacture of the country. Hour of attendance,
ten o'clock."

'Mr Coates, overcome with joy and with pride, recognized that this
invitation was but a natural sequel to the gracious interest shown by
the Prince Regent on the occasion of the levee; so he ordered that his
diamonds should be polished, that a suit of unparalleled magnificence
should be made "in order to do honour to so illustrious a host, the
prince of connoisseurs as well as of the Realm".

'On the evening of the ball, Mr Coates could hardly contain himself
till the moment of his departure. We are told that he left his lodgings
in Craven Street "a blaze of splendour; diamonds of the first water
flashed upon his bosom, whilst those on the hilt of his sword, and upon
his fingers, radiated with equal brilliancy. Having taken his seat in the
chair prepared for his conveyance, he proceeded to his destination
accompanied by two footmen in the most superb and costly liveries."

'When he arrived at Carlton House, and presented his card Colonel
Congreve, who was in attendance, told him, with the utmost politeness,
that it was a forgery. So Mr Diamond, or Curricle, Coates, passed out
of Carlton House into the brilliantly lighted street, where his splendours

and his forlorn condition attracted the attention of the huge crowd that was waiting to stare at the guests; and having found, at last, a hackney carriage (his own magnificent chair had gone, long ago), this poor harmless kindly creature found his way back to his lodging. There he knew the utmost miseries of humiliation, remembering the horrors of his stage appearances, the cruel and perfectly unnecessary mockery, the pain that the crowds had inflicted upon him. But the humiliation on this occasion was not to be perpetual, for the Prince Regent, when told of the circumstances, was made so angry by the heedless and needless cruelty of the hoax, that he sent his secretary, the next day, to apologise to Mr Coates for the disappointment, which, had His Royal Highness known of the occurrence, would not have been inflicted; and Mr Coates was invited to come and view the decorations of the fête, which were still intact.

'Fortune relented on this occasion, it is true, but on others her attitude became more and more harsh. And as the fame of Mr Coates increased, so did the terror of those who appeared on the same stage as the Gifted Amateur. The audiences knew this, and revelled in it, relying on mass hypnotism in order to terrify Mr Coates' fellow-actors into making the strangest admissions. One gentleman, for instance, driven half out of his mind with fear by the menacing attitude of the audience, substituted for the words "I would I were a beggar, and lived on scraps" the phrase "I wish I were a baker, and lived on sprats", an admission which was greeted with rapturous applause and the fall of the curtain . . .

'There was a fresh scene, and this time of unexampled pathos, when Mr Coates appeared at the Haymarket Theatre in *Romeo and Juliet* . . . Miss FitzHenry, as Juliet, became so terrified by the menacing attitude of the audience, that, shrieking, she clung to the scenery and pillars in great agitation; and could not be dislodged. Another time, in the duel scene where Romeo kills Tybalt, all was ruined, and the house was convulsed with laughter at the appearance of a bantam cock, which strutted at the very feet of Romeo, at whom it had been thrown. Mr Coates was in despair, but luckily, at the last and darkest moment, old Capulet seized the cause of the trouble and bore him, crowing loudly, and flapping his wings, off the stage . . . The play continued, though, when Romeo left the stage after killing Tybalt, he stood in the wings and shook his sword at the box from which the cock had been thrown on to the stage, with the result that the occupants of the box yelled that he must apologise for shaking his sword. Mr Coates, very naturally, refused to do so, and the interruptions continued until the occupants of the pit turned on to the interrupters and pelted them with orange peel. The play continued, then, without any further interruption until the moment came when Romeo kills Paris. Then the latter, lying dead upon the ground, was raised to life by "a terrific blow on the nose from an orange". The corpse rose to his feet and pointing in a dignified way to the cause of his revival, made his way off the stage. Mr Coates, we are told, was "considerably annoyed" during the Tomb Scene, by shouts of "Why don't you die?"

'Amidst such scenes of unparalleled ferocity did Mr Coates woo the Thespian Muse, but not for much longer, for his love remained unrequited, and he was growing tired. Besides, the situation grew more and more dangerous, until at last he decided no longer to risk life and limb in this hopeless courtship, but to place his purse, instead of his person, at the disposal of his needy fellow-actors.' [1]

One of the penalties of an actor's fame, though I imagine few of them would see it in such a light, is that they are compelled to live a large part of their lives in public, with an inevitable loss of both dignity and sincerity. Like popular parsons, TV performers, politicians and others of their kind, they seem to find publicity a stimulus. Some politicians, in fact, like most stars, find it unendurable to be eclipsed by time or events and cling to any spar that will serve to keep them in the public eye, often in the pathetic assumption, or so it seems, that personal publicity offers a substitute for the power which, for a brief spell and in however short a measure, they once enjoyed. For those, like the members of our own royal family, who have their greatness thrust upon them, the perpetual glare of publicity must often be distasteful as well as tedious. When you know that every syllable that you utter in public, every hat that you wear, every friend that you make, every unpremeditated smile, every blush, will go on record, it demands self-control of a very high order not to give an occasional sign of boredom or resentment, and it is greatly to the credit of our over-publicised and over-exploited royalty that no such feelings are ever allowed to show. It is not that they are hidden by over-animation or disguised by excessive charm; it is simply as though they did not exist, which is hard to believe. Yet regal restraint is something comparatively new. The Georges were none of them conspicuous for their patience or their good manners. Victoria was probably the first English sovereign since Charles the First to appreciate the incomparable asset that personal dignity must be to one in the unenviable situation of a monarch. The sharp, retentive eye of Greville, who was clerk of the Council, never missed a trick in the game of social deportment.

His diary records that on June 21, 1837, after the death of her uncle the King, 'the young Queen met the Council at Kensington Palace at eleven. Never was anything like the first impression she produced, or the chorus of praise and admiration which is raised about her manner and behaviour, and certainly not without justice. It was very extraordinary, and something far beyond what was looked for. Her extreme youth and inexperience, and the ignorance of the world concerning her, naturally excited intense curiosity to see how she would act on this trying occasion, and there was a considerable assemblage at the Palace, notwithstanding the short notice that was given. The first thing to be done was to teach her her lesson, which for this purpose Melbourne had himself to learn. I gave him the Council papers and explained all that was to be done, and he went and explained all this to her. He asked her if she would enter the room accompanied by the Great Officers of State, but she said she would come in alone. When the Lords were assembled the Lord President informed them of the King's death, and suggested, as they were so numerous, that a few of them should repair to the presence of the Queen and inform her of the event, and that their Lordships were assembled in consequence; and accordingly the two Royal Dukes [of Cumberland and Sussex], the two Archbishops, and the Chancellor, and Melbourne went with him. The Queen received them in the adjoining room alone. As soon as they had returned the proclamation was read and the usual order passed, when the doors were thrown open and the Queen entered, accompanied by her two uncles, who advanced to meet her. She bowed to the Lords, took her seat, and then read her speech in a clear, distinct, and audible voice, and without any appearance of fear or embarrassment. She was quite plainly dressed, and in mourning. After she had read her speech and taken and signed the oath for the security of the Church of Scotland, the privy Councellors were sworn, the two Royal Dukes, first by themselves; and as these two old men, her uncles, knelt before her, swearing allegiance and kissing her hand, I saw her blush up to the eyes, as if she felt the contrast between their civil and their natural relations, and this was the only sign of emotion which she evinced. Her manner to them was very graceful and engaging; she kissed them both, and rose from her chair and moved towards the Duke of Sussex, who was farthest from her and too infirm to reach her. She seemed rather bewildered at the multitude of men who were sworn, and who came one after another to kiss her hand, but she did not speak to anybody, nor did she make the slightest difference in her manner, or show any in her countenance, to any individual of any rank, station, or party. I particularly watched her when Melbourne and the Ministers and the Duke of Wellington and Peel approached her. She went through the whole ceremony, occasionally looking at Melbourne for instruction when she had any doubt what to do, which hardly ever occurred, and with perfect calmness and self-possession, but at the same time with a graceful modesty and propriety particularly interesting and ingratiating. When the business was done she retired as she had entered, and I could see that nobody was in the adjoining room.' [2]

Greville, with his gregarious disposition, his curiosity, and his well-sharpened faculty of observation would have made a fine journalist, though probably not of the kind that nowadays draws down the big money, because he would never have let his enjoyment of scandal get the better of his discretion or arrogated to himself the intimate friend-ship of those whom he scarcely knew. You often hear, especially if you keep an ear to the pulpit, voices denouncing the gutter press as though it were a phenomenon unknown before the days of Hearst or the *Sunday Graphic*, which is, of course, quite untrue. Though Wilkes had more regard for syntax than Walter Winchell, he was his equal in scurrility and impertinence. He also happens to have been a far more able journalist, as well as a man of extraordinary parts, and usually had a better excuse than one would expect nowadays for the violation of a confidence or of personal privacy. The insolent and predatory type of journalist who makes a point of turning the limelight on people's private lives seldom achieves anything except contempt for his lack of scruples. His comments, which are usually trite and superficial, tell one next to nothing about the disposition or motives of the people whose personalities he pretends to explore. To do this with lasting effect is a fine art, and you could count on the hand of a three-toed sloth the number of journalists now living who could turn out a paragraph as telling, as incisive and as artfully observed as this:

'Baudelaire took supper tonight at the next table . . . He was without a cravat, his shirt open at the throat, his head shaved, absolutely the toilette of a man ready for the guillotine. At bottom, however, the whole appearance carefully staged, his little hands washed, their nails cleaned, as tended as the hands of a woman; and with this the face of a maniac, a voice that cuts like steel, and an elocution aiming at the ornate precision of a Saint-Just, and hitting it. He protests obstinately, and with a kind of harsh anger, that he has not offended good taste in his verse.' [3]

That seems to me descriptive journalism of the best kind, in which exact observation is coupled with disciplined and objective writing.

It is a knack that newspaper editors have done their best to kill because it leaves meaningless and romantic trivia out of account, and when it concentrates on details, does so because they are significant, not because they are sensational. A writer who had this same knack and elevated it to the dignity of biography was William Bolitho. I do not know whether anyone reads his books nowadays, or indeed whether he was ever rated as high as, in my opinion, he deserves to be. As a biographer I would put him not far below, though for psychological reasons on a different shelf to that occupied by, Lytton Strachey. Though he may have lacked Strachey's keen but dispassionate gaze, I think he was perhaps a better psychologist, although given now and then to conjecture, which I suppose is to be regarded with suspicion if it is merely the facts of life that one looks for in a biography. To me the interest in Bolitho's studies lies in his extraordinarily vivid gift for conveying, without undue elaboration, an *impression* of character and appearance, in much the same way as Sickert characterized his sitters by the methods of impressionism, among others a startling and sometimes almost miraculous handling of tones, adjusting those of reality to the more sombre key of his own palette. I suppose you might say that this in its way was suppositious too, since the effect it produced was not always in strict accordance with appearance. But the vigour and immediacy of the impressions that Sickert created left most fashionable academics, with their traditions of soapy realism, floundering in their well-worn tracks.

Bolitho's style is spare and his eye selective. In spite of his preoccupation with the psychological side of his subjects, they are lit as much from without as from within, so that one sometimes has the feeling of seeing them illumined by a flash-bulb. His descriptions, particularly of appearances, are brief but sharp-etched. Alexander the Great, he tells us, 'was red-haired, with that illusive appearance of openness that goes with the colour, sunburnt. The turn of his head, which leaned a little to one side, and the quickness of his eye, were best hit off, we are told, by the sculptor Lysippus. He was not tall, nor heavy. He usually fought with the cavalry, and his mounting was always the signal for the charge. His favourite weapon was a light sword with a razor edge. In set battles Aristander, his soothsayer, rode beside him in a white robe, with a gold crown, to point out the omens in the skies. When he began he wore no other armour than a quilted coat, and an iron helmet that was polished like silver.' [4]

If it is possible to be a dictator without being a tyrant I suppose Alexander may be put in that class. Most dictators, with the possible exceptions of Caligula and Hitler, seem to have shown (and some still show) certain redeeming features that modify, however slightly, the odious and brutal autocracy of their natures. Even Stalin, when the moment was propitious, could put on an act of bonhomie. But the complex of 'infallibility', conceit and a messianic sense of personal destiny that makes a dictator tick must also make him rather a boring companion for anyone who had to spend much time in his company. The only dictator that I would have given a fig to have known would have been Napoleon. Not that he was less conceited, or believed himself less infallible, or was less conscious of being the chosen instrument of destiny, than, no doubt, was Genghis Khan. But Napoleon somehow managed to command the true and undying devotion of both men and women, which puts him well ahead of most other dictators, because the dominion of a dictator seldom rests upon confidence or respect, but only upon fear.

I should think that more has probably been written about Napoleon as an individual than about almost any other dictator. Captain Ussher, who commanded the *Undaunted* which took Napoleon to Elba in 1814, gave, in a letter to a friend, as good a description of him as any that exists:

'On the 25th [June] Colonel Campbell drove into Marseilles, being commissioned by Lord Castlereagh to attend Napoleon. He said he came by the express wish of Napoleon himself to request I would go round to St Tropez, where it was intended he should embark, as he did not consider himself safe on board a French frigate. Next day I arrived at St Tropez, but found that he had altered his route, and was at Frèjus . . . Soon after my arrival Count Bertrand, his Grand Marshal, informed me that it was the Emperor's wish to see me (he is still acknowledged Emperor, and Sovereign of Elba).

'When I was presented he said that he was once a great enemy to England, but now he was as sincere a friend. He said we were a great and generous nation. He asked me about the wind, weather, distance to Elba, and other nautical questions; he then bowed and retired. He was very dignified—still the Emperor . . .

'That night we embarked all his numerous baggage. In the morning he sent for me. He asked how the wind was, and said he had made up his mind to embark at eight in the evening. At seven o'clock he sent for me, and I remained alone with him (an immense mob had gathered round his hotel). His sword was on the table, and he appeared very thoughtful; there was a very great noise in the street. I said to him, "The French mob are the worst I have seen." He answered, "They are a fickle people." He appeared in deep thought; but, recovering himself, rang the bell, and ordering the Grand Marshal to be sent for, he asked if all was ready. Being answered in the affirmative, he turned to me and said in his usual quick way, "Allons".

'The stairs were lined at each side with ladies and gentlemen. He stopped a moment, and said something to the ladies which I could not hear. He walked to his carriage ... then called the Austrian commissioner and the Grand Marshal. I sat opposite to him in the carriage, and we drove off. My boats were almost two miles from the town. We were accompanied by an Hungarian regiment of cavalry. It was a delightful moonlight night, the country we passed through a paradise. Then the carriage stopped, the bugle sounded, and the regiment was drawn up.

'An interesting scene now opened—bugles sounding, drums beating, horses neighing, and people of every nation in Europe witnessing the embarkation of this man who had caused so much misery to them all.

'I informed him that the boat was ready, and we walked together to where she was ...

'When we got on board he walked round the ship. My people crowded about him, and he said "for the first time in his life he felt confidence in a mob". His spirits seemed to revive, and he told me next morning that he had never slept better. Next day he asked me a thousand questions and seemed quite initiated in nautical matters. At breakfast and dinner there was a great deal of conversation ...

'When we were sailing by the Alps he leaned on my arm for half an hour, looking earnestly at them. I said he had once passed them with better fortune. He laughed, and liked the compliment. He told me he had been only once wounded: it was in the knee, and by an English sergeant. He looks uncommonly well and young, and is much changed for the better, being now very stout. He showed me a portrait of the King of Rome; he is very like his father. He likewise showed me one of the Empress, which is rather pretty. We had a smart gale when off Corsica: he asked me to anchor at Ajaccio, the place of his birth; but the wind changing made it impossible. In the gale I told him I had more confidence than Caesar's pilot: the compliment pleased him.

'He dresses very plain, wearing a green coat with the decoration of the Legion of Honour. The portrait of him with the cocked hat and folded arms is the strongest likeness I have seen ...

'General d'Alheme, the governor [of Elba], said he would do whatever was agreeable to Bonaparte. At eight in the evening we anchored, and a deputation came off consisting of the governor, generals, prefect, and civil authorities. At daylight nex morning Bonaparte was on deck, and remained with various officers, asking questions as to the anchorage, fortifications, etc., etc. At eight he asked me for a boat, as he intended to take a walk on the opposite side of the bay, and asked me to go with him. He wore a greatcoat and round hat. Count Bertrand, Colonel Campbell, and Colonel Vincent went with us. When about half-way he remarked that he was without a sword, and soon afterwards asked if the peasants of Tuscany were addicted to assassination.

'We walked about two hours, and the peasants, considering us all as Englishmen, cried "Vive les Anglais!" We returned on board to breakfast, and he afterwards fixed the flag of Elba, and ordered two to be made immediately, and one might be hoisted at one p.m. on the fortifications, and at two p.m. he would disembark with the other. (What a childish vanity!) The flag is a white field with a red band running diagonally through it, with three bees in the band. The bees were in his arms as Emperor of France.

'The boats of the island now began to assemble round the ship, crowded with people, bands of music, etc., and shouting "Vive l'Empereur!" . . . as soon as the barge shoved off a royal salute was fired, and the same by each of the French corvettes. On the beach he was received by the mayor, municipality, and the authorities, civil and military. The keys were presented on a plate, and the people seemed to receive him with great welcome, and shouts of "Vive l'Empereur!" We proceeded to the church in procession; thence to the Hotel de Ville, where all the authorities and principal inhabitants assembled, with each of whom he conversed. After that he mounted his horse, attended by a dozen persons, and visited part of the outworks, and dined at seven o'clock.

'Next morning he was up at four, and from that [sic] until ten was on foot visiting the fortifications, storehouses, magazines, etc. At two he mounted his horse, and I rode with him about two leagues into the country, over mountains and precipices, but nothing is impassable to him. He examined the country houses, and stopped at a planter's (wine merchant) and had a cold collation. He helped me to different things, which he never does to any one else. A lady came in and offered him strawberries, which he gave to me.

'I took an opportunity afterwards of offering him a sprig of laurel, which pleased him much. He asked me here how I liked the wine I said it was excellent; and he immediately ordered 2,000 bottles to be sent on board to the men. In short, his manner is always most agreeable and polite, and it's only when anxious to carry any point that he is passionate . . .

'His constitution is of iron—always up at four, and seldom in bed before eleven. The day the transports arrived with his carriages, horses, and guards he was on his legs from four in the morning until four in the evening, under a hot sun. He then mounted his horse and rode over two or three mountains— returned at eight o'clock, and was not twenty minutes at dinner. He sent for Colonel Campbell and myself. He stopped me for a moment in the library, and hurrying over some magnificent drawings of Egypt, stopped at Cairo, and asked my opinion of it. He then said in his quick way, "Allons!" and we walked into the garden; and there we walked for three hours, talking of Egypt . . .' [5]

And also, no doubt, of Nelson and the battle of the Nile. Nelson surely ranks among the most unaccountable of English heroes, a breed that tends to follow a pattern of enigmatic modesty, simple in feeling and outlook, and largely indifferent to applause. Departures from this pattern, like General Gordon and Lawrence of Arabia, are usually men of quixotic temperament and remain unabashed by controversy, praise or censure. Though Nelson coveted honours, he was otherwise no exception. Those that were showered upon him he took as no more than his due. The dividing line between inordinate vanity and supreme self-confidence is sometimes not easy to perceive and which of the two prompted him to say on the eve of the battle of the Nile: 'Before this time tomorrow I shall have gained a peerage, or Westminster Abbey' is anybody's guess.

Considering the possibilities of its subject, Southey's *Life of Nelson* is a rather dull book, but it does give one an understanding of the dedicated spirit and superhuman physical courage that carried Nelson to glory and the grave. For many days before the battle, during which the British Fleet had been shadowing the French, he had hardly any sleep or food: 'During the pursuit, it had been Nelson's practice, whenever circumstances would permit, to have his captains on the *Vanguard* and explain to them his own ideas of the different and best modes of attack, and such plans as he proposed to execute on falling in with the enemy . . . "First gain the victory," he said, "and then make the best use of it you can." . . . "If we succeed, what will the world say?"' Captain Berry asked. '"There is no *if* in the case," replied the admiral; "that we shall succeed is certain, who may live to tell the story is a very different question".' [6]

Not long after the battle had begun, Nelson, who had already lost the sight of an eye at Calvi and an arm at Teneriffe, 'received a severe wound on the head . . . the great effusion of blood occasioned an

apprehension that the wound was mortal. Nelson himself thought so.
A large flap of the skin of the forehead, cut from the bone, had fallen
over one eye; and the other being blind, he was in total darkness.
When he was carried down, the surgeon—in the midst of a scene
scarcely to be conceived by those who have never seen a cockpit in
time of action, and the heroism which is displayed among its horrors—
with a natural and pardonable eagerness, quitted the poor fellow then
under his hands, that he might instantly attend the admiral. "No,"
said Nelson; "I will take my turn" . . . When the surgeon came in due
time to examine his wound (for it was in vain to entreat him to let it
be examined sooner), the most anxious silence prevailed; and the joy
of the wounded men, and of the whole crew, when they heard that
the hurt was merely superficial. The surgeon requested, and, as far as
he could, ordered him to remain quiet; but Nelson could not rest.
He called for his secretary, Mr Campbell, to write the dispatches.
Campbell had himself been wounded; and was so affected by the blind
and suffering state of the admiral, that he was unable to write. The
chaplain was then sent for; but before he came, Nelson, with his
characteristic eagerness, took the pen, and contrived to trace a few
words, marking his devout sense of the success which had already been
obtained. He was now left alone; when suddenly a cry was heard on
deck, that the Orient the French flagship was on fire. In the confusion
he found his way up, unassisted and unnoticed; and, to the astonishment of everyone, appeared on the quarter-deck, where he immediately
gave orders that the boats should be sent to the relief of the enemy.' [7]

Seeing valour as the better part of discretion, Southey concentrates
upon Nelson's professional exploits and skates, with eyes downcast
and only the faintest moue of disapproval over his relations with Emma,
a woman whose meddlesome and ambitious instincts would have
mitigated for me a good deal of her charm. A beauty whose good
looks and gaiety would, I feel sure, have appealed to me far more was
the wife of Dr John Overall, a seventeenth-century divine, who was
Dean of St Paul's. According to Aubrey, she was 'the greatest beautie
in her time in England. That she was so I have it attested from the
famous limmer Mr Hoskins and other old painters, besides old
courtiers. She was not more beautiful than she was obligeing and
kind, and was so tender-hearted that (truly) she scarce denie any one.
She had (they told me) the lovliest eies that ever were seen, but wondrous wanton. When she came to court or to the playhouse, the gallants
would so flock round her. Richard, the earle of Dorset, and his
brother Edward, since earle, both did mightily adore her. And by

their report he must have had a hard heart who did not admire her ...
the good old deane, notwithstanding he knew well enough he was
horned, loved her infinitely: in so much that he was willing she should
enjoy what she had a mind to ...

> Face she had of filberd hue,
>   And bossom'd like a swan;
> Back she had of bended ewe,
>   And wasted by a span.
> Haire she had as black as crowe
>   From head unto the toe
> Downe, downe, all over her
>   Hy nonny nonny noe.[8]

If one has the patience to look for the plums in Aubrey's indigestible
pudding, they are there to be found, sweetened with intimate and
often amusing detail, as in his description of Sir John Suckling, who
'went to the university of Cambridge at eleven yeares of age, where he
studied three or four yeares (I think, four). By 18 he had travelled
France and Italie, and part of Germany, and (I thinke also) of Spaine.

'He returned into England an extraordinary accomplished gentleman, grew famous at court for his readie sparkling witt which was
envyed ... He was incomparably readie at repartyng and his witt
most sprakling when most sett-upon and provoked ...

'He was of middle stature and slight strength, brisque round eie,
reddish fac't and red nose (ill liver), his head not very big, his hayre
a kind of sand colour; his beard turnd-up naturally, so that he had a
brisk and gracefull looke ...

'He was the greatest gallant of his time, and the greatest gamester,
both for bowling and cards, so that no shop-keeper would trust him
for 6d., as to-day, for instance, he might, by winning, be worth 200li,
the next day he might not be worth half so much, or perhaps be
sometimes minus nihilo ... when he was at his lowest ebbe in gameing,
I meane when unfortunate, then would make himselfe most glorious
in apparell, and sayd that it exalted his spirits, and that he had then
best luck when he was most gallant, and his spirits were highest ...

'Anno Domini 163—there happened, unluckily, a difference between
Sir John Suckling and Sir John Digby (brother to Sir Kenelme) about
a mistresse or gameing, I have now forgott. Sir John was but a slight
timbered man, and of midling stature; Sir John Digby a proper person
of great strength, and courage answerable, and yielded to be the best
swordsman of his time. Sir John, with some 2 or 3 of his party assaults

Sir John Digby goeing into a play-house; Sir J. D. had only his lacquey with him, but he flew on them like a tiger, and made them run. 'Twas pitty that this accident brought the blemish of cowardise to such an ingeniose young sparke.' [9]

An older spark, no less ingenious, I daresay, in his own way, was Mr J. Dance, of Warwick, whose name I fancy few people will have heard of. Until the war I had never heard it myself. I was listening to the radio one evening when a talk was announced on 'Making Eyes'. It was the ambiguity of the title, coupled with the speaker's name—the vision of Mr Dance making eyes seemed oddly and romantically appropriate—which stopped me from switching off, and I have always been glad that I hesitated to do so, for to listen to J. Dance talking shop was a revelation of character as distinct and as expressive as a Hogarth portrait; as ineffably English too, and as full of bright-eyed gusto and independence:

'I am a man with a rather peculiar trade,' Mr Dance began: 'I make glass eyes for wild animals, stuffed ones . . . I sometimes think that mine is one of those dull, uninteresting jobs, because I never see my customers. I am wholesale, you see. I make a dozen gross of antelopes' eyes or a gross of tigers', but it is the naturalists and taxidermists who see what you might call the human side of the story. They have all the old ladies coming in saying, "Please put my cat down just as she used to sleep", and so on . . . You can see "Eyes by J. Dance" in every part of the Empire: Africa, India, New Zealand, Canada and North America—I supply them all, not to mention the hundreds of museums and naturalists in the British Isles.

'I have made every eye from a mouse to an elephant and every animal under the sun. Someone asked me the other day if I had ever made an octopus's eye: well, I haven't done that one. Has an octopus got an eye anyway? That's something I cannot answer. I am not a naturalist; I am an eye-maker. And another eye I have never given anyone is a black eye: not even my wife.

'But I make all the others—lions', tigers', crocodiles', elephants', as well as all the small stuff like humming-birds', snakes', cheetahs', bush-babys', bats' and the like; and I make them all in Warwick in the middle of England, where you don't get such a thing as a crocodile from one year's end to another. I have got a little one-man workshop in an old timber yard. It's all old cottages covered with roses where I live, and the country round about is very leafy, full of elm trees and lanes with high hedges. We are right in the middle of the fox-hunting country; and that's where my eyes come in again . . .

'The fox, of course, is of the dog tribe and has a round pupil, but to give it a cunning expression I give it an elliptical pupil—a slit pupil. That's one of the things I do: I put the *expression* into my eyes. For instance, my lions' eyes have a fierce expression. A lion's is a yellow eye and it is always looking at the sun, so it has a tiny pupil. Well, by making the pupil round, I make it fierce. Or perhaps a customer wants a wall eye, blue and white (although I don't know that you would call a wall eye an expression) or a couple of albino eyes, say. The albino eye is always pink, and you get an albino in everything; although I don't remember doing an albino lion. You get albino foxes, of course, and albino baboons, and many a time I have done an albino crow or sparrow. Well now, if a customer wants anything like that, I can give it to him. Customers can have any eye or any expression they want.

'Usually the colour of the eye is taken from the coat of the animal. Colourful eyes go mostly to the tropics, and dark eyes—for bears, moose and the like—to the cold countries. The stag's eye is a cold-country eye, and it is a real quality eye; the bison, the elk, the gazelle and the antelope are all quality eyes. A "quality eye" is a concave eye, and it is my speciality. It is my own invention. It is far more natural than the old-fashioned eye, which was flat at the back. Making it concave shows the colours, whether you are looking sideways or in front, just like the natural eye. The biggest eyes of all are the giraffe's: they must be specially blown. But you only get, say, four pairs of giraffe's eyes in a hundred years. I have been in the trade now forty years, and there have been only two pairs wanted . . . The elephant's eye is a big eye too. It is small compared to the animal, a bit bigger than the ordinary cow or bull, just about the same size as a moose. Then some of the smallest eyes I make are snakes' eyes. They have got a sparkling sort of eye . . .

'All the eyes for the fox furs—and I make thousands of those—go to Canada . . . and I have just done twelve gross of white and yellow birds' eyes for the Sudan Government. I do a lot of work for Africa —I always have: nearly all antelopes and lions. Also quite a number of crocodiles. They have a different sort of eye: dark green with a little slit pupil, and they are not round. Crocodiles' and alligators' eyes are the only eyes I make oval. But the alligator is different altogether from the crocodile; it has a buff-coloured eye.

'When I am making kittens' eyes I do ten gross at a time, because all kittens' eyes are the same, and are always blue. All young creatures have blue eyes. But a cat is quite different. It is one of the few animals you cannot stock eyes for, because every kind of cat has a different kind of eye. They vary as much as human eyes, and much more than dogs'. Dogs' eyes are always hazel.

'I make kittens' eyes in the same way that they used to be made a hundred years ago, and I use a bunsen burner over a hundred years old. With all the modern inventions, they have not been able to improve on it. As far as my workshop is concerned, there are eyes to the left of me and eyes all round me. There are eyes in every ornament in the house, and eyes in all my pockets. I feel in my waistcoat pocket for a spanner perhaps, and I bring out a lion's eye. Or I take out a handful of change to pay for a glass of beer, and there are two or three foxs' eyes in the middle of it.' [10]

I never met Mr Dance. I wish that I had. I think he must have been a delightful as well as a dedicated man. Such a man may sometimes seem a bore, although as likely as not his single-mindedness is the reflection of a character of uncorrupted simplicity. Mr Dance, I feel, would have got along well with Whitman, whose lack of affectation was paradoxically almost an affectation in itself. It was probably the instinctive perception of a character fundamentally similar to his own that attracted him strongly to the personality of Lincoln, whom he often used to see when he himself was living in Washington. With his alert, well-trained and penetrative eye he registered, besides the immediate details of the scene, the deep humanistic gravity of Lincoln's spirit:

'I see the President almost every day, as I happen to live where he passes to or from his lodgings out of town. He never sleeps at the White House during the hot season, but has his quarters at a healthy location some three miles north of the city . . . He always has a company of twenty-five or thirty cavalry, with sabres drawn and held upright over their shoulders. They say this guard was against his personal wish, but he let his counsellors have their way. The party makes no great show in uniform or horses. Mr Lincoln on the saddle generally rides a good-sized, easy-going grey horse, is dress'd in plain black, somewhat rusty and dusty, wears a black stiff hat, and looks about as ordinary in attire, etc., as the commonest man . . . His cavalry men, are generally going at a slow trot, as that is the pace set by the one they wait upon. The sabres and accoutrements clank and the entirely unornamental *cortège* as it trots towards Lafayette Square arouses no sensation, only some curious stranger stops and gazes. I see very plainly Abraham Lincoln's dark brown face, with the deep-cut lines, the eyes, always to me with a deep latent sadness in the expression.

We have got so that we exchange bows, and very cordial ones ... None of the artists or pictures has caught the deep, though subtle and indirect expression of this man's face. There is something else there. One of the great portrait painters of two or three centuries ago is needed.' [11]

It would be hard to find two men more vividly contrasted in their characters and dispositions, more unalike in what each other had to offer and to seek in life, than Lincoln and George Brummell. It is easy to dismiss Brummell as a waster and a snob, but the fact remains that it was his scrupulous taste in matters of dress that gave undying impetus to the belief that Englishmen are the best dressed in the world. Mass production methods of tailoring and the influence of American flamboyance in clothes has done a lot to kill this idea, but there is still some truth in it, and since being well dressed is in some degree a matter of self-respect, it seems a tradition worth trying to preserve. Brummell set himself and posterity a standard of discretion in clothes that has survived the negligence of twentieth century appearances, and for this, if for nothing else, we should be thankful.

For a man to whom fashion and friendship were almost the only resources that existence had to offer, no more unkind fate could be imagined than exile and poverty. However shallow and worthless Brummell may have been, he was not without feeling, and the circumstances of his declining years, which were spent at Caen, even though clouded by a merciful decay of mind, can hardly fail to arouse one's pity. Towards the end, the squalor of his surroundings and the confusion of his brain made it necessary for friends to arrange for his removal to a place where he could be properly looked after:

'When the day arrived for his departure, some fears were entertained that he would object to leave his rooms at the hotel, and every precaution was taken to induce him to go quietly. His landlord a day or two before, invited him to take a drive on the Cours, to which he consented, and a day and hour were named. At the appointed time, therefore, Monsieur Fichet, accompanied by Mr Armstrong and his servant, went to his apartment, having previously had the carriage drawn up close to the door of the staircase, which was immediately under the *porte-cochère*.

'On entering his room, they found poor Brummell in his dressing-gown, seated in his easy chair ... near the fireplace, but without his wig; this he had placed on one knee, which he had raised, by setting his foot on the rail of a chair that stood in front of him. An old pewter shaving-box stood on the table close to him, and into this he kept dipping his brush, and working up a lather, which he transferred to his peruke. So intent was he on what he was doing, that he never observed the entrance of the party, but continued painting away; his great object apparently being to make every hair of the wig lie flat. "Bonjour, Monsieur Brummell," said the landlord, desirous of withdrawing his attention from his occupation; contrary, however, to his usual habit, which even now was courteous in the extreme, he replied, without turning his head, or ceasing to ply his brush: "Laissez-moi tranquille". "But I have ordered a carriage for you to take a drive with me," continued the landlord; "you promised me that you would go, and the carriage is now at the door." Brummell, however, would not go, and excused himself by saying he was not well, and would go another day. They then praised the weather, and a garden that he was to see; it was the merry month of May but he knew it not. Expostulation, however, and every proposition that was likely to tempt him to move, failed—he went on lathering and painting, evidently determined not to budge.

'At length, finding all attempts at persuasion unsuccessful, Monsieur Fichet approached him, and, snatching the wig from his knee, threw it on the table. This so irritated the poor fellow that he ordered them to leave the room instantly, and threatened, if they did not, to turn them out: they had therefore, no alternative left but to use force, and, taking him in their arms, for he would not walk, they carried him down the stairs. This rough usage turned his thoughts into another channel; he imagined they were taking him to jail, and the scene on the staircase was most distressing. It was in vain that they tried to pacify him, by assuring him that he was going to a much better and handsomer residence: he kicked and fought as violently as his swollen legs and reduced strength would permit; screaming and shouting at the top of his voice, "You are taking me to prison—loose me, scoundrels! I owe nothing": and then a shriek followed that was heard at the end of the court; but his resistance was, of course, futile, and this, happily, he appeared to be aware of directly he was put into the carriage, for he suddenly became perfectly tranquil.

'On their way across the Place Royale they met Monsieur de St M——, with whom he had been intimate, though he had not seen him for two years; Brummell, however, to the utter astonishment of those who were with him, recognised him instantly, and, with the feeble ray of reason that flickered over the wreck of intellect, he showed, and for the last time, that the ruling passion even then predominated;

for he immediately drew away from the window, and said, "That is Monsieur de St M——"; and, looking at his tattered dressing-gown, added, "I did not bow to him, for I am not fit to be seen in such a déshabillé as this". When they arrived at the gates of the Bon Sauveur, and the unfortunate Brummell heard the bolts withdrawn, he again thought that he was going to be incarcerated, and wept bitterly, muttering between his teeth: "A prison—a prison". His tears, indeed, fell fast, and did not cease until the carriage drew up in the courtyard and, descending, he found himself surrounded by the nuns, whose kind and gentle manners soon dispelled his grief and fears. When the Superior came up, and took him by the hand, Brummell was quite delighted, and immediately after allowed one of the sisters, a young woman, to lead him into the house.

'Though in a religious habit, he at first imagined she was the wife of Auguste, Mr Armstrong's servant; and turning to him, for he was supporting him on the other side, he said: "N'est-ce pas Madame?" Auguste was rather abashed at this remark, but the nun smiled, while Brummell, totally unconscious of its absurdity, slyly added, "Ah, vous êtes marié! eh bien, je vous félicite; car"—and he turned towards the nun as he spoke—"vous êtes bien une jolie femme". Thus accompanied he was taken to his apartments, where every comfort was awaiting him, and a blazing fire with an armchair in front of it; of this, he immediately took possession, expressing himself greatly delighted with his new quarters . . .

'In this oasis, poor Brummell, surrounded by comforts that he had long been a stranger to, passed the remainder of his days, not, however, destined to be numerous, but which, thanks to the humane conduct of the inmates of the institution, were spent in perfect tranquility. The few friends who charitably paid him an occasional visit always found him sitting before a blazing fire, and his man-servant or one of the *sœurs*, for he was never left alone, sitting in the room to anticipate his every want. When asked by an old acquaintance, whom he did not, however, recognise, whether he was comfortable, Brummell replied, "Oh, yes," and, turning to the nun, who was standing by his chair, and taking her hand, he said, "This excellent nurse of mine is so kind to me that she refuses me nothing; I have all I wish to eat, and such a large fire; I never was so comfortable in all my life."

'To the last he retained a confused recollection of those persons whose countenances had been most familiar to him, and they could occasionally bring to mind the remembrance of those friends from whom he had, during his residence at Caen, received obligations and kindness.

In this state of second childhood he remained till the spring of the following year, apparently perfectly happy, and capable of answering questions relating to his wants, but wholly unconscious of his real position. Though one or two of his most intimate friends called to see him after he was placed in this asylum, the only visits that he received towards the immediate close of his life were those of the English clergyman . . .

'About a week before Mr——— paid him . . . his last visit, his debility had continually increased; his hour was evidently approaching fast; nature was too completely worn out; and her lamp, which had burnt too frequently before the altars of folly and pleasure, was now on the eve of expiring. This . . . description of his last moments . . . I learned from the nun who had attended him from the time he entered the Bon Sauveur. "On the evening of his death," said that amiable woman, "about an hour before he expired, the debility having become extreme, I observed him assume an appearance of intense anxiety and fear, and he fixed his eyes upon me, with an expression of entreaty, raising his hands towards me, as he lay in the bed, and as though asking for assistance . . . but saying nothing. Upon this, I requested him to repeat after me the *acte de contrition* of the Roman ritual, as in our prayer books. He immediately consented, and repeated after me in an earnest manner that form of prayer. He then became more composed, and laid his head down to one side; but this tranquillity was interrupted, about an hour after, by his turning himself over, and uttering a cry, at the same time appearing to be in pain; he soon, however, turned himself back with his face laid on the pillow towards the wall, so as to be hidden from us who were on the other side; after this he never moved, dying imperceptibly." It was a quarter past nine in the evening of the 30th of March 1840.' [12]

If Brummell's life had been more worthwhile his end, instead of coming merely as a pitiful release, might be remembered as a tragedy. But he had no recollections of a useful or even industrious past to compensate for the bitterness of oblivion and poverty. Whatever may be said of the Goncourts' faithful servant Rose, whose death some twenty years later than Brummell's was a tragedy no less sordid, she had worked her fingers to the bone in their exacting service and had earned their lasting affection. Not even Flaubert, for whose acute insight into problems of moral weakness the Goncourts had much respect, could have conceived a more pitiless tragedy than that of Rose; a tragedy which, unknown to them, was happening for years on their own doorstep. There is something curiously ironic in the spectacle of their grief for the victim. Even to a temperament more earthy or robust than theirs, the shock of such a discovery would have been a painful one, but that they, for whom contact with the world beyond their own carefully cushioned universe was like brushing a peach against a thistle—that they should have lived, without knowing it, on the edge of a cesspool must have made the discovery, when it came, unspeakably revolting. Self-pity, more especially when it results, as in their case, from a morbid degree of introspection, seldom arouses much sympathy, but in this instance one cannot help feeling some compassion for the brothers in their distress.

'*July 22:* Little by little disease is accomplishing its ruinous work in our poor servant, Rose.

'*July 31:* Dr Simon will be telling me shortly whether our old Rose is to live or to die. I am waiting for his ring, which will be, to me, the verdict of an assizes jury coming into the courtroom . . . "It's all over. No hope. A question of time. The disease has worked quickly. One lung gone and the other about as bad."

'*August 11:* Rose refuses to go to Dubois's nursing home, where we offered to send her. Twenty-five years ago, when she came to us, she went there once to see Edmond's nurse. The nurse died there, and that nursing home represents to Rose the house of death. I am waiting for Simon, who is to bring Rose a card that will pass her into the Lariboisière Hospital. She spent a good night, almost. She is all ready, even gay. We have hidden the truth from her as best we could. She breathes freer at the idea of going. She is impatient. It seems to her that she will recover there. Simon arrived at two o'clock. "All arranged." In the cab she sat with her hand on the window ledge. I held her up against the pillow we had put behind her. Eyes blank and wide open, she looked vaguely at the houses as we passed. She stopped speaking.

'When we reached the gate she insisted upon getting down without being carried. "Can you walk that far?" the porter asked. She nodded affirmatively and went on. I have no notion where she gathered the strength to walk. Finally we came into a large, high-ceilinged, cold, rigid, clean room with a stretcher in the middle of it. I sat her down in a cane-bottomed chair near a glazed window. A clerk opened the window, asked me her name, her age, and spent a good quarter hour writing on a dozen sheets of paper, all of which had a religious symbol at the top. Finally, that was over. I kissed her. A man took one arm, a charwoman the other. That was the last I saw of her.

'*Saturday, August 16:* At ten o'clock this morning there was a ring at the door. I heard a colloque between the maid and the porter. The door opened. The porter came in with a letter. I took the letter. It bore the stamp of Lariboisière. Rose died this morning at seven o'clock.

'What a void! What a gap in our life! A habit, an affection, twenty-five years old. A servant who knew our whole life, opened our letters when we were away; to whom we told everything about ourselves. When I was very small I rolled a hoop with her, and when we went out she would buy apple pies for me out of her own money. She would wait up for Edmond until daylight to open the door for him when he went to the Opera Ball, unknown to mother. It was this woman, this admirable nurse, whose hands our dying mother put into our hands. She had the keys to everything; she decided and did everything in our home. For twenty-five years she had tucked us into our beds, and every evening we made the same joking remarks about her ugliness and her ungainly body. She shared our joys and our sorrows. Hers was one of those devotions one hopes will be present to shut one's eyes for the last time, when that time comes. Our bodies, in our distress or illness, were accustomed to her tending. She shared all our manias. She had known all our mistresses. She was a chunk of our life, a piece with which our apartment was furnished, a survival of our youth; something tender and grumbling and *watchman-like*, a kind of watchdog, that we were accustomed to have beside us, around us, and that we somehow expected to end only with the end of us.

'*Thursday, August 21:* In the course of a dinner saddened by a conversation that went back again and again to the subject of our dead Rose, Maria, who was dining with us this evening, after two or three nervous pattings of her tightly curled puffed-out hair, exclaimed abruptly, "Look here! So long as the poor woman was alive, I kept my mouth shut because . . . well, call it professional ethics. But now that she is dead and buried, I think you two ought to know the truth about her."

'And with that we heard things about our unfortunate Rose that took away our appetite, that filled our mouths with the acid bitterness of fruit cut with a steel knife. Maria revealed to our ignorance a whole odious, repugnant and lamentable life. Those bills Rose signed, those debts she left with every kind of shop-keeper, were due to an absolutely inconceivable, a most astounding, a most incredible circumstance. Rose kept men. One of them was the son of our creamery woman, for whom she had taken and furnished a room. Another was given our wine, our chickens, our food. A secret existence of nocturnal orgies, nights out, uterine frenzies that actually prompted one of her lovers

to say, "It's going to croak one of us—me or her". A passion, a sum
of passions, that took in all of her—her head, her heart, her senses,
with which went the ailments of the wretched woman, her consump-
tion lending a sort of fury to her sensuality, a kind of hysteria, a
beginning of madness. By the creamery woman's son she had two
children, one of which lived six months. When a few years back,
she told us she was going home for a bit, it was to be delivered of a
child. And her ardour for these men was so excessive, so unhealthy
and demented even, that she, who was ordinarily the soul of honesty,
robbed us, stole twenty-franc pieces which she would give to her lovers
to persuade them not to desert her.

'Following these involuntary spurts of dishonesty, these little crimes
offensive to her natural uprightness, she would sink into such self-
reproach, such remorse, such despondency and black fits of despair,
that in this inferno, going desperately and unsated from transgression
to transgression, she began to drink in order to escape from herself,
to flee the present, to sink and drown for a few hours in one of those
slumbers, those lethargic torpors in which she would lie all day long
on a bed onto which she had collapsed while making it up.

'Poor woman! What predispositions and motives and reasons she
found in herself to devour herself and bleed inwardly as she did!
First, there was the intermittent recoil of religious ideas, with terror of
hell-fire and brimstone; and then jealousy, that quite particular
jealousy that raged in her with regard to everything and everybody;
and finally, the disgust which, after a time, men would brutally betray
her for her ugliness, and which drove her more and more urgently to
drink and led to a miscarriage one day as she fell dead drunk on the
floor. This horrifying tearing of the veil before our eyes was like the
autopsy of a pocket bursting with disgusting things in a suddenly
opened corpse.

'From what we were told I could see all at once all that she had been
through these past ten years: the fear that we might receive anonymous
letters about her; the fear that she would be denounced by some
shopkeeper; the constant trepidation over the demands for money
made upon her and that she could never pay back; and the shame felt
by this proud creature, perverted by the abominable Saint-Georges
quarter in which we live, by the company of low people whom she
despised, and the painful consciousness of premature senility brought
on by sodden drinking, and the inhuman exigencies and meannesses
of the gutter-rats she frequented, and the temptation to suicide (so
that one day I pulled her back from a window out of which she was all

but falling); and all those tears that we used to think had no cause —all this mixed up with a very deep-seated affection she felt for us and an almost feverish devotion when one or the other of us felt ill.

'And there was in this woman an energy, a strength of will, an art of concealment, that was incomparable. There was absolute success in keeping these frightful secrets hidden and locked up within her, without a single betrayal to our eyes or our ears or our general sense of observation, even when she had an attack of nerves (at which times nothing but moaning would come forth from her), a mystery that continued to her very death and which she must have thought buried with her.

'And what did she die of? Of having stood all night in the rain in Montmartre, some eight months ago, spying on the creamery woman's son, who had driven her out, to find out who the woman was that had taken her place: a whole night spent staring at the window of a ground-floor room, from which she had come away with her clothes soaking, chilled to the bone, and mortally ill of pleurisy.' [13]

I do not much care for fact being mixed with fiction, hence my reluctance to read historical novels, and as a result my indifference to Scott, Harrison Ainsworth and others with whom no doubt I ought to be better acquainted. But as my object here is to please myself as well, I hope, as pleasing the reader, I make no apology for my inconsistency in now referring to fact and fiction in the same breath, in this case to a story by Ludwig Bemelmans.

Bemelmans' natural habitat is what is called (though not by me) the 'luxury' hotel. For giving one a cosmic view of the virtues and frailties of the human race there can be no place like it. Man in every variety of mood and circumstance is somewhere there, in the marble bathroom or the refrigeration plant, at the switchboard or in the bar, in the manager's office or at the masonic banquet, in the grill room or the stokehold. Not since Arnold Bennett anatomized the luxury hotel has anyone done it as thoroughly or as sympathetically as Bemelmans. It would be a mistake, however, to imagine him merely as a glorified reporter, as his story of the Brave Commis shows:

'In the locker next to mine in the waiters' dressing-room hung the clothes of a young French commis who worked in fat Monsieur Victor's restaurant. This young man had a dream; for every waiter, like every prisoner, has a dream. With the older ones it is about a chicken farm, or becoming rich through an invention, or various small businesses, or a return home to a little house, and peace; with relatively few is it a hotel or a restaurant—of this they say: "*Sale métier*, filthy profession." But the young ones have more daring dreams: becoming an aviator, a detective, a movie actor, an orchestra leader, or a dancer; and because the French champion prize-fighter is visiting America, a certain young blond *commis de rang* is going to lead a very healthy life and become a boxer.

'He has the boxer's picture pasted up on the inside of his locker door; he does not eat stews and dishes that are made with sauces; when he comes down with his chef to the employees' dining-room, he brings that man's food, but runs up again for plain vegetables, cheese, and a cutlet for himself; he drinks no wine and empties a quart of milk into himself at every meal. He arrives at the hotel in a trot, his fists at the sides of his chest . . . In the locker-room he makes a few boxing motions—*l'uppercut, le knockout*—dancing and twisting his head and then with a loud: "Ah, brr, bhuff," and: "*Ca, c'est bon,*" he takes a cold shower. He has immaculate linen, fine muscles, and he brings his chest out of the shower as if it were a glass case full of jewels.

'Up in the restaurant he looks fine, first because he is tall and handsome, secondly because he stands straight and the mess-jacket and the long apron look good on him, and thirdly because he is always clean. Victor likes him because he is always smiling and is as quick as lightning. He takes the stairs up from and down to the kitchen—thirty iron steps, of which every other man complains—as if they were built for him to train on. He makes the run up in two seconds flat, pushing four steps at a time from under him and flying past the heavily loaded older men so that he almost upsets their trays. They stop and curse him, but he laughs back over his shoulder, takes a stack of hot plates out of the heater, and worms his way to his station through the crowded dining-room with an elegant twist. To reward him, when the visiting French champion comes to the restaurant with his friends, he is seated at the young commis's station and gets service such as no one else receives.

'Victor has also promised the young man a future: he will make him a *chef de rang* at the next opportunity, then in a little while *maître d'hôtel*. Men so engaging, so fine-looking, who, moreover, know their business well and are quick-thinking and intelligent, are few. And he is a Frenchman, and so does not underestimate the value of such a future, and the advice of Victor. He is, besides, very sober in his estimate of the boxing profession. He will try it while he keeps one foot in the Splendide. If all goes well, if he should be another champion, fine. For lesser rewards, no. Meanwhile, he will have had fun, and acquired a well-trained body, which is a good possession, especially since most *maîtres d'hôtel* and managers are fat, bald, pale, and flat-footed. For one so youthful he shows much good sense in his planning.

'He asked me once to go to the Young Men's Christian Association with him. This institution seemed to me far from a benevolent undertaking ... The guests were nice clean-cut earnest boys who wished to get ahead, but the atmosphere of the place, I thought, was commercial, unhospitable, and false.

'The commis introduced me to the gym instructors with the casualness of an old habitué, and for my benefit he put on a little boxing show with one of them and with a ball suspended from a parquet board, which to me, who understood little, seemed very good. When it was time to get back to the hotel to set the tables for dinner, he took another shower and we arrived at the Splendide in a hurry. I was out of wind and perspiring, but he took his shoulders out of his narrow athletic undershirt and asked me in loud French to tell those others what I had seen this afternoon in the way of *"le boxe"*.

'The brave commis did finally become a *chef de rang* with a good station, being jumped over the heads of several older men. He made very good money, but more of it went into boxing, and he became stronger and stronger. Because he was such a good, swift, smiling waiter, he received some of the most difficult guests, and one day during a rush, he had to serve a man who was generally feared, for he had had many men dismissed. Mr Mistbeck, a blanket manufacturer, lived in the hotel. He should never have been allowed in the hotel at all, but he had millions. He was on some kind of diet, and everything had to be cooked for him without salt or sugar; a long list of how his food was to be prepared hung down in the kitchen. Also he had his own wines and his own mustard; he mixed his own salads; and all this, in the middle of a rush, was always difficult. The cooks cursed; there was sometimes delay.

'Mr Mistbeck then became abusive. He knocked on his glass, shouted: "Hey", or "Hey, you", said: "Tsk, tchk, tchk," or: "Psst", and pulled his waiter by the apron or the napkin at luncheon or by the tailcoat at dinner. His wife, a little frowsy, scared, but kindly woman, would try to calm him. That only made him madder; he spoke so loud that the people at the tables around him looked up in surprise; his face turned red and blue, and a vein on his forehead stood out; he moved the silver and glasses, bunched the napkin into a ball, pounded on the table, and sometimes got up and walked to the door, his napkin in his hand, to complain to Victor.

'His complaints always started: "I have been coming here for the last five years, and goddam it, these idiots don't know yet what I want, you charge enough in this lousy dump!" Or it would go: "Listen, you"—he held the waiter while he said that—"listen, you old fool, one of these days I'll buy this goddamn joint and fire every one of you swine and get some people that know how to wait on table; now get going!" With that he would push the man loose. During these embarrassing moments, his poor wife would turn red and look down on her plate and behave as if she were not there. When the waiter was gone, Mr Mistbeck would continue to shout at her, as if she too had kept him waiting or brought him something he did not like.

'One of the dreadful things about the hotel business is that it offers no defence against such people. The old waiters, who have families, just mumble: "Yes, sir. No, sir. Right away, sir. I'm sorry, sir." They insult the guest outside the room, on the stairway down to the kitchen; that is why one sees these poor fellows talking so much to themselves—they are delivering a long repartee and threatening to throw out some imaginary customer and telling him what they think of him . . .

'Mr Mistbeck sat at the station of the new waiter, the former brave commis. He was for some reason unusually abusive, nothing suited him, and finally he pushed back his chair, threw away his napkin, and getting up, took hold of the young man's lapels to deliver his usual speech. Now the brave commis could not stand being touched; his hands leaped up in fists. In a second, Mr Mistbeck had *l'uppercut* and le *knockout*, and had fallen into his chair with his arms hanging down, his face on his fork, and his toupée on the floor.

'That ended the Splendide career of the brave commis. Downstairs, he was congratulated by all the waiters; in the barber's shop he had to show Frank the engineer just how he had done it; and Victor gave him a good recommendation. But in a week the brave commis came back—in uniform. He had enlisted in the American army.

'All the men looked at him with great envy; for a waiter it was so wonderful to be brave, and to be where there were no guests.

'I thought . . . about Mr Mistbeck, and how much I hated this business. Then one evening there was a banquet at which Marshal Joffre spoke. When he was leaving I helped him on with his coat in the lobby, and because it was raining, I said: "*Ça pleut dehors.*" He turned, smiled, and said in German: "*Mein lieber Kleiner, es is nicht 'ça pleut dehors'. Es ist 'il pleut dehors!*'" And because of that, and the brave commis, and other reasons, I enlisted in the American army the next day.' [14]

As we began, so let us end these glimpses of the tiger, the ass, the pig and the nightingale, with Dame Edith Sitwell once more letting the fountain of her irony, tempered with jets of sympathetic amusement, play upon another of the English eccentrics. Again the subject is one of such vast absurdity that no character in literature could compete with him:

'In the flat countryside near Doncaster, stout Mr Jemmy Hirst, the Rawcliffe tanner, who had retired from business with a large fortune, might have been seen any autumn day about the year 1840, leaving his house to go shooting. His jolly, if coarse, face was as round as the autumn sun, and shone like brightly polished leather, whilst everything about him had a strong, horsy, leathery smell. But Mr Hirst did not approve of horses excepting on the racecourse, and he went shooting mounted on the back of a bull of ample proportions and uncertain temper, whilst for pointers, he made use of the services of a crowd of vivacious and sagacious pigs, all of whom answered to their names, and did their duty irreproachably. It is said that Mr Hirst rode the bull when hunting with the Badsworth hounds. If he did, his presence must, I imagine, have lent animation to the scene, and speed to the chase. But we cannot be certain of the truth of the story.

'His household staff consisted of a valet, a female general servant, a tame fox, and an otter, whilst he possessed, as well, a large stud of mules and dogs. The house itself was rendered cheerful by the presence —in the dining-room, which was redolent of leather, and was hung about with rusty agricultural instruments—of a large coffin. Mr Hirst had shown a long foresight in buying this coffin, for he was to live till the age of ninety years; but meanwhile, it proved useful as a sideboard, and Mr Hirst, when visited by his racing friends and others, would produce spirits from the inner recesses of this.

'Mr Hirst's sporting activities did not stop at going shooting and hunting, mounted on a bull, for he was as well, a very well-known figure on the Doncaster racecourse, to which he drove in a very odd carriage, perched on extremely high wheels, shaped like a palanquin, and innocent of nails. His arrival was pleasant, since he was extremely popular on the racecourse, and he would swagger about the enclosure in his glossy shining waistcoat, made of drakes' feathers, from the pockets of which, when making bets, he would draw bank-notes, made by himself, and bearing the responsibility of payment to the amount of fivepence-half-penny.

'His last ride was as remarkable as any he had taken. The coffin was withdrawn from the dining-room and, the spirits having been ejected from it, and the body of the ninety-year-old Mr Hirst substituted for these, it was borne to the grave by eight stout widows, followed by a vast procession of sporting men and racing tipsters, to the accompaniment of a lively march played by a bagpipe and fiddle. Mr Hirst's wish had been to be carried to the grave by eight old maids, and he went so far as to try to bribe ladies to perform this service by the promise of a guinea each; but unluckily the bribe was not large enough to overcome the shyness habitual to the maiden state; so, in the end, Mr Hirst had to fall back upon widows, who, being more accessible, were regarded by him as not being worth more than half a crown each.' [15]

SOURCES

1   Dame Edith Sitwell, *The English Eccentrics*.
2   Charles C. F. Greville, *The Greville Memoirs*, vol. iii.
3   Edmond and Jules de Goncourt, *Journals*.
4   William Bolitho, *Twelve Against the Gods*.
5   Captain Thomas Ussher, letter to Mrs M —, from *Napoleon Banished*.
6   Robert Southey, *The Life of Nelson*.
7   Ibid.
8   John Aubrey, *Brief Lives*.
9   Ibid.
10 J. Dance 'Making Eyes', *The Listener*, April 13, 1943.
11 Walt Whitman, *Specimen Days*.
12 Captain Jesse, *The Life of Beau Brummell*.
13 See 3.
14 Ludwig Bemelmans, *Life Class*.
15 See 1.

A Bill of Fare

*

Cookery, in our era, has been thought beneath the attention
of men of science; and yet, was there ever a political, commercial, or even a domestic event, but what always has been, and
always will be, celebrated either by a banquet or a dinner?
And pray, who is answerable for the comfort and conviviality
of the guests of such festivals but the cook, who has been
entrusted with such important duties? The selection of good
and proper beverages will, of course, greatly assist the cook's
endeavours; but these may be purchased months, or even
years, before you require them, which would of course give
you an ample chance of remedying any error; while the
dinner is the creation of a day and the success of a moment.
Therefore you will perceive that nothing more disposes the
heart to amicable feeling and friendly transactions, than a
dinner well conceived and artistically prepared.

ALEXIS SOYER in a letter to a friend,
from *A Shilling Cookery for the People*

ALTHOUGH I enjoy a good meal as much as I am bored by a bad one, I have never had much of an appetite, and as a carnivore I am by English standards a poor specimen. Until I was about twelve years old I seldom ate meat, not because of vegetarian principles but simply because I did not like it, and to this whim my parents foolishly acceded. Even to this day, meat, except for venison, means less to me as a rule than fish or fowl, and I could live quite happily on either for the rest of my life. But if my appetite is small the enjoyment I get from reading about food and feasts is considerable: a vicarious enjoyment which avoids the penalties of eating and drinking more than is good for me.

No one ever wrote about food with more obvious enthusiasm than Dickens: and not about food only. The circumstances of the meal, the preliminaries and anticipations, are as important to its description as the succulent prose that describes the food and drink itself. No great effort of imagination is needed to seat oneself at the dinner table, to enhale the savoury odours wafting from the kitchen, to hear the clink of glasses and the rattle of silver, or sense the anticipation of Bailey, the youthful factotum, on that Sunday afternoon when Mr Pecksniff's daughters made their debut before the 'commercial gentlemen' who lodged at Mrs Todgers's:

The night before, 'Todgers's was in a great bustle ... There was always a great clinking of pattens down stairs, too, until midnight or so, on Saturdays; together with a frequent gleaming of mysterious lights in the area; much working at the pump; and a constant jangling of the iron handle of the pail. Shrill altercations from time to time arose between Mrs Todgers and unknown females in remote back kitchens; and sounds were occasionally heard, indicative of small articles of ironmongery and hardware being thrown at the boy. It was the custom of that youth on Saturdays, to roll up his shirt sleeves to his shoulders, and pervade all parts of the house in an apron of coarse green baize; moreover, he was more strongly tempted on Saturdays than on other days (it being a busy time), to make excursive bolts into the neighbouring alleys when he answered the door, and there to play at leap-frog and other sports with vagrant lads, until pursued and brought back by the hair of his head ...

'Benjamin was supposed to be the real name of this young retainer, but ... he was generally known among the gentlemen as Bailey junior ...

'The usual Sunday dinner-hour at Todgers's was two o'clock . . . but on the Sunday which was to introduce the two Miss Pecksniffs to a full knowledge of Todgers's and its society, the dinner was postponed until five, in order that everything might be as genteel as the occasion demanded.

'When the hour drew nigh, Bailey junior, testifying great excitement, appeared in a complete suit of cast-off clothes several sizes too large for him, and in particular, mounted a clean sh rt of such extraordinary magnitude that one of the gentlemen (remarkable for his ready wit) called him "collars" on the spot. At about a quarter before five a deputation, consisting of Mr Jinkins, and another gentleman whose name was Gander, knocked at the door of Mrs Todgers's room, and, being formally introduced to the two Miss Pecksniffs by their parent, who was in waiting, besought the honour of conducting them upstairs . . .

'There was a general cry of "Hear, hear!" and "Bravo, Jink!" when Mr Jinkins appeared with Charity on his arm; which became quite rapturous as Mr Gander followed, escorting Mercy, and Mr Pecksniff brought up the rear with Mrs Todgers.

'Then, the presentations took place. They included a gentleman of a sporting turn, who propounded questions on jockey subjects to the editors of Sundaypapers, which were regarded by his friends as rather stiff things to answer; and they included a gentleman of a debating turn, who was strong at speech-making; and a gentleman of a literary turn, who wrote squibs upon the rest, and knew the weak side of everybody's character but his own. There was a gentleman of a vocal turn, and a gentleman of a smoking turn, and a gentleman of a convivial turn; some of the gentlemen had a urn for whist, and a large proportion of the gentlemen had a strong turn for billiards and betting. They had all, it may be presumed, a turn for business; being all commercially employed in one way or other; and had, every one in his own way, a decided turn for pleasure to boot . . .

'There was considerable delay in the production of the dinner, and poor Mrs Todgers, being reproached in confidence by Jinkins, slipped in and out, at least twenty times to see about it . . . until dinner was announced by Bailey junior in these terms:

'"The wittles is up!"

'On which notice they immediately descended to the banquet-hall; some of the more facetious spirits in the rear taking down gentlemen as if they were ladies, in imitation of the fortunate possessors of the two Miss Pecksniffs.

'Mr Pecksniff said grace—a short and pious grace, invoking a blessing on the appetites of those present, and committing all persons who had nothing to eat, to the care of Providence: whose business (so said the grace, in effect) it clearly was, to look after them. This done, they fell to, with less ceremony than appetite; the table groaning beneath the weight, not only of the delicacies whereof the Miss Pecksniffs had been previously fore-warned, but of boiled beef, roast veal, bacon, pies, and an abundance of such heavy vegetables as are favourably known to house-keepers for their satisfying qualities. Besides which, there were bottles of stout, bottles of wine, bottles of ale; and divers other strong drinks, native and foreign.

'All this was highly agreeable to the two Miss Pecksniffs, who were in immense request; sitting one on either hand of Mr Jinkins at the bottom of the table; and who were called upon to take wine with some new admirer every minute. They had hardly ever felt to pleasant and so full of conversation, in their lives; Mercy, in particular, was uncommonly brilliant, and said so many good things in the way of lively repartee that she was looked upon as a prodigy. "In short", as that young lady observed, "they felt now, indeed, that they were in London, and for the first time too".

'Their young friend Bailey sympathized in these feelings to the fullest extent, and, abating nothing of his patronage, gave them every encouragement in his power: favouring them, the general attention was diverted from his proceedings, with many nods and winks and other tokens of recognition and occasionally touching his nose with a corkscrew, as if to express the Bacchanalian character of the meeting. In truth, perhaps even the spirits of the two Miss Pecksniffs, and the hungry watchfulness of Mrs Todgers, were less worthy of note than the proceedings of this remarkable boy, whom nothing disconcerted or put out of his way. If any piece of crockery—a dish or otherwise— chanced to slip through his hands (which happened once or twice), he let it go with perfect good-breeding, and never added to the painful emotions of the company by exhibiting the least regret. Nor did he, by hurrying to and fro, disturb the repose of the assembly, as many well-trained servants do; on the contrary, feeling the hopelessness of waiting upon so large a party, he left the gentlemen to help themselves to what they wanted, and seldom stirred from behind Mr Jinkins's chair, where, with his hands in his pockets, and his legs planted pretty wide apart, he led the laughter, and enjoyed the conversation.' [1]

In those days people undoubtedly ate much more than was good for them. Yet when Dickens writes about gluttony he makes it seem almost a virtue, or at any rate necessary to the proper conduct and enjoyment of life. Intemperance likewise. It was Percy Fitzgerald who drew attention to the fact that Mr Pickwick, so often regarded as the epitome of benevolent respectability, was, if not an habitual drunkard, certainly a toper and frequently drank so much that his judgement and responses were impaired. 'We can hardly count up how many times Mr Pickwick was drunk,' [2] he says, and then sets out a long and ignominious catalogue of Mr Pickwick's lapses. But if, as a race, we have since all become more abstemious, it can hardly be said that the Englishman's palate has much improved. Nor can the inconveniences that came with wartime rationing or the dismal austerity of a balanced diet be blamed for this. Somewhere between this century and the last we seem to have fallen out of love with food. English fare and English cooking have never made much appeal to foreigners, which is understandable if you have ever lived, even for a short while, in France or Italy, or indeed in most other European countries. The trouble is that in England we tend to regard cookery merely as a means, that of satisfying hunger, rather than an end, namely the concoction of something that is appetizing to contemplate and delicious to eat. Yet it was not always so. In the sixteenth century those who could afford to eat well often ate magnificently, which is certainly not the rule nowadays. In matters of food and cooking, our imagination, and consequently our interest, has sadly declined.

'The defence of English cooking is sometimes based on the argument that, since we possess the best meat and butter and vegetables in the world, we have no need to imitate foreigners in their attempts to disguise the poverty of their food. I deny both the premise and the conclusion of this argument. There may have been a time in the eighteenth and early nineteenth centuries when our beef and mutton were in fact superior to that obtainable abroad; but in any case that is not true today. I deny that our vegetables are better, even in their natural state, than French vegetables; and we all admit, sometimes defiantly, sometimes in passive regret, that few English cooks know how to treat vegetables.

'We are careless about food because we do not care about it; and we do not care about it because we have lost the habit of greediness. Why should we have lost that habit?

'In Tudor times the art of cooking was still considered an important element in civilised life. I do not suggest that we today would care for Tudor cooking, since the difficulty of preserving meat and fish in those days induced our cooks to add too many spices, too much nutmeg, cinnamon and saffron, to the dishes they prepared. The Elisabethans had dulled palates, since they were accustomed to tastes that were sharp and scented. But the idea was there all right. Why did it die out? I suggest it was all due to the Puritans. For them the pleasures of the table were pleasures of the flesh; all pleasures of the flesh were to be condemned; therefore it was regarded as gluttonous to be greedy. Mr Robert May, whose father had been cook to Lady Dormer and had travelled abroad, published a cookery book in 1665 in which he regrets the days before the Commonwealth "wherein were produced triumphs and trophies of cookery". It is evident that with the advent of Puritanism the tradition of English cooking was interrupted; it has never been recovered.' [3]

Fortunately for the rest of the world, the Puritans were poor evangelists and did not get as far afield as some other well-meaning but equally meddlesome sects. The peoples of the Levant were spared or at least managed to resist their benevolent interference and consequently have preserved traditions of hospitality and cooking the like of which have long since passed from the Western world. Lawrence of Arabia, whose eye for domestic detail was perpetually alert, recorded an account of a feast that was given in his honour and that of Nasir, Sherif of Medina, by the chiefs of the Fitenna:

'Howeitat hospitality was unlimited . . . and importunate, and left us no honourable escape from the entirety of the nomad's dream of well-being . . . We would reach the tent which was to be our feast-hall . . . The tribal rugs, lurid red things from Beyrout, were ready for us, arranged down the partition curtain, along the back wall and across the dropped end, so that we sat down on three sides of an open dusty space. We might be fifty men in all . . .

'At last, two men came staggering through, . . . carrying the rice and meat on a tinned copper tray or shallow bath, five feet across, set in a great brazier on a foot. In the tribe there was only this one food-bowl of the size, and an incised inscription ran round it in florid Arabic characters: "To the glory of God, and in trust of mercy at the last, the property of his poor suppliant, Auda abu Tayi". It was borrowed by the host who was to entertain us . . .

'The bowl was now brim-full, ringed round its edge by white rice in an embankment a foot wide and six inches deep, filled with legs and ribs of mutton till they toppled over. It needed two or three victims to make in the centre a dressed pyramid of meat such as honour prescribed. The centre-pieces were the boiled, upturned heads, propped on their severed stumps of neck, so that the ears, brown like old leaves, flapped out on the rice surface. The jaws gaped emptily upward, pulled open to show the hollow throat with the tongue, still pink, clinging to the lower teeth; and the long incisors whitely crowned the pile, very prominent above the nostrils' pricking hair and the lips which sneered away blackly from them.

'This load was set down on the soil of the cleared space between us, where it steamed hotly, while a procession of minor helpers bore small cauldrons and copper vats in which the cooking had been done. From them, with much-bruised bowls of enamelled iron, they ladled out over the main dish all the inside and outside of the sheep; little bits of yellow intestine, the white tail-cushion of fat, brown muscles and meat and bristly skin, all swimming in the liquid butter and grease of the seething. The bystanders watched anxiously, muttering satisfactions when a very juicy scrap plopped out.

'The fat was scalding. Every now and then a man would drop his baler with an exclamation, and plunge his burnt fingers, not reluctantly, in his mouth to cool them: but they persevered till at last their scooping rang loudly on the bottom of the pots; and, with a gesture of triumph, they fished out the intact livers from their hiding place in the gravy and topped the yawning jaws with them.

'Two raised each smaller cauldron and tilted it, letting the liquid splash down upon the meat till the rice-crater was full and the loose grains at the edge swam in the abundance: and yet they poured, till, amid cried of astonishment from us, it was running over, and a little pool congealing in the dust. That was the final touch of splendour, and the host called us to come and eat.

'We feigned a deafness, as manners demanded: at last we heard him, and looked surprised at one another, each urging his fellow to move first; till Nasir rose coyly, and after him we all came forward to sink on one knee round the tray, wedging in and cuddling up till the twenty-two for whom there was barely space were grouped around the food. We turned back our right sleeves to the elbow, and, taking lead from Nasir with a low "In the name of God the merciful, the loving-kind", we dipped together.

'The first dip, for me, at least, was always cautious, since the liquid fat was so hot that my unaccustomed fingers could seldom bear it: and so I would toy with an exposed and cooling lump of meat till others' excavations had drained my rice-segment. We would knead between the fingers (not soiling the palm), neat balls of rice and fat and liver and meat cemented by gentle pressure, and project them by leverage of the thumb from the crooked fore-finger into the mouth. With the right trick and the right construction the little lump held together and came clean off the hand; but when surplus butter and odd fragments clung, cooling, to the fingers, they had to be licked carefully to make the next effort slip easier away.

'As the meat pile wore down (nobody really cared about rice: flesh was the luxury) one of the chief Howeitat eating with us would draw his dagger, silver-hilted, set with turquoise, a signed masterpiece of Mohammed ibn Zari, of Jauf, and would cut criss-cross from the larger bones long diamonds of meat easily torn up between the fingers; for it was necessarily boiled very tender, since all had to be disposed of with the right hand, which alone was honourable.

'Our host stood by the circle, encouraging the appetite with pious ejaculations. At top speed we twisted, tore, cut and stuffed: never speaking, since conversation would insult a meal's quality; though it was proper to smile thanks when an intimate guest passed a select fragment, or when Mohammed el Dheilan gravely handed over a huge barren bone with a blessing. On such occasions I would return the compliment with some hideous impossible lump of guts, a flippancy which rejoiced the Howeitat, but which the gracious, aristocratic Nasir saw with disapproval.

'At length some of us were nearly filled, and began to play and pick; glancing sideways at the rest till they too grew slow, and at last ceased eating, elbow on knee, the hand hanging down from the wrist over the tray edge to drip, while the fat, butter and scattered grains of rice cooled into a stiff white grease which gummed the fingers together. When all had stopped, Nasir meaningly cleared his throat, and we rose up together in haste with an explosive "God requite it to you, O host", to group ourselves outside among the tent-ropes while the next twenty guests inherited our leaving.' [4]

As a small boy I was taken two or three times during its tremendous run to see *Chu Chin Chow*, and although I can hardly remember anything about it now, in spite of having enjoyed it hugely at the time, a few words from one of the songs have somehow lodged themselves in my memory and whenever I think of them I am reminded of the banquet which the chiefs of the Fitenna gave to Nasir:

Here be lambs' tails baked in butter,
And plovers' eggs from afar,
Here be humming birds in jelly,
And lizards from Zanzibar.[5]

This is hardly the sort of menu that would have been approved by Soyer, the great Victorian chef on whose skill the fortunes of the Liberal Club are said to have been founded, for although imagination is as indispensable to the art of cooking, in spite of the impermanence of its delights, as it is to more lasting achievements in the other arts, I feel that Soyer would probably have drawn the line—and so, no doubt, would they—at the Liberal leaders of the day being served with *lézards en broche*.

It was Soyer's aim, and one that must then have seemed a good deal less hopeful of achievement than it seems today, to raise the standard of English cooking, and with this purpose in view he toured the country to find out for himself just how appalling our native cuisine could be.

'In the course of my peregrinations,' he says, 'I have made a point of visiting the cottages and abodes of the industrious classes generally and have also closely examined the peculiarities and manners which distinguish each country, as well as the different kinds of labour; and I have viewed with pleasure the exertions made by philanthropic individuals to improve the morals of the labouring class, and render their dwellings more comfortable. But still I have found a great want of knowledge in that one object which produces almost as much comfort as all the rest put together, *viz.*, the means of making the most of that food which the great Architect of the Heavens had so bountifully spread before us on the face of the globe . . .

'In ancient times, a cook, especially if a man, was looked upon as a distinguished member of society; while now he is, in the opinion of almost everyone, a mere menial.' [6]

That is how the English have tended for a long time to regard their cooks, although since the war there have been signs of a growing interest in food and cooking; which is just as well, for I firmly believe it is true that 'the destiny of nations depends on the manner in which they eat'.[7] It is impossible to imagine that the character of the English, and hence their history, would be what it is if their traditional foods were the same as those that nourish the peoples of the Mediterranean, and even further beyond the bounds of credibility that the French would be as they are if porridge, puddings and potatoes had ever been as important to them as they are to us—or wine as unfamiliar. How much pleasanter the world, or at any rate Europe, would be if Germany's diet had always been the same as that of, say the Tahitians, who are not particularly carnivorous, though like the Germans, fond of pig, and also great eaters of fruit. And I refuse to believe that it is either their geographical or their economic position among the nations of the world that accounts solely for the peaceable nature of the Portuguese. Eire too is a small nation, but it is touchy, intransigent and backward, and the cooking there is as vile as any I have ever come across.

On his last visit to Portugal in 1794, Beckford ate and drank, though unaccustomed to the cooking, with true eighteenth-century relish. In June of that year he set off, with the Grand Prior of Aviz and the Prior of St Vincent's as his travelling companions, to visit the great monastery of Aleobaca. There they were welcomed by 'a most tremendous ring of bells of extraordinary power ... The whole community, including fathers, friars and subordinates, at least four hundred, were drawn up in grand spiritual array on the vast platform before the monastery.' [8]

While the ecclesiastics wended their way to the high altar, Beckford himself went to examine one of the chapels: 'Presently in came the Grand Priors hand in hand, all three together. "To the kitchen," said they in perfect unison,—"to the kitchen, and that immediately; you will then judge whether we have been wanting in zeal to regale you".

'Such a summons, so conveyed, was irresistable; the three prelates led the way to, I verily believe, the most distinguished temple of gluttony in all Europe. What Glastonbury may have been in its palmy state, I cannot answer; but my eyes never beheld in any modern convent of France, Italy or Germany, such an enormous space dedicated to culinary purposes. Through the centre of the immense and nobly-groined hall, not less than sixty feet in diameter, ran a brisk rivulet of the clearest water, flowing through pierced wooden reservoirs, containing every sort and size of the finest river-fish. On one side, loads of game and venison were heaped up; on the other, vegetables and fruit in endless variety. Beyond a long line of stoves extended a row of ovens, and close to them hillocks of wheaten flour whiter than snow, rocks of sugar, jars of the purest oil, and pastry in vast abundance, which a numerous tribe of lay brothers and their attendants were rolling out and puffing up into a hundred different shapes, singing all the while as blithely as larks in a corn-field.

'My servants, and those of their reverent excellencies the two Priors, were standing by in the full glee of witnessing these hospitable preparations, as well pleased, and as much flushed, as if they had been just returned from assisting at the marriage at Cana in Galilee. "There," said the Lord Abbot,—"we shall not starve: God's bounties are great, it is fit, we should enjoy them".' [9]

God's bounties were even greater when, on 9 November 1837, the

year of Queen Victoria's accession, she was entertained to dinner at
the Guildhall by the Lord Mayor and Corporation. The bill for food,
wine and service for some eight hundred guests amounted to what
must then have been the enormous sum of £1971.17.6. This provided
a general bill of fare which included 220 tureens of turtle soup, 2 barons
of beef, 50 boiled turkeys and oysters, 80 pheasants, 60 pigeon pies,
45 hams, 140 jellies, some 90 dishes of tarts and pies, besides a very
large assortment of other delicacies. The wines included 35 dozen of
champagne, 20 dozen of claret, 10 dozen of burgundy and a good many
more. 'Sherry one hundred and ten years old was presented to the
Corporation expressly for the Queen's use, by a Mr William Lawson,'[10]
whose brief moment of fame begins and ends here, like that of several
others who were concerned in preparations for this great occasion;
Mr Harper, for instance, who was paid £11.3.0 for 'Trumpets in the
Hall, and for Banners, etc.', Mr J. Hunt, who received £14.0.0 'for
Waiters' Collars,' and Mr R. Armfield, £24.15.0 'for Buttons'. The
whole affair, for which arrangements were made on a fabulous scale,
must have been one of the most expensive ever got up by the Corporation. The total cost was £6870.3.8. For the young Queen, still not
fully accustomed to exhausting ceremonial, it must have been a very
great ordeal. Dressed in 'a pink satin robe, shot with silver, and a
magnificent diamond tiara' [11] she took her place at the Royal Table
at twenty minutes past five and did not rise from it till eight o'clock.

The purgatory of pinching oneself to keep awake throughout an
after-dinner speech, to be compelled for the sake of politeness to linger
over port and brandy when all that you ask is to get up and stretch
your legs, are forms of torture to which my resistance is very low.
But a still worse fate is to find oneself among well-acquainted strangers
and to feel conscious of the uncertainty of one's manners. It was in this
unhappy position that Roger Lowe once found himself. Lowe was the
dutiful conscience-stricken Lancashire lad in whose *Diary* are recorded
a number of quaint and curious happenings. He was extremely shy,
invariably there was something pathetic about his misadventures, and
anyone who has endured the secret and incommunicable pangs of
acute shyness will understand how miserable he must have felt as a
prisoner of his host's hospitality when he was sent on an errand to a
nearby village and was asked to stay to a meal:

'When I lived with Mr Livesey, he sent me to High Lee to Mr Henry
Lee about a minister for his chapell, and going from Budworth to
High Lee without victuals I came just att diner's time. Mr Lee was att
diner . . . he sent word I should stay diner, which I did, and was very

hungery. I was sett att table with servents. Every servent a great bowlefull of podige, anon a great trencher like a pott lid I and all others had, with a great quantity of podige. The dishes else ware but small and few. I put bread into my podige thinking to have a spoone, but none came. While I was thus in expectation of that I could not obtaine, every man haveing a horne spoone in their pocketts, haveing done their pottage, fell to the other dishes. Thought I, these Hungery Amallakites that I am gotten amongst will devoure all if I doe not set upon a resolution. I, lookeing towards them to see theire nimblenes in the exercise of their hands from dish to their mouth, made me forgett my hunger, but I cast my eyes from them, thinkeing it ware best to bethinke my selfe of my one hungery condition. What would it advantage me though I was sat there to table and not satisfie hunger? I cast an eye to my trencher—there was a whole sea of pottage before. Thought I, what must I do with all these; wished in my hart many times that those hungery Rogues had them in their gutts, but that would not doe, for still they ware there before me, and I durst not set them away, tho it was manners so to have done. Well, I resolved: "Hodge, if thou will have any victualls here, thou sees how the case is and into whose company thou art falne into, what a hungery spirit possesses these men. Thou must now resolve upon action;" and a speedy dispatch with these pottage accordingly I did, and sweeped them as if I would have drunke. Than when I had them in my mouth I was in such a hott fiit in my mouth [as] turned meditation into action, but att last, to my lamentation, I was werse than before. I would gladly have given 5s. that I had but had the benefitt of aire or a northern blast. My tongue in my mouth was in a sad condition; helpe my selfe I could not, for table was before me and a wall behind me upon my backe, a woman with her flasket upon right hand, and a man with his codd peece upon the other, and in this sad condition I sat blothering, knew not what to doe best. Those few pottage I tasted was both diner and supper. I att last rise from table with a hungery belly but a lamenting heart, and ere since I have beene cautious how to supp pottage, and likewise wary. Nothing werser to a man then over hastiness, especially in hott concernements: hott women, hott poggage ... beware of and pray to be delivered frome.' [12]

In most of his predicaments Lowe shows himself to have been a young man of sweet but rather heavy and anxious disposition, not really the man for a spree. For my part, I think I should have preferred Francis Hale, particularly if it was he who chose the food for that memorable meal on the orchard slope:

'"The Bull, the Fleece are cramm'd, and not a room
For love or money. Let us picnic there
At Audley Court."
　　　　　　I spoke, while Audley feast
Humm'd like a hive all round the narrow quay,
To Francis with a basket on his arm,
To Francis just alighted from the boat,
And breathing of the sea. "With all my heart,"
Said Francis. Then we shoulder'd thro' the swarm
And rounded by the stillness of the beach
To where the bay runs up its latest horn.

We left the dying ebb that faintly lipp'd
The flat red granite; so by many a sweep
Of meadow smooth from aftermath we reach'd
The griffin-guarded gates, and passed thro' all
The pillar'd dusk of sounding sycamores,
And cross'd the garden to the gardeners' lodge,
With all its casements bedded, and its walls
And chimneys muffled in the leafy vine.

There, on a slope of orchard, Francis laid
A damask napkin wrought with horse and hound,
Brought out a dusky loaf that smelt of home,
And, half-cut-down, a pasty costly-made,
Where quail and pigeon, lark and leveret lay,
Like fossils of the rock, with golden yolks
Imbedded and injellied; last, with these,
A flask of cider from his father's vats,
Prime, which I knew; and so we sat and eat
And talk'd old matters over . . .' [13]

Not a very substantial meal perhaps, but how delicious it sounds.
In any case, picnics should be simple because they must be easy to eat.
The sort of spread you see in Frith's *Derby Day*, with lobster and
champagne set out by a footman, is not my idea of a picnic. Some of
the best meals that I remember have been ones that I have eaten beside
the road in France or Italy—a few slices of cold meat (perhaps a mouth-
ful of paté to start with), a well dressed salad, cheese, butter and crisp
bread, with a bottle of *vin du pays*, makes as good a meal for out-of-
doors as any that you could wish for. Of course, if you are a hearty

eater, which I am not, then such a meal may not do. Your appetite
will probably need to be fortified with

> ' . . . *Oysters; and a kind of stuff*
> *Called Cassouletto (good enough!)*
> *And Mutton duly steeped in claret*
> *(Or jumped with young shallot and carrot),*
> *And chicken livers done with rice,*
> *And Quails (which, I am told, are nice)*
> *And Peaches from a sunny wall* . . .' [14]

If that is the sort of thing you fancy, your salivary glands may be
pleasantly stimulated by Lady Fanshawe's account of food and drink
in Spain. With her husband Sir Richard Fanshawe, who had been
appointed Ambassador to the Spanish Court, she arrived at Madrid
in 1664:

'There is not in the Christian world better wines,' she says, 'than
their midland wines are especially, besides sherry and Canary. Their
water tastes like milk; their corn white to a miracle, and their wheat
makes the sweetest and best bread in the world; bacon beyond belief
good; the Segovia veal much larger and fatter than ours; mutton most
excellent; capons much better than ours. They have a small bird that
lives and fattens on grapes and corn, so fat that it exceeds the quantity
of flesh. They have the best partridges I ever eat, and the best sausages;
and salmon, pikes, and sea-breams, which they send up in pickle,
called *ashe veche*, to Madrid, and dolphins, which are excellent meat,
besides carps, and many other sorts of fish. The cream, called *nuttuos*,
is much sweeter and thicker than any I ever saw in England; their eggs
much exceed ours; and so all sorts of sallads, and roots and fruits. What
I most admired are, melons, peaches, burgamot pears, grapes, oranges,
lemons, citrons, figs and pomegranates; besides that I have eaten many
sorts of biscuits, cakes, cheese, and excellent sweetmeats. I have not here
mentioned especially *manger-blanc*; and they have olives, which are no
where so good.' [15]

Such unpalatable recollections of *manger-blanc* linger in my own
memory that I have never been able to eat it with any enjoyment since
I got out of my nursery. It seems to epitomise the flabby and flavourless
character of most English cooking. Perhaps the truth is that you have
to be English to appreciate the unctuous solidity of *manger-blanc*, just
as the sheep's eye, *bonne bouche* of Arab gastronomy, is less appetizing
to the Western palate than to that of the Levant, and birds'-nests and
eggs of venerable age appeal to the Chinese, but not to us.

Chinese food is an acquired taste, of course, but the Western world is familiar with its principle dishes and their ingredients. Less easy to acquire is the elasticity of the Chinese appetite. A meal of twenty-six courses, oriental courtesy making it imperative that one should eat at least part of every dish, is a digestive ordeal from which most Westerners would shrink. It takes a man of William Burke's moral and physical stamina to get through such a meal without loss of face. Burke was a Methodist minister who left his home in the State of Georgia in 1887 to become a missionary in China. He stayed there nearly fifty years and when he retired in 1936, both Christians and non-Christians joined in praising his efforts among the people with whom he had lived and worked for so long and in regretting his departure. Towards the end of 1937, at the age of seventy-three, his indignation at the atrocities committed by the Japanese invaders of China drove him to return there, in spite of every official obstacle, to see what he could do to alleviate the horrors of the invasion. He was known to be still in China in 1941, living at Sunkiang, where he had spent a lifetime of humane and disinterested service that must have struck the Japanese as quite inexplicable. What finally became of him, no one knows. His story, which has been told by his son, gives a remarkable impression of domestic life in China sixty years ago. Here, for instance, is an account of a party given in honour of Burke's thirtieth birthday at the house of a young friend of his, named Lok Kwe-Liang:

'The round feast table was set in the rear compartment. Lok invited the guests to take off their outer garments and relax in their cotton pants and jackets. They did, for Chinese went about eating with a gusto not best achieved in their full-sleeved silk gowns. Guests and hosts now battled genially, but vigorously, for four or five minutes over who should occupy the "high" seats, the seats farthest from the entrance ranking higher. Burke was finally forced into the "highest" seat, directly opposite the entrance, since the party was in his honour. Lok and his father fought their way to the "lowest" seats and the others took the intermediary places.

'There was no tablecloth of any sort. Each man's place was supplied with a white porcelain ladle, or spoon, a saucer, and a pair of red-bone chopsticks. When the diners were seated, servants began bringing in the opening cold dishes, or hors d'œuvres, and setting them on the table. Six of the dishes were uncovered, and displayed such edibles as ham, pork ribs, smoked fish, preserved crab, century eggs, and dried pork. The seventh dish had a lid on it and Burke discovered why when the guest next to him partly raised the cover and invited him to try some. The dish was full of live crawling shrimp.

'Burke had never run into such a dish in his seven years in China, but he refused to be abashed. He invited the guest to eat first and carefully watched him reach under the lid with his chopsticks, draw out a wriggling shrimp, dip it in a dish of black soybean sauce and thrust it in his mouth, all in a few deft movements. Burke tried. He got through the initial steps all right, though not so deftly, but somehow his mouth wouldn't close quickly enough and the shrimp squirmed out on his lower lip. A chill or two pricked his back, then he got the defiant little crustacean in and clamped down on it stoically. He didn't try any more.

'The so-called "main dishes" were next placed separately in the centre of the table—shark's fins, fresh ham, whole chicken, whole duck, more ham, whole fish, and mutton. After each dish had been sampled by all the guests, it was moved aside to make way for the succeeding one. Then came the courses termed "hot dishes"—shell shrimp, bird's-nest soup, sliced chicken, clam sinews, kidneys and pork brains, bamboo sprouts, pigeon eggs, and roast duck.

'Burke was hoping the courses would come to an end. It wouldn't have been so bad if the Chinese didn't have an almost irritating way of constantly forcing him to eat. The guest at his right and the guest at the left picked up food with their chopsticks and laid it on the minister's saucer—and he was too polite not to eat it. Everyone reached into the same dishes with their chopsticks, put the sticks and food in their mouths and reached back into the dishes with the sticks—a cycle which would clash with most modern hygiene laws. But the Chinese enjoyed themselves immensely, chewing loudly, sipping soup from their porcelain ladles, spitting out bones on the table and floor and belching thunderously—the latter being particularly acceptable indication of gastronomic satisfaction. Now and then a guest would rise, stretch and walk around the room a bit.

'Hot rice wine, served in a small pewter pot, was drunk during the meal in individual thimble-cups. Burke turned his cup down at the start and Lok didn't urge any wine on him, knowing that intoxicants were against Methodist principles. Instead, he had a servant bring tea for him.

'The dessert followed the last "hot dish" and it virtually stopped the feast. Conversation and belching suddenly ceased as a servant brought it on a platter and made a place for it in the centre of the table. It was an eight-precious-rice pudding, but not the sort the feasters were accustomed to. The top of the glutenous delicacy glittered with candles—thirty of them. This was Lok's *pièce de résistance*.

'"This is the Occidental birthday custom," the young scholar announced, breaking the awed silence. "It is specially for our honourable teacher, Mr Burke, who observed his thirtieth birthday last week. Foreigners, you know, recognize their birthdays years before we Chinese do. But I think it is a good idea. Please, now, I invite you to eat." And Lok gestured at the lustrous pudding with his ladle. The lighted candles were taken out by guests as they ate.

'After the dessert came the staple course—rice. It was served in bowls the size of three English teacups and the Chinese miraculously stored away three, four and five heaping servings. They raised the bowls to their mouths and shovelled the rice in with the chopsticks. Burke could scarcely manage one serving. Chinese capacity for rice after a full meal always amazed him. When he had finished his one bowl, he followed the native custom of dipping his chopsticks in a sort of salute to each of the men still eating and saying, "*man yoong* (eat slowly)". Then he put his sticks on the table. He had learned not to lay them horizontally across his empty rice bowl. That, for some reason, was considered too polite and someone would certainly put them on the table for you.

'The rice wasn't all. There remained an end-up course of fruit and nuts—pears, oranges, and pomelos; sugared peanuts, apricot kernels, walnut candy, and watermelon seed. And tea.' [16]

If you are not surfeited by this time with descriptions of food and feasting, here to end with is a recipe that was used by Henry VIII's cook for the king's coronation banquet. But unless you are an ambitious cook, also something of a surgeon, and have plenty of time on your hands, it would probably be best to turn your attention to plainer fare:

TO DIGHT A PEACOCK

'Take and flay off the skin with the feathers and tail, leaving the neck and crest still upon the bird, and preserving the flory of his crest from injury when roasting by wrapping it in a linen bandage. Then take the skin with all the feathers upon it and spread it out on a table and sprinkle thereon ground cinnamon. Now roast the peacock and endore him with the yolks of many eggs, and when he is roasted remove him from the fire and let him cool for a while. Then take and sew him again into his skin and all his feathers, and remove the bandage from his crest. Brush the feathers carefully and dust upon them and his comb gilding to enhance his beauty. After a while, set him upon a golden platter, garnish with rosemary and other green leaves, and serve him forthwith as if he were alive, and with great ceremony.' [17]

SOURCES

1　Charles Dickens, *Martin Chuzzlewit.*
2　Percy Fitzgerald, *The Pickwickian Dictionary and Cyclopædia.*
3　Sir Harold Nicolson, 'The Importance of Being Greedy', *The Listener,* February 8, 1951.
4　T. E. Lawrence, *Seven Pillars of Wisdom.*
5　Frederick Norton, *Chu Chin Chow.*
6　Alexis Soyer, *A Shilling Cookery for the People.*
7　Anthelme Brillat-Savarin, *La Physiologie du Goût.*
8　*The Travel-Diaries of William Beckford.*
9　Ibid.
10　*Reports Relating to the Entertainment of Her Majesty the Queen in the Guildhall of the City of London,* November 9, 1837.
11　Andrew W. Tuer and Chas. E. Fagan, *The First Year of a Silken Reign.*
12　*The Diary of Roger Lowe.*
13　Alfred, Lord Tennyson, *Audley Court.*
14　Hilaire Belloc, *New Cautionary Tales.*
15　*The Memoirs of Anne, Lady Fanshawe.*
16　James Burke, *My Father in China.*
17　*Court Favourites,* edited by Elizabeth Craig.

INDEX OF AUTHORS AND SOURCES